D1616984

ENVIRONMENTAL COMPLIANCE
HANDBOOK

J.I. Bregman
Craig Kelley
James R. Melchor

LEWIS PUBLISHERS
Boca Raton   New York   London   Tokyo

Acquiring Editor:	Ken McCombs
Project Editor:	Carole Sweatman
Marketing Manager:	Greg Daurelle
Direct Marketing Manager:	Arline Massey
Cover design:	Denise Craig
PrePress:	Kevin Luong
Manufacturing:	Sheri Schwartz

Library of Congress Cataloging-in-Publication Data

Bregman, Jacob I.
    The environmental compliance handbook / by J.I. Bregman, Craig Kelley, James R. Melchor.
        p.   cm.
    Includes bibliographical references and index.
    ISBN 1-56670-146-5
        1. Environmental law--United States. 2. Environmental auditing--United States. I. Kelley,
Craig. II. Melchor, James R. III. Title.
    KF3775.B72 1996
    344.73′046--dc20
    [347.30446]   96-4961
                                                                    CIP

AUTHOR

Company president, university professor, political gadfly, and devoted grandfather, **Jack I. Bregman**, B.S., M.S., and Ph.D., is the epitome of the American success story. The only son of Russian immigrants, he is the author of over 60 publications, holds several patents and has written 7 books. An internationally recognized expert in his field, Dr. Bregman is listed in several of the "Who's Who" publications, has been elected to membership in the honor societies of Sigma Xi and Phi Lambda Upsilon, and is a Fellow of the American Institute of Chemists.

After "doing his bit" in a devastated Europe during World War II, Dr. Bregman was awarded his Ph.D. in Chemistry, worked for several years in prominent research laboratories, and served in the Johnson Administration as Deputy Assistant Secretary for Water Quality. Since the mid-sixties he has founded two highly successful environmental consulting firms, the second of which bears his name.

Happily married for almost 50 years, Dr. Bregman and his wife, Mona, reside in Bethesda, MD, where their company is also located. When the question of retirement is raised, Dr. Bregman's standard comment is that perhaps when he reaches the $3/4$ century mark, he may consider semi-retiring to 40 hours per week in order to concentrate a little more on his writing.

AUTHOR

In 1984, armed with a history degree and an ROTC leadership award, **Craig A. Kelley** joined the ranks of "the proud and the few" as a U.S. Marine Corps Infantry Officer. Five years of service later, he entered Boston College Law School, where he managed to make a name for himself as an ardent advocate of conservation issues and environmental law and earned yet another leadership award.

1993 was a banner year for him in which he graduated cum laude from law school, embraced the bonds of matrimony, was admitted to the Massachusetts Bar, and embarked on a career in environmental law, policy, and justice.

As Environmental Manager for the 94th Army Reserve Command, Mr. Kelley is in the happy position of combining both vocation and avocation, monitoring the environmental compliance status of over 50 reserve centers throughout New England, and ensuring that compliance programs (with an emphasis on Clean Air and Clean Water Act issues) are adequately implemented and maintained.

In addition to being an avid cyclist (he recently completed a cycling tour of New Zealand with his wife, Hope), Mr. Kelley is a member of the Environmental Law Section of the Boston Bar Association, the American Bar Association, and is a Founding Member and Past President of The New England Environmental Law Society. Mr. Kelley lives in Cambridge, Massachusetts and is heavily involved in local planning issues, with an emphasis on zoning and environmental permitting concerns.

The Environmental Compliance Handbook is Craig Kelley's first author-collaboration effort.

AUTHOR

Geological oceanographer, professional geologist, commercial pilot, and history buff, **James R. Melchor** heads up the Environmental Analysis Branch and is second-in-command of the Planning Division of the U.S. Army Corps of Engineers in Norfolk, Virginia.

In the 24 years that Mr. Melchor has served the U.S. Army Corps of Engineers (he served in that other Corps for six years — Semper Fi!), he has managed projects for civil works and military projects involving the environment, shoreline erosion control, inlet stabilization, waterway and port development, solid waste management, and tidal and riverine flood control. He presently manages and directs a $30 million-per-year worldwide environmental and planning program, employing approximately 250 people. This effort focuses on providing professional management support to various military installations and commands for environmental and base operations (BASOPS) programs, such as environmental compliance, installation restoration, cultural resources management, real estate planning, hazardous wastes management, and base closure and realignment.

He and his wife of 33 years, Marilyn (also a cultural resource scholar and consultant), live in Norfolk, Virginia, where together they have ample opportunity to further develop their love of history, archeology, traditional crafts, and colonial architecture. Both have published extensively, including a book on 18th century Eastern Shore, Virginia furniture.

ACKNOWLEDGMENTS

As in any sizable project, the writing of a book involves a great deal of support, both professionally and personally, for the writers. Often, it is only when the home stretch is actually in sight that acknowledgments and appreciation come to the fore.

In that light, the authors would like to express their deep gratitude for the wealth of patience and understanding of their life partners, Mrs. Mona Bregman, Mrs. Hope Kelley, and Mrs. Marilyn Melchor. Their support has provided the backbone of this book.

The accuracy and flow of information on these pages owes much to the technical review and input of the following members of the Norfolk District, Corps of Engineers environmental staff : Ms. Kris Holderied, Mr. Tim Thompson, Ms. Gina Foringer, Mr. Richard Muller, and Mr. Craig Seltzer. The authors stand in their debt.

The expertise offered by Ms. Christina Carlson, project manager and ambassador-at-large for BREGMAN & COMPANY, Inc., was also of immeasurable value in the technical editing of *Environmental Compliance Handbook*. Her help is gratefully acknowledged.

Special thanks must also go to Ms. Terry Spencer for her cheerful efficiency in undertaking the sometimes laborious tasks of typing, editing, and proofing these pages. Her unflagging enthusiasm, as she kept the writing team synchronized and running true to form, was a pleasure to witness.

Lastly, the authors must acknowledge the tremendous wealth of information and technical expertise that they have been privileged to draw upon from each of their backgrounds. The teamwork that became the trademark of this book is exemplified in the spirit of cooperation that can exist between education, industry, and the government of this country. It is that spirit that makes *Environmental Compliance* possible, and ultimately, successful.

CONTENTS

1   Purpose

INTRODUCTION

Personnel in every organization subject to federal, state, and local environmental laws and regulations are faced with the difficult task of making certain that they understand these laws and regulations and conform to them. This situation applies to virtually every governmental, industrial, and commercial organization in this country.

The number and complexity of these regulations is further complicated by the fact that they are being modified and expanded frequently. In addition, the technical and legal jargon in which environmental requirements are couched, often is unintelligible to the average person.

It is the purpose of this handbook to present a rational approach to compliance with these laws and regulations. A portion of the handbook will be devoted to a description of the major federal laws and regulations, with a description of some of the more critical state requirements appended. Information also will be given on where the other state and local regulations may be found. Suggested techniques for auditing an operation for environmental compliance will be presented using graphs, figures, tables, and listings to ease record keeping.

An example of the complexity and possible lack of knowledge of environmental compliance requirements was observed by one of the authors of this book while waiting for an airplane at an airport. He noticed on the tarmac below, a worker was taking handfuls of SpeedyDry® from a 50-pound bag and casting it to the ground next to a maintenance vehicle. The author observed and critiqued the worker's actions.

Obviously there had been a release of some sort, and this worker was carrying out the remediation action. Several important questions immediately sprang to mind. Had the worker received proper training to conduct this action? Had the release been reported? If so, to whom and how quickly? Was the release, and its subsequent cleanup, documented in any particular manner? Once swept up, how would the worker handle the used SpeedyDry? Would he store it in properly labelled, closed, and contained drums? Would the disposal company properly manifest the SpeedyDry when it transported the drum to a disposal site? Did the disposal site have the proper permit?

It seemed appropriate that such an incident would mark the start of this environmental compliance manual. For an attorney and environmental compliance specialist, the importance of these questions is critical. Even a small incident, such as that described here, can invoke mind-numbing complex laws and regulations. On a practical level, the impact of environmental violations on individuals, corporations, and governments can be ruinous financially and may even result in prison sentences. Furthermore, liability to nongovernmental parties resulting from improperly disposed waste or noxious emissions can add up to additional millions in legal fees and remediation costs. In many cases, even unintentional environmental violations or degradation can result in civil and criminal liability.

Fortunately, despite the intimidating nature of many environmental laws and regulations, there is no reason for despair. Manufacturers, builders, and others often can comply with environmental standards without significantly altering their work habits. In fact, some compliance strategies, such as recycling or reducing a company waste stream, can result in increased productivity and savings. Proper training of relevant personnel, solid documentation, and where feasible, close coordination with regulatory authorities, help to lay the foundation for effective environmental compliance. Guided by management that understands and fulfills its ultimate responsibility for environmental compliance, most public and private organizations should be able to make compliance an easily met norm. Education throughout an organizational structure is the key.

HOW ENVIRONMENTAL LAWS AND REGULATIONS DEVELOP

While protecting the environment is something we all support in theory, when it comes to the actual "nuts and bolts" of environmental compliance, enthusiasm often wanes. Properly labeling hazardous waste drums, properly storing flammable material, and ensuring that site development does not threaten endangered species can be time-consuming, frustrating, and, above all, confusing to the worker who approaches these issues solely from a traditional profit-based standpoint. To lessen this confusion, it is important for workers and supervisors to understand how these environmental regulations developed, and why they frequently may seem somewhat arbitrary.

The most important entity in creating today's environmental compliance issues has been the United States Congress. Any law, environmental or otherwise, is the result of numerous compromises. For Congress to pass a law, a majority of the House of Representatives and the Senate must agree on the specific language. After Congress agrees on the language, the bill is sent to the President of the U.S. If the President signs the bill, it becomes law. If the President vetoes the bill, it is sent back to Congress, which may override the presidential veto by a two-thirds majority, at which point the bill becomes law.

Even if congressional members agree with the overall plan of a bill, they may not like certain parts that negatively impact their home districts. To reflect hometown political realities and pressure brought to bear by lobbyists, citizen action groups, and other politicians, lawmakers may force the authors of a bill to modify it before agreeing to support it. Lawmakers who disagree with a bill also may force changes by threatening to fight its passage as written. This "give and take" spirit of compromise is very strong in environmental laws, since stricter environmental laws may threaten jobs in fields ranging from logging to automobile manufacturing.

Once Congress passes a law, the task of putting that law into action falls into the hands of a regulatory agency. Agency action is important because laws do very little by themselves. Instead, laws usually set general guidelines or goals while giving a specific federal agency the power to develop the regulations which actually implement the laws. For example, Congress passed the Resource Conservation and Recovery Act (RCRA), but the Environmental Protection Agency (EPA) is responsible for determining the exact details of how much hazardous waste can be left in an "empty" container. Congress also passed the Endangered Species Act, but it is up to the Department of the Interior to decide, within guidelines set by the law, which species are actually endangered.

Agencies promulgate regulations in much the same manner as Congress passes laws. In addition to being limited by the enabling legislation that originally created the regulatory program, agencies must ensure that their regulations do not violate the U.S. Constitution and thus be declared void in court. An agency such as the EPA will be told by Congress to develop regulations in a certain area, such as hazardous waste storage. In the enabling legislation, Congress may tell the agency to finish its regulations by a certain date. The agency will then conduct studies, trying to determine the best way to store hazardous wastes in accordance with the will of Congress.

While devising its regulatory approach, the agency will be subjected to much of the same pressures, both internal and external, with which Congress had to deal when originally passing legislation. Industrial groups may argue that a certain level of parts per million (PPM) is too low to be considered waste, while environmental groups may claim that the same level poses an extreme hazard to human health and to the environment. Citizens will write and call EPA with their comments, and members of Congress will urge EPA to develop some other level that matches their particular political needs. Each side will have mountains of reports, statistics, surveys, etc. It is up to EPA to sift through this material, as well as their own studies, and decide exactly how to phrase the regulatory language.

It is impossible to overemphasize that definitions are the key to the legislative and regulatory processes. As a musician consults the music sheet prior to playing to see what notes are flats and sharps, anyone looking at an environmental law or regulation must consult the relevant definitions to see what areas are affected and what are not. Just as a C-sharp can change an entire piece of music, one regulatory definition can alter an entire regulatory program. Even seemingly concrete terms take on a whole new meaning under the law. "Solid waste" regulated by the RCRA, for example, includes some types of liquid waste. Thus, to understand a law or regulation, one must first understand and apply any relevant definitions.

Once an environmental regulation is passed, it has the effect of law and will be enforced by the regulatory agency. People who violate a regulation can be charged with violating the original statute that created the regulation, and will be subject to whatever penalties Congress decides in that statute. Like laws, regulations tend to be somewhat vague or subject to different interpretations, despite their all-inclusive and detailed appearance. Therefore, although it can be somewhat exasperating, the exact wording of a regulation may be critical to its implementation and enforcement. A comma in a certain position, or the use of a singular noun rather than a plural noun, could mean a difference of millions of dollars in compliance costs or fines.

To define exactly what an environmental regulation requires, or to get it invalidated completely, an industry group or environmental organization may mount a court challenge to the regulation by suing the relevant agency. Once again, just as when the agency originally promulgated the regulation, each side will have experts who say different things about the regulation. This time, however, the court will decide if the regulation is valid or not. If the regulation is valid, the court will enforce it. If the regulation is invalid, the court will declare it void.

This type of court action creates what is known as "case law." Enforcement actions, if they reach court, also create case law. Regardless of how it develops, case law is important because it provides another set of definitions through which compliance personnel must analyze environmental laws and regulations. Analysis by the courts of such purely legal terms as "joint and several" and "knowing and willful" have had a major impact on the implementation of environmental laws and regulations. This impact exists because any subsequent compliance efforts or enforcement actions must reflect relevant case law in that jurisdiction. Case law from one jurisdiction, be it a state or an EPA region, does not govern issues in a different jurisdiction. Case law is advisory only, and the trial jurisdiction may or may not follow it.

As a result of case law being binding within its jurisdiction, it is possible to have conflicting interpretations of statutes, regulations, and case law in different jurisdictions. When these conflicts occur, senior courts, including the United States Supreme Court, may hear a case to decide the conflicting issue, or Congress or the relevant agency may issue additional guidance in an effort to resolve the conflict. Naturally, this conflict resolution is, as it logically should be, never-ending. Each court case or agency guidance opens new questions of meaning, which in turn must be resolved by the courts, Congress, or the agency.

Combined with legislative reauthorizations, statutory amendments, and updated agency guidelines, changing case law makes environmental compliance a very dynamic field. On the positive side, this constant change may result in laws and regulations that more accurately reflect current popular desires and the best of modern technology. On the negative side, this dynamism requires never-ending vigilance on the part of the compliance personnel to ensure compliance strategies are up-to-date.

STATE AND LOCAL ENVIRONMENTAL LAWS

State environmental laws and regulations develop in much the same manner as federal ones, but there are some crucial differences. In addition to having to stay within the guidelines set by U.S. Constitution, state laws and regulations must follow the state's constitution. Furthermore, state programs cannot be contrary to federal laws, since federal laws are supreme. Not surprisingly, there is a large grey area where it is not clear whether a state program is counter to a federal law or the state or the U.S. Constitution. By and large, it is up to the state or federal courts to decide whether a challenged state law is valid or not, just as with federal laws and regulations.

Although, they cannot run counter to federal laws, state laws and regulations can be stricter than federal guidelines. Absent a constitutional problem, such as an undue burden on interstate commerce, a state has considerable flexibility in developing its environmental standards. Some states, most notably California, frequently develop environmental programs that are much stricter than similar federal programs. Other states may essentially follow or simply adopt federal programs. No state, however, can set standards lower than the federal guidelines, as the federal standard sets the absolute floor in that regulated area. In some instances, an area may be regulated only by the federal government or only by the state government. In others, e.g., National Pollutant Discharge Elimination System (NPDES) permits, the responsible federal agency may delegate authority for a program to a state upon the presentation of evidence by the state that it is capable of managing the program and willing to do it. In those cases, the federal agency retains oversight of the state's program and has the ability to revoke the delegation of authority if it has cause to believe that the state is not carrying out the program properly.

Local governments also may have environmental controls. These controls are usually in the form of town bylaws, and reflect the same political concerns as any other law or regulation. Like state and federal laws and regulations, these local ordinances must not violate the U.S. Constitution or any other valid law from a superior governing body. As long as these local laws are valid, they have all the power of any other law, and violations may result in fines and possibly imprisonment. For the most part, local environmental controls focus on land use issues such as minimum lot size, wetlands protection, and industrial zoning.

ENFORCEMENT AND CRIMINAL LIABILITY ISSUES

Nobody would comply with a statute or regulation if there were no enforcement. Accordingly, Congress provided for heavy civil and criminal penalties for violations in most of its environmental statutes. For example, RCRA's criminal provisions include up to $50,000 in fines per day of violation and a two year imprisonment for first-time violators who misrepresent relevant documents, while criminal violations of the Clean Water Act could result in repeat offenders being fined up to $50,000 per day of violation and imprisoned up to two years. State and local environmental laws and regulations likewise can carry heavy sanctions.

While in the past, businesses used to regard environmental fines as just another cost of doing business, enforcement has recently begun to focus more on the criminal aspect of violations. Although the standards of proof are more difficult for the government to meet in criminal proceedings than in civil ones, a guilty verdict is a much more chilling prospect than mere civil liability. Responsible parties may go to jail for environmental violations; criminal fines are severe and criminal convictions may even affect stock offerings.

Environmental laws and regulations raise unusual criminal liability issues because they are public health-type laws. Public health statutes do not require the criminal intent of other laws in order to obtain a criminal conviction. Unlike embezzlement, for example, environmental crimes generally require neither evil purpose nor criminal intent to accompany the doing of the wrongful act. The defendant's state of mind is of relatively little importance except to the extent that the defendant must know it is carrying out a specific action. In essence, these environmental laws create strict liability for offenses.

Nor is ignorance a reliable excuse for environmental violations. There is generally no knowledge requirement for civil sanctions and the violation taking place is enough, by itself, to result in fines or court orders. The level of knowledge the government must prove to obtain a criminal conviction for an environmental violation is higher, but not exceptionally so. Under the doctrine of *respondeat superior*, corporations can be criminally liable for an employee's violating an environmental statute if that employee is operating within the scope of his or her duty at the time of the violation.

Even if no one employee satisfies all of the elements of a crime, especially all of the knowledge of intent elements, finding corporate liability is still possible through the Collective Knowledge Doctrine. Under this doctrine, a corporation may be liable for criminal offenses, even though no single agent intended to commit the offense or knew all of the relevant facts. Basically, a company cannot claim innocence because a variety of employees had bits and pieces of the relevant information, rather than one employee knowing everything. Instead, the corporation is considered to have acquired the collective knowledge of its employees and is held responsible for its failure to act accordingly. While this doctrine is relatively unused in the environmental arena, it may become more important in the future.

The government may prove knowledge through the use of circumstantial evidence. It is not unreasonable to state that, under RCRA, anyone who knows that they are dealing with hazardous materials automatically has all of the knowledge necessary to prove a "knowing" violation of any of RCRA's criminal provisions. It is important to remember, however, that in a crime, having knowledge as an express element, a mere showing of official responsibility, is not an adequate substitute for direct or circumstantial proof of knowledge. Still, a defendant's position and responsibilities within a corporation can help to prove knowledge, and a willful blindness to the facts probably will be considered actual knowledge.

Like most organizations, environmental enforcement agencies do not have unlimited resources. Agencies must use their prosecutorial discretion to decide which cases to pursue, which cases to settle, and which cases to drop altogether. Factors influencing these decisions include the type of violation, the difficulty of proving the agency's case, the attitude of the potential defendant, etc. Since only a small percentage of cases go to trial, a would-be defendant should not assume all is lost merely because an enforcement agency is expressing interest in company activity.

CIVIL LIABILITY AND PRIVATE PARTIES

As stated above, environmental violations can result in civil fines and court orders without raising any criminal issues. Fines can be very high, and court orders can be anything from injunctions prohibiting certain activities to a command to "clean up" thousands of cubic meters of earth. While not as threatening physically as imprisonment, civil liability can be devastating financially to both corporations and individuals. In general, complying with environmental regulations should negate fines, but it is possible that a court still may halt activities that do not actually violate any regulations if it believes that the activity would result in some sort of unreasonable damage.

Polluters also can be liable to nongovernmental parties for trespass, physical injury, devalued property, and so forth. If waste stored by "Company X" leaks onto "Neighbor B's" land, that neighbor may go to court to force Company X to clean up B's land. If B has suffered physical harm, such as contracting a cancer traceable to Company X, X also may pay personal damages. Air pollution, water pollution, hazardous products, and a variety of other methods all have the potential to result in tort claims for property damage or personal injury.

Although personal tort claims can be financially significant, they are independent of compliance issues. It is possible to comply with all relevant federal, state, and local hazardous material storage regulations and still have an accident that results in a tort claim. Depending on the rules of the court which hears the tort claim, the defendant's past compliance with relevant regulations may be evidence of a lack of negligence. Equally, proof of noncompliance, such as past "Notices of Violations," may be strong or even conclusive evidence of the defendant's negligence. Thus, while issues of personal civil liability are beyond the scope of this book, it is important to emphasize that a solid record of environmental compliance may be helpful in avoiding significant civil tort claims.

FEDERAL FACILITIES COMPLIANCE ACT

Congress added a new twist to environmental compliance when it passed the Federal Facilities Compliance Act (FFCA) in October, 1992. Traditionally, the federal government has exempted itself from the civil fines contained in many environmental laws. Congress managed this exemption by using the doctrine of "sovereign immunity," which means that the federal government (the sovereign) is immune to legal assaults from junior governments, such as states. By waiving sovereign immunity, the Congress made it clear that it expects all federal facilities to be in compliance with environmental laws and regulations. FFCA allows states to levy civil fines against federal facilities for not complying with RCRA. Given the hazardous waste/hazardous material management issues at many federal facilities, FFCA promises to be a very popular tool for state environmental agencies to enforce federal compliance.

HOW TO USE THIS BOOK

This book is a tool that will assist the person responsible for environmental compliance at a facility by removing the guesswork and worry from environmental compliance. Like any other tool, this book will perform a variety of functions quite effectively when used properly. Also, like any other tool, this book will not do everything. In those cases, and there are many, where the vagaries of the law prohibit complete coverage, the authors have provided detailed instructions for finding further guidance. At a minimum, the user of this tool will gain a working familiarity with the development, content, and implementation of environmental laws and regulations. This familiarity will enable the reader to understand the general regulatory thrust of an environmental program, to ask the right questions of media experts, and to plan and respond properly on a day to day basis, as well as in the event of an environmental emergency.

The authors have analyzed most major federal environmental laws from two perspectives: (1) a discussion of the law and (2) instructions on how to comply with the law. Most major environmental laws have a complete chapter devoted to them, and some share a chapter. While state laws will vary widely from state to state and subject to subject, the authors have highlighted salient points from the most relevant state laws. The authors have also included detailed guidance, including current points of contact, on where to obtain more information on relevant state and local issues.

After reading the relevant portions of the text, the reader should know how to find more information on important items such as the past use of the property, the location and test results of past or current underground storage tanks, potential air emission sources in the area, etc. The reader also will know who to contact from local and state agencies, and how to properly document any responses he or she carries out.

This book is also intended to give the reader a solid background on environmental issues that could delay projects if improperly handled. If, for example, a company's Chief Executive Officer wants to expand a factory, he or she should read the sections on noise, wetlands preservation, and so forth. While the reader might not be the person who in fact is going to deal with these particular issues on a daily basis, he or she will understand these issues and any relevant permitting processes and will be able to better supervise whichever subordinate is doing this work.

In essence, this book is adaptable to the needs of its readers. For those readers who just want to get the general idea behind some issue, a glance at the relevant sections of this book should suffice. For those readers whose needs are more complex, a thorough reading of relevant sections of this book will provide the needed information. Like any other tool, this book is made to be used. Write notes in it, jot down important phone numbers of points of contact, highlight especially relevant parts, and take it on trips to the field. The only thing for which this book is not to be used is collecting dust—environmental compliance is far too important not to utilize such an effective piece of equipment.

2   The Environmental Compliance Assessment

INTRODUCTION

As discussed in Chapter 1, having a sound environmental compliance program is increasingly vital to the success of any organization. Many organizations, however, are unsure of how to proceed with an effective plan of action. This uncertainty is magnified by the myriad of federal, state, regional, and local environmental laws and regulations. This chapter, therefore, will explain the basics of starting and maintaining an environmental compliance program. While the specific details will vary from organization to organization, the overall theme will remain the same and the techniques discussed below can be modified to meet the needs of any organization.

To develop and monitor an effective environmental compliance program, an organization must first assess its environmental requirements. The environmental compliance assessment is referred to in this chapter by the abbreviation ECA. The present U.S. Army description is "environmental assessment" and is described at length in *The Environmental Assessment Management (TEAM) Guide* (Dec., 1994). Other government agencies use similar terms such as ECAAR, ECAP, etc. The term ECA will be used for an environmental compliance assessment throughout this book. An ECA helps the organization determine which legal requirements, out of a vast number of federal, state, and local environmental laws and regulations, are relevant to its activities. Additionally, the ECA should catalog all resources available to support the organization's compliance program. By determining which environmental regulations are the most relevant, including the ones most likely to lead to unwanted enforcement actions, and by cataloging available resources, an ECA will enable the organization to expend its environmental energies in the most efficient manner.

Intuitively, one would suspect that smaller entities, such as a local camera shop or a family-run restaurant, would face fewer environmental requirements than larger organizations such as General Motors or federal government agencies. While this suspicion may be correct in theory, the camera shop owner would probably be surprised to learn just how many environmental laws and regulations affect his shop. Since even small violations of environmental regulations can result in costly fines and delays, all organizations must try to remain in 100 percent compliance. Therefore, even the smallest organization should conduct a thorough initial review of its environmental program to determine its compliance status.

The ECA is the tool that allows an organization to determine what additional steps it must take to comply with environmental laws and regulations. It is possible that some of these steps may involve expensive remediation projects or entail considerable plant redesign. The cost justifications for such actions by themselves may be difficult, but once the ECA has noted the area of non-compliance, management must address the issue within a reasonable amount of time so that it attains compliance. When management knows of a compliance issue, such as an illegal release under CERCLA, improperly stored hazardous waste under RCRA, or endangered species impacts, subsequent failures to act in accordance with regulatory standards could result in increased fines and possibly criminal sanctions for knowing violations of these statutes. Additionally, if a neighboring property is polluted or a worker is hurt, in part because an organization was not complying with environmental laws, an ECA report noting the compliance problem would be a tort lawyer's dream in establishing the negligence needed to prove liability.

Many insurance policies now have a very comprehensive pollution exclusion. Under these exclusions, an organization could find itself paying devastating remediation fees and tort awards out of its own pockets. If the environmental officer does not know if his organization's insurance policy contains a pollution exclusion, he should determine that fact immediately. He also should consult with his legal officer and the insurance company to determine the scope of such an exclusion.

This caution is not intended to discourage the reader from enthusiastically conducting a thorough environmental review. Such a review, as noted above, is instrumental in best allocating organizational resources to avoid environmental degradation and liability. Instead, this caution is intended to be a guide to the organization's environmental officer, assisting him or her in painting an honest picture of the potential risks and probable benefits of conducting an ECA. Once they have been properly briefed on the pros and cons of performing an environmental compliance assessment, an organization's management will be able to better determine when and if to do an ECA. Because managers are frequently the responsible parties in many organizations, their concerns about the possible liability ramifications of an ECA are understandable. The environmental officer should make sure to remind the organization's management, as discussed in Chapter 1, that the law will treat people as if they had actual knowledge in cases where those people should have known of the compliance problems. Since the position, responsibility, job title, and a variety of other circumstantial evidence may be used to prove "constructive" knowledge, management may find that postponing an ECA does not lessen liability exposure.

WHO DOES AN ENVIRONMENTAL ASSESSMENT?

In deciding who should conduct its ECA, an organization should consider many factors. Are hazardous wastes or hazardous materials issues? Are there any wetlands on site? Since many OSHA requirements are closely related to environmental requirements, especially in the areas of hazardous materials and hazardous waste, should the assessors also conduct at least a partial OSHA assessment? Are Department of Housing and Urban Development regulations, such as those concerning lead-based paint, a concern? How does the organization plan to use its ECA results and what report format will most facilitate such use? How much money is the organization willing to spend for the overall ECA? The organization's environmental officer, along with other relevant management staff such as budgeting, production, and public affairs personnel, should discuss these factors at length. Eventually, management should translate the list of relevant factors into a working paper to assist in setting out the scope of work and other issues for the ECA.

Having decided on what it wants to gain from an ECA, an organization needs to find a firm, or an internal team, to conduct the assessment. It is critical that qualified professionals perform the ECA, as an inaccurate assessment will not assist, and may damage, an organization's environmental compliance program. Personnel conducting environmental assessments should be environmental specialists. Given the wide array of compliance issues, it would be virtually impossible to find someone who has all the answers, but at the very least, an assessor should have a working familiarity with most federal environmental laws such as the Clean Water Act and RCRA. The assessor should be knowledgeable of local, regional, and state environmental laws and regulations, and know how they may affect the organization's activities. Ideally, the assessor will have special expertise or experience in the compliance areas that most affect an organization. For example, an auto shop probably would want an environmental assessor to have more competence in RCRA issues than in wetlands permitting issues. Conversely, a country club may be much more concerned about wetlands and Clean Water Act compliance than it is about hazardous waste. When naming an environmental assessor, an organization should list its special concerns to ensure it selects an assessor with relevant expertise.

Actual experience in the regulated industry, such as working as a shop foreman or as a grounds-keeper, is a plus, as it will give the assessor special insights into the organization's day-to-day actions and compliance problems. An assessor who has worked in an auto body shop in all probability would be more likely to look in all the right corners to find improperly stored hazardous items than someone who has never even changed his car's oil. Similarly, an assessor with some golf course experience would be more likely to know that the dead grass on the fairway is the result of a pesticide spill rather than the mere summer burn that a less sophisticated assessor might assume.

In addition to noticing more compliance issues than their counterparts, assessors with experience in the regulated field should be less likely to accept inaccurate or misleading answers to their probing questions. These assessors also may be able to provide useful, ground-level compliance suggestions. In our auto shop and golf course examples, these ideas could range from methods of properly storing solvents while maintaining accessibility, to providing spill protection in golf courses when applying pesticides.

Larger organizations will probably find that assessor teams, rather than individuals, will conduct the most thorough and the quickest review. These teams should consist of environmental specialists with varied fields of expertise reflecting the organization's unique environmental concerns. A harborside boatyard probably would want assessors with expertise in hazardous waste and hazardous material management due to the organization's use of hazardous materials such as anti-fouling paint and solvents. The boatyard also would be well advised to ensure that one of its assessors had expertise in dealing with wetlands protection and Clean Water Act issues, due to the organization's proximity to the water.

An organization should have its ECA done by individuals who not only can spot compliance issues, but also can translate those issues into a format which the organization can use. If an organization works with certain computer programs such as Dbase IV™ or WordPerfect 6.0™, it should request ECA results in those formats. If the ECA will involve presentations to an organization's management, workers, or shareholders, someone involved with the ECA must be capable of giving those presentations. If presentations must be in certain languages, the assessors should have that language capability. If certain technical aspects must be explained, such as detailing effluent monitoring techniques to the lawyers and bankers constituting the board of directors, the persons doing the ECA must have the relevant expertise to effectively explain these issues.

When engaging a firm to conduct its ECA, an organization should consider the ability of a firm to keep the results confidential. Since some environmental compliance issues, such as hazardous material handling, involve severe financial risks, an organization must ensure that its ECA is not made public unnecessarily. In some cases, an organization may be able to shield its ECA by claiming that the ECA involves a privileged relationship. Draft working documents are frequently shielded from the public eye, so nonfinalized ECAs may remain private even during a court case. The environmental manager should consult with the organization's counsel during the ECA planning stages to determine if and how an ECA can remain private. The ability of other parties to gain access to an ECA report should be openly discussed with an organization's management. Thus, for example, the army's draft reports, as well as those of other branches of the federal government, are not available for public distribution even under a Freedom of Information Request.

Just as an organization must ensure confidentiality in undertaking an ECA, it also must ensure reliability. No one is perfect, and an organization must understand that an inaccurate ECA does not relieve the organization of its duty to comply with all environmental laws and regulations. If an ECA team incorrectly determines that a manufacturing plant has no RCRA compliance issues, that determination will not give the plant complete protection from prosecution when EPA inspectors show up the next day and discover unlabelled hazardous waste. Such an ECA could be useful in convincing EPA, or a judge, that the violation is less egregious due to the organization's good faith attempts to comply. As discussed in Chapter 1, good faith, or the lack thereof, is one of many mitigating factors agencies and courts consider when deciding on potential fines or prosecution.

COORDINATING AN ASSESSMENT

While the approach below is presented in terms of the employment of an outside firm to do the ECA, the same principles apply if the ECA is done in-house.

An organization's environmental officer should personally contact assessors well in advance of an ECA. This initial contact may be by phone or by mail, and is primarily to allow the environmental officer to review the organization's special concerns with the assessors. If a schedule does not already exist, the environmental officer should develop a rough schedule for the assessment and a tentative timeline for post-assessment reports. If the officer has any special instructions or requests, such as asking the assessors not to give on-the-spot corrections to workers, or making sure at least one assessor speaks a certain language, he should note those requests at this time. The representative should stress that while he expects the organization's special environmental concerns to receive the most attention, he still wants a thorough evaluation of all other compliance areas. Of course, if the organization's management has properly evaluated its ECA needs and reflected those needs in the contract, there should be no major surprises for either the ECA firm or the environmental officer. Nonetheless, constant communication between all parties and frequent reiteration of crucial points will maximize the value of an ECA and is well worth the small added cost of redundancy.

Before the start of the ECA, the environmental officer should meet with the assessors to review ECA goals and time schedules. If he has not yet provided the assessors with a written list of all his special concerns and requests, the representative should give them one now. The officer should reemphasize his concern that the ECA be thorough. Ideally, this meeting will take place far enough in advance of the assessment to allow the assessment team to finalize any special arrangements. This advance time also may prove useful to solve any contractual disagreements that may arise concerning the ECA. It would be wise to ensure that any required special items should be in the original contract, including such matters as previewing the presentation, special expertise required, timelines, and so forth.

At some point prior to the assessment, possibly during the initial coordinating meeting, and certainly before the final pre-ECA meeting, the organization's representative should provide the assessors with a written list of potential hazards at the assessment site(s). If the organization has a safety officer, the environmental officer should obtain his or her input on this hazard list for potential OSHA concerns. This is because the organization that is the direct employer of the personnel carrying out the ECA has a duty of care towards the assessors. Even specific language in the ECA contract that provides for indemnification or immunity concerning workplace hazards may not shield the organization from liability for injuries suffered by assessors, or damage to their equipment, during an ECA. The environmental officer should consult with his legal officer concerning such potential liability and attempt to minimize any dangers through workplace safety, clear instructions, and close supervision.

Possible hazards include inhalation of dangerous chemicals such as muriatic acid, explosions, excessive heat in boiler rooms, friable asbestos, or peeling lead-based paint, etc. Ideally, the organization representative will be able to provide the assessors with a master list of the facility's chemicals, its hazardous waste and hazardous storage facilities, gasoline storage and dispensing facilities and any other information that would allow an assessor to best plan a safe site visit.

This information may be most readily available in the form of an existing goal and hazardous waste contingency/spill plan. Prior to sending such a plan to the assessor, the organization's compliance officer should revalidate the plan's information and ensure that it contains no proprietary information that is unsuitable for dissemination to the assessing firm.

An organization's environmental representative will have the responsibility of coordinating the assessment with facility personnel and management. The representative should make sure that, on the day, or days, of the assessment, the assessors have ready access to all areas of the facility. This coordination is especially important for inspecting hazardous waste and hazardous materials, as they are frequently in locked areas. The representative will also want to make sure he can locate all relevant environmental records for the assessors. While doing this coordination, the representative must not overly alarm facility personnel, as even the best-intentioned staff may think that they are doing everyone a favor by camouflaging compliance issues.

Camouflaging compliance problems is counterproductive, since the assessors must see the facility as it operates on a daily basis to evaluate compliance effectively. An ECA is designed to create a compliance "snapshot," and an unnaturally clean or well documented facility will not allow assessors to provide accurate guidance on how to improve daily compliance. The assessors need to see the paint cans in the dumpster, the hazardous material drums with no labels, and the effluent flowing untreated into the local sewer.

Only by viewing all of the compliance problems can the assessors help the organization determine what sorts of compliance issues need what sort of action. The organization must emphasize — to its management and to its ground-level employees — that it is having an ECA for one reason only. This reason is to note compliance issues and suggest corrective actions **before** an environmental agency comes aboard with its civil and criminal enforcement powers. That reason is the heart of a compliance program.

In some cases, it will be necessary for work to stop during an assessment. Machinery may be too loud or too dangerous to approach while running. Filters may be inaccessible, requiring removal for proper evaluation. Workers may need to concentrate on answering questions from the ECA team. If it is necessary to stop work during all or part of an ECA, the environmental manager should attempt to coordinate this requirement beforehand. Besides the obvious safety issue of evaluating an operating piece of machinery, the environmental officer should be concerned with potential releases or discharges due to removed filters or disconnected ducts. By closely coordinating with the work supervisor, the environmental manager can plan the assessment for a time when a work stoppage would have the least negative impact.

THE MECHANICS OF AN ENVIRONMENTAL ASSESSMENT

An environmental compliance assessment does not have to be an expensive and time consuming activity. Naturally, the larger an organization or the more complicated its daily activities, the more complex an ECA should be. The United States Army, an extraordinarily large organization with very complicated activities, has spent many millions of dollars assessing environmental compliance issues at its many bases and reserve centers. The Army's environmental compliance assessment program, known as TEAM, employs a large number of people on a full time basis, in addition to employing numerous consultants to assist with specific assessment projects. A variation of this TEAM program might well be suitable for many other large organizations. For smaller organizations, though, such as our hypothetical camera shop, an environmental compliance assessment should be a relatively simple and inexpensive affair, causing little havoc to either the work schedule or the financial bottom line.

The overall compliance assessment procedure should not vary significantly from organization to organization, although it may vary in scope and intensity. Internal environmental experts or outside consultants will visit sites owned or operated by an organization and review its records, inspect the site for environmental issues, and evaluate the organization's overall environmental practices. The assessor may evaluate compliance using a specialized assessment critique form or else may work from generic manuals and personal expertise. The U.S. Army's environmental assessment specialists base their assessments on 13 compliance categories which, in effect, comprise a list of all major federal environmental statutes and regulations such as the Clean Water Act and the Clean Air Act. Army assessors also use state compliance manuals to supplement the larger federal TEAM manual. With our hypothetical camera shop, an assessor could probably work from a checklist of only two or three pages.

The assessor may take photographs or videos of compliance issues. These can provide compelling evidence of what the assessors saw. For example, at the ECA out-briefing, a floor manager may deny that his unit followed certain unsatisfactory work practices. A video documenting such practices would prevent any further debate. Conversely, a videotape of workers emptying 55 gallon barrels of an unknown substance into a floor drain would make a prosecutor's job a lot easier. And once created, ECA photos and film may be quite difficult to destroy without negative implications. Union officials, legal staff, and the public affairs officer will all have their opinions on whether photography would be an appropriate tool for an ECA, and an environmental officer should solicit their advice during the initial ECA planning stages. Photography issues should be covered in the ECA contract and, if appropriate, during pre-ECA coordination meetings.

Environmental assessors also should catalog an organization's environmental resources. This catalog should include the quantity, type, capability, and location of all environmental compliance materials as well as the names, work areas, numbers, and environmental training of all personnel involved in environmental issues. How many hazardous waste storage facilities does it have? Where are they? What types are they? What types of material do they contain? Which employees have received what sort of training? Does the facility have spill response kits? If so, what types and where are they located? Does the organization have portable spill pods? Where are they? By determining what environmental resources it has, an organization will be better able to allocate those resources or obtain additional ones as needed to further compliance.

Note that many training requirements concerning such things as hazardous materials handling are actually OSHA requirements. Many nonenvironmental regulations are closely related to environmental issues and should be a part of any environmental compliance program.

Compliance assessments should follow a uniform pattern. Assessors should work from the same compliance worksheets for similar installations whether the assessment is in Connecticut or in Colorado, with appropriate variations for state and local laws and regulations. Assessors also should follow the same assessment techniques from installation to installation. If Assessment Team A starts a site visit by talking with the site manager and then progresses to reviewing training records and associated environmental paperwork, Team B should do the same thing at a different facility three months later. Although different sites almost always will raise different compliance issues, the final ECA reports should look as identical as possible. Consistent assessments and reports will give an organization's environmental compliance officer more confidence in the work product and a more accurate understanding of his/her overall compliance status.

The assessors will generally ask "yes" or "no" questions concerning the relationship between the organization and environmental laws. A positive answer indicates that a particular environmental regulation is relevant and requires more investigation, while a negative answer indicates that the regulation is not relevant to the organization and needs no further evaluation. To evaluate compliance under the Clean Water Act, for example, an assessor would ask if the organization discharges anything into the local sewer system. If the answer, found by questioning employees, reviewing plans and checking permits, is yes, then the assessor must ask follow-up questions about effluent testing procedures, discharge permits, and the organization's spill response capabilities. These follow-up questions will require answers in far greater detail than yes or no.

Similarly, if an assessor is reviewing an organization's compliance under the Clean Air Act (CAA), an initial question would be whether there are any potential sources of air emissions. If the answer is no, the assessor would move on to other aspects of the CAA. If the answer if yes, the assessor may have to determine the levels of discharge for these sources, the types of filters used, etc. The assessors should keep clear and detailed notes, rather than relying on memory, to ensure the assessment remains as accurate as possible. If assessors are taking photographs or videos, they should attempt to do so as unobtrusively as possible.

POST-INTERVIEW ENVIRONMENTAL COMPLIANCE ASSESSMENT ACTIONS

Once the interview portion of the ECA is over, the assessors will need a certain amount of time to review their results. Because this review may take some time, an organization may wish to specify in its ECA contract that an exit briefing will immediately follow the assessment. In an exit briefing, the ECA team provides an informal, verbal evaluation of the ECA to the organization's environmental compliance officer and any other interested personnel. This informal assessment should allow the environmental officer to get an immediate start on following up with any pressing compliance issues while beginning to formulate a long term compliance strategy.

The final ECA report and any related presentation(s) should be delineated in the ECA contract. The environmental officer should help the ECA firm coordinate, with the help of the contracting officer if appropriate, the distribution of draft and final ECA reports and the scheduling of any presentations.

It cannot be overemphasized that the best presentation in the world is of no value if it is above the target audience's ability to comprehend. To ensure maximum effectiveness, an organization's environmental officer should insist on approving the final presentation prior to displaying it to the target audience. Board members, bankers, and lawyers generally tend to be busy people who will not appreciate slides that are illegible, handouts that are mislabelled, and technical details that are incomprehensible. While these people may not have much sway over the actual assessors, they generally have considerable input into the environmental officer's career. Furthermore, in addition to emphasizing an environmental officer's competence, a professional presentation will be more likely than a sloppy performance to build support for an organization's environmental program.

Armed with the final ECA report, the environmental officer must aggressively start putting together corrective action plans for noted compliance deficiencies. The compliance officer should also ensure that environmental commendations are given where appropriate. Any corrective action plans should refer to specific deficiencies noted in the ECA, as well as to any relevant local, state, or federal laws and regulations. Because there may be more than one way to implement a corrective action, the environmental officer should get other departments to review his plans prior to implementation.

USING THIS BOOK TO HELP DEVELOP
CORRECTIVE ACTION PLANS AFTER AN ECA

Upon completion of an ECA, facility environmental compliance officers will have an accurate idea of what types of compliance issues they face. Since an effective ECA should note all areas of environmental compliance, not just areas that are in a noncompliance status, compliance officers should have evidence of what their facilities are doing properly as well as what areas need more work. Obviously, areas that are now in compliance will not need corrective action plans, but compliance officers should ensure that the workers responsible for the acceptable state of compliance are commended. Additionally, compliance officers should realize that compliance status may change on a daily basis.

Most facilities will focus on problem areas noted by the ECA. Missing permits, inadequate safety measures, faulty equipment, and nonexistent filter systems are examples of a few of the problems an ECA may reveal. Compliance officers must immediately tackle the job of correcting any non-compliance issues.

When approaching these compliance issues, compliance officers should develop a written corrective action plan. This plan should reflect the various priorities of both the environmental issues and the facility s overall production program. In some cases, environmental issues may be an automatic immediate priority, regardless of what else is going on at the plant. Examples of such important environmental issues include the mixing of incompatible hazardous wastes, the use of leaking tank systems, the unpermitted discharging of hazardous chemicals into surface water, or any other instance where public health and the environment may suffer immediate and severe harm. In such extreme cases, compliance officers should do whatever is necessary to mitigate the damage, making sure to document their efforts. Other environmental compliance issues, such as having the proper documentation for an underground storage tank (UST), may not warrant such immediate attention. Complying with these less pressing environmental issues may be worked into a facility s larger operating plan. For example, obtaining the tightness testing results for a UST may be postponed until after the facility finishes a reorganization of its administrative and archival staff. The exact priorities of a corrective action plan will differ from site to site, depending on the results of the ECA, the relevant state and local laws and any other influences particular to a certain facility.

The corrective action plan should be a well researched, comprehensive description of a facility s problems as noted by the ECA, the relevant regulatory standards, and all potential compliance strategies. Compliance officers also may find that even the most comprehensive ECA overlooks some compliance issues—these issues, too, should be covered by the corrective action plan. For facilities with fairly simple compliance issues, such as lack of documentation for a UST, the compliance officer may be able to develop and implement the corrective action plan singlehandedly. Facilities experiencing more complex compliance concerns, such as lack of a Title V air emissions permit or NEPA documentation for a proposed development, may have to turn to outside consultants to finalize and implement the plan. In such a situation, the compliance staff of the facility would need to have enough knowledge of the regulatory program to provide adequate oversight of the contracted help.

Whether the corrective action plan is done in-house or with outside assistance, compliance officers will find that this book provides a good *starting point* for plan development. After reviewing the ECA results, compliance officers should turn to the relevant sections of this book to determine what regulatory issues exist. For example, if the ECA notes that the facility is discharging wastes into an underground injection well and suggests that this action might present a problem, the compliance officer would review the discussion of injection wells in Chapter 4 and drinking water protection in Chapter 5. The compliance officer would learn that there are two types of permits available for injection wells. Each of these types has specific monitoring and reporting requirements, which are referred to in this book. Using this book, the compliance officer would know to review the permit, if any, for applicable conditions of monitoring, injection rates, and so forth to compare against actual operation. The compliance officer would also know that if there is no permit, or if fuel is being improperly injected, this particular compliance issue would have a higher priority than if there were only some minor monitoring issues.

This book frequently refers the compliance officers to specific sections of the Code of Federal Regulations (CFR) as part of its discussion of a regulatory program. In the example above, while the discussion would enable a compliance officer to understand the broad regulatory program, if there were major compliance problems, such as injection without a permit, the officer would probably want to review the CFR personally. In this case, the CFR section noted is 40 CFR §146. Other compliance issues relate to different CFR sections. The discussion in this book on hazardous waste treatment, for example, discusses the basic requirements for a hazardous waste generator to receive a permit, and then refers the reader to 40 CFR §262 for more information.

It is up to the compliance officer to determine whether this book has provided enough information for any given situation. If the compliance officer is the one developing the corrective action plan, reading the appropriate CFR sections and contacting the relevant environmental agency probably would be a good idea if the compliance issue is of any complexity. In such a case, this book would give the compliance officer a general understanding of the regulatory program, some of the highlights of compliance concerns and, in some cases, important suggestions for putting together a compliance program. This should minimize the frustrations most people experience when trying to fathom a regulatory program without having much background in the subject.

On the other hand, merely reading the appropriate sections of this book may be enough for compliance officers who have minor compliance issues. For example, if a facility in a developed area has not addressed endangered species concerns, the book may provide enough information on putting together a compliance program without having to refer to the CFR. Following the checklist in the compliance portion of that chapter, the compliance officer would review any literature relevant to natural resources on the facility. The officer then would contact the state and federal agencies that deal with natural resources, such as the U.S. Department of Fish and Wildlife. If this research indicates that no endangered species potentially occur on the facility, then the compliance officer should document this research and move on to the next compliance issue.

This book also will prove useful as a stand-alone document, when a facility decides whether to contract out its Corrective Action Plan and, if so, how much of the plan should be contracted. By reviewing ECA findings against the relevant chapters in this book, the compliance officer should have a good idea about which compliance issues are too complicated to handle without outside assistance. If the ECA notes that there is no noise control program, for example, a quick review of the section on noise in this book would give compliance officers a good idea of how this program impacts their facilities. For a compliance officer in charge of several small food stores, the major noise concern is likely to arise from delivery trucks. There are no airfields, blasting operations, or major construction operations to worry about. In all probability, after reviewing this section, compliance officers in such a situation would decide that they could handle noise compliance in-house. On the other hand, compliance officers for airports may well read the description of noise meters, mitigation plans, and projected noise levels and realize that a specialist is needed for proper compliance.

In the latter case, this book serves an important role by allowing facility environmental compliance personnel to quickly apportion the parts of the corrective action plan which can be done in-house without starting an extensive research project just to determine that outside assistance is needed. By reading the relevant sections of this book, facility compliance staff should be able to contact contractors and intelligently discuss the ECA results, relevant regulatory programs, and corrective action plan requirements. Will the contractor measure the noise in specific areas? Is the contractor experienced in mitigation plans? Has the contractor worked in an area where noise comes from a variety of sources at unpredictable intervals? The discussion in this book of general standards with key specific regulatory requirements will allow compliance officers to select competent assistance and also to monitor that assistance without having to be subject matter experts themselves.

ECA CHECKLIST

A truly comprehensive ECA checklist should cover every major federal environmental law as well as relevant state and local laws, regulations and ordinances. The detailed "yes" and "no" checks for the Clean Air Act, the Clean Water Act, the National Historic Preservation Act, etc., would total in the hundreds of pages. Therefore, there is not enough room to enclose a detailed ECA checklist in this book. However, the compliance portions of each chapter provide a detailed alternative ECA system and may be used in conjunction with the abbreviated checklist that follows at the end of this section.

Compliance officers should be able to make good use of a condensed ECA checklist, one which highlights key areas of concern and which will allow compliance officers to quickly determine which areas of their facilities need more immediate attention. This checklist does not indicate any particular priority of importance of the compliance issues discussed. If this list indicates that a facility has specific compliance concerns, the compliance officer should refer to the chapter which discusses those concerns for further, more detailed guidance. If this checklist indicates that a facility has no environmental compliance concerns, the compliance officers should still refer to this book to double-check compliance issues, but there would not be the same level of immediacy as in the first instance.

A positive answer to any of the questions below indicates that further research on that issue is appropriate. Negative answers should be well documented, not just word-of-mouth intuitive responses without factual support. In fact, in many cases a negative answer may require considerable amounts of research, such as conducting a survey to determine that there are no PCBs in concentrations of greater that 50 PPM at the facility. The suggested general checklist is shown below. More detailed checklists designed specifically for Department of Defense personnel may be found in the December, 1994 *TEAM Guide*.

GENERAL CHECKLIST

1. SURFACE WATER
   a. Does the facility have a state or federal discharge permit?
   b. Does the facility have any offsite discharges?
      If so
         Do these discharges run into wetlands?
         Do these discharges run into the public treatment works?
         Are these discharges the result of stormwater runoff?
   c. Does the facility treat wastewater prior to discharge?
   d. Are there wetlands on site?
   e. Does the facility carry out, or plan to carry out, any dredging activities?
2. GROUNDWATER
   a. Does the facility have potential sources of groundwater contamination such as leaching field, sanitary landfills, pesticide spraying operations, storage tanks or injection wells?
   b. Is groundwater contamination potentially or actually occurring on the site?
   c. Is any of the facility covered by a Wellhead Protection Area?
   d. Does the facility sit on top of an aquifer? If so, is it a sole source aquifer?
3. DRINKING WATER
   a. Is drinking water supplied at the facility(ies)?
   b. Is the facility responsible for providing drinking water to anyone?
4. AIR
   a. Does the facility have any state, federal or local air permits?
      If so
         Are these permits up-to-date?
         Do emissions ever exceed permit limitations?
         Are appropriate fees paid promptly?
         Are appropriate cleaning mechanisms in place and properly utilized?
   b. Does the facility operate large central heating plants or other potentially large emitters of air pollutants?
      If so
         Have actual emissions been measured?
   c. Does the facility operate fuel dispensing facilities?
   d. Does the facility emit any toxic or hazardous air pollutants?
   e. Does the facility use or maintain equipment which contains ozone depleting chemicals?
   f. Is the facility located in an area that is designated as non-compliant for any air pollutants?
5. HAZARDOUS WASTE MANAGEMENT
   a. Does the facility generate any amount of hazardous waste?

If so

    Is the facility a Conditionally Exempt Small Quantity Generator?

    Is the facility a Small Quantity Generator?

    Is the facility a Large Quantity Generator?

  b. Does the facility have a hazardous waste generator number?

  c. Does the facility treat hazardous waste or store it longer than 90 days?

  d. Does the facility have any hazardous waste generation, treatment, disposal, or transportation permits?

6. HAZARDOUS SUBSTANCE CONTAMINATION REMEDIATION

  a. Has there been a release of a Reportable Quantity of a hazardous chemical?

    If so

      Were the proper authorities notified?

      Were proper response actions/remediations actions undertaken?

  b. Does the facility have any land which is contaminated with hazardous substances?

  c. Has the facility ever remediated a contaminated area?

7. TOXIC SUBSTANCES CONTROL

  a. Does the facility make, distribute, or import chemical substances?

  b. Does the facility contain Threshold Planning Quantities of specific hazardous or extremely hazardous substances?

  c. Is the facility large enough, of the right type, and with enough toxic chemicals to meet the Toxic Chemical Release Reporting requirements?

  d. Does the facility make, distribute, or use pesticides?

  e. Is the facility an agricultural establishment?

8. STORAGE TANKS

  a. Does the facility have any underground storage tanks?

  b. Does the facility have any aboveground storage tanks?

  c. Has an SPCC plan been prepared if the answer to either A or B is yes?

9. ARCHEOLOGY AND CULTURAL RESOURCES

  a. Does the facility have any cultural resources that are either on or eligible for listing on the National Register of Historic Places?

  b. Does the facility have any sites that appear to have historic value?

  c. Is the facility sited in an area and in such a condition that would support the likelihood of archeological resources?

10. BIOLOGICAL RESOURCES

  a. Does the facility have any biological resources?

  b. Does the facility have any threatened or endangered species?

  c. Does the facility have, or have an impact on, any wetlands?

  d. Is the facility located on the ocean shore?

11. NATIONAL ENVIRONMENTAL POLICY ACT

  a. Is the facility a Federal facility or is the facility proposing a project that requires federal, state, or local permitting?

  b. Is the proposed action likely to have an environmental impact?

12. OTHER FEDERAL AND STATE LAWS AND REGULATIONS

  a. Does the facility have any asbestos on site?

  b. Does the facility contain any lead paint?

  c. Does the facility create any noise that may adversely affect its surroundings?

  d. Does the facility have any areas needing to be surveyed for radon or high levels of radon?

  e. Does the facility have any equipment that contains PCBs in concentrations greater than 50 PPM?

GLOSSARY

Code of Federal Regulations . .   Series of books containing all of the regulations that are current for each federal agency.

Effluent . . . .   Liquid or air discharge from an industrial facility.

Friable Asbestos . . . .   Asbestos that can be crumbled in one's hand; it is the *most toxic* type of asbestos.

Mitigation . . . .   Reduction of a negative environmental impact, but not necessarily its total elimination.

Remediation . . . .   Correction of environmental problems.

REFERENCES AND SELECTED READINGS

U.S. Army Corps of Engineers, Construction Engineering Research Laboratories, Revised, Sept., 1995, "The Environmental Assessment and Management (TEAM) Guide," USACERL Special Report EC-95/05, Champaign, IL.

U.S. EPA, 1989, "Basic Inspectors Training Course: Fundamentals of Environmental Compliance Inspection," U.S. Environmental Protection Agency, Office of Compliance Monitoring, Washington, D.C.

3   Surface Water

The nation's history of the control of water pollution goes back to the River and Harbor Act of 1899, which was the first federal water pollution control legislation. Section 13 of the Act made it unlawful to discharge any refuse matter other than that flowing from streets and sewers into navigable waters. The U.S. Army Corps of Engineers could grant permission for the deposit of any material that might otherwise violate the language of Section 13. The Department of Justice was given authority to enforce the provisions of the River and Harbor Act of 1899 as they pertain to water pollution (Mackenthun and Bregman, 1991).

On December 23, 1970, Executive Order 11574 was issued proclaiming that the executive branch of the Federal government would implement a permit program under Section 13 to regulate the discharge of pollutants and other refuse matter into the navigable waters and that the U.S. Army Corps of Engineers was to be the permitting authority. In October, 1972, this matter was transferred to the U.S. EPA by authority of Section 402 of the Federal Water Pollution Control Act (FWPCA) Amendments, which established the National Pollutant Discharge Elimination System (NPDES).

The Public Health Service Act of 1912 contained provisions authorizing investigation of water pollution relating to the diseases and impairment of humans. In 1924, the Oil Pollution Act was enacted to control oil discharges in coastal waters that might be damaging to aquatic life, harbors and docks, and recreational facilities. In 1948, Public Law 845 created pollution control activities in the Public Health Service. This law also required the consent of the Congress for two or more states to enter into agreements or contracts for pollution abatement, and it provided for loans to any state, municipality, or interstate agency for the construction of necessary treatment works. Interstate conference mechanisms and other enforcement measures followed in the Federal Water Pollution Control Act Amendments of 1956.

Amendments to the FWPCA in 1961 extended federal authority to enforce the abatement of pollution in interstate, as well as navigable, waters. They provided that, in the planning for any reservoir, consideration shall be given to inclusion of storage for regulation of stream flow for the purpose of water quality control, except that any storage and water releases were not to be provided as a substitute for adequate treatment or other methods of controlling wastes at the source. In other words, the solution to pollution was not to be dilution.

The Water Quality Act of 1965, which further amended the Federal Water Pollution Control Act (FWPCA), established the Federal Water Pollution Control Administration and provided for the creation of water quality standards.

The Water Quality Improvement Act of 1970, which also amended the FWPCA, changed the name of the Federal Water Pollution Control Administration to the Federal Water Quality Administration. New sections were added to the FWPCA on the control of pollution by oil, control of hazardous polluting substances (principally hazardous substances spills) and the control of sewage discharge from vessels. Although all of these programs made some progress toward controls at that time, substantial control programs did not develop until after the passage of the Federal Water Pollution Control Act Amendments of 1972. In 1970, all federal water pollution control programs were transferred to the Environmental Protection Agency (EPA), an independent agency, reporting to the U.S. President (Mackenthun and Bregman, 1991).

THE CLEAN WATER ACT

The legislation governing surface water pollution control (streams, rivers, lakes, coastal areas, etc.) today started with the Federal Water Pollution Control Act Amendments of 1972. They have since been amended 17 times. With the amendments in 1977, the governing act became known as the Clean Water Act. Certain key elements of that legislation as it exists today are presented below in detail.

Water Quality Standards

The Clean Water Act calls upon the states to establish programs for water quality planning and management. The first part of that is the development of water quality standards. Each particular reach of each body of water found in the state is given a set of goals by the state for what the use of that water body should be. These goals could include any of the following: cold-water fishing, warm-water fishing, recreation, drinking water, aesthetics, etc. The cleaner the body of water, the higher the goal for its use that the state would establish.

Having determined what the use of a particular reach of water is to be, the state then decides what the chemical and physical criteria should be for the water constituents that will allow attainment of that use. For example, dissolved oxygen values of at least 6 ppm or higher are necessary for cold-water fisheries. Generally, 5 ppm of dissolved oxygen is required for practically every use except the water that may serve an aesthetic purpose only (Bregman and Mackenthun, 1992). Temperature is another sensitive indicator. For cold-

water fisheries, temperature requirements may be in the sixties (degrees Fahr-
enheit). Warm-water fisheries may allow temperatures to go up into the eighties.

The bacterial count is particularly important in terms of the use of water
for recreational purposes. The fecal coliform count is generally kept below 2
per cubic centimeter (cc) so that swimmers do not get dysentery; 0.14/cc
protects shellfish harvesting. Total dissolved solids are regulated, as is turbidity,
because water clarity is a desirable item, both for aesthetics and for fish
habitats. In almost every case, grease, scum, and oil on the surface is forbidden.

Once these criteria for attaining the standards are set by the state, they
must be approved as a part of the water quality standards by the administrator
of EPA, along with the proposed uses. They then become the standards for
each particular water body.

Another aspect of water quality standards is the "nondegradation" issue.
That particular requirement ensures that water bodies that have numerical
values (such as for temperature and dissolved oxygen) that are better than the
minimum criteria for best uses, will not be degraded to the minimum levels
without adequate consideration of the reasons for degradation and public input.
The senior author of the book was one of the authors of that nondegradation
requirement, which is now a part of every state water quality standard.

Having established water quality standards, the states now are expected
to establish and maintain a continuing water quality planning process that will
ensure that those standards are met. The planning process may include such
items as the following:

- Total daily maximum loads
- Effluent limitations
- Descriptions of best management practices for municipal and indus-
  trial waste treatment
- Provisions for nonpoint sources

The states make certain that discharges into water bodies will not upset
the water quality standards requirements.

Under the Clean Water Act, EPA has established effluent limitation guidelines for existing sources of water pollution, standards of performance for new
sources and pretreatment standards for certain types of both sources. These
guidelines place limits on the quantities, rate, or concentration of pollutants
that may be discharged from point sources into a water body. They are based
on the best available treatment technology. In addition, a large list of toxic
pollutants that must not be discharged above threshold amounts into receiving
water bodies has been published by EPA.

The state evaluates the potential effects that discharges will have on water
quality by doing very sophisticated water quality modeling on the body of
water that will receive discharges. Based on the modeling, determinations are
made of how much in the way of contaminants can be introduced into a specific

stretch of water without violating water quality standards. The state then determines how to best distribute the available quantities that may be discharged by the point sources that have discharge requirements. The amount allocated to each source is written into permit requirements.

The situation is much more difficult in the case of non-point sources such as fertilizer runoff from farmlands or discharges from animal feedlots. Nevertheless, the state calculates how much in the way of pollutants from these sources may enter the water bodies, and what their effects will be on water quality.

Section 404 of the Clean Water Act is the mechanism for issuing permits for the discharge of dredged or fill material to navigable waters of the state or the United States. In order to make this coverage as broad as possible, "navigable" waters are defined as those that can support any form of navigation, e.g., as small as canoes or rafts. It is the principal means within the Clean Water Act to prevent the destruction of wetlands, since wetlands are classified as "waters of the state/U.S." Section 404 begins with four significant provisions; it states that: (1) The U.S. Army Corps of Engineers may issue a permit, after notice and opportunity for public hearings, for the discharge of dredged or fill materials into navigable waters "at specified disposal sites"; (2) in specifying disposal sites, the Corps of Engineers must use guidelines developed by EPA in conjunction with the Corps; (3) where the guidelines would prohibit the specification of a site, the Corps could issue a permit regardless, based upon the economic impact on navigation and anchorage; and (4) EPA is authorized to veto permitting a site based upon environmental considerations. Regulations have been promulgated specifying how each of these actions will be managed.

A key feature of the Clean Water Act is the National Pollution Discharge Elimination System (NPDES), which requires that anyone who discharges material into the navigable waters of the U.S. must first obtain a permit issued by EPA or the state to whom permitting authority has been delegated. These permits limit the amount of pollution from each point source.

Applicants must provide the permit-issuing agency with information on the production processes of their facilities, the characteristics of the effluents that result from these processes, and a description of the treatment methods they propose to use to control the pollution. The EPA Regional Administrator or responsible state official prepares a draft permit that consists of the appropriate effluent limitations for the point source, monitoring requirements, record-keeping requirements, and reporting obligations. It is then published for public comment, following which a final permit is issued. The permittee must retain records, available to EPA or the state, that reflect all monitoring activities that are required in the permit.

Section 401 of the Clean Water Act is a significant section because it requires any applicant for a federal license or permit to obtain a certification from the state that any discharge connected with the action will not violate certain sections of the Clean Water Act, including existing water quality standards. No license or permit will be granted if certification has been denied by the state, interstate agency, or the Administrator of EPA, as the case may be.

In order to prevent industrial discharges from either (a) ruining the biological processes in a municipal wastewater treatment plant, or (b) using up an overwhelming amount of the plant capacity, requirements may be imposed for the pretreatment of industrial discharges that flow to municipal waste treatment plants. These requirements are set by each local authority that operates the plants and must conform to EPA pretreatment regulations. The purpose of the pretreatment program is to control pollutants that may pass through and interfere with the operations of the wastewater treatment plants, or that may contaminate wastewater sludge (Bregman and Mackenthun, 1992).

Stormwater

General

Section 402(p) of the Clean Water Act Amendments of 1987 required EPA to establish regulations setting forth National Pollutant Discharge Elimination System (NPDES) permit application requirements for stormwater discharges associated with industrial activity. This was done and proposed rules were published in the November 16, 1990 issue of the *Federal Register* as the initial requirements (Tier I) of the stormwater permitting program. They became effective on December 17, 1990. The Nationwide Urban Runoff Program was funded by EPA from 1978 to 1983 to study the quality of stormwater runoff from commercial and residential areas. The results of the program are cited by EPA in the preamble to the general permit rule as the main impetus for the stormwater regulations (Simon and Dockter, 1993).

EPA has defined stormwater as "stormwater runoff, surface runoff, street washwater related to street cleaning or maintenance, infiltration (other than infiltration contaminated by seepage from sanitary sewers or by other discharges), and drainage related to storm events or snow melt."

Section 402(p)(2) of the Clean Water Act (1987) listed five types of stormwater discharges which were required to obtain permits:

(A) A discharge with respect to which a permit has been issued prior to February 4, 1987

(B) A discharge associated with industrial activity

(C) A discharge from a municipal separate storm sewer system serving a population of 250,000 or more

(D) A discharge from a municipal separate storm sewer system serving a population of 100,000 or more, but less than 250,000 or

(E) A discharge for which the EPA administrator or the state agency, as the case may be, determines that the stormwater discharge contributes to a violation of a water quality standard or is a significant contributor of pollutants to the waters of the United States (*Federal Register*, 1990)

The Water Quality Amendments of 1987 to the Clean Water Act (WQA) stated that permit standards for discharges from municipal storm sewers may be issued on a system- or jurisdiction-wide basis; shall include a requirement to effectively prohibit nonstormwater discharges into the storm sewers; and shall require controls to reduce the discharge of pollutants to the maximum extent practicable, including management practices, control techniques, and system design and engineering methods for the control of pollutants.

The EPA follow-up regulations to these amendments state that whenever EPA decides that an individual permit is required, it shall notify the discharger in writing that the discharge requires a permit and the reasons for the decision. In addition, an application form is sent with the notice. A 60-day period is allowed from the date of notice for submitting a permit application. Site specific factors may dictate that the EPA provide additional time for submitting a permit application.

Since the stormwater permit is an NPDES permit, states that already have been delegated NPDES permitting authority also have this authority. As of September 1995, 41 of the 50 states had NPDES-delegated authority. This means that they are the bodies authorized to grant NPDES permits for storm-water.

Industrial

The EPA regulations cover different categories of stormwater discharges, with major distinctions between industrial, construction and municipal facilities. The approach to industrial activity is tiered in that stormwater discharges must comply with Sections 301 and 402 of the CWA (requiring control of the discharge of pollutants that utilize the Best Available Technology [BAT] and the Best Conventional Pollutant Control Technology [BCT] and where necessary, water quality-based controls), but permits for discharges from separate municipal storm-sewer systems must require controls to reduce the discharge of pollutants to the maximum extent practicable, and must include a requirement to effectively prohibit nonstormwater discharges into the storm sewers. General permits for industrial activities also prohibit nonstormwater discharges.

EPA has developed three industrial permit application options. Industries may submit an individual application, a group application, or a notice of intent to comply with a general permit. The individual permitting option allows a single facility to apply for a permit. This option includes mandatory facility-specific monitoring requirements, which often are extensive in scope. The group or multisector permits cover facilities with the same type of processes and mandate monitoring at a percentage of the facilities. Certain facilities also have the option of filing a Notice of Intent to comply with the general permit requirements. EPA has provided general permit requirements and states may add additional requirements.

The individual permit is a costly alternative to filing a Notice of Intent for a general permit, because stormwater sampling and analysis is usually required at each facility that submits an individual permit application. However, compliance with the general permit can be as extensive as an individual permit application for some industries because the general permit rule also mandates stormwater monitoring for certain facilities (Simon and Dockter, 1993). Certain facilities may not have the option to apply for a general permit due to the type and/or amounts of their stormwater discharges.

Operators of facilities with stormwater discharges associated with industrial activity who did not participate in a group application or did not obtain coverage under a general permit, must submit an individual application consisting of EPA Forms 1 and 2F. The information required in Form 2F includes a site drainage map, a narrative description of the site identifying potential pollutant sources, and quantitative testing data. There are specific requirements for construction activities, oil and gas operations, and mining operations (EPA, October, 1993). Additional detailed information on the contents of an individual permit is presented later in the Environmental Compliance section of this chapter.

Under the group application process, similar industrial facilities are allowed to submit a single application for the development of a model stormwater discharge permit. Approximately 700 groups covering 44,000 industrial facilities are in the group application process (Hamm, 1994). This group application permit process reduces the burden on the regulated community by requiring the submission of quantitative data from only selected members of the group. Where general permits are not appropriate or cannot be issued, a group application can be used to develop model individual permits, which can significantly reduce the burden of preparing individual permits. Many states are not accepting group applications in certain cases, e.g., U.S. Army facilities.

Using the group application information, EPA has developed an industry-specific multisector stormwater general permit. Group application information includes descriptions of industrial activities, materials stored outdoors, best management practices and stormwater sampling data. To develop the multi-sector permit, EPA divided the 44,000 facilities into 29 industrial sectors based on similar industrial activities. EPA incorporated the permit requirements for all 29 sectors into a uniform single stormwater permit. This draft permit was proposed in November 1993, and finalized and published in the *Federal Register* in September 1995.

Industrial stormwater dischargers that submit a Notice of Intent (NOI) to be covered by the general permit are not required to submit an individual permit application or participate in a group application, provided the discharger is eligible for the permit, and an individual permit application is not required by the director on a case-by-case basis. Submitting an NOI represents a significantly smaller burden than submitting an individual application or participating in a group application. The NOI requirements for general permits usually address only general information and typically do not require the collection of monitoring data. Submittal of an NOI is only possible where applicable general permits have been issued by the permitting authority. EPA has finalized general permits for construction and industrial activity in the states without NPDES authorization (57 FR 41176, September 9, 1992 and 57 FR 44412, September 25, 1992) As of mid-1995, 40 of the 41 authorized NPDES states have general permit authority (EPA, May, 1995).

In August, 1995, EPA issued a final rule for regulating small or "Phase II" dischargers under the Clean Water Act. The regulation establishes a two-tiered application process for the class of dischargers. Phase II dischargers are point source discharges of stormwater from commercial, retail, light industrial and institutional facilities, construction activities less than five acres, and municipal separate storm sewer systems serving fewer than 100,000 people.

The new rule establishes a sequential applications process in two tiers for all Phase II stormwater discharges. The first tier provides the NPDES permitting authority flexibility to require permits for those Phase II dischargers that are determined to be contributing to water quality impairment or are a significant contributor of pollutants.

Most of these types of dischargers have already been included under Phase I of the stormwater program. All other Phase II dischargers are included in the second tier. This larger group will be required to apply for permits within six years if the Phase II regulatory program in force at that time requires them.

The new rule relieves most Phase II dischargers from citizen suit liability for failure to have an NPDES permit over the next six years.

The heart of each stormwater control permit is a plan for pollution prevention. This plan is intended to reduce contamination in stormwater discharges. The plan addresses specific conditions at the site. It includes identification of pollution sources on a map, preventive measures, monitoring and periodic inspections, maintenance schedules for pollution controls and in some cases, training. The controls to be used are Best Management Practices (BMPs). BMPs can also include housekeeping measures.

Stormwater discharges from parking lots associated with industrial activities also are required to be included in stormwater permits. The same applies to stormwater discharges from RCRA Subtitle C facilities. Landfills that contain industrial wastes also are covered. Examples of other activities at industrial facilities that are covered by the stormwater permit requirements include fueling stations, vehicle and equipment washing and maintenance, painting operations, materials loading and unloading, aboveground storage tanks, outdoor manufacturing and industrial waste management, outdoor storage, and salt storage (Simon and Dockter, 1993).

Stormwater sampling from all stormwater outfalls was addressed by the EPA general permit regulations to provide information on two sets of conditions: data collected during the first thirty minutes of discharge and flow-weighted composite grab samples of storm event concentrations. However, one outfall can be sampled to represent those that are substantially similar.

Sampling must be done at facilities such as the following:

- Primary metal industries
- Land disposal units, incinerators, and boiler and industrial furnaces
- Wood treatment facilities
- Industrial facilities with coal piles
- Battery reclaiming facilities
- Airports
- Coal-fired steam electric facilities
- Animal handling and meat packaging facilities
- Chemical and allied product manufacturers and rubber manufacturers
- Automobile junkyards
- Lime manufacturers
- Oil-fired steam electric power generating facilities
- Cement manufacturing facilities and cement kilns
- Ready-mix concrete facilities
- Ship-building and repair facilities

(Simon and Dockter, 1993)

Construction

Permits are required for stormwater discharges from construction activities that disturb more than 5 acres of total land. This places them in the same situation as industrial discharges and leaves only the **uncontaminated** runoff as exempt. It should be noted that the 5-acre construction requirement has been challenged in court and may be lowered or eliminated.

For individual stormwater discharge permits, applications must be filed 90 days prior to the commencement of construction. If a contractor has not been selected at the time of application, the owner of the project site would initially file the application, and the contractor would sign on when selected. Under an individual stormwater permit for construction, multiple operators would have to sign onto the permit, instead of submitting a new application. These are the EPA requirements. Authorized NPDES states may have different permit requirements and should be contacted on this issue.

As was the case with industrial permits, pollution prevention plans are required for both individual and general permits. Thus, EPA stormwater construction general permits require subcontractors to implement the BMPs stated in the pollution prevention plan and to certify that he/she understands the terms and conditions of the permit requirements.

If a developer buys a 20-acre lot and builds roads, installs pipes, and runs electricity with the intention of constructing homes or other structures sometime in the near future, this would be considered a "common plan of development or sale." If the land is parceled off or sold, and construction occurs on plots that are *less* than 5 acres by separate, independent builders, their activities still would be subject to stormwater permitting requirements if the smaller plots were included on the original site plan.

A number of construction activities are not covered by the stormwater permitting programs. For example, repaving is not regulated under the stormwater program unless five or more acres of underlying and/or surrounding soil is cleared, graded, or excavated as part of the repaving operation.

Agricultural stormwater discharges also are exempted from NPDES permitting requirements. The clearing of land for agricultural purposes is specifically associated with agricultural activity. However, activities occurring on agriculture lands that meet the description of any of the 11 categories of industrial activity at 40 CFR 122.26(b)(14)(i)–(xi) are subject to permit application requirements.

For general construction permits, as with industrial permits, a Notice of Intent (NOI) to comply with the general permit must be filed before construction is planned to start. The NOI specifies the site location. For most construction activities, this requirement is simple, however in extreme cases, e.g., a 100 mile highway construction project, the midpoint of the linear construction project would be used as the site location on EPA's NOI form. For construction projects that span across more than one state, the project must meet the application requirements of each state.

Construction activity is defined very broadly. For example, if grading, clearing, or excavation activities disturb five or more acres of land either for an individual project or as part of a long-term maintenance plan, then the activity is subject to stormwater permit application requirements. Similarly, at a demolition site, disturbed areas might include those where building materials, demolition equipment, or disturbed soil are situated, which may alter the surface of the land. Therefore, demolition activities that disturb 5 or more acres of land would be subject to stormwater construction permit application requirements.

Under EPA's stormwater construction general permits, issued on September 9, 1992, and September 25, 1992, the following nonstormwater discharges are conditionally authorized (57 *FR* 41219) and (57 *FR* 44419): discharges from fire fighting activities; fire hydrant flushings; waters used to wash vehicles or control dust; potable water sources including waterline flushings; irrigation drainage; routine external building washdown which does not use detergents; pavement washwaters where spills or leaks of toxic or hazardous materials have not occurred (unless all spilled material has been removed) and where detergents are not used; air conditioning condensate; springs; uncontaminated groundwater; and process materials such as solvents. These discharges, except for flows from firefighting activities, must be identified in the pollution prevention plan and the plan must address the appropriate measures for controlling the identified nonstormwater discharges. Other nonstormwater discharges not listed above or not identified in the stormwater prevention plan, must be covered by an individual NPDES permit (EPA, July, 1993).

Stormwater permits are effective as long as the construction continues, but no longer than 5 years. If the construction continues beyond 5 years, the owner/operator must apply for a new permit.

Municipal Facilities

The Clean Water Act requires that NPDES permits for discharges from municipal separate storm-sewer systems include a requirement to effectively prohibit nonstormwater discharges into the storm sewers, and controls to reduce the discharge of pollutants to the maximum extent practicable (including management practices, control techniques, and system design and engineering methods, and other provisions appropriate for the control of such pollutants). EPA or authorized NPDES states may issue system-wide or jurisdiction-wide permits covering all discharges from a municipal separate storm-sewer system. The November, 1990 stormwater final rule established requirements for a two-part permit application designed to facilitate development of site specific permit conditions. The permit application requirements provide municipal applicants an opportunity to propose appropriate management programs to control pollutants in discharges from their municipal systems (EPA, October, 1993). This increases flexibility to develop appropriate permit conditions and ensures input from municipalities in developing appropriate controls.

There are some other municipal facilities that are subject to stormwater permitting that were not included in the industrial and construction categories that were described above, e.g., sewage treatment works, onsite vehicle maintenance/washing facilities, etc. These facilities should be treated in a manner similar to the industrial category as far as permitting is concerned.

ENVIRONMENTAL COMPLIANCE

Water Quality

The first step for the Environmental Compliance (EC) Officer in regards to surface water is an evaluation of the existing situation. He/she must determine whether there are any discharges to surface waters (or which will wind up in surface waters, such as through municipal sewers) in his/her area of responsibility. Where are they? What do they discharge? What is the condition of the receiving water body or treatment plant? Are there any permits in place or new ones required? Any monitoring systems? Are permit requirements being met? Are corrective measures necessary? These are the types of questions to which the EC Officer must seek answers as shown in the checklists that follow.

Surface Water Discharge Locations

Checklist :

- Does the facility(ies) for which the EC Officer has responsibility have any locations where discharges to surface waters may occur, either directly or through the municipal treatment facilities?
  - If answer is no, stop here.
  - If answer is yes, proceed as below.

- Where are these surface water discharges?

  Locate them on a map at the facility(ies).

- What is being discharged?

  Analyze the effluent for types and amounts of contaminants on a time basis.

- What is the condition of the receiving water body if the discharge is directly to one?
  - Name of water body
  - Flow rate
  - Chemical analysis
  - Water quality standards set for that reach of water being met?
  - Impact on the discharge on the water body
    - i) Size of mixing zone?
    - ii) Effect on standards?

- Is there a permit for the discharge (NPDES or otherwise)?
  - Date (still current?)
  - Requirements
  - Monitoring system
  - Are permit requirements being met?
    - i) If yes, stop here.
    - ii) If no, determine why not, how long this has been going on, extent of violations, etc.

If existing permit conditions are not being met, then the EC Officer is faced with the requirement to plan and take corrective actions and to notify the Federal or State agency that issued the permit. This is an extremely delicate situation in terms of both possible fines and adverse publicity. In such an event, it is critical that the EC Officer keep his/her management apprised of the situation and obtain their acquiescence for the corrective measures and the discussions with the permitting agency.

Corrective Actions for Permits

Checklist :

- What will need to be done to meet the permit requirements?
    - Explore all possibilities, including variations in processes, partial or full periodic shutdowns, effects on plant production, costs for new equipment, etc.

- Prepare action plan and discuss it with management.

- After management approval is obtained, put plan into action.

- Notify permitting agency.
    - Give them all the facts; do not hold anything back.
    - Preferably, meet with them and have your management representative with you.
    - If revisions to permit are required, prepare suggested revisions and submit them to permitting agency.

- Carry out decisions of permitting agency.

There may be situations where the EC Officer discovers a discharge that requires a permit and which has never been reported to the permitting agency. In that unfortunate event, the EC Officer should follow a procedure similar to the above checklist, but on a much more accelerated time schedule.

A discussion on dredging permits follows. It will assume that the EC Officer is responsible for a new requirement for such a permit. The EC Officer will be taken through a step-by-step procedure for obtaining the permit and complying with it.

Dredging Permits

Checklist :

- Obtain all possible information on the proposed dredging activity such as
    - Where?

Dredging Permits (continued)

Checklist (continued):

- When?
- How long a stretch of bottom?
- How deep?
- How long will the dredging continue?

- Next, develop information on the dredged "spoil" solid material that will have to be placed.
  - Chemical composition of that material
  - Amount of material to be placed

- Determine whether the act of dredging will contaminate the water body or wetlands.
  - Will polluted dredged material be dissolved or suspended in a water body, or placed on wetlands?
  - If so, what will be the extent of the pollution?
  - Can it be avoided?

- Next, determine how much of the dredged material (whose degree of contamination was determined above) will have to be removed and placed elsewhere.

- Determine possible disposal locations.
  - Distance vs. economics
  - Mode of transport
    - i) Will any polluted material be lost during transport?

  - Condition of the site(s) where the dredged material would be placed
    - i) More than one alternative site, if possible, in case your preferred site is not approved by the permitting agency
    - ii) Location(s) of the land (or water) where the dredged material will be placed
    - iii) Present chemical conditions of those locations and amount of pollution that disposal of the dredged material would create. Effects of that pollution on the local ecology
    - iv) Period of time before the site is filled. Alternative site in that event

Dredging Permits (continued)

Checklist (continued):

- Determine whether placing the dredged material on wetlands must be done.

- Prepare suggested permit and develop the case for approval of that permit.

- Obtain approval from your management.

- Approach and negotiate with permitting agency (usually the local District Office of the Corps of Engineers) and apply for permit. Simultaneously, talk to state, regional, or local agencies if any coastal or wetlands permits will be required.
  - If so, what requirements will the permitting agency place, such as the construction of new wetlands elsewhere?

- If new wetlands must be created, develop a plan to do so, estimate costs, obtain EPA approval and proceed.

- Develop monitoring system to ensure that all permit requirements are met and that you are notified of any violations. In case of violations, follow a procedure similar to that described above for other permits.

When the discharged liquid is to be sent to a municipal wastewater treatment plant, the EC Officer must be conversant with all factors concerning the discharge and its eventual treatment at the municipal plant.

Discharge to a Municipal System

Checklist :

- What is being discharged?
  - How much?
  - What are chemical and physical compositions of effluent?
  - What is its potential for corrosion of the sewer system?
  - What is its potential to upset the municipal treatment system?
  - Is the discharge combined with stormwater flow?

If the discharge is of high volume, contains a large amount of pollutants, and may corrode the sewer system or cause upsets of the treatment plant (e.g., toxics that would destroy the bacteria that are the heart of the secondary treatment process), then the municipality may require that the discharge be pretreated, monitored, and a permit obtained. In that event, the EC Officer must go through the pretreatment permitting process as described below.

Pretreatment Permitting Process

Checklist :

- Obtain complete information on discharge that must be treated:
  - Amount
  - Volume
  - Flow rate
  - Chemical, physical and biological composition
  - Potential for causing sewer corrosion of treatment plant upset.

- Determine the extent to which the discharge should be pretreated and the manner of that treatment, as well as its cost.

- Develop suggested pretreatment permit and obtain management approval.

- Negotiate permit with treatment plant authority. It is desirable to have management or legal counsel participation in those negotiations.

- Set up system to comply with permit requirements. Emphasize monitoring, both for permitting agency and for yourself.

- Check monitoring system frequently. Have procedures set up for
  - Your immediate notification when violation occurs
  - Corrective actions for violations
  - Permitting agency and management notification?

Stormwater

The most current permitting activity relates to stormwater discharges. A determination must first be made of whether the facility(ies) is(are) subject to stormwater permitting.

Is a Stormwater Permit Required?

> **Checklist:**
>
> - Is there anywhere on the facility(ies) where stormwater (as defined earlier in this chapter by EPA for industrial activities, construction or municipal facilities) discharge may occur?
>   - If no, then stop here
>   - If yes, continue this checklist
>
> - Does the stormwater discharge fall into any of the categories listed earlier in this chapter [as in Section 402(P)(2) of the Clean Water Act as Amended in 1987] that require permits?
>   - If no, stop here
>   - If yes, proceed with activity towards permit application

In developing the information for possible stormwater permits, it must be remembered that stormwater discharges may occur in several locations and may have characteristics that are more similar to nonpoint sources than to point sources.

Gathering Information for the Stormwater Permit

> **Checklist:**
>
> Obtain appropriate sample permit form(s) from appropriate agency. For each form, check items listed below
>
> - When is the deadline for filing the permit?
>
> - Where is the stormwater?
>
> - What pollutants (and how much) get washed into it from those locations?
>
> - Where does the stormwater runoff go (water body, sewer, etc.)?
>
> - What is the frequency of this occurrence?
>
> - Show all of the above on a map of the facility(ies).

Gathering Information for the Stormwater Permit (continued)

Checklist:

- Include anything else called for on the sample permit form.

- What can be done to collect and treat the stormwater, as well as preventing its discharge into municipal waste treatment plant sewers?
  - Types of collection devices
  - Types of treatment facilities, etc.
  - Costs and time involved

- Review situation with management and arrive at tentative approach.

Permit Requirements

The checklist below describes requirements of the stormwater pollution prevention plan that is to be prepared by the applicant. EPA and some states do not require submission of the pollution prevention plan, even though it must be prepared and followed.

Industrial Pollution Prevention Plan

Checklist :

Pollution Prevention Plans Requirements for Industrial Activities

Each industrial facility covered by the general permit must develop a plan, tailored to the site specific conditions, and designed with the goal of controlling the amount of pollutants in stormwater discharges from the site.

- *Pollution Prevention Team* - Each facility will select a Pollution Prevention Team from its staff, and the Team will be responsible for developing and implementing the plan

Industrial Pollution Prevention Plan (continued)

Checklist (continued):

- *Components of the Plan* - The permit requires that the plan contain a description of potential pollutant sources, and a description of the measures and controls to prevent or minimize pollution of stormwater. The description of potential pollutant sources must include:
  - A map of the facility indicating the areas which drain to each stormwater discharge point
  - An indication of the industrial activities which occur in each drainage area
  - A prediction of the pollutants which are likely to be present in the stormwater
  - A description of the likely source of pollutants from the site
  - An inventory of the materials which may be exposed to stormwater
  - The history of spills or leaks of toxic or hazardous materials for the past 3 years

  The measures and controls to prevent or minimize pollution of stormwater must include:
  - Good housekeeping or upkeep of industrial areas exposed to stormwater
  - Preventive maintenance of stormwater controls and other facility equipment
  - Spill prevention and response procedures to minimize the potential for, and the impact of, spills
  - Testing all outfalls to insure there are no cross connections (only stormwater is discharged)
  - Training of employees on pollution prevention measures, controls, and record keeping

  The permit also requires that facilities:
  - Identify areas with a high potential for erosion and the stabilization measures or structural controls to be used to limit erosion in these areas
  - Implement traditional stormwater management measures (oil/water separators, vegetative swales, detention ponds, etc.) where they are appropriate for the site

---

Industrial Pollution Prevention Plan (continued)

Checklist (continued):

- *Inspection/Site Compliance Evaluation* - Facility personnel must inspect the plant equipment and industrial areas on a regular basis. At least once every year, a more thorough site-compliance evaluation must be performed by facility personnel
  - Look for evidence of pollutants entering the drainage system
  - Evaluate the performance of pollution prevention measures
  - Identify areas where the plan should be revised to reduce the discharge of the pollutants
  - Document both the routine inspections and the annual site compliance evaluation in a report

- *Consistency* - The Plan can incorporate other plans which a facility may have already prepared for other permits including Spill Prevention Control and Countermeasure (SPCC) Plans, or Best Management Practices (BMP) Programs

- *Signature* - The Plan must be signed by a responsible corporate official such as the president, vice president or general partner

- *Plan Review* - The Plan is to be kept at the permitted facility at all times. The Plan should be submitted for review only when requested by EPA

Semi-Annual Monitoring/Annual Reporting Requirements

- EPCRA Section 313 facilities

- Primary metal industries Standard Industrial Classification (SIC) 33

- Land disposal units/incinerators/BIFs

- Wood treatment facilities

- Facilities with coal pile runoff

- Battery reclaimers

Industrial Pollution Prevention Plan (continued)

Checklist (continued):

Annual Monitoring/No Reporting Requirements

- Airports with at least 50,000 flight operations per year

- Coal-fired steam electric facilities

- Animal handling/meat packing facilities

- Additional facilities, including:
  - SIC 30 and 28 with storage piles for solid chemicals used as raw materials that are exposed to precipitation
  - Certain automobile junkyards
  - Lime manufacturing facilities where stormwater comes into contact with lime storage piles
  - Oil handling sites at oil-fired steam electric power generating facilities
  - Cement manufacturing and cement kilns
  - Ready-mix concrete facilities
  - Shipbuilding and repairing facilities

Additional Monitoring Requirements

- Testing parameters for facilities are listed in the general permits

- At a minimum, all dischargers must conduct an annual site inspection of the facility.

Alternative Certification

- A discharger is not subject to the monitoring requirements for a given outfall if there is not exposure of industrial areas or activities to stormwater within the drainage area of that outfall within a given year

- The discharger must certify, on an annual basis, that there is no exposure to stormwater, and such certification must be retained in the stormwater pollution prevention plan. Facilities subject to semi-annual monitoring requirements must submit this certification to EPA in lieu of monitoring data

Industrial Pollution Prevention Plan (continued)

Checklist (continued):

Numeric Effluent Limitations

- Coal pile runoff: 50 mg/l Total Suspended Solids (TSS) and 6–9 pH

Available Guidance

Stormwater Management for Industrial Activities, Developing Pollution Prevention Plans and Best Management Practices, available from NTIS (703) 487-4650, order number PB 92-235969; *Summary Stormwater Management for Industrial Activities, Developing Pollution Plans and Best Management Practices*, available from the Stormwater Hotline, (703) 821-4823.

Construction General Permit Requirements

Checklist :

Coverage

- Stormwater discharges from construction sites that are authorized by this permit include those that will result in the disturbance of 5 or more acres of land

Pollution Prevention Plan Requirements for Construction Activities

Each construction activity covered by the general permit must develop a plan, tailored to the site specific conditions, and designed with the goal to control the amount of pollutants in stormwater discharges from the site

- *Components of the Plan* - The permit requires that the Plan contain a site description, and a description of the measures and controls to prevent or minimize pollution of stormwater. The site description must include:
  - A description of the nature of the construction activity
  - A sequence of major construction activities

Construction General Permit Requirements (continued)

Checklist (continued):

- An estimate of the total area of the site and of the area to be disturbed
- An estimate of the runoff coefficient of the site after construction is complete
- Any existing data on the quality of stormwater discharge from the site
- The name of the receiving water
- Any information on the type of soils at the site; and
- A site map indicating drainage patterns and slopes after grading activities are complete, areas of soil disturbance, the outline of the area to be disturbed, the location of stabilization measures and controls, and surface waters at the discharge points

- *Measures and Controls* - Measures and controls to prevent or minimize pollution of stormwater must include three different types of controls: erosion and sediment controls, stormwater management controls, and other controls:
  - Erosion and Sediment Controls

    * Stabilization (seeding, mulching, etc.) - Disturbed areas where construction has permanently or temporarily ceased must be stabilized within 14 days of the last disturbance or as soon as practicable in semi-arid and arid areas (areas which will be redisturbed within 21 days do not have to be stabilized)

    * Structural Controls - Sites with common drainage locations that serve 10 or more disturbed acres must install a sediment basin where it is attainable (where a basin is not attainable, sediment traps, silt fence, or other equivalent measures must be installed). Sediment basins must provide 3,600 cubic feet of storage per acre drained. Drainage locations which serve less than 10 disturbed acres must install either a sediment basin, sediment trap, or silt fence along the down slope and side slope perimeter.

- Plan shall be completed prior to submittal of an NOI and updated as appropriate

Construction General Permit Requirements (continued)

Checklist (continued):

- The plan shall provide for compliance with the terms and schedule of the plan beginning with the initiation of construction activities

Available Guidance

Stormwater Management for Construction Activities, Developing Pollution Prevention Plans and Best Management Practices, are available from NTIS (703) 487-4650, order number PB 92-235951; *Summary: Stormwater Management for Construction Activities, Developing Pollution Prevention Plans and Best Management Practices* (October, 1992), available from the Stormwater Hotline (703) 821-4823.

Municipal Permits

Checklist :

The municipal stormwater permit must contain the following items:

Part 1

- General information (name, address, etc.)

- Existing legal authority and any additional authorities needed

- Source identification information

- Discharge characterization including:
  - Monthly mean rainfall and snowfall estimates
  - Existing quantitative data on volume and quality of stormwater discharges
  - A list of receiving water bodies and existing information on the impacts of receiving waters
  - Field screening analysis for illicit connections and illegal dumping

Municipal Permits (continued)

Checklist (continued):

- Characterization plan identifying representative outfalls for further sampling in Part 2

- Description of existing management programs to control pollutants from the separate municipal storm sewer and to identify illicit connections

- Description of financial budget and resources currently available to complete Part 2

Part 2

- Demonstration of adequate legal authority to control discharges, prohibit illicit discharges, require compliance, and carry out inspections, surveillance, and monitoring

- Source identification indicating the location of any major outfalls and identifying facilities that discharge stormwater associated with industrial activity through the municipal separate storm sewer

- Discharge characterization data including
  - Quantitative data from 5–10 representative locations in approved sampling plans
  - For selected conventional pollutants and heavy metals, estimates of the annual pollutant load and events
  - Proposed schedule to provide estimates of seasonal pollutant loads and the mean concentration for certain detected constituents in a representative storm event
  - Proposed monitoring program for representative data collection

- Proposed management program including descriptions of:
  - Structural and source control measures that are to be implemented to reduce pollutants in runoff from commercial and residential areas
  - Program to detect and remove illicit discharges

Municipal Permits (continued)

Checklist (continued):

- - Program to monitor and control pollutants from municipal landfills, hazardous waste treatment, disposal, and recovery facilities; EPCRA Section 313 facilities; and other priority industrial facilities
- - Program to control pollutants in construction site runoff.

- • Estimated reduction in loadings of pollutants as a result of the management program

- • Fiscal analysis of necessary capital and operation and maintenance expenditures

Available Guidance

Guidance Manual for the Preparation of Part I of the NPDES Permit Application for Discharges from Municipal Separate Storm Sewer Systems and NPDES Stormwater Sampling Guidance Document available from NTIS (703) 487-4650, order number PB 92-114578; *Guidance Manual for the Preparation of Part 2 of the NPDES Permit Applications for Discharges from Municipal Separate Storm Sewers Systems*, available from the Stormwater Hotline, (703) 821-4823 (EPA, October, 1993)

Submitting the Individual Stormwater Permit

Checklist :

- • Check sample permit application(s) to be certain you have prepared all the required information

- • Prepare draft application(s)

- • Meet with permitting agency and ask them to review the draft application(s)

- • Make any required changes and submit the application(s)

Notice of Intent (NOI)

As part of the general permit procedure, facilities must file Notices of Intent (NOIs) for industrial and construction activities. These NOIs must be filed at least 2 days prior to the commencement of the industrial or construction activity.

Notice of Intent (NOI) Contents

Checklist :

Contents of NOIs are presented below. After each item, their inclusion in Industrial activities is shown as *I*, and in Construction activities as *C*. Most requirements are common to both types of activities.

Contents of NOI

- Street address or latitude/longitude (I, C)

- SIC code or identification of industrial activity (I, C)

- Operator's name, address, telephone number, and status as federal, state, private, public, or other entity (I, C)

- Permit number(s) of any existing NPDES permit(s) (I, C)

- Name of receiving water(s) (I, C)

- Indication of whether the owner or operator has existing quantitative data describing the concentration of pollutants in stormwater discharges (I, C)

- A certification that a stormwater pollution prevention plan has been prepared for the facility (I, C)

- An estimate of the project start date and completion date (C)

- An estimate of the number of disturbed acres (C)

Once the stormwater permit(s) is (are) issued, it becomes necessary to make certain that compliance is achieved and necessary corrections are made promptly. The same procedures for accomplishing these goals that were described earlier for other permits should be followed.

Finally, the monitoring program called for in the permit needs to be put in place and performed. These procedures were included in the permitting checklists presented earlier.

Compliance with Permit Conditions

Checklist:

- Make any necessary equipment or facility changes that will ensure compliance with permit requirements

- Check the operation and maintenance of the facility(ies) in accordance with permit requirements and make corrections rapidly when they are required. Notify permitting agency about those corrections

- Put monitoring systems called for by permits in place and adhere to the schedules rigorously

GLOSSARY

Bacterial Count . . . . Concentration of bacteria in water expressed as number of bacteria per cubic centimeter (cc) of water.

Coliform . . . . Bacteria that are found in the human colon.

Combined Sewers . . . . Sewers carrying both human wastes and stormwater.

Conveyance . . . . A pipe, sewer, or other device that carries water from one location to another; it can also be a swale or other non-man-made structure.

Disposal Sites . . . . Locations where dredged or fill materials are placed.

Dredged Material or Spoil . . . . Solid or solid/liquid material that is removed from a dredged water body.

Dysentery . . . . An epidemic-type disease characterized by severe diarrhea and often with abdominal pain, caused by bacteria spread chiefly through contaminated food or water.

Effluent . . . . The discharge from a facility to a receiving water system.

Effluent Limitations .... Limits on the amounts of specific contaminants that are allowed to be in the discharge from a facility to a water body.

Fecal Coliform .... Coliform found in human feces.

Infiltration .... Seepage of water into sewer pipes.

Interstate Waters .... Water bodies that include more than one state.

Mixing Zone .... Three-dimensional volume of receiving water body in which pollutants in discharged effluent are permitted to exceed water quality standard limitations.

Navigable Waters .... These are defined as waters that are capable of allowing navigation by boats. For purposes of regulation, this definition usually is expanded to include the smallest boats possible, e.g., canoes.

New Sources .... New or greatly modified facilities that will add contaminants.

Non-Point Sources .... Sources of pollutants that cover a wide area, e.g., farms, cattle feed areas, and lawns, that are not discharged at a single identifiable point.

PPM..................... Concentration expressed in terms of parts per million on a weight basis.

Point Source Pollution .... Pollution that comes from a single identifiable source, usually coming out of a pipe from that source.

Pretreatment .... Treatment of liquid wastes to reduce pollutant concentrations before the wastes are discharged into a sewer or a water body.

Primary Treatment .... Removal of solids at a municipal wastewater treatment plant.

Private or Federally Owned ... A pipe, sewer, covered gutter, or other
Stormwater Conveyance   means of collecting and transporting stormwater that is privately or federally owned and is not a municipal stormwater sewer.

Reach.................... A portion of a water body (a portion of a stream) that is uniform with regards to size, flow, water quality, uses, etc.

Runoff . . . . Water that "runs off" a flat surface like a parking lot into a gutter, sewer, water body, or other receiving source.

Sanitary Sewers. . . . . Sewers carrying human wastes.

Secondary Treatment . . . . Removal of 85–95% of the liquid contaminants at a municipal wastewater treatment plant, usually by biological processes.

Sludge . . . . A solid/liquid material that is the residue left after treatment of human or certain industrial wastewaters.

Stream Flow . . . . The rate of movement of the water in a stream.

Total Daily Maximum Load . . . The maximum amount of specific contaminants that are allowed to be in the discharge from a facility to a water body.

Water Quality Modeling . . . . . . Mathematical predictions of the concentrations of various water chemical and physical constituents at various distances and depths.

Water Releases . . . . A specific amount of water that has been stored behind a dam is released into the river that flows away from the dam.

Watershed . . . . A region in which the water drains to a specific water body.

Waters of the United States . . . Those waters over which the federal government has jurisdiction; in the present context this is usually limited to "navigable" waters, and in some cases this may be interpreted to include wetlands.

REFERENCES AND SELECTED READINGS

Bregman, J.I. and Mackenthun, K.M., 1992, "Environmental Impact Statements," CRC Press, Boca Raton, FL.

Environmental Protection Agency, Nov. 16, 1990, *Federal Register*, NPDES Permit Application Regulations for Stormwater Discharges, Final Rule, Washington, D.C.

Hamm, E.L. and Associates, 1994, "Stormwater Law Sourcebook," U.S. Army Training and Doctrine Command, Prepared for U.S. Army, Norfolk, VA, District Corps of Engineers.

Mackenthun, K.M. and Bregman, J.I., 1992, "Environmental Regulations Handbook," CRC/Lewis Publishers, Boca Raton, FL.

Simon, J.A. and Dockter, G.N., Spring, 1993, "Complying with the New General Stormwater Permit Rule," *Environmental Permitting*, 235–245.

U.S. EPA, September 9, 1992, "Part II, Construction Permit Language," *Federal Register*, 41209-41233, Washington, D.C.

U.S. EPA, September 9, 1992, "Part III, Non Construction-Industrial Permit Language," *Federal Register*, 41297-41342, Washington, D.C.

U.S. EPA, March, 1992, "NPDES Stormwater Program – Question and Answer Document," Volume 1, Washington, D.C.

U.S. EPA, July, 1993, "NPDES Stormwater Program – Question and Answer Document," Volume 2, Washington, D.C.

U.S. EPA, October, 1993, "Overview of the Stormwater Program," Washington, D.C.

4   Groundwater

The vast amount of present and potential usage of groundwater as a source of supply of drinking water, both internationally and in the United States, is largely unknown by the general public. It has been stated that more than 97% of the world's fluid fresh water is underground (Briggs, 1976). Obviously, this amount of water is not all available as a source of future drinking water, but its magnitude defines underground water as a precious resource to be husbanded for future needs (Bregman and Mackenthun, 1976). EPA has estimated that half of all Americans get their household water supplies from underground sources of water. Groundwater also is used for about half of the nation's agricultural irrigation and nearly one-third of its industrial water needs.

Groundwater is found in many types of geologic situations. Areas where groundwater exists in sufficient quantities to supply wells or springs are called aquifers. Aquifers store water in the spaces between particles of sand, gravel, soil, and rock as well as cracks, pores, and channels in relatively solid rocks. The storage capacity of an aquifer is controlled largely by its porosity, or the relative amount of open space present to hold water. Its ability to transmit water, or permeability, is based in part on the size of these spaces and the extent to which they are connected.

There are two basic types of aquifers; **confined** and **unconfined**. If the aquifer is located between layers of relatively impermeable materials (e.g., clay), it is called a confined aquifer. Confined aquifers are frequently found at greater depths than unconfined aquifers, whose upper boundaries are generally closer to the surface of the land (EPA, 1990). In a number of locations, only one aquifer appears to be suitable as a potential or actual source of drinking water. Aquifers of this type are called sole source aquifers.

A key element in the need for protection of groundwater is the fact that, in contrast to surface water, groundwater moves very slowly and in a variety of directions. Groundwater can move sideways as well as up or down. This movement is in response to gravity, differences in elevation, and differences in pressure. The slow movement is frequently as little as a few feet per year, although it can be as much as several feet per day in very permeable zones. Groundwater can move even more rapidly in karst aquifers, which are areas of water soluble limestone and similar rocks where fractures or cracks have been widened by the action of the groundwater to form sinkholes, tunnels, or even caves (EPA, 1990). Even that movement, however, is very slow compared to surface water and, coupled with the absence of oxygen, does not allow self-cleansing as is the case with surface water.

During the past 10 years, great concern has arisen concerning the increasingly rapid contamination of U.S. groundwater. In contrast to fast-moving freshwater streams, underground water moves so slowly that when it is contaminated it tends to remain in that condition. The result is often the loss of a major source of water supply for public or industrial purposes (Bregman and Mackenthun, 1992).

Between 1971 and 1985, 245 groundwater-related disease outbreaks, with 52,181 associated illnesses, were reported. Most of these diseases were short-term digestive disorders. In addition, approximately 74 pesticides, a number of which are known carcinogens, were detected in the groundwater of 38 states. The situation has become much worse since 1985, as the extent of groundwater contamination from abandoned hazardous waste sites has become recognized. EPA (1990) has presented a listing of activities that could cause groundwater contamination, shown below in Exhibit 4-1.

A discussion of some of these activities and their effects on groundwater contamination follows (EPA, 1990):

Septic Tanks, Cesspools, and Privies

A major cause of groundwater contamination in many areas of the United States is effluent from septic tanks, cesspools, and privies. Approximately one-fourth of all homes in the United States rely on septic systems to dispose of their human wastes. If these systems are improperly sited, designed, constructed, or maintained, they can allow contamination of the groundwater by bacteria, nitrates, viruses, synthetic detergents, household chemicals, and chlorides. The sheer number of such systems and their widespread use in areas that do not have public sewage treatment systems makes them serious contamination sources.

Surface Impoundments

More than 180,000 surface impoundments (e.g., ponds, lagoons) are used by municipalities, industries, and businesses to store, treat, and dispose of a variety of liquid wastes and wastewater. Although these impoundments are supposed to be sealed with compacted clay soils or plastic liners, leaks can and do develop.

Exhibit 4-1   Possible Groundwater Contamination Activities

Location where contamination starts	Source of contamination	
Ground surface	Infiltration of polluted surface water Land disposal of wastes Stockpiles Dumps Sewage sludge disposal Animal feedlots	De-icing salt use and storage Fertilizers and pesticides Accidental spills Airborne source particulates
Above water table	Septic tanks, cesspools and privies Holding pools and lagoons Sanitary landfills Waste disposal in excavations	Underground pipeline leaks Artificial recharge Sumps and dry wells Graveyards Underground storage tanks
Below water table	Waste disposal in wells Drainage wells and canals Underground storage Mines	Exploratory wells Abandoned wells Water-supply wells Groundwater withdrawal

Agricultural Activities

Contamination may come from the millions of tons of fertilizers and pesticides spread on the ground, and from the storage and disposal of livestock wastes. Homeowners contribute to this problem by the chemicals they apply to their lawns and gardens.

Landfills

In 1990, there were approximately 500 hazardous waste land disposal facilities and more than 16,000 municipal and other landfills nationwide. To protect groundwater, these facilities are now required to be constructed with clay or synthetic liners and leachate collection systems. Unfortunately, these requirements are comparatively recent, and thousands of landfills were built, operated, and abandoned in the past without such safeguards. A number of these sites have caused serious groundwater contamination problems and now are being cleaned up by their owners, operators, or users; State governments; or the Federal government under the Superfund program.

Underground Storage Tanks

Between five and six million underground storage tanks in the United States are used to store a variety of materials, including gasoline, fuel oil, and numerous chemicals. The average life span of these tanks is 18 years, and over time, exposure to the elements causes them to corrode. Hundreds of thousands of these tanks were estimated to be leaking in 1990.

Abandoned Wells

If drinking water wells are abandoned without being properly sealed, they can act as direct channels for contaminants to reach groundwater.

Accidents and Illegal Dumping

Accidental chemical or petroleum product spills occur that, if not handled properly, can result in groundwater contamination. Frequently, the automatic reaction of the first people at the scene of an accident involving a spill will be to flush the area to dilute the chemical. This washes the chemical into the soil around the accident site, allowing it to work its way down to the groundwater. Washwater is frequently dumped on soil deliberately. The washwater, e.g., from washing trucks that contain pesticides or from washing down empty chemical barrels, may eventually cause serious contamination of groundwater. In addition, there are numerous other instances of groundwater contamination caused by the illegal dumping of hazardous or other potentially harmful wastes.

Highway De-Icing

More than 11 million tons of salt are applied to roads in the United States annually. As ice and snow melt or rain subsequently falls, the salt is washed into the surrounding soil where it can work its way down to the groundwater. Salt also can find its way into groundwater from improperly protected storage stockpiles.

Contamination of groundwater is difficult to overcome and, in many cases, may be considered to be almost irreversible. There are five generally accepted approaches to cleaning up contaminated groundwater (EPA, 1990):

- Containing the contaminants to prevent their migration from their source.
- Withdrawing the pollutants from the aquifer.
- Treating the groundwater where it is withdrawn or at its point of use.
- Rehabilitating the aquifer by either immobilizing or detoxifying the contaminants while they are still in the aquifer.
- Abandoning the use of the aquifer.

All too often, the last approach is the only practical one.

FEDERAL LEGISLATION AND REGULATIONS

In contrast to other types of pollution, groundwater pollution is legally controlled by parts of several different federal laws. A listing of the more important ones, together with a brief discussion of how each one affects water pollution control follows (EPA, 1990):

- *The Safe Drinking Water Act* regulates the underground disposal of wastes in deep wells, designates areas that rely on a single aquifer for their water supply, and establishes a program to encourage the states to develop programs to protect public water supply wells (i.e., wellhead protection programs).
- *The Resource Conservation and Recovery Act*, which prevents contaminants from leaching into groundwater from municipal landfills, underground storage tanks, surface impoundments, and hazardous waste disposal facilities.
- *The Comprehensive Environmental Response, Compensation, and Liability Act (Superfund)*, which authorizes the government to clean up contamination caused by hazardous waste sites.
- *The Federal Insecticide, Fungicide, and Rodenticide Act*, which authorizes EPA to control the availability of pesticides that have the ability to leach into groundwater.
- *The Toxic Substances Control Act*, which authorizes EPA to control the manufacture, use, storage, distribution, or disposal of toxic chemicals that have the potential to leach into groundwater.
- *The Clean Water Act*, which authorizes EPA to make grants to the states for the development of groundwater protection strategies.

STATE LEGISLATION AND REGULATIONS

States play a key role in the protection of groundwater. The U.S. EPA has defined the roles of federal and state governments in regulating specific sources of contamination as follows (EPA, 1991):

1. In general, state and local governments should play the prominent *regulatory* role. This is especially appropriate when: (a) the activities of concern are numerous (e.g., 23 million septic tanks), or highly localized (e.g., vary in impact and number from state to state), and nationally present a low to medium risk potential; (b) when land use management is a principal protection approach; (c) when technologies currently exist or are easily developed to address the problem. Further, state and local governments should play the primary role in the implementation of federally-mandated groundwater protection regulations.

2. EPA should take a prominent regulatory role as currently authorized by law when: (a) there is a need to establish regulatory consistency (e.g., to limit adverse impacts on interstate commerce); (b) when the scope of the effort requires national resources (e.g., research, regulations addressing technically complex environmental problems); (c) when state-by-state efforts would create unwarranted and inefficient duplication (e.g., bans, research); and (d) when national security is involved (e.g., the disposal of radioactive waste).

According to the U.S. EPA, most of the states have passed groundwater protection legislation and developed groundwater policies. State groundwater legislation can be divided into the following subject categories (EPA, 1990):

- Statewide strategies — Requiring the development of a comprehensive plan to protect the state's groundwater resources from contamination.
- Groundwater classification — Identifying and categorizing groundwater sources by how they are used to determine how much protection is needed to continue that type of use.
- Standard setting — Identifying the level at which an aquifer is considered to be contaminated.
- Land-use management — Developing planning and regulatory mechanisms to control activities on the land that could contaminate an aquifer.
- Groundwater funds — Establishing specific financial accounts for use in the protection of groundwater quality and the provision of compensation for damages to underground drinking water supplies (e.g., reimbursement for groundwater cleanup, provision of alternative drinking water supplies).
- Agricultural chemicals — Regulating the use, sale, labeling, and disposal of pesticides, herbicides, and fertilizers.
- Underground and aboveground storage tanks — Establishing criteria for the registration, construction, installation, leak and overflow prevention, monitoring, repair, closure, and financial responsibility associated with tanks used to store hazardous wastes or materials. The state also approves spill contingency plans, as well as spill prevention control and countermeasure plans.
- Water-use management — Including groundwater quality protection in the criteria used to justify more stringent water allocation measures where excessive groundwater withdrawal could cause groundwater contamination.

Some of the federal laws cited earlier require very specific legal and regulatory actions by state and local authorities. A discussion of some of the more important ones follows:

Wellhead Protection

The 1986 amendments to the Safe Drinking Water Act established the **wellhead protection** program and require each state to develop programs to protect public water supply wells from contaminants that could be harmful to human health. Wellhead protection is the protection of all or part of the area surrounding a well from which the well's groundwater is drawn. This is called a **wellhead protection area** (WHPA). The size of the WHPA will vary from site to site depending on a number of factors, including the goals of the state's program and the geologic features of the area (EPA, 1990).

The law specifies certain minimum components for the wellhead protection programs:

- The roles and duties of State and local governments and public water suppliers in the management of wellhead protection programs must be established.
- The WHPA for each wellhead must be delineated.
- Contamination sources within each WHPA must be identified.
- Approaches for protecting the water supply within the WHPAs from the contamination sources must be developed.
- Contingency plans must be developed for use if public water supplies become contaminated.
- Provisions must be established for proper siting of new wells to produce maximum water yield and reduce the potential for contamination as much as possible.
- Provisions must be included to ensure public participation in the process.

Underground Storage Tanks (USTs)

The U.S. EPA has developed a series of regulations for USTs as a result of the requirement by Subtitle I of the 1984 Amendments to RCRA. These, in turn, have become the basis from which state regulations have been set across the country. The EPA regulations have the following major points (EPA, 1988):

- USTs installed after December 1988, and new USTs, must have correct installation, spill and overfill prevention, corrosion protection, and leak detection.
- USTs installed before December 1988 must be modified to meet the same requirements as above.
- Corrective action must be taken in response to leaks.
- Specific closure requirements for tanks temporarily or permanently closed have been set.

- UST owners are financially responsible for the cost of cleaning up a leak and compensating other people for bodily injury and property damage caused by their leaking UST. They must demonstrate their ability to pay these costs.

Most state regulations follow these EPA requirements very closely. They also impose severe fines for UST owners not complying with the regulations after the dates set by the states (usually about 1988).

Leaking USTs are receiving a considerable amount of attention from state regulators because of the magnitude of the problem. It has been estimated that in 1988, the date when most state UST regulations went into effect, 1.4 million USTs, approximately two-thirds of the country's tanks, were leaking.

The new federal regulations define USTs as tanks whose volume is 10% or more beneath the ground surface, including piping, and are being used to accumulate hazardous substances. Excluded from regulation, under 40 CFR 2280 and 281 are farm or residential tanks with capacities of 1,100 gallons or less which are used to store motor fuel for non-commercial use; tanks of any size used to store heating oil for consumptive use on the premises; storage tanks on or above an underground floor; septic or flow-through process tanks; pipeline facilities, gas production-related traps or gathering lines or surface impoundments and stormwater/wastewater collection systems.

A comparison of state and federal regulations on USTs (Stabilito, 1993) has shown that several states have adopted the EPA regulations verbatim, whereas others have developed more stringent ones. This includes such areas as compliance deadlines, the use of specific corrosion protection devices, a lack of the EPA exemptions for secondary containment, expanded leak detection requirements, and more rapid release reporting. The result is that owners of USTs must be sure to check their state's regulations as well as the federal ones.

Sole Source Aquifers

Sole source aquifers receive a good deal of attention in environmental laws and regulations because they represent the only possible source of future (and, on occasion, present) drinking water supplies for a large population covering a wide area. Large portions of Florida and New Jersey are examples of heavily populated areas that are dependent on sole source aquifers. The Safe Drinking Water (SDW) Act calls on State and local governments to identify critical aquifer protection areas that are eligible for special protection. Regulations provide criteria for state and local governments to use for the identification of such aquifers.

Landfills

As discussed earlier, a major source of contamination of groundwater is by leachates from landfills. Existing landfills are covered by RCRA and abandoned ones by CERCLA. Existing landfills now are stringently regulated insofar as to what toxic materials may be placed in them. Liquids are banned. Further, double liners are usually required around the landfills in order to trap liquids leaching from the wastes. These liquids then are pumped up into suitable containers and disposed of properly.

In order to obtain permits under RCRA, owners and operators of hazardous waste facilities usually must install groundwater monitoring wells to detect contamination from the facilities and undertake the necessary corrective measures.

EPA has adopted a two-fold approach to RCRA permitting standards:

- liquids management
- groundwater monitoring and response

The first, liquids management, minimizes the generation of leachate that might contaminate groundwater. The second compares groundwater contamination to that which occurs naturally in the uppermost aquifer or the Maximum Contaminant Levels (MCLs) for contaminants listed under the Safe Drinking Water Act, whichever is less. If those values are exceeded, then corrective actions must be undertaken.

EPA regulations at 40 CFR 264, Subpart G, contain procedures for closing permitted TSD facilities. Regulations at 40 CFR 265, Subpart G, contain procedures for closing hazardous waste accumulation sites and TSD facilities that have interim status. Tanks which are used for the accumulation of hazardous wastes must be closed in accordance with the RCRA regulations which require that all waste residues, contaminated containment system components such as liners, and contaminated soils, structures and equipment, must be decontaminated or removed and managed as hazardous waste.

Injection Wells

For many years the injection of wastes (e.g., cyanide and heavy metals from the steel industry) into wells going deep into the ground was a commonly accepted practice. These wastes were injected into aquifers that thus became contaminated and unsuitable for future use as public water supplies. EPA, therefore, has placed increasingly stringent restrictions on this practice and has drastically reduced the amounts of permitted underground injection activity. The purpose behind these restrictions ultimately is to eliminate all underground injection wells that may serve to introduce hazardous constituents to future water supplies. Permits for such injection wells, which are approved by EPA, must undergo very rigid scrutiny before they are granted.

For those applicants who desire to start or continue underground injection, EPA has placed underground injection wells in three categories or "classes" according to the nature of the substance and the threats they pose. EPA considers whether or not to allow operation of those wells through one of two mechanisms: by general rule or by individual permit.

In the cases of those underground injection wells that EPA allows to function *by general rule*, the owner/operator is required to submit to EPA or the state that has been delegated authority, an inventory of the underground injection wells and, for certain classes, the rates of injection. Reports also may be required on groundwater monitoring and analyses of fluids injected into wells.

When authorized *by permit*, EPA or the state must require a form of monitoring that will produce data representative of the activity being monitored. The permittee is required to present these results (40 CFR 146). The permit will also require the owner/operator to report any changes in the facility. Any incident of noncompliance with permit conditions that endangers an underground source of drinking water must be reported to the agency within 24 hours.

These regulatory controls ensure the mechanical integrity of the injection well operations, as well as ensure that none of the well's contents migrate into underground sources of drinking water. Information collected subsequent to authorization by rule or permit enables EPA or the states to remain informed about the contents and operating characteristics of these wells and the status of groundwater in the area. In this way, changes in rules or permits can be made, and, when necessary, enforcement actions can be taken (Bregman and Mackenthun, 1992).

A 1994 EPA Fuel Rule placed new restrictions on dumping ignitable wastes in underground injection wells. The Rule bans injection of wastes with ignitable characteristics — those with high organic carbon content and toxic pesticide wastes — unless wells meet EPA's no-migration standards. These wastes may also be injected if they are first treated according to RCRA land disposal regulations.

ENVIRONMENTAL COMPLIANCE

The information presented in this section on groundwater must be utilized by the environmental compliance officer (ECO) together with those of the chapters on drinking water and storage tanks. Each of these three cited chapters may make an impact upon groundwater and the ECO therefore must be concerned with each of them. For those reasons, this section will not be lengthy or all-inclusive.

As with other situations, the ECO first must determine whether his/her facility has the potential for groundwater contamination, as well as whether it already exists.

Potential Groundwater Contamination

> **Checklist :**
>
> - Does the facility have sources of potential groundwater pollution? Check against possible sources of contamination listed in Exhibit 4-1 plus any other possible sources peculiar to the facility.
>
>   No.   Move on to the check of whether actual contamination exists.
>
>   Yes.   Identify potential sources on map of facility. Describe potential on paper in terms of items such as nature of origin of contaminant; volumes of liquid; type of pollutant, its concentration and toxicity; description of groundwater that could be contaminated, effects on that groundwater, etc.

If the facility has a potential for groundwater contamination but has not yet contaminated the groundwater, the next step for the ECO is to determine how to prevent that potential from occurring. In that determination, he/she must consider costs and the possible degree of prevention. He/she then should present management with the information on the potential contamination and the most cost-effective method of preventing it. Finally, the ECO should arrange for the construction of the approved approach and oversee that construction.

Prevention of Potential Groundwater Contamination

> **Checklist :**
>
> - What is the source of the possible contamination (e.g., septic tank, surface impoundant, landfill, underground storage tank, abandoned well, de-icing salts, etc.)?
>
> - What is the likely extent of the contamination (amount, time, effect on groundwater use, etc.)?
>
> - What are the normal approaches to preventing contamination from that particular source?

Prevention of Potential Groundwater Contamination (continued)

Checklist (continued):

- Draw up a tentative prevention plan. Be specific about possible effectiveness and costs of construction.

- Review plan with management. Obtain approval/disapproval for proceeding further.
  - If disapproved, stop here, but monitor for possible contamination.
  - If approved, develop detailed plans, select a contractor, and oversee construction. Set up monitoring devices to determine effectiveness of process as a function of time.

The possible existence of groundwater contamination poses an entirely new set of complex problems for the ECO. First, let us consider the case of proven existence of contamination during the past period of time.

Existing Contamination

Checklist :

- Questions to be answered are
  - What?
  - Where?
  - Since when?
  - Type and amount of contamination?
  - Source?

- Next, the ECO must determine whether or not actions, such as remedial activities, have already been taken
  - If no action taken to date, treat as described below for newly discovered sources of groundwater contamination
  - If previous action has been taken, review the action and any contacts with regulatory agencies. Is the action
    - i)   Still in effect?
    - ii) Working properly?
    - iii) Complying with regulatory requirements?
  - If the answer to any of the above three questions is positive, then monitor the action until it is completed

Existing Contamination (continued)

> **Checklist (continued):**
>
> - If the answer is negative, proceed as described below for newly discovered cases of groundwater contamination

The determination of possible new groundwater contamination is a difficult one. It may involve considerable well boring, sampling, and modeling. The problem is not the fact that groundwater is contaminated, but rather the need to show the amount of that contamination, the volume of water that is already contaminated (including pinpointing its location), and the direction and rate at which that water will spread in the foreseeable future. The question of whether it does or will contaminate drinking water supplies is paramount.

Determination of Previously Unknown Groundwater Contamination

> **Checklist :**
>
> - Review the information that has led to the belief that groundwater may be contaminated
>
> - Based on the above information, develop a program of well drilling and water sampling that will show, at least empirically, the degree of contamination and the area/volume of groundwater that may presently be contaminated
>   - In doing the above, a detailed study of the known geology of the area is essential
>
> - Groundwater modeling is performed next to take the developed information and to predict the direction and rate of flow of the contaminated groundwater. Particular emphasis is placed on location of nearby present or potential drinking water supplies and the possibility that they may become contaminated

Having found that previously unknown contaminated groundwater exists, the ECO should then determine which of several acts may cover his/her situation and proceed accordingly.

Legal Coverage of Contaminated Groundwater

Checklist :

- Is the contaminated groundwater subject to coverage under any of the following Acts?
  - Safe Drinking Water Act
  - RCRA
  - CERCLA
  - FIFRA
  - TSCA
  - Clean Water Act

  If so, go to the chapters in this book that cover those Acts, as well as proceeding as described later in this section.

- Is the contaminated groundwater subject to any state legislation or regulations that are not covered by these Acts?

  If yes, obtain the proper information on the legislation and regulations, contact state officials, and proceed according to their requirements.

  If no, proceed to the next step.

The next several checklists describe procedures for complying with the Acts listed above. The first item to be discussed here will be the *wellhead protection program* required by the Safe Drinking Water Act. This is required if the drinking water supply for a facility comes from a well. It protects the area around the well from pollution that could lead to contamination of the drinking water. The protection programs with which the ECO must comply are developed and enforced by the state and local governments. The minimum components for such programs have been listed earlier in this chapter.

Wellhead Protection Programs

Checklist :

- Does the water supply for the facility come from a well?
  - If no, stop here
  - If yes, learn what the wellhead protection plan is and follow it including the following items

Wellhead Protection Programs (continued)

Checklist (continued):

- Identify contamination sources within the wellhead protection area (WHPA)

- Develop and enforce approaches for protecting the water supply within the WHPA from the contamination sources
  - Check to see if the state or local government has such a program
    - i) If yes, make your program fit into theirs, including contingency plans if the well becomes contaminated
    - ii) If no, work with them in developing yours in such a manner that they will adopt it as theirs

- If you will need to develop new wells in the future, work with the state or local authority to ensure siting
  - To obtain maximum water yield
  - To minimize potential for contamination

Procedures that the ECO must follow with regard to the prevention of *leakage from underground storage tanks (USTs)* are described later in this book in the chapter on storage tanks. For the purposes of the present chapter, the ECO must be concerned with the following checklist.

Contamination by Leaking USTs

Checklist :

- Are there any underground storage tanks (USTs) in the facility?
  - No. Stop here
  - Yes. Continue as below

- Make certain they have spill and overflow prevention devices, corrosion protection systems (usually sacrificial cathodes or impermeable liners), and procedures for detecting leaks

- In case of a leak

Contamination by Leaking USTs (continued)

> **Checklist (continued):**
>
> - Have an emergency program for leak-corrective action ready ahead of time. Depending on the size of the leak, this may include repair, closure, or removal of the tank
>
> • In case of closure, follow the closure requirements that have been set for the tank. See the chapter in this book on storage tanks for more details
>
> • If repairs are required, obtain bids and oversee the construction
>
> • If a leak has developed, the ECO will be responsible for overseeing removal of the tank and the contaminated soil, as well as for making plans for appropriate treatment of contaminated groundwater. The approaches to these requirements will require State approval. The state may impose fines on the tank owners

The ECO is responsible for determining which aquifer may be contaminated by activities at the facility. The ECO also must determine whether any of those activities will contaminate *a sole source aquifer.*

Sole Source Aquifer

> **Checklist:**
>
> • Determine from which aquifer your groundwater comes
>
> • Is it a sole source aquifer, identified by the state or local government?
>   - No. Stop here
>   - Yes. Check with the state and local authorities on their regulations for sole source aquifers and comply with them

The ECO must determine whether there are any *landfills* on the property that may be contaminating groundwater and take appropriate actions to comply with EPA and state requirements.

Landfills

Checklist :

- Any landfills on property?
  - No. Stop here
  - Yes. Proceed

- Abandoned or existing?
  - Abandoned. Proceed as in Chapter 8 on abandoned hazardous waste facilities
  - Existing. Proceed as below

- Double liners and pumping systems in place?
  - Yes. Proceed as below
  - No. Close landfill as in Chapter 8 dealing with RCRA

- Groundwater monitoring wells nearby?
  - Yes. Proceed as below
  - No. Install wells in accordance with state requirements

- RCRA permitting
  - Details in later chapter
    - i) Liquid management to minimize leachate
    - ii) Groundwater monitoring. Compare contamination with maximum contaminant levels (MCLs) in the Safe Drinking Water Act or with natural contamination in upper aquifer level, whichever is less. If value is exceeded, take corrective action

- Closure of Tanks
  - Follow procedures shown in Chapter 10

If the facility contains an *underground injection system*, the ECO may be certain that it will be required to be closed out in the not too distant future and should start planning accordingly. Meanwhile, compliance measures must be taken as indicated below.

Underground Injection of Wastes

Checklist :

- Are wastes injected underground?
  - If no, stop here
  - If yes, follow procedures listed below

- Do you have a permit for the underground injection?
  - If yes, check to make certain the permit conditions are being observed
  - If no, confer with EPA on the need for a permit, the type of permit (i.e., general rule or individual), and the requirements to be imposed by EPA on the permit

- If you have a permit, is the monitoring requirement being carried out properly?
  - If no, arrange to have it done right
  - If yes, make periodic checks

- For new permits, arrange monitoring system in accordance with EPA requirements

- Whether the permit is old or new, make sure that no ignitable wastes (see definition earlier in this chapter) are dumped in wells unless first treated according to RCRA land disposal regulations

GLOSSARY

Aquifer . . . .   A water-bearing bed or stratum of permeable rock, sand, or gravel, capable of yielding considerable quantities of water to wells or springs.

Carcinogen . . . .   Chemical reputed to be involved in causing cancer.

Feedlot. . . . .   An area in which a large number of animals, e.g., cattle, are kept penned while being fed.

Groundwater Modeling........	A mathematical prediction of the quantity and degree of contamination of groundwater, coupled with a projection of its rate of flow and the direction of that flow.
Groundwater Monitoring ..... Well	Very small artificial well from which samples of groundwater are drawn periodically for analysis of the contaminants in the water.
Particulates	Very tiny airborne solid materials.
Septic Tank	Tank buried in the ground that serves as a receptacle for human sewage.
Sole Source Aquifer	Aquifers that are the only source of actual or potential drinking water supply for a populated area.
Sump	A pool or puddle.
Surface Impoundment........	Artificial pool, lake, or lagoon created to contain wastewater.
Underground Storage Tanks ...	Storage tanks, 10% or more of which have the tank and associated piping below ground level.
Wellhead	The area surrounding a well from which water seeps into the ground to replenish the well.

REFERENCES AND SELECTED READINGS

Bregman, J.I. and Mackenthun, K.M., 1992, "Environmental Impact Statements," CRC Press, Boca Raton, FL.

Briggs, G.F., 1976, "Developing Groundwater Resources," in *Handbook of Water Resources and Pollution Control*, Gehm, H.W. and Bregman, J.I., Editors, Van Nostrand Reinhold Company, New York.

Conservation Foundation, 1987, "Groundwater Protection," Washington D.C.

Stabilito, Stephen, May, 1993, "Managing Underground Storage Tanks: State vs. Federal Regulations," Focus, Vol. 9, Issue 3, Consulting Services, 2c., Exton, PA.

U.S. EPA, May 8, 1991, "Protecting the Nation's Groundwater: EPA's Strategy for the 1990s," Final Report of the EPA Ground-Water Task Force, Washington, D.C.

U.S. EPA, April, 1990, "Citizens Guide to Ground-Water Protection," EPA/440/6-90-004, Office of Water, Washington, D.C.

U.S. EPA, September, 1988, "Musts for USTs," EPA/530/UST-88/008, Office of Underground Storage Tanks, Washington, D.C.

5   Drinking Water

Since the beginning of civilization, mankind has recognized the need for purifying its water supply to reduce health risks. As early as 2000 B.C., a physician in India stated that "impure water should be purified by being boiled over a fire, or being heated in the sun, or by dipping a heated iron into it, or it may be purified by filtration through sand and coarse gravel and then allowed to cool" (EPA, April, 1990). A century ago, man knew almost nothing about water-borne disease. Most infections were explained by vapors or miasmas and often were treated by draining blood from a diseased body. In the wake of two devastating epidemics of cholera in 1831 and 1848, a few English physicians noted that the dreaded diseases often cropped up in river towns downstream from the initial outbreak, suggesting that water might be the carrier of cholera. A sudden outbreak of cholera in 1853 gave Dr. John Snow, a London physician, an opportunity to test the theory by mapping the occurrences of the cholera cases. Snow found all were in households which drew their water from one well located on Broad Street in the Soho District. Therefore, he proposed that the pump handle of the Soho well be removed. City officials decided to test his hypothesis. The epidemic was quickly brought under control and probably saved hundreds, if not thousands of human lives (Bregman and Lenormand, 1966).

Although it was three decades before the etiology of cholera was established by the German bacteriologist, Robert Koch, sanitary engineers in England soon focused their efforts on providing hygienic sources of municipal water. By 1883, when the causal agent of the disease was isolated and studied, cholera had been effectively curbed in both England and the United States. Our inability to learn from history is shown by the recent (1993) outbreak of cholera in South America on a massive scale. This epidemic has been traced to contaminated water supplies.

In World War II, army doctors were concerned about the traditional camp epidemics of infectious hepatitis, generally known as jaundice. Despite an intensive research program, 180,000 American soldiers were hospitalized by this infection. Experiments revealed that hepatitis viruses survived chemical treatment unless the chlorine level was significantly increased. The laboratory work was supported by studies of hepatitis epidemics. The reports included analyses of outbreaks in Grangesburg, Sweden, where 400 persons succumbed to the disease and in the spectacular New Delhi, India, epidemic which affected 30,000 residents in a city of 2,000,000. In both cases, the highly suspected sources of infection were the municipal supplies of water.

A documented case of hepatitis from drinking water occurred in a small town in Daviess County, Kentucky, where an outbreak occurred in several adjacent houses. Investigation revealed that the disease was almost certainly caused by the movement of the pathogens from a single septic tank to a series of seven neighboring wells (Bregman and Lenormand, 1966).

Waterborne diseases caused by microbial contamination remain a matter of great concern to this day. From 1961 through 1983, there were over 575 reported cases of waterborne disease outbreaks in the U.S. involving more than 153,000 individual cases of illness resulting in 23 deaths. From 1981 through 1985, 351 cases of outbreaks were reported from public systems. And yet, as of 1986, there were still over 1,300 community water systems and more than 1,500 noncommunity water systems using surface water as a source of drinking water and not providing filtration (EPA, 1986). In 1989, EPA estimated that there were still over 89,000 cases each year of waterborne diseases in the U.S. that are caused by microorganisms (EPA, June 19, 1989).

In 1994, the Natural Resources Defense Council (NRDC) stated that 20% of the nation's drinking water was unsafe to drink. California, Florida, Georgia, Illinois, Massachusetts, and Pennsylvania were cited as states with the nation's dirtiest drinking water (Environmental Conference Alert, Aug. 11, 1994).

Exhibit 5-1 lists some of the diseases that are caused by micro-organisms in water supplies (EPA, April, 1990). *Giardia lamblia* is now the most commonly identified organism associated with waterborne disease in this country. Over 20,000 water-related cases of this disease have been reported in the last 20 years (Ryan, 1987) with probably many more cases going unreported.

Chemical contaminants, both natural and synthetic, might also be present in water supplies. Contamination problems in groundwater (used by 85% of small systems) are frequently chemical in nature. Common sources of chemical contamination include: minerals dissolved from rocks; pesticides and herbicides; leaking underground storage tanks; seepage from septic tanks, sewage treatment plants, and landfills; and any other improper disposal of chemicals in or on the ground. In some systems, the water quality can promote corrosion of materials in the distribution system, possibly introducing lead and other materials into the drinking water (EPA, April, 1990).

Among the carcinogens that have been identified in many sources of water are such pesticides as DDT, dieldrin, and chlordane, in addition to the aromatic hydrocarbons, benzopyrene and benzanthracene. At least three carcinogenic elements — arsenic, beryllium, and chromium — are found in some waters. Water contamination by radioactive elements — iodine, strontium, cesium — is well documented and widely known (Bregman and Lenormand, 1966).

Exhibit 5-1   Waterborne Diseases

Waterborne disease	Causative organism	Source of organism in water	Symptom
Gastroenteritis	Rotavirus	Human feces	Acute diarrhea or vomiting
	Salmonella (bacterium)	Animal or human feces	Acute diarrhea and vomiting
	Enteropathogenic *E. coli*	Human feces	Acute diarrhea or vomiting
Typhoid	*Salmonella typhosa* (bacterium)	Human feces	Inflamed intestine, enlarged spleen, high temperature – sometimes fatal
Dysentery	*Shigella* (bacterium)	Human feces	Diarrhea – rarely fatal
Cholera	*Vibrio comma* (bacterium)	Human Feces	Vomiting, severe diarrhea, rapid dehydration, mineral loss – high mortality
Infectious hepatitis	Hepatitis A (virus)	Human feces, shellfish grown in polluted waters	Yellowed skin, enlarged liver, abdominal pain – low mortality, lasts up to 4 months
Amoebic dysentery	*Entamoeba histolytica* (protozoan)	Animal or human feces	Mild diarrhea, chronic dysentery
Giardiasis	*Giardia lamblia* (protozoan)	Animal or human feces	Diarrhea, cramps, nausea, and general weakness – not fatal, lasts 1 week to 30 weeks
Cryptosporidiosis	*Cryptosporidium* (protozoan)	Animal or human feces	Diarrhea, stomach pain – lasts an average of 5 days

Adapted from American Water Works Association, *Introduction to Water Treatment: Principles and Practices of Water Supply Operations*, Denver, CO, 1984.

Radionuclides in drinking water occur primarily in those systems that use groundwater.

Ingestion of uranium and radium in drinking water may cause cancer of the bone and kidney. While radium and uranium enter the body by ingestion, radon (a gas) is usually inhaled after being released into the air during showers, baths, and other activities such as washing clothes and dishes. Although radon can be ingested as well as inhaled, it is estimated that inhalation is far more toxic than the ingestion route. The main health risk of concern due to inhalation of radon is lung cancer (EPA, 1986).

LEGISLATION AND REGULATIONS

Laws in the United States to protect the quality of drinking water have been in existence for a long time. Since their inception, they have required the issuance and enforcement of drinking water standards to protect the health of the consumer. First adopted in 1914, Public Health Service Drinking Water Standards were designed only to protect the health of the traveling public. The Drinking Water Standards were revised in 1942 and 1962, but they remained applicable only to interstate carriers, such as buses, trains, and airplanes. Finally, the Safe Drinking Water Act of 1974, P.L.93-523, made drinking water standards applicable to all public water systems with at least 15 service connections and serving at least 25 individuals for at least 60 days each year.

The SDWA directed the U.S. Environmental Protection Agency (EPA) to identify and regulate substances in drinking water that, in the judgment of the EPA administrator, may have an adverse effect on public health. It included interim regulations (National Interim Primary Drinking Water Regulations - NIPDWRs) to be established within 180 days of enactment of the SDWA and National Primary Drinking Water Regulations (NPDWRs) to be finalized over a period of years. National Interim Primary Drinking Water Regulations were promulgated in 1975 (Mackenthun and Bregman, 1992), which also created a National Drinking Water Advisory Council to assist EPA. The National Drinking Water Regulations were subdivided into primary regulations, affecting public health, and secondary regulations, affecting aesthetic qualities relating to the public welfare (EPA, June, 1990).

In 1976, EPA issued a *National Safe Drinking Water Strategy* for implementing drinking water protection programs authorized by the SDWA. These were the Public Water System (PWS) and Underground Injection Control (UIC) programs. The strategy, developed "to clarify EPA policy," was designed to be "an operational plan" and to describe "what EPA plans to do in light of its legislative mandate and the realities of existing federal, state, and local capabilities and resources" (EPA, February, 1977).

The 1986 Amendments to the Safe Drinking Water Act (SDWA)

The SWDA, as amended in 1986, Public Law (PL) 99-339, 42 U.S. Code (USC) 201, 300f–300j-25, 6939b, 6979a, 6979b, 7401–742, etc, is the federal legislation which regulates the safety of drinking water in the U.S. States have primary enforcement responsibility for the provisions of the Act.

Congress significantly expanded and strengthened the SDWA in 1986. The 1986 amendments include provisions on the following:

- **Maximum Contaminant Levels.** The Safe Drinking Water Act required EPA to set numerical standards, referred to as Maximum Contaminant Levels (MCLs), or treatment technique requirements for contaminants in public water supplies. Maximum Containment Level Goals (MCLGs), which are considered as non-enforceable health goals, also were to be set. The 1986 amendments established a strict schedule for EPA to set MCLs or treatment requirements for previously unregulated contaminants. The 1986 Amendments to the Act resulted in the regulation of a large number of contaminants, broken down into the following categories:

  - inorganic compounds
  - synthetic organic compounds
  - volatile organic compounds
  - radionuclides
  - turbidity
  - microbiological activity

  National primary drinking water regulations apply to each public water system in each state. However, such regulations do not apply to a public water system which:

  1. consists only of distribution and storage facilities (and does not have any collection and treatment facilities)
  2. obtains all its water from, but is not owned or operated by, a public water system to which such regulations apply
  3. does not sell water to any person
  4. is not a carrier which conveys passengers in interstate commerce (42 USC 300(g)).

- **Monitoring.** EPA must issue regulations requiring monitoring of all regulated and certain unregulated contaminants, depending on the number of people served by the system, and the contaminants likely to be found.

- **Filtration.** EPA must set criteria under which systems are obligated to filter water from surface water sources if the following contaminants do not meet EPA criteria:

  - total and fecal coliform
  - turbidity

  It must also develop procedures for states to determine which systems have to be filtered.

- **Disinfection.** EPA must develop rules requiring all public water supplies to disinfect their water.

- **Use of lead materials.** The use of solder or flux containing more than 0.2% lead, or pipes and pipe fittings containing more than 8% lead, is prohibited in public water supply systems. Public notification is required where there is lead in construction materials of the public water supply system, or where the water is sufficiently corrosive to cause leaching of lead from the distribution system/lines.

- **Wellhead protection.** The 1986 SDWA amendments require all states to develop wellhead protection programs. These programs are designed to protect public water supplies from sources of contamination as well as to identify anthropogenic sources of contamination to wells (EPA, April, 1990). Early versions of the SDWA provided for the protection of underground sources of drinking water through the issuance of regulations for state underground injection programs, the provision of petitions by citizens for no new underground injection programs, and the sole-source aquifer protection where the vulnerability of an aquifer is in question.

The U.S. EPA has been very active in issuing the required SDWA regulations. This regulatory effort is divided into the following five phases:

- Phase I: Volatile organic compounds
- Phase II: Synthetic organic compounds, inorganic compounds, and unregulated contaminant monitoring
- Phase III: Radionuclide contaminants
- Phase IV: Disinfectant and oxidant by-products
- Phase V: Inorganic compounds and synthetic organic compounds

EPA is setting regulations for these phases as rapidly as possible, but not all at one time. This will be apparent from the discussion that follows. The requirements vary from one phase to another, but they all must meet values that are considered safe for consumption. In the cases of the particularly toxic chemicals, the amounts of contamination may be set at zero.

Federal Facility Requirements

Each department, agency, and instrument of the executive, legislative, and judicial branches of the federal government having jurisdiction over any potential source of contaminants identified by a state program must be subject to and observe all requirements of the state program applicable to such potential source of contaminants, both substantive and procedural, in the same manner, and to the same extent, as any other person, including payment of reasonable charges and fees (42 USC 300h-7(h)).

If a Federal agency has jurisdiction over any federally owned or maintained public water system, or is engaged in any activity resulting, or which may result in, underground water injection which endangers drinking water, it is subject to, and must observe, any Federal, state, and local regulations, administrative authorities, and process and sanctions respecting the provision of safe drinking water and respecting any underground injection program in the same manner, and to the same extent, as any nongovernmental entity. This requirement applies:

1. to any rules substantive or procedural (including any record keeping or reporting, permits, and other requirements)
2. to the exercise of any Federal, state, or local authorities
3. to any process or sanction, whether enforced in federal, state, or local courts or in any other manner (42 USC 300j-6(a)).

States have primary responsibility ("primacy") to enforce compliance with national primary drinking water standards and sampling, monitoring, and notice requirements in conformance with 40 CFR 141. U.S. EPA executes the enforcement responsibilities until individual state programs are approved.

States under primacy may establish drinking water regulations, monitoring schedules, and reporting requirements more stringent than, or in addition to, those in the Federal regulations. Federal public water systems in these states are required to comply with these additional requirements. Most states have adopted drinking water regulations that closely reflect the federal requirements. Almost all states have achieved authorization from U.S. EPA to administer drinking water compliance programs including Underground Injection Control (UIC) programs (U.S. ACERL, 1993). However, EPA has expressed dissatisfaction with programs in certain states (e.g., Colorado and North Carolina) and may take over those state programs (Environment Compliance Alert, September 22, and August 11, 1994).

The 83 regulated contaminants (plus others) under the 1986 SWDA Amendments and their proposed values are shown in Exhibit 5-2 (Metcalf and Eddy, 1990), on the following pages.

In 1989, EPA also proposed nine new secondary maximum contaminant levels (SMCLs), which are listed in Exhibit 5-3.

In June, 1988, EPA issued proposed regulations to define MCLs and MCLGs for lead and copper. The MCLG proposed for lead is 0 mg/l, and 1.3 mg/l for copper. The proposed MCLs applicable to water entering the distribution system were 0.005 mg/l for lead and 1.3 mg/l for copper.

In June, 1989, the Surface Water Treatment Rule (SWTR) and the Coliform Rule were promulgated by EPA. According to the SWTR, all public water systems using surface water or ground water under direct influence of surface waters must disinfect and may be required to filter if certain source water quality requirements and site-specific conditions are not met. These source water criteria necessary to avoid filtration cover coliform and turbidity limits as follows:

**Exhibit 5-2 Regulated Contaminants
Under 1986 SWDA Amendments**

Parameters[a]	MCL[b]	MCLG[c]	Proposed MCL	Proposed MCLG	SDWA 1986	1/22/88 Changes
Inorganic Compounds						
Aluminum					×	−
Antimony					×	
Arsenic	0.050			0.050	×	−
Asbestos				7.1E+06 Fibers/liter	×	
Barium	1.000			1.500	×	
Beryllium					×	
Cadmium	0.010			0.005	×	
Chromium	0.050			0.120	×	
Copper				1.300	×	
Cyanide					×	
Fluoride	4.000	4.000			×	
Lead	0.050			0.020	×	
Mercury	0.002			0.003	×	
Molybdenum					×	−
Nickel					×	
Nitrate	10.000			10.000	×	
Nitrite				1.000		+
Selenium	0.010			0.045	×	
Silver	0.050				×	−
Sodium					×	−
Sulfate					×	
Thallium					×	
Vanadium					×	−
Zinc					×	−
Microbiological						
Coliform	1–4Clfm/ 100ml			Zero	×	
Giardia lamblia				Zero	×	
Legionella					×	
Standard plate count					×	
Viruses				Zero	×	
Synthetic Organic Compounds						
1,2-Dichloropropane				0.006	×	
2,3,7,8-TCDD Dioxin					×	
2,4,5-TP Silvex	0.010			0.052	×	
2,4-D	0.100			0.070	×	
Acrylamide				Zero	×	

**Exhibit 5-2   Regulated Contaminants
Under 1986 SWDA Amendments (continued)**

Parameters[a]	MCL[b]	MCLG[c]	Proposed MCL	Proposed MCLG	SDWA 1986	1/22/88 Changes
Adipates					×	
Alachlor				Zero	×	
Aldicarb				0.009	×	
Aldicarb sulfone				0.009		+
Aldicarb sulfoxide				0.009		+
Altrazine					×	
Carbofuran				0.036	×	
Chlordane				Zero	×	
Dalapon					×	
Dibromochloro-propane				Zero	×	
Dibromomethane					×	–
Dinoseb					×	
Diquat					×	
Endothall					×	
Endrin	2.0E–04				×	
Epichlorohydrin				Zero	×	
Ethylbenzene				0.680		+
Ethylene dibromide					×	
Glyphosate					×	
Heptachlor				Zero		+
Heptachlor epoxide				Zero		+
Hexachlorocyclo-pentadiene					×	
Lindane	0.004			2.0E–04	×	
Methoxychlor	0.100			0.340	×	
Pentachlorophenol				0.220	×	
Phthalates					×	
Pichloram					×	
Polychlorinated biphenyls				Zero	×	
Polynuclear aromatic hydrocarbons					×	
Simazine					×	
Styrene				0.140		+
Toluene				2.000	×	
Total trihalomethanes	0.100					
Toxaphene	0.005			Zero	×	
Vydate					×	
Xylenes				0.440	×	

**Exhibit 5-2   Regulated Contaminants
Under 1986 SWDA Amendments (continued)**

Parameters[a]	MCL[b]	MCLG[c]	Proposed MCL	Proposed MCLG	SDWA 1986	1/22/88 Changes
Volatile Organic Compounds						
1,1,1-Trichloroethane	0.200	0.200				×
1,2-Dichloroethane	0.005	Zero				×
1,1-Dichloroethylene	0.007	0.007				×
Benzene	0.005	Zero				×
Carbon tetrachloride	0.005	Zero				×
Chlorobenzene						×
cis 1.2-Dichloro-ethylene				0.070		×
Methylene chloride						×
p-Dichlorobenzene	0.750	0.750				×
Tetrachloroethylene				Zero		×
Trans 1,2-dichloro-ethylene				0.070		×
Trichlorobenzene(s)						×
Trichloroethylene	0.005	Zero				×
Vinyl chloride	0.002	Zero				×
Radionuclides						
Radon						×
Uranium						×
Gross alpha particle activity	15 pCl/l					×
Radium-226 & Radium-228	5 pCl/l					×
Particles & photon radioactivity	4 mrem/yr					×
Other						
Turbidity	1.0 NTU	0.5 NTU	0.1 NTU			×

Note: All values are mg/l unless otherwise stated. Under 1/22/88 Changes column: + indicates addition to the list; – indicates deletion.

[a] Numbers indicate items required by the Act.

[b] Maximum Contaminant Level (MCL); as defined by the Safe Drinking Water Act (SDWA).

[c] Maximum Contaminant Level Goal (MCLG); nonenforceable health goal, as defined by the SDWA.

Taken from Metcalf and Eddy, 1990.

Exhibit 5-3   Proposed SMCLs

Contaminant	Level (mg/l)
Aluminum	0.05
o-Dichlorobenzene	0.01
p-Dichlorobenzene	0.005
Ethylbenzene	0.03
Pentachlorophenol	0.03
Silver	0.09
Styrene	0.01
Toluene	0.04
Xylene	0.02

From U.S. EPA, 1989

Source water coliform requirements are:

- fecal coliform limit of <20 colonies per ml sample of raw water in 90% of the samples

- total coliform limit of <100 colonies per 100 ml of raw water in 90% of the samples

- if both fecal and total coliforms are monitored:
  - total coliform can exceed the limit
  - fecal coliform cannot exceed the limit

- coliform sampling frequency is:

Population	Samples/week
<500	1
501–3,300	2
3,301–10,000	3
10,000–25,000	4
>25,000	5

- coliform sampling must include a sample on every day the raw water turbidity exceeds 1 Nephelometric Turbidity Unit (NTU); however, this sample counts toward the required weekly total

Source water turbidity sampling frequency and turbidity limit requirements prior to disinfection are:

- <5 NTU per sample based on a least one grab sample every 4 hours

- not to exceed 5 NTU more than:
  - two periods for 12 months, or
  - five periods for 120 months

- period is defined as the number of consecutive days on which a sample exceeds 5 NTU

Site-specific criteria necessary to avoid filtration are as follows:

A. Disinfection

The EPA site disinfection requirements are:

- water system practice disinfection
- have a redundant disinfection capability with auxiliary power supply and alarm
- system demonstrates that a minimum of 0.2 mg/l disinfectant residual is maintained in the water entering the distribution system
- system demonstrates inactivations of:
  - 99.9% of Giardia cysts
  - 99.99% of enteric viruses

The MCLGs established in the EPA rule are

- Giardia Lamblia - 0
- Viruses - 0
- Legionella - 0

B. Watershed Control

The site watershed control program must prove to the state authorities that the potential for Giardia cyst and enteric virus contamination is minimized. A watershed control must address the following:

- watershed hydrology
- watershed property ownership
- identification, monitoring, and control of characteristics and activities which may be detrimental to water quality

C. Sanitary Surveys

The site sanitary survey requirements are

- annual sanitary survey, which is a general inspection of the facility to assess compliance
- survey must be done by the State or a state-approved agent

D. No Waterborne Disease Outbreaks

The site waterborne disease requirement is that the water system, with its present facilities, has not had a waterborne disease outbreak as identified by the State.

E. Long-term Coliform Requirement

The coliform rule requires all public water systems to meet the coliform MCL and monitor total coliform with frequencies depending on population served. To comply with the coliform MCL, no more than 50% of all total coliform samples per month can be total coliform-positive (EPA, April, 1990).

F. Total Trihalomethane Requirement

The site trihalomethane (THM) requirement in community water systems is a total THM less 100 µg/l (Metcalf and Eddy, 1990). This is sampled at least annually, and usually more often, depending on the source type.

Drinking Water Standards

In September, 1988, EPA published a schedule for the setting of drinking water standards in accordance with the 1986 SDWA Amendments. This schedule is shown in Exhibit 5-4 (EPA, September, 1988). EPA has adhered to that schedule fairly closely.

Recent Developments

EPA has issued proposed rules that will require the water utilities of the nation either to replace chlorine as a disinfectant or else to install new filtering devices that reduce chlorinated byproducts of water purification. These byproducts are stated to have the ability to cause cancer, liver and kidney damage, heart and neurological effects, and reproductive problems. Maximum containment levels would be set as follows:

- trihalomethanes at 0.080 mg/liter
- haloacetic acids at 0.060 mg/l
- bromate at 0.010 mg/l
- chlorite at 1.0 mg/l
- chlorine at 4.0 mg/l
- cloramines at 4.0 mg/l
- chlorine dioxide at 0.8 mg/l
  (Environmental Compliance Alert, June 30, 1994).

EPA plans to finalize these rules on December 15, 1996.

These new rules were triggered by concern over the parasite outbreak that killed several people in Milwaukee in 1993. The proposal would specifically require "enhanced surface water filtration" to help control *Cryptosporidium* (the parasite). The proposal seeks to strike a delicate balance between using enough disinfectant to kill "crypto" and the other bacteria, while at the same

Exhibit 5-4   Drinking Water Standard Setting Schedule

Contaminant/requirement	Promulgation date	Effective date	First mandatory review/amendment (and every 3 years thereafter)
Fluoride	4/86	10/87	1989
Lead ban	—	6/88	1991
Volatile organic chemicals (VOCs)[a]	6/87	1/89	1990
Public notification	10/87	4/89	1990
Surface water treatment rule (SWTR)[a]	6/89	Fall 90	1992
Microbial WQ MCL[a]	6/89	Fall 90	1992
Lead[a]/corrosion control	Early 89	Fall 90	1992
38 Inorganic and synthetic organic chemicals (I/SOCs)[a]	Fall 89	Spring 91	1992
6 Radionuclides[a]	Spring 90	Fall 91	1993
24 Chemicals[a]	Spring 90	Fall 91	1993
1st List (1/88) of 25-plus contaminants (including "substituted" contaminants, disinfectants, byproducts, VOCs and pesticides, "SARA list" haz substances)	Winter 91	Summer 92	1994
Disinfection treatment rule[a]	Winter 91	Summer 92	1994
2nd List (1/91) of 25-plus contaminants	1/94	6/95	1997

Note: VOC = volatile organic chemical; I/SOC = inorganic and synthetic chemical contaminants; CWS = community water systems; NT(NC)WS = nontransient (noncommunity) water systems; MCL = maximum contaminant level.

[a] Contaminants/NPDWRs specifically mandated by SDWA Amendments

From U.S. EPA, September, 1988

time making sure that the disinfectant itself does not pose a threat (Environmental Managers Compliance Advisor, July 4, 1994).

EPA also is developing draft regulations for the following industrial contaminants in drinking water: boron, manganese, molybdenum, zinc, acifluorfen, acrylonitrile, 2,4/2,6-dinitrotoluene, ethylene thiourea, 1,3-dichloropropene and 1,2,3-trichloropropane. (Environmental Compliance Alert, August 25, 1994)

In 1994, the U.S. House of Representatives approved an SDWA reauthorization that revised EPA's contaminant selection process. The new bill, HR 3392, dropped the requirement that EPA identify 25 new contaminants every three years. Instead, the agency would list 15 unregulated contaminants and then update the list with 12 additions every four years.

The House version would also create a state revolving fund to help local communities meet SDWA requirements. About $15 million would be for technical assistance. The House bill would also give water systems three years to start monitoring water for pesticides, PCBs, dioxins, and other unregulated contaminants (Environmental Compliance Alert, October 13, 1994).

A bill passed the Senate at the same time that would force EPA to conduct risk assessments to weigh costs vs. benefits of all its future regulations. The two bills went to a House-Senate Conference Committee and died there. It is anticipated that a new SDWA bill will pass the Congress in the near future.

ENVIRONMENTAL COMPLIANCE

The responsibility of the Environmental Compliance (EC) Officer with respect to drinking water is a very serious one. It is the EC Officer who must be certain that the water is fit to drink and that no diseases are caught by members of his/her organization as a result of drinking inferior water. These diseases, as shown in Exhibit 5-1 of this book, range from causing unpleasant after-effects to those that are life-threatening. Probably none of the EC Officer's duties are more important than assuring the safety of the drinking water for his/her charges. This especially applies to viruses and bacterial contaminants, corrosion products, toxic chemicals, and even radioactive materials.

An EC Officer first must determine the extent of his/her responsibility for drinking water safety. Is this a responsibility and, if so, where does the water supply come from?

Drinking Water Supply

Checklist :

- Is drinking water supplied at the facility?

    - No. Go to the next chapter in this book
    - Yes. Continue as below

- Where does the drinking water supply come from?

    - City supplies
    - Wells
    - Small treatment units

Assuming that there is a drinking water supply for which the EC Officer has responsibility, the extent of that responsibility will vary as described below.

Water Supply Responsibility - City

Checklist :

- If the water is supplied by the city

  - Stay in close contact with the water treatment authority so that you receive early notice of problems

  - Have the water that comes out of the tap analyzed (including for lead and chlorine) to be certain that it meets drinking water standards. If it does not, then notify the city water authority and they (or you) take appropriate measures

  - If the analysis for lead is high and the city disclaims responsibility, check the distribution lines at the facility as well as water bubblers to determine if corrosion of piping or leaching of lead solder may be the source of the lead

  - If either proves to be the source, take action to replace the pipes or the bubblers with non-lead containing ones if this is possible. If this cannot be done, then insist that all water taps and bubblers be run for about 5 minutes first thing in the morning before they are used. This will eliminate high concentrations of lead that may have accumulated overnight

Water Supply Comes from Wells

Checklist :

- Has the water supply been analyzed and approved by the State (usually the Department of Health) or local authorities?

Water Supply Comes from Wells (continued)

Checklist (continued):

- If yes, then conduct frequent analyses for meeting requirements listed earlier in this chapter for regulated contaminants (Exhibit 5-2), Maximum Contaminant Levels (MCLs), the Surface Water Treatment Rule (SWTR), and the Coliform Rule. Call attention of the state and facility management to violations of these requirements and take appropriate corrective actions. These actions may involve deepening the supply wells to lower aquifers or even abandoning them and finding new sources of drinking water supply

- If no, then analyze the drinking water supply for the above listed requirements. If it does not meet them, then proceed as above to find a new drinking water supply source. If it does meet the requirements, contact the appropriate federal, state, and/or local authorities to obtain the necessary permits and to establish the monitoring requirements

Water Supply from Small Treatment Units

Checklist :

- Is the treatment unit functioning properly?

  - Check the quantities for the unit against its performance

  - Check, as above, for wells on the approval by state authorities. Take the same actions

A watershed control program must be carried out similar to the wellhead protection program described earlier in this chapter if the facility supplies its own drinking water.

Watershed Control Program

Checklist :

- Does a watershed control program already exist?

  - If yes, check to see that it is up-to-date and effective

  - If no, institute such a program, covering the following topics:

    i) Map watershed hydrology as it affects drinking water supply

    ii) On the map, show the watershed property ownership

    iii) Determine factors in the watershed that could affect the drinking water supply in an adverse manner. Develop and institute approaches to overcome those problems to the extent possible. Where not possible, estimate when they may render the water supply unusable for drinking purposes and plan for treatment methods to overcome them. If treating will not be effective, start a search for future alternative water supplies

Annual sanitary surveys must be made of all drinking water facilities by the state. The Environmental Compliance Officer must prepare for these surveys to be certain that the facility meets all requirements.

Sanitary Surveys

Checklist :

- Determine when the state will make its annual sanitary survey

- Prepare for the survey by correcting all obvious deficiencies

- Accompany the state agent on the survey. Note any deficiencies that are found. Take corrective actions

In view of the desire of EPA to replace chlorine as a disinfectant at some future date, or else to install new filtering devices that will reduce chlorinated byproducts, the EC Officer should be moving in that direction. This means keeping abreast of developments and possibly experimenting either with new disinfectants, filtering devices, or both.

Chlorine Reduction

Checklist :

- Is chlorine used as a disinfectant for the drinking water supply?

    - If no, stop here

    - If yes, proceed as below

- Are any other promising disinfectants available to the EC Officer?

    - If yes, obtain state or EPA approval for pilot scale testing. Anything beyond that will require state and EPA approval

    - Whether yes or no, examine the possibility of pilot scale testing for better filtration systems that would reduce chlorine byproducts. Submit results of any tests to state authorities and EPA. Take no further actions without their approvals

Finally, the EC Officer must be concerned with whether any of the industrial contaminants listed earlier in this chapter as the subjects of EPA possible draft regulations are present in the drinking water. If so, a determination must be made of their quantities and methods for their removal from that water examined.

Industrial Contaminants

Checklist :

- Are any of the contaminants listed earlier present in the drinking water?

Industrial Contaminants (continued)

> **Checklist (continued):**
>
> - If no, stop here
>
> - If yes, examine possible methods either for
>
>   i) Prevention of their entry into the drinking water
>   ii) Removal from the drinking water
>
> • Obtain approval from the state and EPA for any of the above experimentations. Keep them apprised of the results. Do not go any further without their approval

GLOSSARY

Anthropogenic. . . . . Involving the impact of man on nature.

By-Product . . . . Something produced in addition to the principal product in a chemical reaction.

Carcinogens. . . . . Chemicals suspected of causing cancer.

Coliform . . . . Bacteria found in the human colon.

Community Water Systems . . . Systems that provide treated drinking water to one or more communities.

Dioxin . . . . A toxic chemical found on occasion in very small quantities in the air or water environment.

Disinfectant. . . . . As used in this chapter, it is a chemical that will eliminate infectious bacteria or viruses from a drinking water supply.

Distribution System . . . . The system of pipes by which drinking water is conveyed from the treatment plant to the home.

Enteric . . . . Of, or relating to, the intestines.

Etiology. . . . . The science of causation or demonstration of the cause.

Filtration . . . . The process of passing a liquid through a porous solid material.

Hydrology . . . . The science of the properties, distribution, and circulation of water.

Hygienic . . . .   Condition or practices conducive to health.

mg/l . . . .   Milligrams per liter.

Miasma . . . .   A vaporous exhalation (as from a marsh or putrescent material) formerly believed to contain a substance causing disease (such as malaria).

Noncommunity Water Systems   Systems providing drinking water to one or more specific locations, rather than one or more communities.

Pathogens . . . .   A specific cause of disease, such as a bacterium or virus.

Radionuclides . . . .   Chemicals that are radioactive and are derived from the nucleus of a conventional chemical.

Sanitary Engineering. . . . .   A branch of civil engineering dealing with the maintenance of environmental conditions conducive to public health.

Sole-Source Aquifer . . . .   A layer of underground water that is the only possible source of future underground drinking water for a community or region.

Synthetic Organic . . . .   Organic chemicals (those based on a carbon
 Compounds   skeleton) that are man-made.

Turbidity . . . .   The state of being cloudy or muddy in physical appearance.

Volatile Organic Compounds . .   Organic chemicals that can become gases at the normal temperatures and pressures.

Watershed . . . .   A region in which the water drains to a specific water body.

Wellhead . . . .   The top of a well used for drinking water purposes.

> . . . .   Mathematical symbol for "greater than".

< . . . .   Mathematical symbol for "smaller than".

REFERENCES AND SELECTED READINGS

Bregman, Jack and Lenormand, Sergei, 1966, "The Pollution Paradox," Spartan Books, Washington, D.C.

Environmental Compliance Alert, June 30, 1994, Washington, D.C.

Environmental Compliance Alert, August 11, 1994, Washington, D.C.

Environmental Compliance Alert, August 25, 1994, Washington, D.C.

Environmental Compliance Alert, September 22, 1994, Washington, D.C.

Environmental Compliance Alert, October 13, 1994, Washington, D.C.

Mackenthun, K.M. and Bregman, J.I., 1992, "Environmental Regulations Handbook," CRC Press, Boca Raton, FL.

Metcalf and Eddy, 1990, "What You Need to Know About the Safe Drinking Water Act," Wakefield, MA.

Ryan, D., December, 1987, "Water Treatment to Combat Illness," EPA Journal, Washington, D.C.

The Environmental Manager's Compliance Advisor, July, 1994, Issue No. 378, Business Legal Reports, Inc., Washington, D.C.

U.S. Army Corps of Engineers Construction Engineering Research Laboratories, September, 1993 "Environmental Compliance Assessment Army Reserve (ECAAR)," USACERL Special Report EC-93/07, Champaign, IL.

U.S. EPA, February, 1977, "National Safe Drinking Water Strategy: One Step at a Time," Washington, D.C.

U.S. EPA, February, 1986, "Drinking Water at the Tap," Washington, D.C.

U.S. EPA, September, 1988, "Drinking Water Protection – Five Year Implementation Strategy," Office of Water, Washington, D.C.

U.S. EPA, February, 1989, "Fact Sheet – Drinking Water," Washington, D.C.

U.S. EPA, June 19, 1989, "Surface Water Treatment Rule and Coliform Rule," Federal Register (54 FR 27522), Washington, D.C.

U.S. EPA, April, 1990, "Environmental Pollution Control Alternatives: Drinking Water Treatment for Small Communities," EPA/625/5-90/025, Center for Environmental Research Information, Cincinnati, OH.

U.S. EPA, June, 1990, "Seminar Publication – Risk Assessment, Management and Communication of Drinking Water Contamination," EPA/625/4-89/024, Washington, D.C.

U.S. EPA, January 10, 1995, Telephone Response from Safe Water Hotline, Washington, D.C.

6   Air

FEDERAL LAWS AND REGULATIONS

The Clean Air Act was first enacted as Public Law 159 in 1955. It has been amended and strengthened several times since then, with the most recent amendments being signed into law by President George Bush on November 15, 1990.

The purpose of the Clean Air Act is to protect and enhance the nation's air quality as well as to safeguard public health and welfare and the productive capacity of its people. The Act is divided into two basic groupings:

- Control of pollution from stationary sources.
- Control of pollution from mobile sources.

Standards

The Clean Air Act requires the promulgation of certain standards by the U.S. Environmental Protection Agency (U.S. EPA, 1990). Each state then is required to develop a State Implementation Plan (SIP) and related regulations. A discussion of the key regulations and standards follows.

The 1970 version of the Act required that EPA establish **primary and secondary air quality standards** for each of the six common air pollutants, or "criteria pollutants": carbon monoxide, lead, nitrogen dioxide, ozone, particulates, and sulfur dioxide. They are called criteria pollutants because comprehensive air quality criteria documents support and provide the rationale for regulation of those pollutants. Human health-related standards are designated as primary ambient air quality standards, and the welfare-related standards are designated as secondary ambient air quality standards. For each of the pollutants, EPA was (1) to set a maximum concentration level, (2) to specify an averaging time over which the concentration is to be measured, and (3) to identify how frequently the time-averaged concentration may be violated per year. For the ozone standard, for example, the concentration level is now 0.12 parts of ozone per million parts of air (or 0.12 ppm), daily maximum one-hour average, not to be exceeded at each air quality monitor (to be discussed later in this chapter) on the average of more than 1 day per year over a 3-year period.

The national ambient air quality standards are based upon medical and other scientific evidence of health and environmental effects for the six pollutants. Ozone and smog are formed when volatile organic compounds (VOCs) and oxides of nitrogen interact in the presence of sunlight. Ozone irritates the eyes, aggravates respiratory problems, and causes crop damage. Oxides of nitrogen affect the respiratory system and can cause bronchitis, pneumonia, and lung infections. Lead, which can come from battery manufacturing and nonferrous smelters, is a dangerous pollutant because it accumulates in body tissues, particularly in children, and can cause neurological impairment and behavioral disorders. Particulate matter (PM) is a general term for airborne particles, some of which are seen in the form of smoke or dust; some are too small to be seen. Particulates can irritate the respiratory system and may carry metals, sulfates, and nitrates. Sulfur oxides, and particularly sulfur dioxide, come primarily from the burning of coal and oil and various industrial processes. In the atmosphere, they react to form sulfuric acid, sulfates, and sulfides. They can affect the respiratory system, especially when the sulfuric acid settles on a fine particle that is inhaled. Carbon monoxide, which may come from automobile or industrial emissions, is deadly to humans in enclosed areas. Small amounts can cause faintness, vertigo, and other serious illnesses.

The primary standards are (1) uniform across the country, though the states may impose stricter standards if they wish, (2) set with an adequate margin of safety for those especially vulnerable to pollution, such as the elderly and children, and (3) set without regard to the costs or technical feasibility of attainment. A deadline of 1972 was initially set for achieving compliance with the primary air quality standards. It was later extended for ozone and carbon monoxide, first to 1975, then to 1982, and to 1987. These standards still have not been achieved in a number of large metropolitan areas.

The secondary standards are intended to prevent damage to soils, crops, vegetation, water, weather, visibility, and property. No deadlines have been set for attaining the secondary standards, but the Act calls for their attainment as expeditiously as practicable. Present primary and secondary standards for "criteria pollutants" are shown in Exhibit 6-1 that follows.

The Clean Air Act was overhauled substantially by passage of the Clean Air Act Amendments of 1990. In the remainder of this chapter, considerable emphasis will be placed on the requirements of the 1990 Amendments. For that reason a brief discussion of their highlights follows.

Subchapters I, III, IV, V, and VI of the 1990 Amendments relate to stationary sources (Mackenthun and Bregman, 1992). Subchapter I addresses nonattainment areas. In addition to the ozone nonattainment area listings discussed elsewhere in this chapter, EPA has designated all areas of the country as either in **attainment** or **nonattainment** for each of the other criteria pollutants. Nonattainment areas are those that are not in compliance with national

Exhibit 6-1   National Ambient Air Quality Standards (NAAQS)

Pollutant		Averaging time	Frequency parameter	Concentration mcg/m³	ppm
Sulfur dioxide (SO₂)	P	24 hour	Annual maximum[a]	365	0.14
	P	1 year	Arithmetic mean	80	0.03
	S	3 hour	Annual maximum[a]	1,300	0.50
Inhalable particulates	P,S	24 hour	Annual maximum[b]	150	—
(PM-10)	P,S	24 hour	Annual arithmetic mean	60	—
Carbon monoxide (CO)	P,S	1 hour	Annual maximum[a]	40,000	35.00
	P,S	8 hour	Annual maximum[a]	10,000	9.00
Ozone (O₃)	P,S	1 year	Annual maximum[a]	235	0.12
Nitrogen dioxide (NO₂)	P,S	1 year	Arithmetic mean	100	0.05
Lead	P,S	3 month	Arithmetic mean	1.5	—

Note: P, primary standard; S, secondary standard; mcg/m³, micrograms per cubic meter; ppm, parts per million.

[a] Not to be exceeded more than once per year.

[b] Not to be exceeded more than once per year averaged over 3 years.

From U.S. EPA, 1994

air quality standards for one or more of the criteria pollutants. For a proposed source that will emit a criteria pollutant in an area where the new standards are presently being exceeded for that pollutant, even more stringent precon-struction review requirements apply. This review is the primary responsibility of the state where the source is proposed to be constructed, with overview authority vested in EPA.

For the pollutant ozone, the new law establishes nonattainment area clas-sifications for metropolitan areas ranked according to the severity of the air pollution problem. These five classifications are: marginal, moderate, serious, severe, and extreme. EPA assigns each ozone nonattainment area one of these categories, thus triggering various requirements the area must comply with in order to meet the ozone standard. Local officials in those non-attainment areas are required to conduct an inventory of their ozone-causing emissions and institute a permit program. Moderate areas and above must achieve 15% volatile organic compounds reduction within six years of enactment. For serious and above, an average of 3% volatile organic compounds reduction per year is required until attainment. For the City of Los Angeles, for example, this translates to a 20-year ozone-reduction program to achieve attainment (U.S. EPA, 1990). The law established similar programs for areas that do not meet the federal health standards for the pollutants carbon monoxide and particulate matter. VOCs are the major source threshold in this case. Presented below are the various ozone nonattainment classifications based on the "design values" of the U.S. Army Environmental Hygiene Agency, 1993.

Exhibit 6-2   Ozone Class Assignments

Class	Design value (ppm)	Major source threshold (VOC, tpy)[a]	Attainment date
Marginal	0.121 – 0.138	100	1993
Moderate	0.138 – 0.160	100	1996
Serious	0.160 – 0.180	50	1999
Severe	0.180 – 0.280	25	2005–2007
Extreme	>0.280	10	2010

Note: The ozone NAAQS is 0.120 parts per million (ppm).

[a] **VOC**, Volatile Organic Compounds; **tpy**, tons per year.

From U.S. Army Environmental Hygiene Agency, 1993.

Air emission inventories are required for VOC and NO_x sources located in ozone nonattainment areas. Emission inventories must be updated and certified annually. Air emission inventories also are required for all major policies under Subchapter V of the Act.

Subchapter III addresses emissions of toxic pollutants. The Amendments list 189 hazardous air pollutants. EPA must list the source categories that emit one or more of the 189 pollutants, and then publish a schedule for regulation of the listed source categories. For all listed major point sources, EPA must promulgate maximum achievable control technology (MACT) standards. These MACTs are emission standards based on the best demonstrated control technology and practices in the regulated industry. For existing sources, they must be as stringent as the average control efficiency or the best controlled 12% of similar sources. For new sources, they must be as stringent as the best controlled similar source.

Subchapter IV is designed to reduce acid rain. It is intended to result in a permanent 10 million ton reduction in sulfur dioxide emissions per year from 1980 levels. The first phase will affect 100 power plants and will provide them with certain emission allowances. The second phase is estimated to affect about 2,000 utilities. In both phases, affected sources will be required to install systems that continuously monitor emissions in order to track progress and to assure compliance or to install approved alternatives. The law allows utilities to trade emission allowances within their system or to buy or sell allowances to and from other affected sources.

Subchapter V establishes a clean air permit program for toxics similar to the NPDES permit program in water. EPA must issue program regulations. Each state then must submit to EPA a state implementation plan (SIP), meeting these regulatory requirements. After achieving the state submittal, EPA accepts or rejects the program. EPA must levy sanctions against a state that does not submit or enforce a permit program.

All sources subject to the permit program must submit a complete permit application within 12 months. The state permitting authority must determine whether or not to approve an application within 18 months of the date it receives the application. Each permit issued to a facility will be for a fixed term of up to 5 years. The new law establishes a permit fee system whereby the state collects a fee from the permitted facility to cover reasonable direct and indirect costs of the permitting program.

Subchapter VI relates to stratospheric ozone and global climate protection. The law requires a complete phaseout of certain chemicals that affect the ozone layer. Leading up to a phaseout, there will be stringent interim reductions placed upon the specific chemicals. EPA had to list all regulated substances, along with their ozone-depletion potential, atmospheric lifetimes, and global warming potential.

Enforcement, research, and other clean air-associated issues are addressed in other subchapters of the 1990 Amendments.

The 1990 Amendments also established tighter pollution standards for emissions from automobiles and trucks. These standards will reduce tailpipe emissions of hydrocarbons, carbon monoxide, and nitrogen oxides on a phased-in basis (Mackenthun and Bregman, 1992). Automobile manufacturers are required to reduce vehicle emissions resulting from the evaporation of gasoline during refueling. EPA has recently (1994) issued a requirement for canisters on automobiles to do this.

Fuel quality also will be controlled. Scheduled reductions in gasoline volatility and sulfur content of diesel fuel, for example, will be required. New programs requiring cleaner gasoline will be initiated for the nine cities with the worst ozone problems. Other cities can "opt in" to the reformulated gasoline program. Higher levels of alcohol-based oxygenated fuels are being produced and sold during the winter months in 41 areas that exceed the Federal standard for carbon monoxide.

The new law also establishes a clean-fuel-car pilot program in California, requiring the phase-in of tighter emission limits for 150,000 vehicles in model year 1996 and 300,000 by model year 1999. These standards can be met with any combination of vehicle technology and cleaner fuels. The standards become stricter in 2110. Other states can "opt in" to this program, but only through incentives and not through sales or production mandates.

Twenty-six of the dirtiest areas in the country will have to adopt programs limiting emissions from centrally fueled fleets of 10 or more vehicles beginning as early as 1998 (U.S. EPA, 1990).

Under Title II of the Act, §202(a)910, EPA has the authority to establish emission standards for vehicles such as automobiles, trucks, buses, and motorcycles. EPA also has the power to set standards for nonroad engines and vehicles if the Agency believes that the emissions from these units contribute significantly to CO or ozone levels in two or more nonattainment areas. EPA has already set emissions standards for new lawnmower and power boat engines. EPA also may regulate emissions from locomotives.

Although the Act creates only two types of vehicle classes, "light-duty" and "heavy-duty," EPA has subdivided these classes into four distinct sub-categories. These four classes are: (1) light duty vehicles (passenger car capable of seating 12 or fewer people), (2) light duty trucks between 6,000 lbs and 8,500 lbs gross vehicle weight rating (GVWR), (3) light duty trucks under 6,000 lb GVWR, and (4) heavy duty vehicles over 8,500 GVWR. Motorcycle emissions generally are given special consideration under vehicle emission regulations and sometimes even fall under heavy-duty vehicle guidelines. Vehicles that carry over 12 passengers would be one form of light duty trucks. Under §219, urban buses produced after 1993 must have 50% less PM than heavy-duty 1994 diesel engines.

While EPA may set vehicle emission standards for any pollutants endangering public health, it **must** set standards for carbon monoxide (CO), hydrocarbons, and nitrogen oxides (NO_x). EPA also sets standards for heavy-duty vehicles (defined in §202(b)(3) as vehicles having a gross weight of over 6000 lbs) and light duty vehicle particulate matter. The Act itself sets many relevant emissions standards, allowing the Agency little discretion. For example, model year 1988 and later heavy-duty vehicles cannot exceed 4.0 grams of NO_x emissions per brake horsepower hour. Additionally, per §202(g), by 1994, 40% of all light duty vehicles and light duty trucks had to meet very stringent standards that the Act sets for non-methane hydrocarbons, CO, and NO_x, emissions. By 1996, all of these vehicles must meet those standards.

Title II creates specific enforcement mechanisms for EPA. §206(a) gives EPA the power to certify most new motor vehicles or motor vehicle engines. There are limited exceptions for vehicles with projected model year sales of no more than 300 and a use of no more than 160 hours or 5,000 miles — §206(a)(1). Light duty vehicles obtain certification by test-driving a prototype, representing a specific "engine family," under prescribed conditions for 50,000 miles. Every 5,000 miles the prototype is tested to establish the emission factor for that family. Once the prototype and differently configured prototypes have been approved and the certificate granted, the manufacturer cannot alter production models in any material fashion, regardless of whether the change actually affects the vehicle's emissions. Heavy duty vehicles and motorcycles may obtain certificates even if they do not conform to the set standard if the manufacturer pays a nonconformance penalty designed to negate any competitive advantage the maker would otherwise obtain.

§206(b) creates the power for EPA to test vehicles coming off the assembly line and to inspect relevant records to ensure that these vehicles meet certification requirements. In practice, EPA will approve a class of vehicles unless the Agency, through these tests, expects that the failure rate for the whole class would be greater than 40%. §207(c) allows EPA to force the manufacturer to remedy model classes that, as a group, fail to meet regulatory standards. There are no specific guidelines for just how many vehicles within a group must fail the standards to require a recall.

§207(a) and (b) force manufacturers to provide warranties that cars produced since February, 1970 will no have defects which cause the vehicles to fail regulatory standards. These warranties cover all parts of a vehicle that affect its emissions for the first 24 months or 24,000 miles. After this initial period, these warranties only cover problems arising from the failure of components which were installed for the primary purpose of controlling emissions. Additionally, a variety of replacement parts may be certified by EPA so that their use will not void the original manufacturer's warranties.

§211 sets up the authority for EPA to regulate fuels and fuel additives. Prior to marketing fuels or additives, the manufacturer must register the product with EPA. EPA may require testing of these items for their effects on public health and may prohibit sale of items deemed to be overly dangerous or found to excessively interfere with existing emissions control systems. Unless they are very similar to the gasoline used in certifying 1975 or later vehicles, fuels and additives created since 1977 must obtain a waiver prior to being marketed. This waiver indicates that the fuel or additive is compatible with existing emission control systems. This section also provides for injunctive relief and substantial civil penalties.

In specified nonattainment areas, EPA may require the use of reformulated gasoline. §211(k) sets out the requirements for reformulated gasoline regarding heavy metal and oxygen contents, as well as other factors such as performance standards vs. regular gasoline and the creation of a credit program for reformulated gasoline that exceeds the regulatory guidelines.

Sections §241–250 of the Act set up the Clean Fuel Program. Under this program vehicles using "clean alternative fuels," including methanol, ethanol, reformulated gasoline, and natural gas, must meet more stringent emissions standards than those set out in §202.

California is the site of the pilot test program to demonstrate the effectiveness of clean-fuel vehicles (CFVs) in controlling air pollution in ozone nonattainment areas. This program applies only to light duty vehicles and, except where other states "opt-in," applies only in California.

EPA issued a final rule for NO_x (nitrogen oxides, whatever the ratio of oxygen to nitrogen may be) in the Spring of 1994 that was in response to the 1990 Clean Air Act Amendments (U.S. EPA, 1994). The rule is intended to reduce annual emissions of nitrogen oxide by 1.8 million tons annually by 2000. The rule affects 700 dry bottom, wall-fired or tangentially fired coal-burning electric utilities and will require reductions from 170 of those units beginning in 1995. The others have until 2000 to come into compliance with NO_x reductions. The rule allows utilities to join averaging pools in which an overall emissions limit average must be met and leaves it to them to choose which technology to reduce NO_x emissions. Utilities that cannot meet these stringent emissions limits by using approved technologies can apply for a less restrictive emission standard.

Part C of Subchapter I of the Act, **Prevention of Significant Deterioration (PSD)** of air quality, applies in all areas that are attaining the national ambient air quality standards, where a new source or a major modification of an existing source is proposed to be constructed. Its purpose is to prevent air quality in relatively clean areas from becoming significantly dirtier. A clean air area is one where the air quality is attaining the ambient primary and secondary standard. The designation is pollutant specific, so that an area can be in nonattainment for one pollutant, but in attainment for another. There are three classifications of geographical areas for proposed emitters of sulfur dioxide and particulate matter:

- Only minor air quality degradation allowed – Class I.
- Moderate degradation allowed – Class II.
- Substantial degradation allowed – Class III.

In no case does PSD allow air quality to deteriorate below secondary air quality standards. The baseline is the existing air quality for the area. Increments are the maximum amount of deterioration that can occur in an attainment area below baseline. Increments in Class I areas are smaller than for Class II, and Class II increments are smaller than for Class III areas.

For purposes of PSD, a major emitting source is one of 26 categories designated by EPA that emits or has the potential to emit 100 tpy of the designated air pollutant. A source that is not within the 26 designated categories is a major source if it emits more than 250 tpy.

Any proposed major new source or major modification is subject to preconstruction review by EPA, by a state to whom the program is delegated, or by a state that has adopted PSD requirements in its SIP, so that a permit for increases will not be exceeded. The permit describes the level of control to be applied and what portion of the increment may be made available to that source by the state. Where EPA has delegated such review, EPA and the state have concurrent enforcement authority (U.S. EPA, 1989). The Prevention of Significant Deterioration (PSD) program and regulations are designed to ensure that new or modified air pollution sources constructed in clean air areas will not cause ambient air concentrations to rise over the National Ambient Air Quality Standards (NAAQS). The regulations require that a potential source demonstrate that the processes and controls that will be employed will achieve the desired ambient air concentrations. PSD is oriented toward ambient air quality impacts.

REGULATORY PROGRAMS

The Clean Air Act establishes two major regulatory programs for stationary sources. In the first, the **New Source Performance Standards (NSPS)** program establishes stringent emissions limitations for new or substantially modified stationary sources of air pollution in designated industrial categories, regardless of the state in which the source is located or the air quality associated with the area. These new stationary source standards directly limit emissions of air pollutants (or in the case of the pollutant ozone, its "precursors," i.e., chemicals that react to form ozone). The standards apply to categories of sources. For example, EPA has set emission limits for new petroleum refineries.

The owner or operator of a new or modified source must demonstrate compliance with an applicable new source performance standard within 180 days of initial startup of the facility, and at other times as required by EPA. EPA has primary authority for enforcement of NSPS unless authority is delegated to the states. In such cases, EPA and the states have concurrent enforcement authority.

The second program, the **National Emissions Standards for Hazardous Air Pollutants (NESHAP)**, regulates emissions of "toxic" pollutants for which no NAAQS is applicable, but which cause increases in mortality or serious illnesses. Section 112 of the Clean Air Act lists hazardous air pollutants (e.g., chlorine, toluene, methanol) as those for which no air quality standards are applicable, but that are judged to increase mortality or serious irreversible or incapacitating illness. NESHAPs are based on health effects, with strong reliance on technological capabilities. These standards apply to both existing and new stationary sources. The NESHAP program is a Federal permit program, that can be delegated to the states, and is designed to control emission of particular hazardous materials without regard to NAAQS.

Under NESHAP, no person may construct any new source unless EPA determines that the source will not cause violations of the standard. For existing sources, a standard may be waived for up to two years if there is a finding that time is necessary for the installation of controls and that steps will be taken to prevent the endangerment of human health in the interim (U.S. EPA, 1989). NESHAPs, or national emission standards for hazardous air pollutants, at the time of the writing of this book, control arsenic, asbestos, benzene, beryllium, coke oven emissions, mercury, radionuclides, and vinyl chloride. They were developed for particular source categories and regulate more than 25 source emissions categories. §112(d) directs EPA to establish emission standards for all listed source categories by the year 2000.

On March 1, 1994, EPA issued the **Hazardous Organic National Emissions Standards for Hazardous Air Pollutants**, also known as the HON rule (U.S. EPA, 1994). This rule limits emissions of 112 air toxics. An "emission averaging" provision allows plants to average emissions from up to 25 emission points in meeting HON limits, as long as total emissions are reduced by an additional 10%. EPA estimates that 370 existing facilities are affected by the rule, which they have 3 years to meet. New facilities must meet the rule's standards immediately. This rule applies to sources that emit more than 10 tons per year (tpy) of any single hazardous air pollutant (HAP) or more than 25 tpy of any combination of HAPs, gaseous or particulate.

If a stationary source has the potential to emit 10 tpy of any HAP or 25 tpy of any combination of HAPs after using emission controls, it is considered to be a major source. Any stationary source of HAPs that is not major is considered to be an area source. Thus, **all** stationary sources of HAPs are regulated under the Act, regardless of the actual amount of emissions. In actuality, however, many sources of HAPs are not covered by specific NES-HAPs and thus have no regulatory requirements with which to comply.

In late 1993, (U.S. EPA, 1994), EPA promulgated regulations that required the phaseout of production and subsequent use of chlorofluorocarbons (CFCs), as well as other ozone layer depleting chemicals. Affected activities include servicing, maintaining, or disposing of household or vehicle refrigerants. As of August 12, 1993, any persons servicing air conditioning or refrigeration equipment or appliances had to certify that they have acquired approved refrigerant recovery or recycling equipment.

If EPA fails to promulgate a NESHAP within 18 months of its schedule, §112(j) requires the owner or operator of any major source to submit a permit application. 40 CFR §63 Subpart B describes this permit application process.

A second federal statute which has impacts on stationary air emission sources is the Superfund Amendment and Reauthorization Act (SARA) (Mackenthun and Bregman, 1992). Under the Toxic Chemical Release Reporting provisions of SARA Title III, certain facilities (with SIC codes 20-39) that manufacture, process, or otherwise use a SARA listed chemical are required to report annually their release of such chemicals to the Environmental Protection Agency and the state where the facility is located.

STATE LAWS AND REGULATIONS

State air quality laws and regulations are promulgated and enforced by individual state agencies, which usually are a part of a comprehensive overall department, such as a State Department of Environmental Protection. On occasion, the agency may be a separate air quality board known by that name or a similar one. In addition, a number of large counties (e.g., in California), regional authorities and local communities have air quality requirements as well. It therefore becomes the responsibility of the environmental compliance officer to ascertain which state, county, regional, or local agencies exercise control over the area that he/she is examining. Then the environmental compliance officer must obtain copies of their air quality laws and regulations so that he/she has a complete set of the requirements that must be met.

The situation generally is not as complicated as the above paragraph might lead one to believe. Most of the state, regional, county and local laws are derived directly from U.S. EPA requirements. Others are peculiar to the individual states or are a local requirement. The environmental compliance officer should check with the appropriate state officials for air quality requirements for his/her facilities in that state.

A review of state requirements that are derived from the federal laws and regulations described earlier in this chapter follows.

Each state is required to adopt a plan, called a State Implementation Plan (SIP), that limits emissions from air pollution sources to the degree necessary to achieve and maintain the NAAQS (Bregman and Mackenthun, 1992). The Clean Air Act provides that no SIP may be adopted without a public hearing, and sources affected by the SIP are entitled to participate.

State Implementation Plans (SIPs) contain plans, policies, regulations, and schedules of the state for controlling air pollution. They result from a formal requirement for a state to determine if national air quality standards are being attained. States must develop and enforce SIPs that detail measures to be undertaken to achieve compliance with national air quality standards for any nonattainment areas. EPA approves these plans. If a state plan is not acceptable, EPA is required to provide a federal implementation plan that EPA itself must then enforce. When a state has not shown that it can achieve air quality standards by an acceptable date, EPA must disapprove the SIP and propose bans on construction in the area or take other measures. A SIP is federally and state enforceable.

EPA has designated all areas of the country as either in *attainment* or *nonattainment* for each of the criteria pollutants. SIPs must assure attainment of NAAQS by prescribed dates. SIPs must meet federal requirements, but each state may choose its own mix of emission controls for sources to meet the NAAQS. Controls may include: stationary and mobile source emission limits; transportation plans; preconstruction review of new sources; nonattainment areas (NAAs); prevention of significant deterioration (PSD) permits for construction of new sources; monitoring; and inspection and testing of vehicles. Other measures may include emission charges, closing and relocation of plants, changes in operations, and methods of reducing vehicular traffic, including taxes, staggered work hours, and mass transportation.

New construction of major sources or major modifications in an NAA is prohibited unless the SIP provides for all of the following:

- The new source will meet an emission limitation for the nonattainment pollutant that reflects the lowest achievable emission rate.
- All other sources within the state owned by the subject company are in compliance.
- The proposed emissions of the nonattainment pollutant are more than offset by enforceable reductions of emissions from existing sources in the nonattainment areas.
- The emissions offsets will provide a positive net air quality benefit in the affected areas.

Nonattainment and attainment areas vary widely. They may be within a state's boundaries or they may be interstate in nature. They may be small geographically or they may be large. Exhibit 6-3 (BREGMAN & COMPANY, 1992) is an example of a nonattainment area in Summit County, Ohio for total suspended particulates. The map shows nonattainment for both the primary and secondary standards.

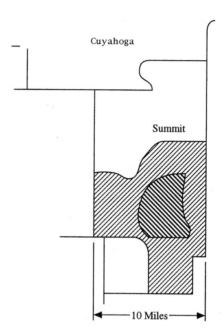

EXHIBIT 6-3. A Sample Map of Summit County, Ohio, Nonattainment Area for TSP. About half of Summit County is in nonattainment for TSP, total suspended particulates. The diagonal hatching represents the nonattainment area based on the secondary standard, and the cross-hatching is that based on the primary standard.

Requirements that a state may impose in connection with ozone-causing emissions or acid rain were described earlier in this chapter in the section on federal laws and regulations. Those requirements must be approved by the U.S. EPA.

A very important source of pollutants that is regulated by the states is known as Volatile Organic Compounds (VOC). VOCs may come from such sources as the storage and transfer of certain petroleum fuels and chemicals (solvents), the operation of incinerators, solvent use, degreasing/metal cleaning, sterilizing, and other processes (paint stripping and metal finishing) that use solvents.

Their importance as sources of pollution varies from state to state. Thus, California has individual Air Quality Management Districts that have stringent VOC emission requirements, because of the role of VOCs in photochemical oxidant (ozone) problems. On the other hand, North Dakota has very little in the way of ozone problems and, therefore, has fewer and less stringent VOC limitations. The limitations for VOCs usually are expressed in pounds of VOC/unit volume of substance used.

State agencies play a very important role with regard to emissions from vehicles in two respects:

(1) Emission testing stations.
(2) Limitations on vehicles in nonattainment areas, in addition to emission testing.

In the first case, many states have set up programs for emission testing of vehicles on an annual or biannual basis. Emissions from tailpipes must meet state standards, or costly adjustments and retesting may be required. States have considerable leeway in terms of how they must comply with EPA limitations on vehicles in nonattainment areas. These limitations on vehicle use tend to predominate, with controls imposed such as:

- High Occupancy Vehicle (HOV) lanes.
- Restrictions on parking spaces and increased rates for parking.
- Subsidies and pressures for car pooling.
- In extreme cases, even designation of days on which some cars may/may not enter the metropolitan area.

Many states and air quality regions have required that industrial firms with more than a designated number of employees must develop and enforce plans that will substantially reduce the number of vehicles driven to work by their employees. In particularly severe cases, land use restrictions have been applied that require new sources of vehicular traffic to locate outside of already congested areas. Mass transit systems also are being created and expanded so as to reduce the number of vehicles on highways.

Fugitive dust emissions are a temporary but annoying source of air pollution. They generally are caused by construction activities. Suppression measures that may be included in the permit granted for construction by the local authorities include restrictions on types of equipment, wetting of roads, etc.

Finally, the clean air permit program, which was described earlier in this chapter, places a heavy burden upon the states to submit proposed permit programs to EPA that meet EPA's regulatory requirements. Once the program is approved by EPA, the state government has the authority and the obligation to enforce this new permit program in a manner similar to that by which it enforces the NPDES permit program for water quality.

MONITORING AIR QUALITY

Air quality is monitored for a number of reasons such as:

- To determine whether a specific region is in compliance with standards.

- To determine the amount of pollutants coming from specific sources.
- To observe variations in time of emissions.
- To develop inventories and concentrations of pollutants coming from specific sources and regions.
- To monitor effectiveness of "emissions trading."

In the most important air monitoring in this country, each of the nation's 242 air quality control regions places one or more air quality monitoring instruments at various sites. The monitors record hourly concentration-level readings. EPA then uses the data to define each region as an attainment (clean) or nonattainment (polluted) area for each pollutant.

To determine whether an area is complying with the ozone standard, for example, EPA counts the number of "exceedances." An exceedance occurs when the ozone level is above the standard level (0.12 ppm) for 1 hour or longer at one or more monitors during a 24-hour day. The standard allows three exceedances at each monitor on separate days over any 3-year period. As soon as any single monitor registers four exceedances, the area is classified as being a nonattainment area (U.S. EPA, 1990).

State and local agencies are required to develop, set up, maintain, and operate a State and Local Air Monitoring Stations (SLAMS) network to provide year-round measurements of the six NAAQS pollutants. A subset of these monitors, specifically designated as National Ambient Monitoring Stations (NAMS), is used by EPA for national trend analyses. The NAMS and SLAMS monitoring must adhere to very specific network design, probe, siting, monitoring method and equipment, and quality assurance requirements stated in EPA regulations. In 1988, there were 3967 SLAMS monitors and 957 NAMS monitors nationwide. The resulting data are used by EPA and the states to determine the attainment status of specific geographic areas, to evaluate air quality trends, and as the basis for the development of air pollution control strategies and regulations to reduce or maintain ambient air quality concentrations of specific constituents. (Bregman and Mackenthun, 1992).

Stationary sources of pollution have been monitored for many years. This type of monitoring, called "static testing," may involve one or more pollutants, measured either sequentially or simultaneously the entire time that the static source is in operation. The results are plotted on a continuous recording system that shows pollutant concentrations as a function of time. For specific stationary source sampling, the analytic procedures are included in quality assurance project plans, which often are called *stack test protocols* in this program. These project plans must be approved ahead of time and must be followed during the testing. In addition, EPA and state personnel are able to arrange for performance evaluation audit samples to improve confidence in the analytical results.

Frequently, gas chromatography/mass spectrometry or high performance liquid chromatography techniques are used for this purpose. However, as time goes by, the techniques for this type of testing of stack emissions have become more and more sophisticated. For example, EPA has recently revised a draft protocol for fourier transform infrared (FTIR) spectrometry as a continuous emissions monitor. This particular technique has the capability of measuring dozens of wastestreams simultaneously.

Perhaps the least sophisticated technique of air monitoring is that which is used for particulates in many cases. Here, the relative opacity of the air is measured by comparison with cards that range from black to pure white. The answer is given as "percent opacity." Interestingly enough, this approach is still frequently used for particulate matter. It is especially important in startup, maintenance and cleaning of systems that generate particulate matter. Generally, higher levels of visible emissions (opacity) are normally permitted during certain startup and maintenance operations for short periods of time (5 min/h).

An example of monitoring requirements is presented in Exhibit 6-4.

EMISSIONS TRADING

In the late 1970s EPA developed a procedure that was designed to assist industry in meeting its obligations concerning new sources of pollution in nonattainment zones. This concept, called "emission trading," was later recognized in the 1990 Amendments to the Clean Air Act as an effective method of preventing additional pollution in nonattainment zones and, instead, allowing for industrial development, while reducing pollution by use of emission banking or trading techniques for the pollutant or pollutants for which the area has been designated in nonattainment. Emissions offsets from existing sources may need to be obtained, especially if the new source will have emissions that would exceed the allowance for the NonAttainment Area (NAA). In this situation, the source would need to obtain enforceable agreements from other sources in the NAA or from its own plants in the NAA.

For new sources or modification of existing sources, the Clean Air Act requires a preconstruction review. One of EPA's requirements for this review is that, in nonattainment areas, pollution from existing stationary sources be reduced enough to more than compensate for the additional pollution expected from the new source. At present, EPA requires an offset of roughly 120%. This means that a company wanting to build a new emissions source has to purchase "emission offsets," that is, pay for emission reductions in someone else's plant if it cannot offset the increase at one of its own plants. In another variation of this approach, EPA has devised an emissions trading policy, called the "bubble policy." One example of its application relates to plants that want to modify their facilities. A plant can modify its facilities (and avoid a new source review) by showing that total emissions under an imaginary bubble covering itself or a group of plants will not exceed a predetermined amount despite the modification. A plant may be able to achieve this by altering the emission controls on existing parts of its operations. The bubble policy may also apply to existing plants faced with meeting new emissions reduction

Exhibit 6-4   Monitoring Requirements for Steam Generators and
Incinerators[a] Standards of Performance, 40 CFR Part 60

Source category	Fuel type	Pollutant	Emission level	Monitoring requirement
Subpart D				
Steam generators[b] (>250 MBtu/h) constructed or modified after 8/17/71	Solid fossil fuel	Particulate	0.10 lb/MBtu	None
		Opacity	20%; 27% 6 min/h	Continuous
		SO_2	1.2 lb/MBtu	Continuous
		NO_x (except lignite and coal refuse)	0.70 lb/MBtu	Continuous
	Liquid fossil fuel	SO_2	0.80 lb/MBtu	Continuous
		NO_x	0.30 lb/MBtu	Continuous
	Gaseous fossil fuel	NO_x	0.20 lb/MBtu	Continuous
	Lignite	NO_x	0.60 lb/MBtu	Continuous
	Lignite mined in ND, SD, or MT, burned in a cyclone fired unit	NO_x	0.80 lb/MBtu	Continuous
Subpart E				
Incinerators (>50 tons/day) constructed or modified after 8/17/71	Incinerators	Particulate CO_2	0.08 gr/dscf[c] corrected to 12% CO_2	Record of daily charging rates and hours of operation

Note: SO_2, sulfur dioxide; NO_x, nitrogen oxides; CO_2, carbon dioxide.

[a] U.S. Army Corps of Engineers, 1993.

[b] Does not include electric utility steam generating units that started construction or modification after 18 September 1978.

[c] gr/dscf - grains per dry standard cubic foot.

requirements. Within the bubble, these plants may make adjustments so long as the new emissions goal is met (Bregman and Mackenthun, 1990).

The 1990 Amendments allow utilities to trade allowances with their systems and/or buy or sell allowances to and from other affected sources. Each source must have sufficient allowances to cover its annual emissions. If not, the source is subject to a $2,000/ton excess emissions fee and a requirement to offset the excess emissions in the following year (U.S. EPA, 1990).

As an example of this allowance, plants that emit SO_2 at a rate below 1.2 lbs/mmBtu will be able to increase emissions by 20% between a baseline year and 2000. Bonus allowances will be distributed to accommodate growth by units in states with a statewide average below 0.8 lbs/mmBtu. Plants experiencing increases in their utilization in the last five years also receive bonus allowances. 50,000 bonus allowances per year are allocated to plants in 10 midwestern states that make reductions in Phase I. This bonus arrangement gives a plant leverage in emissions trading.

Factors that are required by EPA in emissions trading or offsets include the following, which have been stated earlier under the discussion of the State SIPs:

- The proposed emissions of the nonattainment pollutant are more than offset by enforceable reductions of emissions from existing sources in the nonattainment areas.
- The emissions offsets will provide a positive net air quality benefit in the affected areas.

The applying source in an NAA, therefore, must obtain a greater than 1:1 reduction in pollutant emissions.

NEW CLEAN AIR ACT REGULATIONS

The volume of regulations mandated by the 1990 Clean Air Act Amendments is such that proposed and final regulations are being produced in substantial numbers. This large volume of regulations continues through the year 1996. It therefore becomes critical that environmental compliance officers of all organizations stay abreast of the regulations published in the *Federal Register* (FR).

Illustrative of this fact, the National Association of Manufacturers has distributed a listing of following regulations published in the *Federal Register* during the time frame of April 22 through August 5, 1994. These eight regulations form a small portion of the 30 to 50 such regulations that are being published on an annual basis. They are as follows:

1. National Ambient Air Quality Standards for Carbon Monoxide - Final Decision. 49 FR 38906, August 1, 1994. EPA announced that revisions in the NAAQS for CO are not appropriate at this time.
2. National Emission Standards for Hazardous Air Pollutants for Source Categories; Organic Hazardous Air Pollutants from the Synthetic Organic Chemical Manufacturing Industry and Other Processes Subject to the Negotiated Regulation for Equipment Leaks.

59 FR 19402, April 22, 1994. This final rule sets forth the MACT (maximum achievable control technology) standards for 112 of the 189 hazardous air pollutants listed in the tremendously expanded air toxics program under the 1990 Amendments. EPA must establish a national emission standard for each source category of hazardous air pollutant (NESHAP). The hazardous organic NESHAP is referred to as HON.

3. National Emission Standards for Hazardous Air Pollutants for Source Categories: Aerospace Manufacturing and Rework. Proposed rule, 59 FR 29261, June 6, 1994.

4. Hazardous Air Pollutants: Regulations Governing Equivalent Emission Limitations by Permit, Final Rule; 59 FR 26429, May 20, 1994. Effective date was June 20, 1994.

5. Acid Rain Program: Notice of Final Permits, 59 FR 37755, July 25, 1994. EPA is issuing, as a direct final action, 5-year Phase I Acid Rain Permits to 12 utility plants in accordance with the Acid Rain Program Regulations (40 CFR part 72).

6. Selection of Sequence of Mandatory Sanctions for Findings Made Pursuant to Section 179 of the Clean Air Act, 59 FR 39832, August 5, 1994, Final Rule. This regulation sets forth the sequence in which sanctions shall apply after EPA makes a finding of failure specific to any SIP required under the nonattainment area provisions.

ENVIRONMENTAL COMPLIANCE

Because of the complexity of compliance with air quality issues, this section on compliance will be considerably longer than other compliance sections of this handbook. To avoid an unnecessarily complicated compliance program, an organization's compliance officer should start the program by analyzing the applicability of each section of the Act to the organization's activities. Once it is clear which parts of the Act apply, the compliance officer should conduct a more detailed appraisal of those relevant parts. For ease of reference, this compliance discussion will be broken down along the lines of the subchapters of the Clean Air Act.

A specific source may be regulated under multiple subchapters of the Act. For example, a company manufacturing ozone depleting substances would be subject to Subchapter VI, "Stratospheric Ozone Protection." If that company emits 10 tons of chlorine per year, it also would be a major source under Subchapter I's NESHAPs provisions. If the company wants to build a new facility that will affect the air quality in a nearby air pollutant attainment area, it also will have to comply with the Prevention of Significant Deterioration Regulations.

A number of states have air pollution control requirements that are separate from, and in addition to, the federal requirements. The Environmental

Compliance Officer must address those requirements as well as the federal ones.

General Stationary Source Emission Limitations

New Source Performance Standards, New Source Review, standards for emissions of Hazardous Air Pollutants and programs particular to nonattainment areas are the major general programs with which a compliance officer must be concerned. These programs are outlined below – a compliance officer should review the checklist at the beginning of each subsection . If the checklist indicates that compliance with the relevant laws and regulations is an issue, the compliance officer should read the subsection, the appropriate earlier parts of this chapter and related documents such as the CFR.

New Source Review

Checklist :

Are you creating a new source?

No: No need for compliance efforts.

Yes: Will it significantly contribute to air quality deterioration?

No: Double-check with state /EPA. Document.

Yes: Follow permitting procedure in CFR/SIP. Obtain and designate emission offsets.

All new sources may require permitting. §110(a)(2)(C) of the Act requires that each SIP include a program governing the modification and construction of any stationary source. The compliance officer should consult with the state agency to determine whether the organization's proposed new construction or modifications are covered by this section.

Subpart I of 40 CFR §51 sets out the review process for any new sources and modifications that may significantly contribute to concentrations of any pollutants for which the area is designated as being in nonattainment. It also applies to major projects in attainment areas which will affect nearby nonattainment areas. This preconstruction program requires that the owner/operator provide enough information to allow the permitting authority to determine if the proposed project will result in a violation of the Act or interfere with attainment or maintenance of a local or nearby NAAQS. To obtain a permit, the owner/operator may have to provide emission offsets.

New Source Performance Standards

Checklist :

Are you building or going to build something that may emit pollutants?

No:	No compliance effort needed.
Yes:	Check definitions to see if it is a new source modification or reconstruction requiring compliance.
It is not:	Double-check with state/EPA. Document.
It is:	Is your future source specifically covered in 40 CFR Subpart 60?
Not covered exclusions:	Double-check with state/EPA. Document.
Covered by exclusion:	Does the relevant CFR section **exclude** your future source?
Yes:	Double-check with state/EPA. Document.
Not covered by exclusions:	Comply with listed requirements. Also comply with monitoring, performance testing, notification and record-keeping requirements of 40 CFR §§60.7,8,13.

Note: Determine the date construction commenced for relevant regulatory requirements.

§111 of the Act, implemented by 40 CFR §60, sets forth the standards of performance for new stationary sources (NSPS). A substantial modification of an existing source or the reconstruction of an existing facility may bring it under NSPS regulations.

If a facility is constructing a new source or modifying an existing source with a resultant increase in emissions, the environmental compliance officer should review the subparts of §60 to determine if the facility's actions fall under any NSPS regulations. "Construction," according to 40 CFR §60.02, means actual erection or installation while "commenced" means that the owner or operator has started a **continuous** construction/modification program or has entered into a contract to do so within a reasonable time. Thus, merely considering constructing a new source does not trigger NSPS standards, but signing a contract with a company to build or modify a source probably would. Under §60.05, the owner/operator of a facility may request that EPA make a determination of whether an action or a proposed action constitutes construction, reconstruction, or a modification under the NSPS regulations. EPA must respond to this request within 30 days. The actual date that construction commences may be very important, as only NSPS regulations in effect **at the time of commencement** will govern the resulting source.

If the facility's construction program is covered, the compliance officer should read the first section of any subpart of §60 which may regulate the facility. This section describes the subpart's applicability and may exclude the facility from following the regulations. If the subpart is applicable to the facility, the compliance officer should ensure that his/her facility will meet the emissions standards set by that subpart. Additionally, the compliance officer should ensure that any emission and fuel monitoring requirements of either the subpart or of §60.13 are implemented. The compliance officer should also ensure that the facility conducts any performance tests as required under §60.8. Further, the compliance officer must follow the notification and record keeping requirements as set forth in §60.7. Specific requirements include notification of commencing construction within 30 days of doing so, notification of anticipated date of initial startup between 30 and 60 days prior to that date, and notification of the actual date of startup within 15 days after that date.

Prevention of Significant Deterioration (PSD) of Air Quality

Checklist :

Are you building or planning to build a new source of emission?

No: No compliance program needed.
Yes: Does the proposed source meet the regulatory definition of a major new source or major modification?

No: Double-check with state/EPA. Document.
Yes: Does the proposed source fall within one of the many PSD exceptions?

Is under exceptions: Double-check with state/EPA. Document.

Is not under exceptions: Permit needed. Contact state/EPA air staff to determine relevant requirements.

Prevention of Significant Deterioration (PSD) of Air Quality

Checklist (continued):

Is alternative technology feasible?

    Yes: Consider it as an option.
    No: Determine relevant technology on a case-by-case basis.

Note: Construction must be started within 18 months of permitting, and delays/breaks in construction may invalidate the permit.

As stated earlier in this chapter, Part C of the Clean Air Act, implemented by 40 CFR 51.166, creates a program to prevent significant deterioration of air quality (PSD). The basic thrust of this Part is to preserve air quality in areas such as national parks, to keep economic growth from fouling clean air resources, and to keep emissions in one state from contributing to significant deterioration of air quality in another state.

An environmental compliance officer must be aware of the PSD program because it impacts new construction. Under §51.166(i)(1), no major stationary source or major modification thereof shall begin construction unless it meets SIP emission and NSPS limitations and standards. The compliance officer should search §51.166(b)(1)(i)'s definition of "major stationary source" to see whether his/her facility comes under the Act. If emissions potential will not be above 100 tpy of any pollutant regulated by the Act for certain types of sources, if the facility will not have the potential to emit more than 250 tpy of any pollutant regulated by the Act, or, if a physical change at a facility would not constitute a major source by itself, it is likely that PSD regulations will not apply.

A "major emitting facility", as defined in §169(1) of the Act, specifically **excludes** new or modified facilities which are nonprofit health or education institutions which have been exempted by the state. Another major PSD exception is set out by §112(b)(6) of the Act. This section states that PSD regulations shall not apply to the NESHAPS pollutants listed under §112. Finally, the applicant must meet the PSD requirements only for attainment pollutants that would be emitted in "major" and "significant" amounts. While the terms "major" and "significant" are not defined further, the obvious implication is that they refer to quantities of attainment pollutants that could substantially downgrade high quality air.

Once he/she has determined that PSD regulations require a permit prior to starting a construction project, the compliance officer should contact either EPA or the state's SIP implementation agency to determine specific permit requirements. At a minimum, permit applications must include an analysis of ambient air quality in any area affected by the source under §56.166(m). The applicant also may have to conduct a year or more of monitoring for NAAQS pollutants. The owner/operator of a major stationary source or major modification also may have to conduct post-construction monitoring to determine the actual effect that the source's emissions are having on an area's air quality.

Sources affected by the PSD regulations generally will be required to install the best available control technology (BACT) for each pollutant regulated under the Act if that technology would result in a significant reduction of emissions. The term BACT refers to commercially available technology that removes the maximum amount of that pollutant that can be achieved. Major modifications with no net emissions increase, phased construction projects, and sources which can demonstrate that alternative technology would be equally safe and effective may avoid having to install BACT.

If emissions from a proposed major emitting facility will impact a Class I area (parks and wilderness over 5,000 acres) §165(d) requires that EPA give notice of the permit application to the Federal Land Manager and the federal official responsible for managing any lands within that area. If these officials, EPA, or the governor of an adjacent state with an affected Class I area claim that the emissions may contribute to an adverse change in the area's air quality, the permit application must be denied unless the owner/operator proves otherwise.

Once it has received a PSD application, the permitting authority has a year to grant or deny a permit. After receiving a permit under 40 CFR §52.21, the applicant must commence construction within 18 months or the permit becomes invalid. Construction that is interrupted for 18 months or takes an unreasonably long time, may also result in an invalid permit.

Nonattainment Areas

Checklist :

Are you in a nonattainment area for any criteria pollutants?

No: No need for a compliance program.
Yes: Are you building or modifying a source?

No: No need for a compliance program (see note below).
Yes: Does your source meet this section's definition of new or modified major stationary sources?

No: Double-check with state/EPA. Document.
Yes: Permit required. Source will need to use Lowest Available Emissions Rate (LAER). Emissions offsets needed on a greater than 1:1 basis.

Nonattainment Areas (continued)

Checklist (continued):

Note: Additional special requirements are necessary for sources, **currently existing or proposed**, that are located in nonattainment areas for specific pollutants.

Permits are required to build anywhere in a nonattainment area. The permit must show that the source will comply with the lowest available emission rate (LAER), which must be, at a minimum, equal to New Source Performance Standards. The permit must demonstrate that any other major stationary sources owned or operated by the applicant are in compliance, or on schedule for compliance, with all Clean Air Act requirements. Further, there must be an analysis of alternative sites, production processes, sizes, and environmental control techniques for the source that demonstrates its benefits outweigh its costs.

Prior to commencing operations, the owner/operator must obtain emission reduction offsets. There are many requirements for reduction credits, including that they are permanent, quantifiable, and federally enforceable, and are located in areas with EPA-approved attainment plans. Shutting down sources or agreeing to modified production schedules that will decrease emissions are two examples where a facility may gain emission credits, plus it may be possible for a facility to buy offsets from another area.

The facility compliance officer need only be concerned with this part of the Act in special circumstances. If the facility is located in an attainment zone for all pollutants, then this part is not relevant, although PSD permitting, NESHAPS, Title V, New Source Performance Standards, and other permitting processes or emissions controls may apply. If the facility is located in a nonattainment zone for any pollutant, Part D applies. The compliance officer must then make sure that the permit is properly put together and submitted prior to commencement of construction. He/she must also ensure that the facility has enough acceptable offsets to allow for startup of the new facility.

The Act includes special provisions for areas in nonattainment for ozone, CO, particulate matter, sulfur oxides, NO_x, and lead. The facility compliance officer should determine if his/her facility is located in a nonattainment area for any of these pollutants and then review the relevant sections of the Act and its regulations. It would also be wise to contact EPA or the local state air agency to determine if there are any special requirements as a result of the facility's location in a nonattainment area.

National Emission Standards for Hazardous Air Pollutants (NESHAPS)

> **Checklist :**
>
> Do you emit any listed Hazardous Air Pollutants (HAPs)?
>
> No: No need for compliance program.
> Yes: Are you a source category? (Check 57 FR 31576, 16 July, 1993). Double-check with state/EPA.
>
> | | |
> |---|---|
> | Source Category: | Are you a major (10/25 tpy) source or area? |
> | Major Source: | Are you listed in 40 CFR §63 or §61? |
> | Listed Source: | Follow the specific regulations. |
> | Not a Listed Source: | Double-check with state/EPA. Document. |
>
> **Note:** If EPA is 18 months behind schedule in setting out a NESHAP for your source, you may need to apply for a permit via §63 Subpart B.
>
> | | |
> |---|---|
> | Area Source (<10/25 tpy): | Follow same process as for Major Source. |
>
> Do you have specific hazardous materials at or above the threshold levels per 40 CFR §68?
>
> Yes: Comply with regulations.
> No: Double-check with state/EPA. Document.

EPA has designated numerous source categories, although the compliance officer should frequently contact his/her State or EPA representative frequently to ensure he/she has the most up to date category modifications. The initial 124 source categories list was presented in 57 FR 31576, July 16, 1993. If a compliance officer's facility falls into one of these source categories, he/she will have to ensure compliance with any relevant NESHAPs (although EPA may not yet have set out a NESHAP covering the situation).

Major sources of HAPs are regulated by the major source NESHAPs. Area sources are regulated by the area source NESHAPs. Facilities having both major and area sources of HAPs are governed by both sets of standards.

EPA is far behind the NESHAPs setting schedule set out in 58 FR 63941, but they have promulgated numerous standards. 40 CFR §61 sets forth the national emission standards for a variety of hazardous air pollutants. 40 CFR §63 sets forth the national emission standards for hazardous air pollutants for source categories. §63 subsections describe emission requirements for specific categories of stationary sources that have the potential to emit one or more listed HAPs. A compliance officer should review these sections of the CFR to determine if there are any NESHAPs affecting his/her facility. If the facility's pollutants or activities are listed in the CFR, the relevant section will detail the required monitoring, reporting, and other requirements.

Because EPA has not promulgated regulations for NESHAPs for all source categories, it is possible to be a listed source but not to have any relevant NESHAPs with which to comply. While the compliance officer will not have to worry about regulatory compliance in this situation, he/she may wish to participate in EPA's early reduction program before a relevant NESHAP becomes law. Under this program, set forth in 40 CFR §63 subpart D, if a source owner reduces HAP emissions by 90% (particulate HAPs 95%), and keeps them at that level, the owner may avoid having to meet the formal NESHAP requirements for six years. The baseline year against which emissions reductions are measured must be 1987 or later, emission rates must be actual and verifiable and the emissions cannot be artificially or substantially greater than in previous years.

SUBPART II: MOBILE SOURCE REGULATION

Vehicle Emissions

Checklist :

Do you manufacture vehicles, lawnmowers, boat engines, etc?

No: Have your vehicles' emissions been tested in accordance with local law?

Yes: Determine the emission rates of vehicles as shown by the CFR. Ensure vehicles meet these standards.

Do you conduct vehicle emissions testing?

No: No need for a compliance program.

Yes: Conduct testing in accordance with 40 CFR §85 Subpart W.

To determine the regulatory standard applied to a vehicle, a compliance officer would search both §202 of the Act and 40 CFR §86 for the relevant guidelines. For example, a gasoline-fueled Ford Probe would be considered a light duty passenger car, as it typically carries 12 or fewer passengers. 40 CFR §86.094-8 sets emission standards for this year model's light-duty vehicles. Absent a variety of special conditions, which are listed in the CFR and in the Act, the typical 1994 Probe should not exceed 2.0 grams of hydrocarbons per test in fuel evaporative emissions.

Under the regulatory scheme, a vehicle should have an emissions test during its "useful life." Generally, §202(d) is used to set a useful life of 5 years or 50,000 miles, whichever comes first, for light duty vehicles and lighter duty trucks. Post-amendment requirements are 10 years and 100,000 miles, whichever comes first for these vehicles. For heavier light duty trucks, the useful life was 5 years and 50,000 miles, and is now 11 years and 120,000 miles at the time of the preparation of this handbook.

In practice, EPA has allowed short tests since 1980. Subpart W of 40 CFR 85 sets out the variety of short test methods state inspection stations must follow to certify a vehicle's emissions. Although most standards must be met by each individual vehicle, light duty diesel vehicle particulates and heavy duty vehicle NO_x and particulates emissions need only fall within a range determined by EPA to result in an average emission equal to the regulatory standard. Compliance testing is limited, at most, to 7 years or 75,000 miles, but the manufacturer is responsible for honoring relevant warranties for the entire useful life of the vehicle, as defined by the regulations, which does not necessarily reflect actual use.

Generally, states do not have the power to enact their own vehicle emission standards except for California. Under §177, other states may adopt standards that are identical to California's, as long as these regulations do not require the creation of a vehicle other than those authorized under federal or California regulations. Hence, the shorthand reference to the "California Car."

Enforcement

Checklist :

Do you make vehicles, engines, or parts?

No: No need for a compliance program.

Manufacture vehicles: Obtain certificate for vehicles by test driving prototype. Do not subsequently change production models in any material fashion.

Enforcement (continued)

> **Checklist (continued):**
>
> Manufacture parts: Obtain certification per EPA guidelines.

Fuels and Additives

> **Checklist :**
>
> Ensure that any fuel or additive you manufacture or sell is registered with EPA.

Clean Fuel Program

> **Checklist :**
>
> Are you in California or an opt-in state?
>
> No: No need for compliance program (except for fleet vehicle operators).
> Yes: Vehicle dealers must sell appropriate number of Clean Fuel Vehicles (CFVs). Fuel suppliers must make proper fuel available.
>
> Fleet vehicle owners: Are you located in an ozone or CO nonattainment area?
>
> No: Doublecheck with state/EPA. Document.
> Yes: Check to determine if excluded from definition. If not excluded, follow SIP guidance on purchasing appropriate number of CFVs. Consider buying extras for bonus credits.

Operators of "centrally fueled" fleets (the term does not include lease or rental fleets, law enforcement vehicles, sales lots, emergency vehicles, or nonroad vehicles such as those used in farm and construction work) of 10 or more vehicles in many, but not all, ozone and carbon monoxide nonattainment areas, must purchase increasing percentages of clean fuel light vehicles. By the year 2000, 70% of all new light duty trucks/vehicles and 50% of all heavy duty trucks purchased by these operators must be clean fuel vehicles. Federal fleets, other than those certified by the Secretary of Defense to need an exemption for reasons of national security, also must comply with the clean fuel program. By buying additional vehicles that meet more stringent standards, or by purchasing specially listed clean vehicles, fleet operators may obtain credits to sell or trade to other operators within the same nonattainment area. These credits may also be banked for later use by the same operator.

Subchapter IV: Acid Rain

Checklist :

Does your facility have a steam-electric generating unit?

   No: No need for a compliance program.
   Yes: Does this unit sell electricity?

   No: No need for a compliance program.
   Yes: Check definitions to see if your unit is excluded.

Excluded: Double-check with state/EPA. Document.
Not excluded: Comply with regulations.

Note: You may wish to opt into this program to use its allow-
             ance benefits.

A variety of small power plants do not have to comply with these federal regulations. The exceptions focus on plants with a capacity of less than 25 megawatts, which cogenerate steam and electricity and sell less than 25 megawatts of power to a utility, which sells at least 80% of its electricity at wholesale or has simple combustion turbines that have been in operation prior to the date of the Clean Air Act Amendments.

Power plants which emit sulphur dioxide and are not otherwise subject to this section of the Act may wish to opt into the program in order to take advantage of its allowance program. Naturally, once a facility has opted into the program, it must comply with all regulations concerning monitoring, reporting, inventorying, and so forth.

Permitting

Checklist :

Ensure that you have a permit that meets the requirements of §76.9 and §72 Subpart D.
Ensure you have a compliance plan per §76.9 and §72 Subpart D.

Both SO_2 and NO_x emission limitations and allowances must be a part of an affected unit's Title V operating permitting status. An affected unit also must obtain an Acid Rain Permit. These permits require the units to comply with a variety of monitoring requirements, and to keep copies of all reports, compliance certifications, emissions monitoring, and other relevant data as stated in 40 CFR §72.9.

Initial permit applications must be accompanied by a compliance plan. This plan will detail how the affected source will comply with its Subtitle IV requirements at all of its affected units. In many cases, set forth in §408(b) of the Act, a statement by the owner or operator, or the owner and operator's designated representative, that the source will meet all applicable emission limitations will suffice as a compliance plan. Units that have an alternative method of compliance under §404 of the Act must give more detailed descriptions of how they will comply. 40 CFR §76.9 explains the NO_x compliance plan and permitting programs, while §72 Subpart D explains the compliance plan program in general.

Sulphur Dioxide (SO_2) Allowances

Checklist :

Are you regulated by this section? Check Tables I–IV, 40 CFR §73.

No: No need for compliance program.
Yes: Determine your allowances per the tables.
Ensure you are not emitting more than your allowances.
Consider buying, selling, or banking allowances as appropriate per 73 CFR Subparts C, D, and E.
Consider applying for early reduction credits per §73.20.

For those compliance officers whose facilities do fall under this subchapter of the Act, the task is to ensure that no facility exceeds its allowances of emissions. Each allowance is equal to the ability to emit one ton of SO_2 per year. Facilities are issued a certain amount of allowances by EPA and may use these allowances, bank them for a future year, sell them or trade them. By the year 2000, EPA will be unable, with some exceptions, to allocate annual allowances that would result in total emissions from subject units of over 8.9 million tons of SO_2. Unused allowances may be carried over without penalties. Because §403(f) of the Act specifically states that allowances are **not** property rights, EPA may reduce allowances. Additionally, the Act does not affect the power of state utility regulators, who may wish to increase or decrease the amount of allowances transferred into or out of their respective states.

Starting in 1995, EPA assigned allowances to 110 specific large power plants which are listed in §404 (Table A) of the Act and in Table I of §73.10. These allowances are Phase I of the SO_2 reduction program and only apply to these listed units. Phase II of the program, scheduled to start after January 1, 2000, assigns allowances for all affected units based on a variety of formulas. §405 of the Act details which allowance formula applies to which type and size of plant. Table II of 40 CFR §73.10 details the allowances of Phase II affected units. Tables II and IV provide additional allowances for specific units. When determining allowances, EPA works from a "baseline" year's actual emissions. For units in operation prior to 1985, the baseline is the average of 1985–1987 fuel consumption if recorded on DOE Form 767. If they did not use that form, these units may have as a baseline the numbers in the 1985 National Acid Precipitation Assessment Program. Other units may figure out their baseline emissions using Appendix C to 40 CFR §72.

Affected units that are relatively clean may be allowed to increase emissions over their baseline years, and EPA may award limited bonus allowances for a variety of reasons. §73 Subpart B details the provisions for allowance allocations, to include early reduction credits and revision of actual allowances.

If post-2000 SO_2 emissions from these affected sources exceed 8.9 million tons, EPA may limit the basic Phase II allowances as needed to comply with the Act.

Nitrogen Oxide Allowances

Checklist :

Determine NO_x emission limitations per §76.5, §76.10.
Ensure emissions do not exceed limitations.
If emissions exceed limitations, consider applying for an extension in accordance with §76.12.

§407 of the Act, implemented by 40 CFR §76, sets out the legislative guidelines concerning EPA's NO_x emissions reduction program. Any unit that is subject to the Subchapters of the Act because of its SO_2 emissions also is subject to relevant NO_x emission limitations. §76.5 details the actual NO_x emission limitations for a variety of boilers. The emissions limitations depend on the type of boiler and its BTU heat input, which is unlike the set allowances in the SO_2 emissions program. Continuous emissions monitoring, as detailed in 40 CFR §75, is required of affected facilities. Facilities may be able to opt-in under §76.8 and may be eligible for alternative emissions limitations per

§76.10. §76.11 allows affected units, under the control of the same owner/operator, to average their emissions under certain circumstances. Monitoring, record keeping, and reporting procedures are outlined in §76.14

New Fossil-Fuel Fired Power Plants

> **Checklist :**
>
> Ensure you have proper allowances prior to emitting pollutants.

New fossil fuel fired power plants must obtain their emission allowances from non-EPA sources prior to emitting any SO_2. Once EPA has determined NO_x limitations, new plants will have to meet these, too.

Penalties

Affected units that exceed their SO_2 or NO_x emissions limitations or allowances are subject to a penalty of $2,000 per excess ton emitted. The Act states that this penalty does not diminish other potential liabilities, so enforcement under other sections of the Act could also occur. EPA also may require the offending source to offset its excess emissions over future years. If so, the offending source will submit a plan on how it will achieve these proposed offsets. If approved, this plan automatically becomes part of the operating permit.

Monitoring

> **Checklist :**
>
> Ensure monitoring system exists and meets §75's requirements.
> Consider alternative monitoring system if applicable.

Affected units must install continuous emission monitoring systems as specified in 40 CFR §75. These systems must measure the SO_2 and NO_x concentrations in parts per million and the emission rate of these gases in lb/mmBTU (NO_x) or lb/h (SO_2). If post-monitoring emissions data is not available as required, EPA requires the owner or operator of a unit to provide substitute data as detailed in 40 CFR §§75.30–34.

If a source can demonstrate that an alternative monitoring system would be as accurate as a continuous emission monitoring system, EPA may authorize use of the alternative. 40 CFR §§75.40–48 describe the criteria for these alternative monitoring systems.

Designated Representative

> **Checklist :**
>
> Ensure you have a properly designated representative for your acid rain program.

Generally, each affected source, which may include several affected units, may have only one designated representative for its acid rain program. The source must send EPA a certification of representation for this individual. 40 CFR §72.20(b) is detailed in explaining that this designated representative's actions will legally bind the source owner regardless of any agreement between the owner and the representative.

Subchapter V – Permits

> **Checklist :**
>
> Does your facility emit enough pollutants to come under Title V Regulations?
>
> No: Double-check with state/EPA. Document.
> Yes: Permit needed. Conduct inventory, submit permit signed by responsible official, pay fees based on actual emissions.
>
> **Note:** Some sources may be eligible for a general permit.

Title V's "self reporting" theme places the onus of compliance and reporting on the regulated community. While 40 CFR §70 sets out the federal requirements for a Title V permitting program, the programs themselves may be administered by the states. The compliance officer should locate the relevant permitting authority and ascertain the exact specifications of its permitting program.

Title V also requires the permit application and any associated compliance plans to be signed by a "responsible official." The enforcement provisions of the Act, §113, set stiff penalties for anyone who "knowingly" submits a false document to EPA.

Title V operating permits are required only for facilities that meet any of the following criteria:

1. Directly emits, or has the potential to emit, 100 tpy of any air pollutant.
2. Is a major source of criteria pollutants (this threshold lowers as the relevant nonattainment classification increases. See §70.2's definition of a major source, paragraph (3)).
3. Emits, or has the potential to emit, considering controls, 10 tpy or more per year of any hazardous air pollutant (HAP) or 25 tpy of any combination of hazardous air pollutants. EPA may lower these thresholds for certain HAPs based on the potency of the air pollutant, persistence, etc.
4. Is subject to a New Source Performance Standard (NSPS).
5. Is subject to NESHAP requirements.
6. Is subject to a preconstruction review program.
7. Is a solid waste incinerator subject to rules under Title III of the Act.

Further, the facility must be "within a contiguous area and under common control" to be considered a source requiring a Title V permit. Therefore, an organization with numerous unconnected facilities that total over 10 tpy emissions of a listed HAP would not have to apply for a Title V permit as long as no single facility met any of the above listed criteria.

§70.6(d) authorizes states to issue a general permit covering numerous similar sources. If a compliance officer is interested in this program, he/she should contact the relevant permitting authority to determine the status and requirements of its general permits. If it later turns out that the facility did not actually qualify for a general permit, EPA will consider the facility to have been operating without a Title V permit.

Conducting an Air Emissions Inventory

Checklist :

Is it at all possible that your facility's potential emissions could bring it under Title V's regulations?

No: Double-check with State/EPA. Document.
Yes: Conduct an inventory (check to make sure you do not take an inventory of any exempt sources of emissions). Inventory actual emissions as well, if possible.

To determine whether a particular facility emits any pollutants over the relevant threshold levels, a compliance officer should conduct an air emissions inventory. The heart of a Title V compliance program, this inventory should be a simple process for a small facility but will probably require outside assistance for more complex ones.

The inventory consists of determining the potential emissions of all non-exempt sources of air pollution on an installation. (Exempted emission sources are generally noted in the relevant permit program rules.) Since the facility will pay a fee based on its actual emissions, the inventory should determine them as well. Emission sources fall into three categories:

1. *Point Source:* Stationary units which emit air pollutants. Essentially, anything with a discharge stack is considered a point source (e.g., boilers, incinerators). Regardless of a point source's potential emissions, it should be included in the permit unless state or local requirements specifically exempt the source. Because state programs differ, the compliance officer should assess state-regulated sources individually to decide which of those sources must be a part of the permit application.
2. *Area Source:* Several emission sources are too small to be counted as point sources. These sources, while not emitting large amounts of pollutants individually, pose a threat of cumulative significant emissions. Depending on their surroundings, a variety of source categories could be considered area sources because of their frequency in that area. Examples of sources which should be included on an inventory include dry cleaners, gas stations, and pesticide applications. Such sources normally are addressed by statewide programs rather than the Title V permit.
3. *Fugitive sources:* A source which does not emanate from a distinct point such as a vent or stack. Examples of fugitive sources include construction areas (emitting dust), fuel storage and dispensing equipment, paint booths, and wastewater treatment plants. Some sources of fugitives do not count towards threshold determinations, but must be inventoried if a permit is otherwise required.

If the potential emissions, as indicated by the inventory, meet any of the thresholds discussed above, a Title V permit is required. If the thresholds are not met, there is no need for a Title V permit, although other operating permits may be required under the relevant State Implementation Plan.

Once an installation meets one emissions threshold for Title V, its permit application must describe all of its regulated air pollutant emissions, regardless of their potential or actual emissions. These pollutants include NO_x, VOCs, NAAQS pollutants, NSPS pollutants, ozone depleting substances and other substances that EPA has denoted as regulated air pollutants.

Application

Checklist :

Ensure that you actually need a Title V Operating Permit.
Apply in timely manner.
Follow standard application form.
Have permit signed by responsible corporate official.
Submit application to the state agency. Supply additional information as required.
Operate as described in your application to obtain a "permit shield."

Once a compliance officer has determined that an organization meets any threshold level for Title V, he/she should develop a permit application. In general, §70.5(a)(1) requires that this application be submitted to the state twelve months after the source becomes subject to the permit program. While application requirements may vary from state to state, each state should only accept applications under a standard form per §70.5(c). Besides the inventory of potential emissions, the application will have to contain an inventory of actual emissions, a compliance assessment of currently regulated air emissions, a declaration of *de minimus* sources, a compliance plan and schedule to bring non-complying sources into compliance, and a plan for monitoring and reporting its sources and emissions to prove future compliance.

The final application must be signed by a responsible official and sent to the permitting authority. The regulatory agency has 60 days to determine if the application is complete. If the agency finds the application incomplete, it will ask the applicant for additional information. The agency then prepares a draft permit which is reviewed and commented on by EPA, affected states, and the public. An "affected state" is a state which is contiguous to the permitting state *and* whose air is impacted by the applicant's air emissions, or a state within 50 miles of the source noted in the draft permit. The applicant may have to respond to some or all of these comments, and also may have to attend a public hearing. When the comments have been successfully addressed, the regulatory agency may issue the final operating permit.

In the interim between submission of the application and receipt of a final permit, an organization must operate in accordance with all the terms noted in its application, including the emissions inventory, record keeping, monitoring, fee payment, reporting, compliance assessment, and emission control requirements. Failure to meet these requirements can result in enforcement actions. It is important to remember that many, but not all, of a state's air regulations are federally enforceable. While all regulatory guidelines can be bundled into one permit, the compliance officer should ensure that the Title V permit application clearly separates those state requirements that are not federally enforceable from those state requirements which are federally enforceable. Failure to properly separate them in the Title V permit application will result in these state-enforced requirements becoming part of the federally-enforceable operating permits.

Fees

The federal government generally pays reasonable fees, although it will not pay what it believes to be taxes. Thus far, it appears that the federal government will pay these annual air emission fees.

Checklist :

Is your facility operating under a Title V permit?

No: No fees are required under *this* program.
Yes: Pay fees to state based on actual emissions multiplied by cost per ton of pollutant emitted.

---

§70.9 sets forth the mandatory fee program. States must charge enough in fees to cover the cost of running their Title V programs. The Act suggests that states charge up to $25 per tpy (except CO, ODCs regulated under CAA Title VI, and pollutants regulated only because of the Act's accidental release requirements) of pollutant emitted each year, although many states charge less and a few charge more. States may forego charging for emissions above 4,000 tpy. Unlike the air emissions inventory which determines whether Title V is applicable, emissions fees are based on the actual emissions as determined through stack tests, continuous emission monitoring, and surrogate parameters as contained in the permit application of the final permit. Despite their imposing sounding name, surrogate parameters merely allow organizations to use circumstantial facts to indicate their emissions under an EPA-created chart.

Permits

Checklist :

Do you have a Title V permit?

Permits (continued)

> **Checklist (continued):**
>
> No: No compliance program necessary.
> Yes: Ensure you follow all permit requirements and submit
>   for renewal six months prior to the permit's expiring.

§70.6 describes the minimum contents of the final permit. Permits must include a discussion of all emissions monitoring techniques, relevant record-keeping requirements and relevant reporting requirements. The permit will clearly state that violations of the permit are violations of the Act and are subject to enforcement action. The permit also will state that it does not convey any property rights. The permitting agency may terminate or modify a permit for cause. The permit itself requires the facility to provide the information needed to make such a determination.

A facility may modify its Title V operating permit if it meets the conditions set forth in §70.7. Permit modifications are broken down into administrative amendments, minor modifications, and significant modifications. Administrative amendments are for such things as change in ownership, correcting typographical errors, or changing phone numbers identified in the permit. Minor modifications do not violate any applicable requirements and do not involve significant changes to existing requirements in the permit. Significant modifications are all other permit modifications. §70.7 spells out in detail the requirements for a permit alteration, although the permitting authority may alter them.

Permits are generally good for 5 years. Municipal solid waste incinerators may have 12-year permits, which are reviewed every five years. Permit renewal applications should be received by the permitting agency 6–18 months prior to the existing permit's termination.

Subchapter VI - Ozone Compliance

> **Checklist :**
>
> Do you manufacture, import, export, or sell Ozone Depleting Substances (ODS)?
>
> Yes: You must comply with phaseout, reporting, record keeping and labeling requirements per 40 CFR §82.
> No: No compliance program is necessary **unless**:

Subchapter VI - Ozone Compliance (continued)

> **Checklist (continued):**
>
> Do you maintain equipment that uses ODS?
>
> No: No compliance program is necessary.
> Yes: Motor vehicle and nonmotor vehicle ODS-using equipment must be maintained only by certified mechanics using approved equipment.

Not all Ozone Depleting Substances (ODS) are identical, so the compliance officer must be aware that there are essentially two classes of regulated ODS. Class I ODS are listed in §602 (a) and include CFC-11, CFC-12, Halon-1211, carbon tetrachloride, and methyl chloroform. EPA may add to the Class I list, and must add all ODS found to have an ozone depletion potential of 0.2 or greater. Class II ODS are listed in §602 (b) and consist of a variety of hydrochlorofluorocarbons (HCFC). As with Class I ODS, EPA must add to this list any substances which it believes may damage the ozone layer.

Determining the Need for a Compliance Program

> **Checklist :**
>
> Do you: manufacture any Ozone Depleting Substances (ODS)?
>   purchase any ODS?
>
>   own any equipment that utilizes ODS?
>
>   maintain, for yourself or for any other party, any equipment that uses ODS?
>
> No: No compliance program is necessary.
> Yes: Follow the regulatory guidelines.

Generally, ODS are found in refrigerants, fire fighting apparatuses, and solvents. Accordingly, the compliance officer should check freezers, refrigerators, coolers, and air conditioning systems for CFCs. He/she should check portable fire extinguishers and system mounted fire fighting units (such as those on an airplane or an army tank) for halons. Finally, he/she should check with maintenance staff and other places where solvents are used to see if any of the solvents contain ODS. If the organization does maintenance, such as an autobody shop, the compliance officer should determine if any of the systems (e.g., vehicle air conditioners) maintained at the facility contain ODS.

If the organization has no ODS and does not maintain any ODS-using equipment, implementing a Stratospheric Ozone Protection strategy will be simple. The compliance officer should merely draft a memo documenting the negative results of his/her inventory and detailing how the survey was conducted. The officer should also give written guidance to relevant departments, such as procurement or customer service, describing the possibility of future contact with ODS and instructing them to contact him/her should such contact occur.

If the compliance officer's organization does work with ODS, the organization must meet a variety of regulatory requirements.

Class I ODS Producer, Importer, or Exporter Requirements

Checklist :

Do you import, produce or export Class I ODS?

No: No compliance program necessary.
Yes: You must comply with the regulation described below.

Producers, importers, and exporters of Class I ODS must file a report with EPA indicating the amount of the ODS produced, exported, or imported. As new Class I's are listed, the person has 180 days to submit a baseline report for that relevant ODS.

40 CFR §82.6 lists the apportionment of baseline production allowances for a variety of producers. 40 CFR §82.13(i) (j) (k) (l) and (m) contain special requirements and extra allowance opportunities for persons who destroy Class I ODS.

Reports must be mailed to EPA within 45 days of the end of the reporting period. Records and copies of these reports must be kept for at least three years, although it may be a good idea to keep them forever.

Each kilogram of an ODS constitutes a separate violation, so a facility should keep very detailed records and audit them frequently to ensure that the numbers add up as they are supposed to.

Within 120 days after a producer first produces a Class I ODS, the producer must submit a report to EPA as set out in 40 CFR §82.13(f)(1). Among other things, this report must describe the methods by which the producer measures production, quantity of fugitive emissions, and the estimated efficiency rate of the production process. Changes in this information must be submitted to EPA within 60 days.

Class I producers must maintain detailed records in accordance with §82.139(f)(2). These records include copies of invoices documenting the sale of ODS for some use that would result in their destruction, dated records of the quantity of raw materials and feedstock chemicals used for the production of ODS, and records of any ODS release equalling or exceeding 100 lbs.

Class I producers must file a quarterly report with EPA. Detailed in 40 CFR 82.13 (f)(3), this report must contain, among other information, the quantity of each ODS produced and the quantity of recyclable and recoverable ODS containing material actually recovered.

Class I importers have their own record keeping and reporting requirements to meet. These requirements are detailed in 40 CFR §82.13(g). The record-keeping requirements include the quantity of each ODS imported (alone or in a mixture), the date of importation, and a copy of the relevant bill of lading. Reports are detailed in 40 CFR §82.13(g)(2). Under this subparagraph, importers must submit a report each quarter that includes summaries of much of the previous quarter's information, the total quantity of each ODS imported, and the amount of ODS imported for use in processes which resulted in their destruction.

Class I exporters must follow the regulatory requirements of 40 CFR §82.13(h). Exporters have 45 days after the end of the year to report ODS exports that were not previously reported. This report must include, among other items, the names and addresses of the exporter and of the recipient, the exporter's Employee Identification Number and the type and quantity of each ODC exported.

Class II Producers and Importers

Persons who produce, import or export Class II ODS must report quarterly levels of production, imports, and exports within 45 days of the end of the quarter.

Phase-Out Requirements for Class I ODS

Checklist :

Do you *produce* Class I ODS?

No: No compliance program necessary.
Yes: Check definition of "production" to ensure that you are covered. If so, decrease Class I ODS production in accordance with the law.

§604 sets out the percentage of the baseline ODS figures that producers may continue to produce [under §601(11). "Production" does not include the manufacture of an ODC that is used and entirely consumed (except for trace quantities) in the manufacture of other chemicals, nor does "production" refer to recycling or reuse of ODS; an example of this definition's importance is the fact that carbon tetrachloride, to be phased out of "production" by the year 2000, is primarily manufactured in the U.S. for use as feedstock. For example, in 1996 a producer may only produce 40% of its baseline production figure for most Class I ODS, and that figure drops to 0% by the year 2000. Production of carbon tetrachloride and methylchloroform are listed separately, but also decline significantly.

Phase-Out Requirements for Class II Producers and Importers

Checklist :

Do you produce or import a Class II ODS?

No: No compliance program necessary.
Yes: Check to see if any exceptions apply. If not, reduce production or importation in accordance with the regulatory schedule.

Class II ODS producers and importers find their ODS activities limited through 40 CFR §82.4 (e)–(j). While there are some exceptions for medical devices and export to developing countries, most ODS production is prohibited by January 1, 2030 unless the ODS will be used in such a manner as to be destroyed. A variety of Class II ODS are prohibited from importation or production considerably in advance of 2030 unless they are destroyed in use.

Exchange Allowances

§607 of the Act allows transfers of both production and consumption of ODS, subject to a variety of constraints. 40 CFR §82.12 sets out the precise requirements of these transfers. Essentially, a party would request that EPA allow such a transfer, whether of an ODS allowance *between* companies (transfer) or from one type of ODS to a similar type of ODS within the *same* company (conversions) or both. Although the exchange is almost one to one, the exchanging party must subtract 101% of the amount exchanged from its prior unexpended balance. EPA will review the applicant's records to ensure it has sufficient unexpended allowances to cover the exchange claim. If EPA ultimately finds this is not the case, all parties involved in the transaction could be liable for violating the apportionment regulations.

Maintenance, Repair and Sale of ODS and ODS-Using Equipment

Checklist :

Do you maintain or repair any ODS-using equipment?

    Yes: Determine whether you work on vehicle or non-vehicle ODS-using equipment, or both. Ensure that mechanics are properly certified and using regulatory approved equipment.

    No: No compliance program necessary, **unless:**

Do you sell ODS or ODS-using equipment?

    No: No compliance program necessary.

    Yes: Ensure you meet the regulations for labelling and selling these items.

The Act, and the relevant CFR section, break maintenance and repair into two sections. One section focuses on motor vehicle air conditioners while the other section focuses on everything else.

Motor Vehicle Air Conditioners: §609 of the Act and 40 CFR §82.30 detail the requirements regarding servicing of motor vehicle air conditioners. Air conditioning on buses using HCFC-22 refrigerant and hermetically-sealed refrigeration systems of cargo trucks are not covered by these regulations. No paid mechanic may service a vehicle's air conditioning unit unless that mechanic is using regulatorily approved equipment and has been properly trained and certified. The owner of air conditioner repair equipment, or another responsible officer, must certify that anyone working on motor vehicle air conditioners is properly trained and certified to do so. Only approved refrigerant recycling equipment can be used. All records of certification and training, as well as off-site destinations for recycled materials and proof of buyer certification in the case of vendors, must be maintained for at least three years. EPA may inspect commercial organizations that work on vehicle air conditioners.

Nonmotor vehicle refrigeration: §608 of the Act and 40 CFR §§82.150–166 provide the details for servicing everything but motor vehicle air conditioners (small appliances which contain five pounds or less of ODS refrigerant, such as home freezers and window air conditioners, are exempt from many of the CFR's requirements). In addition, these regulations apply to parties disposing of ODS-using appliances (including motor vehicle air conditioners) and virtually anyone else who works with, owns, reclaims, or recycles ODS refrigerants. The program prohibits all releases of ODS refrigerants except for *de minimus* releases during proper, good faith efforts to recycle the substances. The CFR spells out in detail the procedures for working on ODS-containing cooling systems, essentially forbidding any work on such systems unless it is by a properly certified technician using properly certified equipment. Owners of commercial cooling systems or cooling systems containing 50 pounds or more of ODS may have to repair significant coolant leaks and keep various service records. ODS recycling and reclamation operations have a variety of regulatory standards to meet, and everyone must keep detailed records of training and certification for at least 3 years.

Sale of ODS and ODS-Using Equipment: It is illegal for anyone to sell more than 20 pounds of an ODS refrigerant to an uncertified person unless the buyer certifies that the ODS is for resale only. Vendors also must display a special sign prominently, detailed in §8242(c), stating the sale and purchase requirements concerning ODS. Vendors of ODS-using cooling systems must ensure that their systems have special adaptation which facilitate repair and ODS-reclamation without ODS releases.

Under §611 of the Act and 40 CFR §§82.100–124, no container or product containing a Class I ODS and no container with a Class II ODS can be placed into interstate commerce without a clear and conspicuous label stating: **Warning. Contains** [insert name of substance]. **A substance which harms public health and environment by destroying ozone in the upper atmosphere**. If a party can prove that there are no substitute products or manufacturing processes that are potentially available that do not rely on a Class I ODS and which reduce the overall risk to human health and the environment, that party will not have to use such labels prior to 2015. If a proper alternative exists, products containing Class II ODS may have to display this warning label also.

Nonessential Products Containing ODS

Checklist :

Do you sell or distribute listed nonessential items?

No: No compliance program necessary.
Yes: Determine if any of the items are covered by any of several listed exceptions. Doublecheck with State/EPA. Document.

§610 of the Act, implemented by 40 CFR §§82.60–70 prohibits the sale or distribution of a variety of ODS-using items identified in the CFR as being nonessential. A partial list of these items include marine safety horns, cleaning fluids (except those distributed or sold to a commercial purchaser), plastic party streamers, personal safety horns, aerosol cans, and home intruder alarms. Some exceptions exist for items which were in initial inventory by December 31, 1993, which are used for medical reasons (as defined in §601(8) of the Act), or which meet a variety of other requirements.

Substitutes for ODS

> **Checklist :**
>
> Ensure that any materials used in place of ODS are EPA approved.

§612 of the Act and 40 CFR §174 limits the substitution of other substances for Class I and Class II ODS. Appendix A to Subpart G of 40 CFR §82 lists a variety of acceptable and unacceptable substitutes and provides an explanation for these decisions. In general, ODS substitutes should not present adverse effects to the environment or to human health.

Federal Procurement

Under §613 of the Act and 40 CFR §§82.80–86, the federal government must follow specific guidelines when purchasing, or considering purchasing, Class I and Class II ODS. Among these requirements is the need to substitute safe alternatives for these ODS to the maximum extent practicable, the need to have contractual language insist that the contractor abide by certain regulations and the need to avoid purchasing defined nonessential ODS-containing products.

Technology Export and Overseas Investment

§614(c) of the Act prohibits the export of technologies used to produce a Class I ODS, prohibits investments in Class I or Class II producing facilities in nations not party to the Montreal Protocol and prohibits government agencies from aiding programs that produce and Class I substances.

Other Compliance Programs

In addition to the programs described above, the Act has specific sections that apply to the federal government (§116), primary nonferrous smelters (§119), stack heights (§123), solid waste combustion (§129), and gasoline vapor recovery systems (§325).

GLOSSARY

40CFR Part 60 . . . . Section 40, Code of Federal Regulations, Part 60, presents the requirements shown in Exhibit 6-4. The CFR sections cover all EPA environmental requirements. FR is also used instead of CFR.

Acid Rain . . . . Rain that has an acidic pH due to the presence in it of acids such as sulfur dioxide or nitric acid.

Attainment Areas . . . . Areas that are in compliance with national ambient air quality standards.

Best Available Control . . . . Technology for control of a specific pollut-
    Technology ant that is commercially feasible and removes the maximum amount of that pollutant that can be achieved.

Chlorofluorocarbons (CFCs). . . Chemical compounds containing carbon, hydrogen, chlorine, and fluorine that are utilized in household and vehicle refrigerants.

Criteria Pollutants . . . . Six common pollutants (carbon monoxide, lead, nitrogen dioxide, ozone, particulates, and sulfur dioxide). Comprehensive air quality criteria documents support and provide the rationale for regulation of these pollutants.

Emissions . . . . Discharges of pollutants into the air.

Emission Testing Stations. . . . . State stations that test the levels of contaminants in exhaust emissions from automobiles.

Exceedance . . . . When the contaminant level in the air is above the standard level for a specific amount of time over a specific time period.

Fugitive Dust. . . . . Dust that is blown into the air during construction, or from other activities such as tank removal.

Hazardous Organic National. . . These are emission standards for 112 (as of
    Emission Standards for July, 1994) toxic air pollutants.
    Hazardous Air Pollutants
    (HON)

High Occupancy Vehicle . . . . . Highway lanes restricted to use by vehicles
    (HOV) Lanes containing a designated number of occupants.

Hydrocarbons	Various chemical combinations of hydrogen and carbon.
Lowest Available Emission. . . . Rate	A source emits the specific pollutant at the lowest possible emission rate from a technological point of view. At a minimum, it must be equal to requirements of New Source Performance Standards.
M Btu/h	Million British Thermal Units per hour, a measure of the amount of energy generated.
Maximum Achievable Control . Technology (MACT)	The best demonstrated control technology and practices in the regulated industry.
Mobile Sources	Sources of air pollution that can be moved, e.g., automobiles, trucks, etc.
National Ambient Air Quality . Standards (NAAQS)	Standards developed by U.S. EPA for the six criteria pollutants. These include both primary and secondary standards.
National Ambient Monitoring . Stations (NAMS)	A subset of the SLAMS monitors used by EPA for national trend analysis.
National Emission Standards . . for Hazardous Air Pollutants (NESHAPs)	These standards regulate hazardous air pollutants for which no air quality standards are applicable.
New Source Performance . . . . . Standards (NSPS)	Limitations on emissions of air pollutants or their precursors from new or substantially modified stationary sources.
Nonattainment Areas.	Areas not in compliance with national ambient air quality standards.
NO_x	Various combinations of nitrogen and oxygen.
Opacity	Degree of visible emission. Used to measure particulates.
Oxygenated Fuels	Fuels containing chemically bound oxygen, e.g., methanol or ethanol.
Ozone	A compound consisting of three oxygen atoms. It can cause health and crop damage. At ground level, ozone generally is deleterious to health and should be minimized. By contrast, ozone in the upper atmosphere is critical to human health because of its action in blocking ultraviolet rays from the sun.
Particulate Matter	Small airborne particles, generally of carbon, the largest of which may appear to the eye to be smoke or dust.

Precursors . . . . Chemicals that react to form the pollutant being controlled.

ppm . . . . Parts per million measured on the basis of the weight of the pollutant (grams) in a million grams of air.

Prevention of Significant . . . . . Prevention of contamination of air whose
Deterioration (PSD) quality is better than that allowed by primary and secondary air quality standards.

Primary Air Quality Standards . Standards for pollutants designed to protect human health.

SARA . . . . Acronym for the Superfund Amendments and Reauthorization Act of 1986.

SIC . . . . Acronym for Standard Industrial Codes that describe various industrial activities.

Secondary Air Quality . . . . Standards for pollutants designed to prevent
Standards human welfare damage. This includes damage to material things such as soils, crops, vegetation, water, visibility, weather, and property.

Smog . . . . An unpleasant fog-like condition (smoke and fog = smog) caused by a combination of air pollutants and climate conditions.

State and Local Air . . . . A network that provides year-round mea-
Monitoring Stations surements of the six NAAQS pollutants.
(SLAMS) Network

State Implementation Plan . . . . A plan developed by each state to limit
(SIP) emissions from air pollution sources to the degree necessary to achieve and maintain the National Ambient Air Quality Standards.

Stationary Sources . . . . Sources of air pollution that are fixed in position, e.g., incinerators, power plant emissions, papermills, etc.

Sulfur Oxides . . . . Varying combinations of sulfur and oxygen atoms caused primarily by combustion of fuel. These materials tend to be malodorous and damaging to human health.

Total Suspended Particulates . . Weight of suspended particulates per unit
(TSP) volume of air (micrograms per cubic meter).

Volatile Organic Compounds . . Organic chemicals that can easily move
(VOC) from the solid or liquid state to the gaseous state under normal conditions.

REFERENCES AND SELECTED READING

BREGMAN & COMPANY, 1992, "EIS for Proposed Cemetery in Cleveland Area," Bethesda, MD.

Bregman, J.I. and Mackenthun, K.M., 1992, *Environmental Impact Statements*, Lewis Publishers, Boca Raton, FL.

Mackenthun, K.M. and Bregman, J.I., 1992, *Environmental Regulations Handbook*, CRC Press, Boca Raton, FL.

National Association of Manufacturers (NAM), August, 1994, "Recent Significant Clean Air Act Regulations Published in the Federal Register," Washington, D.C.

U.S. Army Corps of Engineers, Construction Engineering Research Laboratories, September, 1993. "Environmental Compliance Assessment Army Reserve (ECAAR)," Champaign, IL.

U.S. Army Environmental Hygiene Agency, May, 1993. "Clean Air Amendments of 1990. Impacts on the Department of the Army," Washington, D.C.

U.S. EPA, 1989, "Basic Inspectors Training Course: Fundamentals of Environmental Compliance Inspection," U.S. Environmental Protection Agency, Office of Compliance Monitoring, Washington, D.C.

U.S. EPA, 1989a, Progress in the Prevention and Control of Air Pollution in 1987," Report to Congress, U.S. Environmental Protection Agency, Research Triangle Park, NC (EPA-450/2-89-009).

U.S. EPA, 1989b, "Status of Selected Air Pollution Control Programs," U.S. Environmental Protection Agency, Office of Air Quality Planning and Standards, Research Triangle Park, NC.

U.S. EPA, 1990, "The Clean Air Act Amendments of 1990. Summary Materials," U.S. Environmental Protection Agency, Office of Air and Radiation, Washington, D.C.

U.S. EPA, 1990a, "Progress in the Prevention and Control of Air Pollution in 1988," Report to Congress, U.S. Environmental Protection Agency, Washington, D.C. (EPA-450/2-90-007).

U.S. EPA, 1994, Private Communication, Office of Administrator for Air and Radiation, Washington, D.C.

7   Hazardous Waste Management

GENERAL OVERVIEW

The heart of any solid waste disposal plan is its hazardous waste management program. Improper handling of hazardous wastes can harm both people and the environment, while at the same time exposing the offending party to a wide variety of civil and punitive actions. A recent example occurred in Florida, where corporate officials were sentenced to 27 months in prison for improperly disposing of toluene in a dumpster where children played. Two children died with massive amounts of toluene in their systems.

The primary national legislation guiding hazardous waste is the **Resource Conservation and Recovery Act (RCRA)** of 1976. The Act was amended in 1984 by the "Hazardous and Solid Waste Amendments of 1984 (HSWA)." While the Act is most frequently referred to as RCRA, it is actually Subchapter III of the Solid Waste Disposal Act, 42 U.S.C. §§6921–6939(e). The authors will refer to Subchapter III as RCRA, with the appropriate section number mentioned as it is referred to in the U.S.C. Most RCRA programs are implemented by 40 CFR §§260–272, although a variety of guidance is found in other sections of the CFR. RCRA is the subject of this chapter except for the portions of RCRA dealing with underground storage tanks which are addressed in other chapters of this book.

The goal of RCRA is to prevent improper disposal of hazardous waste. RCRA accomplishes this goal by tracking hazardous waste from its "cradle" (when the material first becomes hazardous waste) to its "grave" (when the material is finally disposed of). Hazardous wastes must be properly stored, labeled, dated, manifested, transported, disposed of, and accounted for under complex EPA and Department of Transportation (DOT) regulations. The more hazardous the waste, the more complex are the regulatory requirements. Failure to properly fulfill any one of the requirements can subject a facility, *and any responsible officials*, to severe civil and criminal sanctions. These sanctions, spelled out in §6928 of the Act, include penalties of up to $25,000 per day per violation, criminal fines of up to $50,000 per day per violation and imprisonment of up to 5 years.

SOLID WASTE

Under §6903(5) of the Act, a waste must be a solid waste or a combination of solid wastes before it can be regulated as a hazardous waste. However, according to §6903(27), "solid" wastes may be defined as solid, semi-solid, liquid, or contained gaseous materials. 40 CFR §261-2 defines what qualifies as solid waste in greater detail. Essentially, anything that is discarded (i.e., not immediately captured and reused on-site) is likely to be a solid waste. Obviously, something that is thrown in the dumpster qualifies as a solid waste, since it has been disposed of. Other methods of dealing with waste, such as some methods of recycling, are not as clearcut. Recycling an inherently wastelike material, as defined in §261.2, does not keep that material from being a solid waste. Burning listed materials for energy does not remove those materials from the solid waste category. Facilities conducting those activities still have to comply with RCRA.

According to the Act, solid waste does not include solid or dissolved material in domestic sewage, irrigation return flows, or some industrial discharges. Additionally, 40 CFR §§261.2 and 261.4 spell out a variety of situations where an otherwise solid waste is not considered to be such.

If a post-use material is not a solid waste according to the Act or the CFR, it is not subject to RCRA. That is not to say, however, that the non-solid waste material is completely unregulated. Sewage, for example, is not a solid waste, but is regulated under the Clean Water and Safe Drinking Water Acts.

A concept that is frequently difficult to grasp is that virgin products which are intended for future use clearly are not governed by RCRA, regardless of their potential hazards, because they are not yet solid waste. While not covered by RCRA, the compliance officer should check TSCA, OSHA, and other relevant regulations to see if they cover these hazardous items. Unexpended munitions, for example, are not yet considered hazardous waste according to RCRA, but EPA at some point may define unexploded or obsolete ordnance as being a RCRA hazardous waste. Similarly, if a virgin product can no longer be used for its intended purpose, it may become a solid waste.

HAZARDOUS WASTE

Once a material has been designated a solid waste, it must also be designated as being hazardous before it comes under RCRA's regulatory program. 6903(5) defines a hazardous waste as a solid waste, or a combination of solid wastes, which, because of the "quantity, concentration, or physical, chemical, or infectious characteristics" may cause or significantly contribute to increases in mortality or serious illnesses, or pose a substantial threat to human health or the environment when improperly managed. The language in this definition leaves much room for interpretation. 40 CFR §261.3 sets out much more detailed guidance for when a "solid waste" becomes a "hazardous waste," although this guidance, too, is subject to interpretation.

It is up to the generator to determine if its solid waste is hazardous waste or not. For wastes that are not clearly listed as being hazardous wastes, as described below, §262.11 allows a generator to make this determination based on an approved testing method, or based on generator knowledge. If a generator knows that what went into a solid waste is not a hazardous waste, then there is no need to comply with RCRA. Generator knowledge should be carefully documented and access to waste limited to ensure that generator knowledge remains accurate.

There are four basic paths a solid waste takes to become hazardous under RCRA:

1. It exhibits a characteristic of a hazardous waste
2. It is listed as a hazardous waste
3. It is a mixture of a listed hazardous waste and another solid waste
4. It is generated from the treatment, storage, or disposal of a hazardous waste

Each of these four waste groups has many types of hazardous wastes, and each type of hazardous waste has a special EPA Hazardous Waste Number. For example, a waste that is hazardous because it exhibits reactive characteristics has an EPA Hazardous Waste Number of D003. In another example, solvent carbon tetrachloride spent in degreasing has an EPA Hazardous Waste Number of F001. An expanded description of the four basic groups of hazardous wastes follows.

Characteristic Wastes

A solid waste is hazardous under §261.3 if it exhibits any of the four hazardous characteristics set out in §§261.21–.24. (§261.3 specifically excludes some ore and mineral extraction and processing wastes from this definition.) These hazardous characteristics are

> *Ignitability* — A liquid with a flash point of less that 140°F, which under standard temperature and pressure, may cause a fire through friction, moisture absorption, or spontaneous reactions, and burn so energetically that it creates a hazard; or an oxidizer or ignitable compressed gas under Department of Transportation (DOT) regulations 49 CFR §173. Ignitable hazardous wastes have EPA Hazardous Waste Number D001;
>
> *Corrosivity* — A liquid that has a pH of between 2.0 and 12.5 and corrodes steel faster than one-quarter inch per year under certain conditions. Corrosive hazardous wastes have EPA Hazardous Waste Number D002;

Reactivity — The liquid is very unstable and readily undergoes violent change without detonating; it reacts violently, forms potentially explosive mixtures, or generates dangerous toxic gases when mixed with water; it may explode or detonate under certain conditions; it can generate dangerous toxic gases when exposed to a pH level of between 2 and 12.5; or it is a forbidden explosive by 49 CFR §173. Reactive hazardous wastes have EPA Hazardous Waste Number D003;

Toxicity — The extract from a representative sample contains certain contaminants in greater concentrations than permissible as listed in Table 1 of §261.24. This method is the Toxicity Characteristic Leaching Procedure, or TCLP for short. It essentially attempts to predict if the leachate of this material, after its been deposited in a landfill, will be hazardous. Toxic hazardous wastes may have EPA Hazardous Waste Numbers from D004 to D043 depending on their location in Table 1.

Listed Wastes

A solid waste is a hazardous waste if it is listed as such on any of three EPA hazardous waste lists. These lists are located in 40 CFR §261 Subpart D. EPA also provides, in the right-hand columns for F and K listed wastes and in the paragraph above the tables for P and U listed wastes, the hazard code explaining why the Agency found that particular waste to be hazardous. Set forth in §261.30(b), the relevant hazard codes are as follows: "I" means the waste is hazardous because of its ignitability, "C" indicates corrosiveness, "R" stands for reactive, "T" is for toxic, and "H" is for acute hazardous (generally subject to especially stringent regulations regarding treatment, storage and disposal. While most acutely hazardous wastes are P-wastes, other wastes also qualify as acutely hazardous, so it is important to check the hazard code), and "E" is for TCLP results.

The three lists each cover a basic category:

Nonspecific Sources — §261.31. Generic hazardous wastes produced by general industrial, manufacturing, and maintenance operations. Waste solvent carbon tetrachloride spent in degreasing is an example of this list. There are 39 specific wastes listed in this section. They have EPA Hazardous Waste Numbers F001 to F039.

Specific Sources — §261.32. Hazardous wastes produced by particular activities such as spent potliners from primary aluminum reduction. This list is broken into sections by industry to make locating any of its 148 listed hazardous wastes easier. These hazardous wastes have EPA Hazardous Waste Numbers K001 to K148.

Various "Throw Away" Commercial Chemical Products — §261.33. A variety of discarded commercial chemical products, off-specification species, container residues and spill residues when intended to be discarded, used as a fuel or applied to the land in lieu of their original intended use. This particular list is subdivided into two separate lists. Members of the first sub-list, with EPA Hazardous Waste Numbers starting with P are *acute* hazardous wastes and are subject to special regulations under other parts of the CFR. These acute hazardous wastes include materials such as zinc cyanide and phosphine. The second sublist contains U-wastes, which are toxic wastes and which are not subject to the same extra rigorous regulations as acute hazardous wastes. Some examples of these listed U-wastes include toluene and vinyl chloride.

Mixed Wastes

In general, when a listed hazardous waste is mixed with other wastes, the mixture becomes a hazardous waste and must be treated as such. When a characteristic hazardous waste is mixed with other waste, the entire mixture is considered to be a hazardous waste if it demonstrates any hazardous waste characteristics. Since the onus is on the generator to determine what is and is not hazardous waste, it is a wise idea to segregate waste streams to avoid cross contamination. §261.3(a)(2)(iii) and (iv) discuss this mixture concept in detail, and spell out numerous exceptions where the mixture rules do not apply.

Generated by Treatment, Storage or Disposal

These wastes, generated by the treatment, storage or disposal of hazardous wastes, generally are considered to be hazardous wastes themselves unless they do not exhibit any characteristics of a hazardous waste.

EMPTY CONTAINERS

Defining when a container is empty is important because once a material has been discarded, it becomes solid waste. If the material in the container is considered hazardous waste when discarded, it must be treated as hazardous waste **even if it is still in its original container and has not been contaminated with anything**. Therefore, a material that is still usable, which has not been discarded, must be treated only as a hazardous material, but when one uses up that material and throws away the container, the container may have to be treated as hazardous waste unless it is properly "empty." Thus, empty containers that once held regulated RCRA wastes may themselves be considered hazardous wastes, depending on how empty they really are. If a container is truly empty, it is not hazardous waste and does not need to be disposed of under any special RCRA regulations. §261.7 sets out the regulatory guidance for when a container is "empty" for the purposes of the Act.

For all containers that held non-gaseous or non-acute hazardous waste, "empty" means that the containers have been emptied using the traditional methods of emptying such a container and that no more than one inch of residue remains in the container. An alternative to the inch measurement is that containers of no more than 110 gallons may have up to 3% by weight of the total capacity of the container. A container with a capacity of greater than 110 gallons is empty when it contains no more than 0.3% by weight of its total capacity. Containers of gaseous hazardous waste are empty when the container's pressure approaches atmospheric.

Acute hazardous waste containers are empty when they have been properly triple washed or cleaned by some other approved method. If the container had an inner liner that kept the waste from actually touching the container, merely removing that inner liner will empty the container.

LEACHATE

EPA views leachate as a hazardous waste if it exhibits a hazardous waste characteristic or if it comes from the disposal of a listed hazardous waste. Even if the material disposed of became a regulated hazardous waste after disposal, the resulting leachate is considered a hazardous waste.

In the same vein, the §261.3(c) also places spill residue from hazardous wastes in the hazardous waste category. Thus, soil and groundwater that have been contaminated by hazardous waste are likely to be regulated as such. As always, the CFR setting forth this rule also contains exceptions.

HAZARDOUS WASTE RECYCLING

§261.6 sets out the initial standards for hazardous waste recycling. Hazardous waste recyclers also must follow many regulatory requirements listed in §§262–266, 268, 270, and 124 for generators, transporters, owners, and operators dealing with recyclable hazardous waste. Members of this particular regulated community include reclaimers of spent lead-acid batteries and precious metals, facilities that burn hazardous waste for energy recovery, and facilities that use hazardous waste in a manner that equates to disposal.

Some hazardous waste recyclers are expressly excused from the regulatory requirements listed in the above paragraph. According to §261(a)(3), these exempt hazardous waste recyclers include reclaimers of industrial ethyl alcohol, parties who are shipping hazardous wastes to foreign countries for reclamation, battery manufacturers regenerating used batteries, and scrap metal recyclers.

LAND DISPOSAL

§§6924(c)–(g) of the Act and 40 CFR §268 forbid the disposal of certain hazardous wastes on or in land-based facilities. These restrictions are typically called the "Land Ban Restrictions," and wastes regulated under this program are called "Land Ban Wastes." Essentially, Congress decided that some waste is simply too hazardous to dispose of in any type of land-based facility. §268.4 provides an exception for surface impoundments where treatment occurs, sampling is done, and residue not meeting the treatment standards is removed within a year.

Even storage of restricted wastes is forbidden under §268.50 unless the facility is merely accumulating enough waste to handle efficiently. Treatment, Storage and Disposal Facilities (TSDFs) may store Land Ban Wastes for up to a year unless EPA can prove that this storage time was not needed to build up enough waste to handle properly. The responsibility switches after a year, with the facility having to show that it needs more time to accumulate the Land Ban Wastes.

Land Ban Wastes are a very inclusive group, covering virtually all hazardous waste except TCLP wastes that do not have EP toxicity. Certain exceptions to Land Ban Wastes apply. These exceptions are described in §268.1 and include some farming pesticides, *de minimis* losses from normal material handling operations and conditionally exempt small quantity generators. The primary Land Ban Wastes are: noncontainerized liquid hazardous wastes, non-hazardous liquids, California list wastes by §268.32, solvents and dioxins according to §§268.30 and 268.31, and wastes with EPA hazardous waste numbers as listed in §268.33–37.

TREATMENT

Some Land Ban Wastes are given specific exemptions so that they can be disposed of in underground injection chambers, while the majority of wastes must be treated before disposal. Treatment standards for Land Ban Wastes, set forth by §268 Subpart D, generally are based on levels achievable through the best demonstrated available technology (BDAT).

Land Ban Wastes may be land disposed only if one of three conditions is satisfied. The first condition is that an extract of the waste, or of the treatment residue, does not exceed listed values under a TCLP test, at which point the potential to contaminate groundwater will have diminished. These values are listed in Table CCWE of this subpart. The second condition covers wastes with prescribed treatment standards expressed as specified technologies. These wastes and standards are listed in Tables 1 and 2 of §268.42. The third condition is when certain wastes, not their extracts, meet the hazardous constituent levels specified in §268.43 Table CCW. If these constituent levels are unattainable, the generator or TSDF may apply for a variance in accordance with §268.44. In limited cases, mostly for ignitable, corrosive, and radioactive wastes, dilution is appropriate if the residue no longer contains hazardous elements which pose a threat to human health and the environment.

Facilities which treat Land Ban Wastes must follow the waste analysis and record-keeping requirements of §268.7. The type of waste determines the residue or residue extract tests that the treatment facility must perform. When the treatment facility ships the treated waste to a land disposal facility, it must include notification of EPA hazardous waste number, the corresponding treatment standards, relevant manifest numbers and an authorized representative's certification that he/she inspected the treatment procedures and believes that the waste was properly treated.

Hazardous debris is dealt with separately under §268.45. In general, hazardous debris must be treated for each "contaminant" subject to treatment. Contaminants include toxicity characteristic debris, debris contaminated with listed waste, and cyanide reactive debris. Hazardous debris must be treated by either the waste specific treatment standards for the waste contaminating the debris or by alternative, debris-specific methods listed in Table 1 of §268.45. If EPA determines that the debris is no longer contaminated, treatment prior to land disposal is not necessary.

HAZARDOUS WASTE GENERATORS

Overview

Anyone who creates a hazardous waste is a hazardous waste generator and must follow the standards set in 40 CFR §262. The Federal RCRA program breaks hazardous waste generators into three different tiers, depending on how much hazardous waste they generate or store on site. Logically, the more hazardous waste generated or stored on site, the more stringent the relevant RCRA regulations become. States will generally follow the RCRA classification scheme, but they may raise or change the standards somewhat. Some states, such as Massachusetts, regulate used motor oil as a hazardous waste. Many smaller facilities, such as a service station, may find themselves classified as a larger generator than anticipated if their state regulates used oil as a hazardous waste.

Fully Regulated (Large Quantity) Generators

Hazardous waste generators who are not subject to any of §262 or §261.5 exceptions must follow all RCRA regulations pertaining to regulators. Large Quantity Generators (LQGs) generate 1000 kg or more of hazardous waste in one or more months during the year. LQGs must obtain EPA Identification numbers in accordance with §262.12.

LQGs may store hazardous waste on site for up to 90 days without obtaining a permit to operate as a Treatment, Storage and Disposal Facility (TSDF). Generators must still follow storage safety requirements set out in §265 Subparts C and D, as well as a variety of labeling, dating, and training regulations. §270.1(c)(2)(i) states that this 90-day storage is only allowed at the site where the wastes were generated.

The generator must prepare hazardous waste for shipment in accordance with DOT regulations and must prepare a manifest for each hazardous waste shipment. Both DOT regulations and manifests are discussed below.

Generators also must comply with the Land Ban restrictions discussed earlier in this chapter.

Small Quantity Generators (SQGs)

A facility that generates between 100 and 1,000 kg per month of **total** hazardous waste is considered a Small Quantity Generator (SQG). Generators in this category are still regulated under §262, but are exempted from some of this section's requirements by §262.34(d), (e), and (f).

Of primary importance, these generators may store hazardous waste on site for up to 180 days or up to 270 days if the nearest TSDF is over 200 miles away, without the need for a TSDF permit as long as they never accumulate over 6,000 kg of waste on site and comply with a variety of storage regulations listed below.

Conditionally Exempt Small Quantity Generators (CESQGs)

§261.5 sets out special, relatively lenient, regulations for Conditionally Exempt Small Quantity Generators (CESQGs). A generator is a CESQG if it generates no more than 100 kg of hazardous waste in any month and no more than one kilogram of acute hazardous waste. If the CESQG exceeds these amounts for any one month, it becomes a SQG (or, potentially, a LQG). At that point, all regulations applying to the higher category of generator apply to the former CESQG. Any storage deadlines, such as 180-day on-site storage for a SQG, come into existence as soon as a CESQG accumulates enough hazardous waste to be placed in a higher class. A CESQG may accumulate enough acute hazardous waste to bring regulation of that waste to a higher level without increasing regulation of non-acute hazardous waste that remains under the specified accumulation limits.

CESQGs are specifically exempted, in most cases, from having to follow the regulations contained in §§262–266, 268, 270, and 124, as well as RCRA notification requirements of §6930. Unlike the other two types of generators, under §261.5(g)(3), CESQGs may send their hazardous waste to non-TSDF facilities and may store their hazardous waste without worrying about RCRA storage regulations or time limits. However, other legal issues, such as OSHA and generic liability for spills of hazardous waste, generally dictate that hazardous waste be stored in a controlled manner even at CESQGs.

CESQGs may even mix hazardous waste and non-hazardous waste as long as the resulting mixture does not exhibit any of the four hazardous characteristics described above and exceed the CESQG generation limits. If a CESQG mixes its hazardous waste with non-hazardous waste oil, the resulting mixture must be managed according to 40 CFR §279 if it will be used for energy recovery.

HAZARDOUS WASTE STORAGE AND TRANSPORTATION

Overview

Throughout its life, a hazardous waste must be stored according to precise federal or state regulations, except when generated by a CESQG. There are basically three stages to hazardous waste storage. These stages are: satellite accumulation, general storage on site, and storage by a TSDF. Transporters of hazardous waste have special concerns which are discussed in the section on Transportation. Of these three storage stages, the first, satellite accumulation, is the least regulated while the last, TSDF, is the most regulated. On-site storage by the generator, as long as it does not exceed the relevant time frame, is subject to one of two levels of regulation depending on whether the generator is a SQG or a LQG. LQGs must meet higher regulatory standards.

There are certain basic rules that apply regardless of the relevant storage level. Incompatible materials may not be stored in such a manner that they could mix, spills must be contained, hazardous waste accumulation areas must be inspected, hazardous waste buildings and hauling vehicles must be properly placarded, etc. Personnel who handle or are exposed to hazardous waste may have to undergo particular training. Records of everything from personnel training to manifest copies to hazardous waste accumulation area inspection sheets must be kept for a minimum of three years, although it would be wise to retain those records indefinitely.

Small Quantity Generator (SQG) Storage

According to §262.34(d), SQGs may not store over 6000 kg of hazardous waste on site or else they become a LQG. SQGs must legibly and plainly label hazardous waste containers with the words "hazardous waste" and the date accumulation began. According to §265 Subpart I, containers must always be closed except when adding or removing waste, must not be of material that would react with the contained waste, must be in good condition and containers holding incompatible material must be separated by an impermeable barrier. If a container starts to leak, the owner must place the hazardous materials into a good container.

SQGs that accumulate hazardous waste in tanks must comply with the special requirements of §265.201. This regulation forbids SQGs from mixing incompatible wastes in tanks in ways that would threaten the environment. It also requires a variety of features on tanks to prevent accidents and releases. SQGs must inspect tanks which are in use to ensure that they are structurally sound and not leaking. SQGs also must empty hazardous waste tanks upon facility closure and put ignitable/reactive wastes in tanks only under limited circumstances.

SQGs also must comply with §262.35(d)(5) requirements that the facility designate an **accessible** emergency coordinator. This coordinator should be able either to call the fire department or use an extinguisher to put out fires, to contain spills as much as possible, to clean up hazardous waste spills as soon as possible and to promptly and properly inform the National Response Center when a release may threaten human health outside the facility or has reached surface water. The facility must post this coordinator's name next to the telephone, along with information on spill response equipment and fire extinguishers and the local fire department's number if there is no direct alarm.

Large Quantity Generator (LQG) Storage

Like SQGs, a LQG storing hazardous waste in containers must clearly and legibly label those containers with the words "Hazardous Waste" and the date accumulation started. LQGs must also follow the same regulatory procedures as SQGs for storing hazardous waste containers and they also must create a preparedness and prevention program.

LQGs may also, like SQGs, may store their hazardous waste in tanks, although their regulatory requirements are somewhat stiffer. §265 Subpart J explains the regulatory standards which LQG tank storage must meet. This regulatory program is designed to ensure that tank systems do not leak or explode. Accordingly, §§265.191 and 192 set out provisions for inspecting existing tanks and for designing new tanks and components to ensure that tank systems have adequate strength and compatibility with the waste(s) so as to minimize the potential for a release. Tanks and their associated piping, joints and valves, must have secondary containment and leak detection devices except where §265.193 allows otherwise, in which case leak detection devices or leak tests may still be needed. This subsection sets out a timeline for retrofitting existing tanks with containment and leak detection. The owner/operator must inspect overfill/spill equipment, above ground components, data gathered by monitoring equipment and the area around externally accessible portion of tank systems at least once a day to check for any signs of releases (e.g., the waste itself, wet spots, dead vegetation, erosion). Cathodic protection systems must also be inspected on a regular basis under this regulation. The results of all of these inspections must be entered in the facility's operating record.

LQGs may also store their hazardous wastes on drip pads as long as they comply with §265 Subpart W, have a description of how the drip pads will be cleaned, and document all waste removal from the drip pad and any associated equipment. §265.443 sets out the requirements for designing and operating a drip pad, including that they not be made of earth, that they slope to collection systems, that they are bermed and that they have a certain hydraulic conductivity. Existing drip pads must be inspected by a registered professional engineer to ensure that they meet all the requirements of new pads, except those requirements regarding liners and leak detection devices. The pad must be reassessed and recertified annually, until it has been completely upgraded except for the liners and leak detection systems. The owner of an existing pad must provide EPA with a written upgrade plan at least two years before the upgrade is completed. Leaks in any drip pads must be repaired, following prescribed procedures, in a reasonable amount of time. All drip pads should be inspected weekly and after storms to detect evidence of deterioration, malfunctions, leakage, cracking, or any other evidence of a potential release. When the facility closes, the owner must completely clean up the drip pad, to include waste residues, contaminated containment system components and contaminated subsoils in accordance with §265.445.

The fourth manner of storage available for LQGs is to place their hazardous wastes in containment buildings that are certified by a professional engineer to meet the design standards of 40 CFR §265.1101. The owner/operator of this type of storage must ensure that there is a written plan explaining how the waste will be managed to keep any waste from remaining on site for over 90 days. The owner/operator may avoid the preceding requirements by keeping documentation that the unit is emptied at least once every 90 days. §§265.1100–1102 prescribe additional regulations for this type of storage, including that the unit be completely self-enclosed and self-supporting, will not break up under normal and expected use, prevents fugitive dust emissions, and ensures containment. Units built to contain liquid wastes must meet additional standards such as sloping floors and collection systems. When the containment building closes, the owner/operator must remove or decontaminate all waste residues, contaminated containment system components, and so forth as set forth in §265.1102.

In addition to their particular storage requirements, LQGs need contingency plans as provided in 40 CFR §265 Subpart D. Essentially, a contingency plan should minimize human and environmental hazards from hazardous waste releases. The plan must describe what actions facility staff must take should a release occur. The plan must describe arrangements agreed on by local emergency response agencies to coordinate emergency services; it must list the up-to-date names, addresses, and phone numbers of everyone qualified to act as an emergency coordinator; and it must designate one of the coordinators as the primary one. The plan must include a list of all emergency equipment at the facility, as well as a brief discussion of each piece of equipment and its capabilities. If there is a possibility that the facility may need to be evacuated, the plan should include an evacuation plan. The facility should maintain a copy of the plan, with all revisions, and should submit additional plans to all non-facility emergency response teams who may assist the facility should a release occur.

HAZARDOUS WASTE TRANSPORTERS

Transporters of hazardous waste requiring a hazardous waste manifest must comply with both EPA and DOT regulations. EPA regulations, located in 40 CFR §263, detail the applicable requirements for these transporters. These allow them to transport residue from a hazardous waste discharge without manifests or EPA identification numbers if the appropriate agency official determines that immediate removal is necessary to protect human health or the environment.

These regulations specifically exclude on-site transportation of hazardous waste by generators or TSDF owners.

Transporters need an EPA identification number prior to transporting hazardous waste and may not accept a hazardous waste that is not accompanied by a proper manifest (transporters who ship hazardous waste by rail or by water may find somewhat different regulatory manifesting programs apply per §263.20). The transporter must sign this manifest, leaving a signed copy with the generator prior to leaving the latter's property. This manifest must stay with the hazardous waste, while the transporter must retain his/her copy for at least three years from the date the waste was first transported. Additionally, transporters must appropriately respond to and clean up any hazardous waste discharge that occurs during transportation. Federal, state, or local officials may require the transporter to take specific action in the event of a spill to minimize health and environmental risks.

If a transporter is unable to deliver the waste in accordance with the manifest, the transporter must contact the generator for further directions, revising the manifest as appropriate. When the generator delivers the hazardous waste, whether to another transporter, the facility designated on the manifest, the alternate designated facility, or the place outside the United States designated by the generator, he/she must have the manifest signed by whoever receives the waste. At this point, the transporter keeps one signed copy of the manifest and passes the rest of the multi-copy document on to whoever accepted the waste.

Transporters may store manifested hazardous waste shipments in containers acceptable under §262.30 for up to 10 days without being subject to additional regulations concerning TSDFs, interim TSDFs, and some other RCRA programs. However, transporters who mix hazardous wastes of different DOT shipping descriptions or who import hazardous waste into the United States expand their regulatory requirements and must comply with §262 regulations for hazardous waste generators.

Hazardous waste transporters also must follow DOT regulations for hazardous material shipments. These regulations are located at 40 CFR §§172, 173, 178, and 179. This group of regulatory requirements sets the standards for placarding, packaging, marking, and labeling. While the generator has the responsibility, under 40 CFR §262 Subpart C, to ensure that these requirements are met prior to offering hazardous waste to a transporter, the transporter still has the responsibility to make sure that hazardous waste shipments meet DOT regulations.

Hazardous waste shipments must be in approved packaging in order to be properly transported. Proper packaging will differ from waste to waste depending on the specific hazards posed. DOT hazardous material regulations break hazardous materials into several different classes such as explosive (class one) and flammable liquids (class three). There are nine classes in all, many of which are broken down by divisions into particular hazards such as explosives with a projection hazard and explosives with mostly a fire hazard. §173.2 lists the different class and division numbers. §173 Subpart B sets out general requirements of preparing hazardous waste for transportation, with individual sections discussing requirements on issues ranging from transportation by aircraft to hazardous materials in cargo tank motor vehicles. Subparts C through H each discuss particular packaging requirements and definitions, frequently referring to §178's transportation requirements.

§178 sets out the mass of specific requirements for containers in which hazardous materials or wastes are shipped. Cylinders, portable tanks, and radioactive material packaging are covered in great detail. Subparts L and M describe performance standards and testing procedures for non-bulk packaging. Tank cars shipping hazardous waste must meet the special requirements set forth in 49 CFR §179. This section details the specific structural requirements of tank cars used to transport hazardous waste, covering such areas as thickness of plates, bursting pressure, and safety relief valves for certain types of tank cars.

§172 sets out the labeling, marking, and placarding requirements for hazardous waste transport. Bulk and non-bulk containers each have some unique marking requirements, but all marking must be durable, in English, and printed on or affixed to the container in a clear and legible manner. In §172.101 the Hazardous Materials Table describes the shipping name, along with a variety of other useful information. If the proper DOT shipping name does not identify the hazardous substance by name, §172.324 requires that the waste stream number, EPA waste characteristic or the name of the hazardous substance be marked on the package. Containers must have specific labels as described in Subpart E that clearly demonstrate the hazard posed by the waste. Subpart F requires that carriers of hazardous waste place specific placards on their vehicles depending on the dangers posed by the transported hazardous waste. The CFR is detailed in describing the colors, placement, and use of these placards.

HAZARDOUS WASTE MANIFESTS

To keep track of a hazardous waste, EPA has developed a complex manifesting system. Under this system, hazardous waste may not be offered for transportation, transported, or accepted by any party without a proper manifest. As always, there are exceptions. CESQGs do not need to manifest their hazardous waste. In certain cases where the waste is to be transported and reclaimed by the same contracted party, SQGs may not have to use manifests either. §§262.20–23 explains the manifesting process, providing specific instructions on how to fill out the manifest form itself. Hazardous waste shipped to an on-site TSDF may not require a manifest under §§264.70 and 265.70.

In most cases, the basic functioning of a manifest is as follows: When the waste is removed, the owner must fill out manifest forms that will follow the waste to its final destination. The manifest describes the hazardous waste and must contain the designated recipient of the waste plus one alternate recipient. The initial transporter, and any subsequent transporter, signs the manifest, leaving one copy with the party who formerly had the waste (either the generator or another transporter). When the waste and the accompanying manifest reach the designated recipient, the recipient sends a copy of the manifest back to the waste's original owner. The State or EPA receives copies of the initial manifest when the waste hauler picks up the waste and of the final manifest when it is accepted by a proper treatment, storage, or disposal facility.

The generator's representative who signs the manifest certifies that the hazardous waste to be transported is properly marked, packed, classified and labelled and ready for transport. An LQG's generator's representative must also certify, on the manifest, that the generator has a program in place to reduce the volume and toxicity of waste generated as much as feasible. The certification also requires the LQG to ensure it has selected the best method of treatment, storage or disposal for the environment. SQGs merely have to certify that they are making a good faith effort to minimize waste generation and select the best waste management system that they can affordably obtain.

TREATMENT, STORAGE AND DISPOSAL FACILITIES (TSDFS)

Overview

All hazardous wastes, except those from CESQGs, should eventually wind up at a properly permitted Treatment, Storage and Disposal Facility (TSDF). Hazardous waste that is accepted by an overseas facility is an exception to this rule, although there are strict regulatory requirements governing exportation of hazardous waste in 40 CFR §§262.52–58. Additionally, it is not clear that RCRA §6921(i)'s exclusion of facilities which burn only household waste and commercial nonhazardous waste for energy applies to facilities whose byproducts include hazardous waste.

TSDFs are the most regulated parties involved in hazardous waste management, with their operating requirements listed in 40 CFR §§264 (fully permitted TSDFs) and 265 (interim status TSDFs). Both §264 and §265 have lengthy and detailed descriptions about organizations to whom these regulations do not apply or to whom they apply in only a limited fashion. Examples of the latter organizations include farmers disposing of waste pesticides from personal use in compliance with 40 CFR §262.70, generators accumulating waste on site in accordance with §262.34, transporters, and parties responding to hazardous waste releases. Under §265(c)(11)(iii), a party that continues or initiates hazardous waste treatment or containment activities after the immediate response is over becomes subject to the regulations for the duration of those activities.

TSDFs must have permits under §270. When generators store their hazardous waste beyond their allowable timeline they are considered **unpermitted** TSDFs.

Fully Permitted TSDFs

Although fully permitted TSDFs have a separate CFR section from interim TSDFs, the regulatory requirements for each are identical in most areas.

Fully permitted TSDFs are governed by the extensive regulations set forth in §264. Some TSDFs, such as incinerators and landfills, must also comply with special subparts which provide additional regulatory guidance. Most major issues concerning TSDFs are also dealt with in separate subparts.

All TSDFs must have a preparedness and prevention program, a contingency plan, and designated emergency procedures as detailed in subparts C and D. In these areas, as well as in the use and management of containers, waste piles, containment buildings, and drip pads and the need for an EPA identification number, TSDFs must essentially meet the same regulatory standards as Large Quantity Generators. These issues are dealt with in detail in the section on storage for LQGs.

Given their more intimate connection with hazardous wastes, it is logical that TSDFs must also meet standards that are not applicable to LQGs. §264.14 requires extensive security precautions for TSDFs, including a 24-hour surveillance system or a fence and controlled gate unless the TSDF can prove such precautions are unnecessary. §264.15 directs TSDFs to establish a written, regular inspection program, the results of which must be entered into a log. §264.16 specifies that a formal training program, through either on the job training or classroom instruction, must exist to ensure that employees can respond appropriately to hazardous waste releases and incidents at the facility. Management of this program, which must cover each employee within six months of the employees need for the particular training, has exacting standards.

Location of TSDFs is governed under §264.18, which raises concerns about TSDF siting on 100-year floodplains, on faults and in salt domes. Construction at a TSDF must be monitored for quality assurance following the procedures set out in §264.19.

At least four weeks prior to the expected date for accepting a hazardous waste shipment, the facility must notify the EPA Regional Administrator in writing of the expected shipment. The facility must also notify the generator, except where the same company is both the TSDF and the generator, that it has the proper permits and will accept the shipped waste. Before treating, disposing, or storing a hazardous waste, as well as certain nonhazardous wastes, §264.13 dictates that the TSDF obtain all chemical and physical information needed to properly handle that waste. This information may be obtained through analysis or from a knowledge of waste obtained through a similar process. The TSDF must have a written plan for how it plans to obtain and verify this knowledge.

In addition to the manifesting requirements discussed above, TSDFs must follow additional record keeping and reporting procedures spelled out in Subpart E. The TSDF's operating record, detailed in §264.73, must contain the location, type, treatment/storage/disposal methods and dates, relevant manifest numbers, and quantity of all hazardous waste within the facility. The record must also have summaries of all incidents requiring implementation of the contingency plan, closure cost estimates and considerable amounts of other information. The TSDF must submit a variety of reports to EPA, including a detailed operational report by March 1st of every even numbered year, notification of any unresolved manifest discrepancies and reports of certain hazardous waste releases.

TSDFs that include surface impoundments, landfills and/or land treatment units must comply with §264 Subpart F requirement for groundwater monitoring. According to §§264.97 and 264.98, this monitoring must include enough wells to determine the quality of unaffected "background" water as well as the quality of groundwater downgradient of the facility. After establishing "indicator" parameters to help determine hazardous materials in the groundwater, the TSDF must notify EPA if these parameters indicate a significant increase in contamination from the facility. Should such an increase occur, the TSDF must follow §264.99, which focuses on additional monitoring and amending the TSDF permit to include a description of a corrective action plan. At some point, not beyond a reasonable time after the excessive contamination is detected, a TSDF may be required to take corrective actions under §264.100 to achieve the groundwater protection standard specified in the facility's permit.

TSDFs must also be concerned with closure and post-closure requirements. Given the hazardous nature of their business, these facilities cannot close up shop without following very detailed regulatory guidance. According to §264 Subpart G, closure must occur in a manner that protects human health and the environment. Additionally, a facility that is operating any systems governed by specific regulatory subparts, such as tank systems or waste piles, must follow the relevant subpart's closure guidance for those specific systems. Most notable among these closure requirements is that the 30 years of extensive post-closure monitoring required for landfills also applies to most other TSDF systems and subsoils that cannot be completely cleaned.

The facility cannot just carry out the required closure requirements. It also must have a written closure plan. This closure plan should describe how each hazardous waste management unit will be properly closed and should contain a detailed description of the steps needed to remove or decontaminate all contaminated containment systems and equipment. It is the responsibility of the TSDF to amend the closure plan under certain conditions. The TSDF must request the amendment at least 60 days before a planned event, or no later than 60 days after an unplanned event, causes a significant change in the proposed closure process.

§264.113 requires that all hazardous waste must be treated, removed, or disposed of on site within 90 days of a facility's accepting its final shipment of hazardous waste. Within 180 days, all closure action must be finished. EPA may extend these time periods if it so desires. A TSDF may continue to accept *nonhazardous* wastes and may delay completion of closure under certain conditions specified in §264.113(b).

Post-closure plans also are required for TSDFs under §264.118. Like closure plans, post-closure plans must be written. These plans must include a description of planned monitoring activities, procedures to ensure that the cap and any containment systems remain sound and the names and addresses of relevant points of contacts. Post-closure plans may be amended as needed, and the TSDF has an affirmative duty to amend them when certain material conditions change.

TSDFs also must follow exceptionally detailed guidelines concerning financial requirements, except as they can demonstrate that these requirements are not applicable to them. This financial program is set forth in §264 Subpart H. The basic thrust behind this program is that active TSDFs must have insurance to cover accidental and non-accidental occurrences. Also, they must have enough money to cover closure and post-closure expenses as needed. These last expenses may be covered by a designated trust fund, a surety bond, a corporate guarantee, or a variety of other measures listed in §264.143 and §264.145. §§264.142 and 264.144 explain the process for the mandatory closure and post-closure expense analyses.

40 CFR §270.1(c) requires that some land disposal facilities such as landfills, waste pile units, and surface impoundments obtain a post-closure permit. This program applies to facilities that received wastes after July 26, 1982, or that certified closure after January 26, 1983. Post-closure permits incorporate §6924(u) of the Act's requirement that hazardous waste releases, regardless of when they took place, be matched by a corrective action plan (see below).

Interim Treatment, Storage and Disposal Facilities

§6925(e) of the Act allows a facility which was in existence either on November 19, 1980 or at a later time when new RCRA regulations brought it into the regulatory program, to continue in operation in an interim status. To qualify for this status, the facility must have notified EPA of its hazardous waste activity in accordance with §6930(a) of the Act and must have submitted a complete TSDF permit application.

These interim TSDFs are governed by 40 CFR §265, which establishes a regulatory program almost identical to that governing fully permitted TSDFs. Individual sections of §265 tend to mirror the same section numbers in §264.

TSDF Permits

Overview

In order to be either an interim TSDF or a fully permitted TSDF, a facility must apply for and receive a permit as detailed in §6925 of the Act and 40 CFR 270. Permit applications must be signed by a responsible corporate officer, the proprietor, a principal executive officer, or some similarly responsible individual. TSDF permits are expensive. It may cost up to a million dollars just to obtain the permit, not counting the actual costs of construction projects and doing business. EPA or the issuing agency may deny permit applications in whole or in part, and may revoke a permit for failure to meet permit or general TSDF standards. Permitted facilities which generate hazardous waste must certify annually that they have a hazardous waste reduction plan and that the proposed method of treatment, disposal, or storage most efficiently minimizes the threat to human health and the environment. In addition to permit requirements under this section, the issuing authority may incorporate specific technical requirements discussed in 40 CFR §§264, 266, and 267.

TSDF Permit Applications

Permit application requirements for virtually all proposed TSDFs are set forth in §270.13 and §270.14. The first section, part A of the permit application, requires such basic information as the facility's mailing address, the facility's RCRA regulated activities, and a listing of other permits received or applied for. Part B of the permit application is considerably more complicated. §270.14 sets out these general requirements, such as a general description of the facility, a copy of its waste analysis plan(s), a copy of its security procedures, and a description of its release prevention procedures and equipment.

§270.14 also implements §6924(u) of the Act, which requires that any facility seeking a permit must implement a corrective action program for hazardous waste releases. Even if the waste was not considered a hazardous waste at the time it was discarded, if it has since become a hazardous waste, either by being listed or by developing a hazardous waste characteristic, and is leaking, it will require a corrective action program. 40 CFR §270.14(c) explains the requirements for corrective action and groundwater monitoring plans. As the contamination of the groundwater increases, the complexity of the groundwater monitoring and corrective action plans, and their probable expense, increase also. For groundwater contamination above specified levels, subparagraphs §270.14(c)(7) and (8) require corrective action programs. These two subparagraphs incorporate the corrective action program requirements of §264.99 and §264.100, as well as specifically requiring detailed descriptions of the wastes previously handled at the facility, the proposed groundwater monitoring system and the corrective action plan.

Part B of the permit application has specific requirements for a variety of unique hazardous waste management and handling facilities and procedures. These requirements are listed in §270 subpart B, and include specific part B information requirements for drip pads, surface impoundments, landfills, tank systems and other similar areas. These sections also incorporate many of §264 requirements for those systems, which means that the operating requirements of §264 become part of the final permit.

TSDF Permit Requirements

A TSDF permit brings with it a large number of conditions. Under §270 Subpart C, the permitted TSDF has the duty to comply with the requirements of the permit. There is an affirmative duty to reapply prior to a permit running out. TSDFs must operate and maintain their facilities to comply with the permit, including ensuring appropriate funding and staffing levels and adequate quality assurance programs. All reports and information must be signed by the same responsible individual who signed the original application or by a properly designated representative.

Under §270 Subpart D, permits may be changed as conditions dictate. Permit alterations would be probable for such occurrences as a change in relevant laws and regulations, a determination by EPA that a compliance schedule needs modification because of some occurrence beyond the TSDF control, or a material addition to the TSDF that is not covered in the existing permit. TSDFs may request modification in accordance with §270.42 or EPA may modify or revoke/reissue a permit of its own volition, as in §270.43.

TSDF permits may not be granted for more than 10 years, and generally cannot be extended by modification beyond that time. Subpart E allows EPA to issue permits for less than 10 years, and requires the Agency to review land disposal permits every five years to determine if modification is necessary. If a TSDF has submitted its permit reapplication in a timely manner and receives no response, §270.51 allows the TSDF to use a sort of "permit shield" rule and follow the existing permit until the Agency acts on the reapplication.

Special Permits

§270 Subpart F lists several types of special operations that have unique permit requirements. Possibly the most important of these special permits is the temporary emergency permit of §270.61. This permit may be either written or oral, and applies when there is an imminent and substantial endangerment to human health or the environment. These emergency permits should incorporate, as much as is possible under the circumstances, the requirements of

40 CFR §§264 and 266. Other special permits include hazardous waste incinerator and research, development, and demonstration permits.

Used Oil

While used oil is not a RCRA federally regulated hazardous waste, there is a specific regulatory program governing the management of such oil. However, waste oil is a hazardous waste in some states such as Massachusetts. Further, even where normal waste oil is not considered a RCRA waste, contamination in the oil from improperly disposed RCRA hazardous wastes or from unusual operating conditions may make some batches of waste oil hazardous under RCRA. This management program is located at 40 CFR §279 and covers used or waste oil such as that recovered by automobile shops. Used oil regulations also cover materials contaminated with used oil, which are burned for energy recovery, used oil removed from materials contaminated with used oil, and mixtures of used oil and other fuel products. The exception to this rule is that a generator of waste oil may mix the oil on-site with diesel fuel and use it in his/her own vehicles without it being regulated as used oil.

Used oil burned for energy recovery is not subject to federal used oil regulations under §279.11 if it meets certain listed characteristics.

§279.10 states that used oil may be considered a RCRA hazardous waste under certain circumstances. If used oil has been mixed with a listed hazardous waste, the mixture becomes hazardous waste. The exception to this rule is when the waste was listed only because it exhibited hazardous waste characteristics, the waste/used oil mixture will be hazardous only if it also displays hazardous characteristics. If used oil has been mixed with a *characteristic* hazardous waste, it becomes a hazardous waste if the waste/used oil mixture also exhibits hazardous waste characteristics. If used oil contains over 1,000 ppm total halogens, it will generally be considered hazardous waste unless analytical data proves the oil was not mixed with a listed hazardous waste. Used oil that itself has hazardous waste characteristics is considered a hazardous waste unless it is burned on-site in a space heater of under 0.5 million Btu/hour, in which case §279.23 dictates that it be treated merely as used oil.

Used oil that is not considered hazardous waste may be stored in above ground storage tanks (ASTs), underground storage tanks (USTs), or containers. Containers and ASTs must be in good condition and not leaking. These containers must be clearly marked "Used Oil," as must the fill pipes used to transfer used oil into USTs. USTs themselves are subject to considerably more regulatory requirements under 40 CFR §280. Requirements for ASTs and USTs are covered in more detail elsewhere in this book.

If a facility can store over 42,000 gallons of oil (including used oil) in USTs, has the potential to store over 1,320 gallons of oil above ground, or has an AST of over 660 gallons, it may need to have a Spill Prevention, Control, and Countermeasure Plan.

If a facility has a release of used oil from any above ground container or any UST with a capacity of no more than 110 gallons, it must undertake several actions consistent with §279.22. The facility must stop and contain the release, clean up the released used oil, and repair or replace leaking containers as needed prior to reusing them. Releases of used oil from USTs of over 110 gallons are subject to the requirements of §280 Subpart F.

Used oil that is not properly burned on site should be removed from the facility by a transporter with an EPA Identification Number as in §279.24. One exception to this rule is that generators may transport up to 55 gallons of used oil at a time to a proper used oil collection center without needing an EPA identification number. Additionally, a used oil transporter does not need an EPA Identification Number if the oil will be reclaimed by the facility which transports it. There must be a contract stating that the generator will eventually receive the reclaimed oil for use as a coolant, lubricant, or cutting oil.

PCBs

Under RCRA, PCBs are not considered hazardous wastes and thus are not automatically regulated under this program. PCBs are hazardous substances, however, and when present at levels above 50 ppm are regulated under the Toxic Substances Control Act. Additionally, as PCBs are removed from use and become waste, the various states may choose to regulate wastes as hazardous wastes if they have PCB concentrations of over 50 ppm.

STATE RCRA PROGRAMS

Although RCRA is a federal law, most hazardous waste enforcement programs are actually run at the state level. As this book was written, only California, Wyoming, Iowa, and Connecticut did not manage their own hazardous waste regulatory programs.

§3006(b) allows EPA to approve state hazardous waste management programs that are equivalent to the federal program, are consistent with federal and other state programs, and provide adequate enforcement provisions.

40 CFR §271.21 requires that states update their RCRA programs on a periodic basis to keep current with changes in the federal RCRA program. These state modifications generally occur each July. CFR additions implementing HSWA provisions take effect immediately in all states. In §271.1(j), Table 1 provides a list of these additions.

In states which run their own programs, only the state regulations apply, and federal regulations are relevant only when incorporated by reference. States are allowed to promulgate hazardous waste regulations that are more stringent than the federal standards, but their regulations may not be weaker. Some states will follow the federal RCRA program closely, while others will deviate significantly. Although all states must operate within the same general RCRA standards, there is plenty of room for regulatory differences.

Even in states where EPA has ceded the hazardous waste program to the state government, the EPA still retains considerable enforcement powers. If a state is not administering or enforcing its hazardous waste program in keeping with RCRA requirements, EPA may terminate that state's authority to run its own program.

Because state RCRA programs become "federalized" when they receive EPA approval, the Agency may go to court to enforce state RCRA provisions. EPA may also "overfile" and conduct enforcement actions where it believes a state's parallel actions will be clearly inadequate. Under 40 CFR §271.1, however, EPA is limited to enforcing state RCRA provisions that are no broader in scope than the federal RCRA program.

ENVIRONMENTAL COMPLIANCE

RCRA General Overview

By reviewing the major RCRA definitions, a compliance officer should be able to determine if he/she has any regulated RCRA materials. If there are such materials, other definitions should allow determination as to which regulations apply. At that point, the compliance officer will be well on the way to bringing the facility into compliance and making sure it stays there.

Solid Waste

Checklist:

1. Review the facility's wastestream against RCRA's "solid waste" definitions.

2. If there is no "solid waste," no compliance program is needed. **Note:** Other laws may cover nonsolid waste such as sewage.

3. If there is "solid waste," proceed to determine if the waste is hazardous under RCRA.

A compliance officer should study both the Act's and §261's definitions of solid waste, with their respective exclusions, to ensure that the material produced or stored by the company or agency is properly categorized. If the compliance officer has any doubts, he/she should check with the state and EPA and document their comments.

The compliance officer should review the post-use "nonsolid waste" stream to determine if any material may be subject to other regulatory programs. If there are any doubts, they should be voiced to the appropriate state and EPA officials and their responses documented.

Hazardous Waste

> **Checklist:**
>
> Inspect the solid waste stream to determine if any wastes meet the RCRA definition of "hazardous".
>
> 1. No wastes defined as hazardous - no RCRA compliance program needed.
>
> 2. Waste is defined as hazardous - compliance program is needed as discussed in this chapter.

A compliance officer should not be disheartened at the complexities of the hazardous-waste numbering system, since approximately one-third of all calls to the EPA RCRA hotline are from people trying to determine whether a given material constitutes a hazardous waste.

On a daily level, mixtures of hazardous waste contaminating nonhazardous waste are most likely to happen when workers pour hazardous waste in drums full of nonhazardous material such as water or motor oil. Other likely points of contamination are dumpsters and trash cans, where coatings of hazardous waste may be impossible to remove from otherwise nonhazardous solid wastes.

One way to alleviate the risks of improper mixture is by locking facility dumpsters and limiting access to bulk liquid storage areas. Near each disposal site, and in other prominent areas throughout the facility, a flier should warn workers of the dangers of potential hazardous waste contamination, listing likely hazardous wastes to be improperly disposed of in the main waste-stream. This flier should stress that empty containers may actually be considered hazardous waste. People planning to dump questionable objects in the disposal site should be directed to contact a specific person or office prior to disposing of the object. Periodic field checks through the solid wastestream will ensure that the risk of improper disposal and resultant contamination is minimized.

Empty Containers

> **Checklist:**
>
> Does the facility receive hazardous material or hazardous waste in containers?
>
> No: This section is not relevant.

Empty Containers (continued)

> **Checklist:**
>
> Yes: Ensure that containers previously holding hazardous waste or hazardous material are "empty" prior to disposing of them as regular nonhazardous solid waste. If not "empty," dispose of containers as a hazardous waste.
>
> **Note:** Acute hazardous waste containers need special cleaning prior to being "empty."

Leachate

> **Checklist:**
>
> Does the facility have leachate from a landfill or spill residue from a release?
>
> No: No compliance issues present.
>
> Yes: Determine if material is a listed hazardous waste or exhibits hazardous waste characteristics. If it meets these standards for hazardous waste, the material must be managed as such. If the material does not meet hazardous waste standards, it may be managed as regular waste.

Hazardous Waste Recycling

> **Checklist :**
>
> Does the facility recycle hazardous waste?
>
> No: This compliance section is not relevant.
> Yes: Is the recycling program covered by an exemption in the CFR?
>
> Yes: Double-check with state/EPA. Document. No specific recycling compliance program needed.
> No: Follow general hazardous waste and specific recycling regulations.

Land Disposal

Checklist:

Does the facility generate hazardous waste?

    No: No compliance program needed.
    Yes: Determine if hazardous waste is a land ban waste (most are).

If hazardous waste is not a Land Ban Waste, this section does not apply.

If hazardous waste is a Land Ban Waste, do exemptions apply to the facility?

    Yes: Double-check with state/EPA. Document. Land Ban regulations do not apply to the facility.
    No: Treat Land Ban Wastes per CFR prior to disposal.

Treatment

Checklist :

Does waste stream include land ban wastes?

    No: No compliance program needed.

    Yes: Land ban wastes must be treated per specific CFR guidance prior to disposal. Waste analysis and record keeping for treatment facilities must follow regulatory requirements.

    Note: Dilution of wastes is permissible only under limited circumstances.

Under §268.7(a), it is the generator's responsibility to determine if the waste is covered by the land ban, and, if so, to notify the appropriate TSDF of the relevant treatment standard. Generators must retain records of this determination as well as documentation of what happened to its Land Ban Wastes.

HAZARDOUS WASTE GENERATORS

Fortunately for the compliance officer, not all generators are subject to the same regulations. The compliance officer should check with the state agency to ensure that he/she understands how much hazardous waste generation determines the type of hazardous waste generator and the specific regulatory programs that apply to that specific facility.

Types of Generators

Checklist :

Does your facility generate *any* hazardous waste?

No: No compliance program needed.

Yes: Determine how much hazardous waste and acute hazardous waste the facility generates and/or stores on a monthly basis. This amount will determine the generator size and corresponding regulatory requirements.

Extensions

Checklist :

Has hazardous waste been accumulated on site for a period approaching the legal limit?

No: Ensure waste is removed or disposed of on schedule.

Yes: Consider applying for an extension.

If a generator without a TSDF permit retains hazardous waste beyond the allowable 90, 180, or 270 day limits, that generator has, in theory at least, become a Treatment, Storage, or Disposal Facility (TSDF) and is operating as such without a permit. Unpermitted TSDFs expose their owners to considerable liabilities, so a compliance officer who is going to be unable to remove hazardous waste from a site within the relevant time limit may wish to ask EPA for an extension under §262.34. The EPA Regional Administrator may grant an extension for up to 30 days on a case-by-case basis.

Exception Reports

> **Checklist :**
>
> Does your facility have final copies of all hazardous waste manifests indicating that they were accepted by the designated recipient?
>
> Yes: No compliance issues raised.
>
> No: Complete and file exception reports per CFR requirements.

If a generator does not receive its hazardous waste manifest signed by the owner/operator of the receiving facility, §262.42 requires that certain steps be taken. LQGs who have not received the copy of the manifest within 35 days of shipment must contact the designated facility to determine the status of their shipped waste. If the LQG still does not have the signed manifest copy 10 days later, 45 days after initial shipment, the generator must file an exception report with the EPA Regional Administrator. This exception report must include a legible copy of the relevant manifest and a letter explaining the generator's attempts to locate the missing hazardous waste.

Small Quantity Generators have 60 days after shipment before they have to submit an exception report consisting of a copy of the manifest and an indication that there has been no confirmation of the delivery of the waste.

CESQGs do not have to file exception reports as their hazardous wastes do not need to be manifested.

Satellite Accumulation

> **Checklist :**
>
> Does your facility accumulate hazardous waste at the generation point?
>
> No: No compliance issues raised.
>
> Yes: Ensure satellite accumulation area meets CFR requirements, especially regarding the amounts of waste allowed in this area and how quickly wastes must be removed.

All generators are allowed, under §262.34(c)(1), to store small amounts of hazardous waste at the point of generation for over 90 days with no need for a permit or for complying with many of this sub-section's requirements. Generators may accumulate up to 55 gallons of hazardous waste or one quart of acute hazardous waste in their accumulation areas. It is not clear whether the 55 gallons is the total of all hazardous wastes at the satellite accumulation point, or if it is 55 gallons per hazardous waste stream. The compliance officer should check with the state agency to determine the local protocol, making sure to document the response.

These waste containers must be in good repair, be closed when not in use, be marked in a manner identifying the contents as hazardous waste, and be compatible with the waste they contain. Wastes in the accumulation area may remain there until the container is full, at which point the generator has three days during which to bring the container into compliance with general RCRA regulations regarding storage and handling, i.e., move the hazardous waste to the facility's hazardous waste storage area.

Small Quantity Generator (SQG) Storage

Checklist :

Review the hazardous waste stream to determine if the facility is a small or large quantity generator.

SQG: Follow the directions in this section, including preparedness and prevention requirements, storage tank regulations, and designating an emergency coordinator.

LQG: Follow the directions in the next section.

The compliance officer must ensure that hazardous waste containers are inspected on a weekly basis for labeling, that they are being kept closed and not leaking, and that containers holding incompatible material are separated by an impermeable barrier.

SQGs must ensure that their hazardous waste accumulation areas meet preparedness and prevention requirements set forth in §265 Subpart C. This subsection dictates that facilities be operated to minimize risk of explosions, fires, releases, or other threats to human health or the environment. Depending on the hazards the facility handles, it may need portable fire extinguishers, spill control equipment, an internal alarm system or other emergency equipment. Similarly, depending on the hazards handled by the facility, personnel may need immediate access to another employee when handling hazardous waste. Regardless of the hazards in the accumulation area, there must be enough aisle space to allow emergency personnel and equipment to operate there as necessary.

Additionally, the owner of the facility must coordinate with local authorities such as the police and fire departments, local hospitals and state emergency response authorities to familiarize those parties with the risks presented at the facility and possible emergency response actions. If more than one police and fire department may respond to an emergency, the compliance officer should make arrangements as to who will have primary authority and who will provide support. The compliance officer must document those instances where a state or local authority refuses to enter into an arrangement regarding emergency response.

Large Quantity Generator Storage

Checklist :

Review the facility's waste stream to determine if the facility is a small or large quantity generator.

SQG: Follow the requirements discussed above.

LQG: Follow all SQG requirements, plus special regulations concerning tanks, drip pads, containment buildings. Ensure facility has a proper contingency plan, meets prevention and preparedness requirements, and has appropriate emergency coordinator(s).

LQGs have four storage options available to them. These options, with their relevant control requirements, are set forth in 40 CFR §262.34(a). Unfortunately for the compliance officer, this section is actually quite complicated because, in addition to providing specific regulatory guidance, it incorporates many subparts of 40 CFR §265.

LQGs' emergency coordinators, whose qualifications and responsibilities are listed in §§265.55 and 265.56, must be considerably more sophisticated than their SQG counterparts. LQG coordinators must be intimately familiar with all aspects of the facility's contingency plan, must be able to notify state or local responders as needed, must be able to immediately identify the character, source, and amount of released materials, and must be able to perform a variety of other important functions should a release occur. Most importantly, the coordinator must take all reasonable measures necessary to ensure that a release does not occur, recur or spread to other hazardous waste at the facility. These containment measures specifically include stopping operations and processes.

Hazardous Waste Transporters

> **Checklist :**
>
> Do you transport hazardous waste?
>
> No: No compliance issues are raised.
> Yes: Is the hazardous waste transported completely on site by the generator or TSDF?
>
> Yes: No special transporter requirements.
> No: Follow manifesting, storage, spill response, and other requirements per the CFR. Ensure hazardous wastes are packaged, labeled, and placarded according to the particular hazards they present.

A compliance officer shipping hazardous waste should review each subpart of §178 to determine if any of the containers are regulated by these programs.

Because labeling, marking, and placarding requirements are going to vary according to the type of waste and the type of transportation, the compliance officer should review §172's list of contents to determine which particular sections apply to the transported hazardous waste.

Hazardous Waste Manifests

> **Checklist :**
>
> Is hazardous waste shipped offsite by an LQG, SQG, or TSDF?
>
> No: No compliance program needed.
>
> Yes: Manifesting of hazardous waste is required. Ensure manifest is completed, signed, remains with the waste, and, upon arrival at the destination, that the state agency gets a copy. File exception reports as discussed above.
>
> Develop a plan to reduce the volume and toxicity of waste (LQG) or make good faith efforts to minimize waste generation (SQG). Both sizes of generators must select the most effective method of treatment, storage, or disposal.

Fully Permitted TSDFs

Checklist :

Does the facility treat or dispose of hazardous waste or store hazardous waste for longer periods than allowed generators?

No: No compliance program needed.
Yes: Has the facility received a permit for TSDF activities?

No: Refer to section on interim TSDFs.
Yes: Ensure compliance with 40 CFR §264, including requirements for security, training, waste analysis, record keeping, groundwater monitoring, closure and postclosure plans and operations, financial security, and postclosure permits as needed.

While some records, such as manifests, do not have to be kept indefinitely, it would be wise to retain these records forever. Should a TSDF become subject to an enforcement action, all record retention periods are automatically extended as needed by the enforcing agency.

Interim Treatment, Storage and Disposal Facilities

Checklist :

Does the facility treat or dispose of hazardous waste or store hazardous waste for longer periods than allowed generators?

No: No compliance program needed.
Yes: Has the facility received a permit for TSDF activities?

Yes: Refer to section on fully permitted TSDFs.
No: Ensure compliance with 40 CFR §265, including requirements for security, training, waste analysis, record keeping, groundwater monitoring, closure and postclosure plans and operations, financial security, and postclosure permits as needed.

Compliance officers responsible for interim status TSDFs should review the requirements discussed above for fully permitted facilities and then check individual sections of §264 for specific implementation processes.

Land disposal facilities that are granted interim status must certify that they are in compliance with all applicable groundwater monitoring and financial responsibility requirements within 12 months of becoming regulated or they will lose their interim status.

Additional Operating Specifications for Certain Facilities

Checklist :

Determine if the facility is of a type specifically listed in §266 and §267.

If so, additional hazardous waste management guidelines apply.

40 CFR §§266 and 267 set out specific guidelines for particular hazardous waste management facilities and new land disposal facilities. These guidelines are only appropriate to facilities which burn hazardous waste, recycle materials in a manner constituting disposal, reclaim spent lead-acid batteries, and recover precious metals. The new land disposal facilities covered by §267 include facilities utilizing underground injection, land treatment, surface impoundments, and landfills. If a compliance officer's facilities do not fall into any of these categories, he/she does not have to worry about complying with these sections.

TSDF Permit Applications

Checklist :

Is the facility a TSDF?

No: No TSDF permit requirements.

Yes: TSDF permit required. Complete per §§270.14 and 270.15, including a corrective action program for hazardous waste releases.

40 CFR §270.60 contains a lengthy list of facilities which are deemed, by regulation, to already have RCRA permits if they meet certain listed conditions. The compliance officer should review this list to ensure that the facility does not already have an effective "permit" under this section.

TSDF Permit Requirements

Checklist :

Does your TSDF have a permit?

No: Apply for a TSDF permit.

Yes: Ensure that facility meets specific requirements of permit *and* requirements incorporated by reference. Submit permit reapplication prior to the permit expiration.

Given the considerable legal liabilities, both criminal and civil, that RCRA imposes, senior officials will probably want to scrutinize the compliance officer's records to ensure that they will not be getting themselves into trouble when signing documents.

Used Oil

Checklist :

Does the facility create used oil?

No: No compliance program needed.
Yes: Is the used oil considered a hazardous waste per state or federal regulations?

Yes: Manage as hazardous waste in most circumstances.
No: Manage as used oil. Store in properly marked and managed containers or tanks, develop an SPCCP as needed, and remove via a proper transporter.

Note: Some facilities may burn used oil in space heaters even if it exhibits hazardous waste characteristics.

PCBs

A compliance officer should contact the state environmental agency to determine if, and at what level, PCB wastes are governed by RCRA regulations.

State RCRA Programs

Checklist :

Does the facility's state run its RCRA program (most do)?

    No: Follow EPA regulations.

    Yes: Follow state regulations.

Note: State RCRA regulations will mimic EPA regulations in most regards. Some differences may be significant, however, so the compliance officer should double-check requirements with the state.

GLOSSARY

100-Year Floodplains . . . . Geographic locations that are flooded on the average of once every 100 years.

Cathodic Protection Systems . . Inexpensive systems that protect a tank against corrosion by themselves corroding instead of the tank.

Flammable. . . . . Capable of being easily ignited.

Halogens . . . . Chemicals from the group of chlorides, fluorides, bromides, and iodides.

Irrigation Return Flow . . . . The irrigation water that runs off to a nearby water body.

Leachate . . . . The liquid that has percolated out from a solid material.

Recycling. . . . . The reuse of a waste material in the process from which it was derived.

Salt Domes . . . . Intrusion of fossil sedimentary salt into overlying rock resulting from great pressure. Salt domes tend to be located around the Gulf Coast.

Satellite Accumulation . . . . Accumulation of a hazardous waste at a location other than that at which it was generated.

Virgin Products . . . . Materials that have not yet been used.

REFERENCES LISTED AND SELECTED READINGS

Mackenthun, K.M. and Bregman, J.I., 1992, *Environmental Regulations Handbook*, Lewis Publishers, Boca Raton, FL.

National Association of Manufacturers, 1989, "Waste Minimization: Manufacturers' Strategies for Success," Washington, D.C.

U.S. Army Corps of Engineers, Construction Engineering Research Laboratories, November, 1994, "The Environmental Assessment and Management (TEAM) Guide," USACERL Special Report EC-95/05, Champaign, IL.

U.S. Department of Energy, August, 1995, "Guidance Document Publications List," Office of Environmental Policy and Assistance, RCRA/CERCLA Division (EH-413), Washington, D.C.

8   Hazardous Substance Contamination Remediation

GENERAL OVERVIEW

Hazardous substance removal, remediation, and response projects from abandoned sites are governed by the Comprehensive Environmental Response, Compensation, and Liability Act (CERCLA), 42 USC §§9601–9675. Congress instituted this Act, commonly known as "Superfund," in 1980 and reauthorized and amended it in 1986 through the Superfund Amendments and Reauthorization Act (SARA).

There is a fine line between the meaning of the terms "remediation," "removal," and "response." §9601(23) defines "removal" as the cleanup or removal of released hazardous substances from the environment, actions taken in the event of a threat of release, evaluation actions, and so forth. "Remedial action" is defined in §9601(24) as being those actions consistent with permanent remedy taken instead of or in addition to removal actions. "Response" actions include both remedial and removal actions. Although these terms may be interchanged in general discussions without much harm, parties involved with a CERCLA action should be sure to use the correct terms.

CERCLA is unique among environmental laws in that it does not focus much effort on regulating current behavior, but instead sets out a program for "cleaning up" the results of past actions or present day spills. Hazardous substance cleanups must follow certain criteria and sites must be "clean" according to EPA before the cleanup can stop. CERCLA authorizes the federal government, states, private parties, and Indian tribes to clean up polluted sites and to impose liability on others to recover some or all of the cleanup costs. The regulatory program of the Act, along with a variety of interpretory court decisions, sets out the limits of CERCLA liability and defines the rules parties must follow to invoke such liability on others. Because a site is undergoing a CERCLA cleanup does not mean that it cannot be used for other activities at the same time. Many chemical plants, military bases, and arsenals contain "Superfund" cleanup sites but still function in their original capacities.

CERCLA compliance programs may be broken into three main parts. The first part involves the only major behavioral requirement, which in §9603 directs facilities to report certain releases of hazardous substances. The second main compliance issue posed by CERCLA is EPA's ability either to respond to a contamination incident on its own under §9604 or to direct a facility, under §9606, to conduct certain cleanup actions. Finally, a compliance officer must be well versed in the liability issues presented by both CERCLA and by courts interpreting the Act. An interesting, and, to a compliance officer potentially crucial, twist to CERCLA's regulatory scheme are the bounty provisions of §9609(d) which allow awards of up to $10,000 for information leading to the conviction of any person for a violation subject to one of CERCLA's criminal penalties. Similarly, §9610's "Whistle Blower" provisions create statutory protection for employees who provide information to the government concerning CERCLA offenses.

NOTIFICATION REQUIREMENTS

§9603 of the Act requires "any person in charge" of a vessel or "facility" to notify the National Response Center (1-800-424-8802) should an unpermitted release of a hazardous substance above a specific quantity take place. "Facility" is defined as "Any building,...pond,...motor vehicle,...or (B) any site...where a hazardous substance has been...placed..." 40 CFR §302 explains this program in detail, adding the caveats that the release take place within any 24-hour period, that the release not result solely in exposure within the workplace, that the release not be an engine exhaust emission, and that the release not be the result of a defined nuclear incident. Notification is intended to alert the authorities to incidents that may potentially require a response action. It is significant for notification requirements, as well as for liability purposes as discussed below, that the release not be federally permitted. Logically, a federal permit to release hazardous substances precludes a facility from having to report those releases unless directed to do so by the permit. Failure to provide prompt notification of a release after gaining knowledge of it can result in significant criminal and civil liabilities for the person in charge of the relevant vessel or facility. Similarly, knowingly submitting a false or inaccurate notification may also result in significant penalties. These penalties include up to 5 years in prison and fines or penalties of up to $25,000 per day.

REMEDIATION ACTIONS

Overview

The true heart of CERCLA is the manner in which EPA either can conduct remediation actions itself or force a facility to conduct them. CERCLA's primary goal is to speed the cleanup of toxic dump sites.

This remediation portion of CERCLA revolves around EPA's response authority under §9604 and its authority under §9606(a) to issue cleanup orders itself or seek judicial cleanup orders. Additionally, §9659 allows citizens to file lawsuits to seek, among other things, judicial implementation of CER-CLA's remediation program.

Regardless of which section of the Act it looks to for authorization, EPA may act in response to actual or threatened releases of hazardous substances. A "release," defined as including "spilling, leaking, pumping...or disposing into the environment...," is a very broad term that covers any time a hazardous substance gets into the environment and is no longer under a facility's control. Under §9601(22), "release" specifically excludes an occurrence which results in exposure to persons solely within a workplace, engine exhausts, certain nuclear incidents, and the normal application of fertilizer. "Threatened" releases are generally present when a hazardous substance is present at a facility and that facility refuses to assert control over it. Given the great scope of these key terms, EPA's ability to act under CERCLA is broad indeed.

RESPONSE ACTIONS

§9604(a) allows, but does not command, EPA to spend "Superfund" dollars to respond to releases or threatened releases of hazardous substances into the environment. "Superfund" is actually the Hazardous Substance Super-fund, which is a fund created through taxes on certain chemical products under 26 USC §9507. This fund provides dollars for federal actions during hazardous substance cleanups and related activities. The fund may also reimburse private parties for their response costs in certain cases.

§9604(a) also allows EPA to respond to actual or threatened releases of **any** pollutant or contaminant which may present an imminent and substantial danger to the public health and welfare. The only specific limitation to EPA's authority to act under this section is that any response actions must be con-sistent with the National Oil and Hazardous Substances Pollution Contingency Plan, or the National Contingency Plan (NCP). EPA also is directed to give primary attention to those releases it deems the most threatening to public health. This section, reflected in 40 CFR §300.400(d), specifically gives EPA, or any other state or federal agency operating under CERCLA the right to enter any facility and carry out appropriate CERCLA response actions under the NCP. There does not need to be an imminent and substantial danger posed by releases or threatened releases of hazardous substances for the Agency to act.

If the Agency believes that the owner/operator of a site, or some other responsible party, will carry out corrective actions properly and promptly, it may allow that party to do so under §9604(a) with adequate EPA supervision. Responsible parties may also carry out their own remedial investigations and feasibility studies (RI/FS) where EPA specifically finds that they are capable of doing so and where EPA arranges for proper oversight, with EPA receiving reimbursements for any related costs.

While EPA may respond to any release or threat of release that it believes constitutes a public health or environmental emergency that no other party can alleviate, it has some limits on its §9604 authority. Specifically, the EPA will not provide for a removal or a remedial action under §9604 if the release or threatened release is of a naturally occurring, unaltered substance from a location where it is naturally found (e.g., naturally occurring radon). Nor will it use §9604 to respond to releases from products which are part of the structure of, and result to exposure within, residential buildings or business or community structures (e.g., lead in lead-based paint). Finally, the Agency will not look to §9604 to address releases or threatened releases into public or private drinking water supplies due to deterioration of the system through ordinary use (e.g., lead from lead solder in water pipes).

Unless a variety of conditions exist as noted in §9604(c)(1), EPA should not obligate further monies from the Superfund after $2 million has already been obligated by the fund for a specific response action. Nor should the EPA generally spend additional fund monies after 12 months has elapsed from the date of initial response to an incident. One condition that *would* allow for continued Superfund expenditures is that the actions are needed to alleviate an emergency which poses an immediate risk to public health or the environment and which otherwise will not be carried out in a timely manner.

Should a party not carry out proper response actions under §9604 without sufficient cause, it may be liable for up to three times the amount spent from the Superfund to cover its inaction.

ABATEMENT ACTIONS

Under §9606 of the Act, EPA may order a party to respond to a release or a threatened release as needed to protect the public health and welfare. This approach is generally called a "§106 Order" after the section of CERCLA section in which it is located. EPA may follow this course whenever the Agency feels that there *may* be an imminent and substantial endangerment to the public health, welfare, or the environment because of an actual or threatened release of a hazardous substance from a facility. EPA may use §106 orders regardless of whether the site is on the National Priority List (NPL). This section gives EPA considerable power, although not absolute discretion, to direct a company's priorities.

A company that has received a §106 Order has limited options. It can comply with the order without any additional fuss and bear the cost itself. An organization also may comply with the order and then seek cost recovery from the Superfund under §9606(b). Organizations following this route must show, by the preponderance of evidence, that they are not responsible for the response costs under §9607(a) and that the reimbursement is for a reasonable amount. Organizations also may obtain some compensation from the Superfund if EPA's selection of the particular response action was arbitrary and capricious or was not otherwise in accordance with the law. 40 CFR §§305 and 307 explain the process through which a party may seek compensation from the Superfund. The organization also may comply with the §106 order and seek compensation from other Potentially Responsible Parties (PRPs) after the fact. Remediation actions pursued under §9606 are enforced through settlements, called consent decrees, as discussed below.

The response actions ordered by this section must follow the cleanup standards of §9621, which requires EPA to ensure that responses are, as much as possible, consistent with the NCP and cost-effective. Should an organization receive a §9606 order, it is probable that the organization will not be able to obtain a judicial review of the order until EPA attempts to enforce it. Failure to comply with a §9606 order without sufficient cause may result in a fine of up to $25,000 per day. Should a party fail, without sufficient cause, to carry out a §9606 order with the result that Superfund monies are spent instead, that party may be liable for up to three times the amount spent from the Superfund.

EPA may also use §9606 to go to court and ask a judge to grant an order commanding the defendant to carry out certain response actions. Response orders granted by this mechanism must follow the NCP just like any other response actions but, unlike §106 orders, EPA does not need to go to court to enforce the cleanup order. Organizations that incur response costs as a result of a court order under §9606 still may seek contribution from other Potential Responsible Parties (PRPs). Organizations that ignore the judicial orders resulting from §9606 risk subjecting themselves to substantial judicial penalties.

VOLUNTARY ABATEMENT ACTIONS

An organization does not need to wait for an EPA order to commence response actions. If it feels that there is a need to act pursuant to CERCLA, it may do so and still seek reimbursement from other PRPs even where the organization's cleanup actions were of a voluntary nature. If EPA has initiated a remedial investigation and feasibility study (RI/FS) for the site, the organization should obtain authorization from the Agency in accordance with §9622(e)(6) prior to starting its response actions. For a party to obtain compensation for response action costs, those costs must be consistent with the NCP.

CLEANUP STANDARDS

The NCP does not actually define what constitutes a "CERCLA-quality cleanup," but §9621 sets out five requirements that all CERCLA remediation actions must meet. These requirements are that the action must:

1. Protect human health and the environment
2. Utilize permanent solutions and alternative treatment/resource recovery technologies as much as practicable

3. Be cost-effective
4. Attain compliance with applicable or relevant and appropriate requirements (ARARs) where hazardous substances will remain on-site
5. Be in accordance with the NCP as much as possible.

§9621(b)(1) expresses a preference for treatment which significantly reduces the volume, toxicity, or mobility of hazardous substances over reme-diation actions that do not involve such treatment. This subsection also directs that offsite transport and disposal of hazardous substances or contaminated materials without the treatment described above should be the least favored when there are practicable treatment technologies available.

Attaining relevant ARARs is the major barrier of many CERCLA pro-grams. §9621(d)(2) (A)(i) specifically notes that TSCA and the SWDA are two of several Federal environmental statutes which may set specific cleanup standards for CERCLA programs. For example, even though CERCLA does not set any particular contamination level, the Clean Water Act may require best available control technology (BACT) be used or a certain level of parts per million of a contaminant to be attained before a site is considered "clean." §9621(d)(4) allows EPA to ignore ARARs if, among other reasons, the Agency determines that compliance with an ARAR would result in greater risk to human health and the environment, that compliance with an ARAR is techni-cally impractical, or that compliance with an ARAR would use up Superfund monies that would be better spent elsewhere. The use of ARARs in determining permissible contamination levels is quite problematic. While response actions must comply with ARARs in most cases, what requirements are actually "applicable" or "relevant and appropriate" is a professional judgement and, as such, is subject to considerable discretion on the part of the person making the judgement. Should a state have a relevant standard that is stricter than the federal standard, it is likely that the state standard would apply to set the CERCLA cleanup level. As a general rule, the higher the likelihood of ground-water contamination, the more likely a tougher cleanup standard. If the poten-tially polluted groundwater is used, or is likely to be used, as a drinking source, the cleanup standard will be higher still.

Where an ARAR does not specify a more stringent standard, EPA looks at overall protection with regard to toxicity and carcinogenicity. 40 CFR §430(e)(2)(i)(A)(1) states that "acceptable exposure levels [of systemic toxi-cant] shall represent concentration levels to which the human population, including sensitive subgroups, may be exposed without adverse effect." Car-cinogens, according to 40 CFR §430(e)(2)(i)(A)(2), may be present at levels between 10^{-4} and 10^{-6} ppm. These levels mean that, given certain exposure and toxicity levels, between one and 100 people per million would contract cancer. Obviously, the exact level of permissible contamination is going to vary by substance and other factors such as the type of soil, "background" contamination, and precipitation.

What is clean in one area may not be clean enough in another area. To help balance out apparent inequities in CERCLA cleanups, EPA Region I has begun a process to make cleanup standards more easily attainable. By emphasizing the use of more realistic risk assessments based upon future land use assumptions, EPA Region I hopes to use "less costly, common-sense solutions" more frequently than in the past. This approach is sensible, since CERCLA sites that will be re-used as industrial parks do not face the same risks as sites that will be future homes. EPA Region I also is planning to provide "Clean Area Letters" for sites that have some contaminated areas along with some clean areas. These letters would describe the nature and extent of contamination within the site, allowing the clean areas to be treated as such. When no further federal interest is warranted, EPA Region I plans to issue "No Further federal Interest" letters to property owners to help remove the CERCLA stigma from their land. It is quite likely that other EPA Regions will follow the Region I example. This approach is similar to the "Brownfields" approach being promoted by the EPA Administrator. That approach addresses the situation where a large number of pieces of valuable properties located in major urban areas (usually within the inner city) cannot be used for many years because they are Superfund sites or are on state lots. The "Brownfields" approach represents an attempt to cut through red tape and minimize the amount of time before these properties once again can be income and job-producing. It involves a recognition that full cleanup of many of these sites may not be necessary because

- Contaminated groundwater will never be used there as a drinking water supply, and
- The future commercial or industrial uses of many of these sites do not require a full cleanup.

NATIONAL CONTINGENCY PLAN

§9605 creates the National Contingency Plan (NCP), which sets forth a program of substantive and procedural rules governing EPA's responses to both actual and threatened releases. The NCP sets out numerous layers of national and regional responders, with the nerve center of response actions being the National Response Center (NRC). Agency responsibilities for actions in the event of a release requiring a response and specific offices, such as the On-Scene Coordinator, are set up and basic guidelines for response preplanning, coordination, and actions are developed in an effort to make response actions more timely and efficient.

In addition to planning for immediate responses to releases, the NCP governs cleanup and remediation actions. 40 CFR §300 Subpart D sets out the requirements for response actions to oil releases while Subpart E describes the proper response actions for hazardous substance releases. A PRP is only liable for response costs to the extent that those costs were incurred in keeping with the NCP. Parties who clean sites under a §9606 order or under a §9622 consent decree enjoy the rebuttable presumption that their cleanups were in accordance with the NCP. While the NCP does not provide specific timeframes for cleanup completion, it does require that the timeframe be reasonable for each particular site's circumstances. According to EPA, "reasonable" time-frames may be as short as one year or as long as several decades. The NCP allows private parties to deviate a bit from the NCP's specific procedural and public participation requirements, but 40 CFR §300.700(c)(3)(i) absolutely insists that the end result be a "CERCLA-quality cleanup."

CERCLA REMEDIATION

40 CFR Subpart E describes the procedures for developing a remediation plan for hazardous substance contamination. The first step in the remediation procedure is §300.420's remedial preliminary assessment (PA), which may be followed by a remedial site inspection (SI). Both the PA and the SI are designed to gather data concerning hazardous substance releases, concentrating on deter-mining the source and nature of a release, exposure targets, and potential pathways of contamination. PAs and SIs allow the controlling agency to eliminate from further consideration those releases posing no significant threat to public health or the environment and to recommend if further action is warranted.

§300.430 sets out how to establish a remediation plan, explaining how to conduct preliminary studies and select an appropriate remedy. The stated purpose of the remedy selection process is to implement remedies that "elim-inate, reduce, or control risks to human health and the environment." To help with the implementation, EPA has promoted several guiding principles and expectations for program management, set forth in §300.430(a)(ii) and (iii). These principles and expectations include the facts that sites should be reme-diated in operable units to expedite the cleanup, that EPA expects to use treatment to address principal threats wherever practicable and that the Agency expects to use engineering controls, such as containment, for waste that pre-sents a relatively low long-term threat.

Under 40 CFR §430(a)(2), EPA follows its PA/SI with a remedial inves-tigation/ feasibility study (RI/FS) program to assess site conditions and eval-uate alternatives to the extent necessary to select a remedy. Conducting an RI/FS includes project scoping, data collection, risk analysis, treatability studies, and an analysis of alternatives. The purpose of the remedial investigation (RI) is to collect the data needed to properly characterize the site for the purpose of developing and evaluating effective remedial alternatives. The primary purpose of the Feasibility Study (FS) is to ensure that appropriate remedial alternatives are developed and evaluated so that the decision-maker can select a suitable remedy based on a solid knowledge of all possible routes. In other words, after the PA/SI indicates that further work is warranted under CERCLA, the RI/FS should keep the responders from stampeding after the first remediation process that comes to mind by forcing them to rationally develop and consider viable alternatives.

Nine criteria, listed in 40 CFR §300.430, are used to evaluate potential remedies in keeping with the NCP. These criteria include: overall protection of human health and the environment; compliance with applicable or relevant and appropriate requirements (ARARs); long-term effectiveness and permanence; reduction of toxicity, mobility or volume through treatment, short-term effectiveness; implementability; cost; and state and community acceptance. The criteria are not equally important. The first two, ARARs and protection, are threshold criteria which all potential responses must meet prior to being considered any further. ARARs and protection relate to the question of "how clean is clean?" Cost-effectiveness is used as a criterion to help choose from competing remedies that meet the overall protection and ARAR requirements. According to 40 CFR §430(f), cost-effectiveness is determined by evaluating long-term effectiveness, reduction of toxicity, mobility or volume through treatment, and short-term effectiveness. If a remedy's costs are proportional to its overall effectiveness, it is deemed cost-effective. Cost-effectiveness as a criteria for determining cleanup programs is subject to considerable discretion.

The middle five criteria are known as "primary balancing criteria" and are used to balance the pros and cons of competing cleanup options. State and community acceptance are known as "modifying criteria" since a program will have been through public comments before its acceptance is known. Thus, the specific cleanup standards will vary on a site by site basis, depending on the above-noted factors.

Selecting the final remedy is an EPA decision, and, like any agency decision, it must be properly documented. The resulting document, in detail appropriate to the site's situation, is called the Record of Decision (ROD). The ROD explains how the selected remedy is protective of human health and the environment, which ARARs the remedy will attain, which ARARs the remedy will not attain along with relevant waivers, and how the remedy is cost effective.

Before it adopts any plan for remedial action under CERCLA, the agency or organization carrying out the remedy must ensure that there is proper opportunity for public participation as stated in §9617. Public participation includes both notification of the proposed plan(s) and a reasonable opportunity for the submission of oral statements, as well as a public meeting at or near the facility or site in question. When the final remediation plan has been adopted, it must be made available to the public before the commencement of any remedial action. Publishing notification of the remediation plan(s) and a relevant summary in a major local newspaper will probably suffice for public participation as long as people can visit the relevant site and inspect pertinent documents themselves.

Once the remedy has been selected, it is time for remedial design/remedial action (RD/RA), as described in 40 CFR §300.435. The RD/RA stage includes the development of the actual design and construction of the selected remedy. All RD/RA activities must be in conformance with the Record of Decision (ROD) or another relevant decision document for that site. If conditions change significantly, such as the discovery of new major sources of contamination, the ROD must be formally amended so that the selected remedy may be adjusted accordingly. When implementing the remedy, prime contractors or subcontractors must not have conflicts of interest that could significantly impact their work.

STATE INVOLVEMENT

State involvement in Superfund cleanups is guided by §9221(f) and implemented by 40 CFR §300 Subpart F. Under these guidelines, EPA must ensure "meaningful and substantial state involvement" in hazardous substance response. Specifically, EPA must provide an opportunity for state participation in removal, pre-remedial, remedial, and enforcement response activities, and it must encourage states to enter into an EPA/State Superfund Memorandum of Agreement (SMOA). States may be the lead agency for CERCLA actions. They identify potential sites, evaluate them, and make up a list that ranks the severity of sites in that state, which they give to EPA for use in setting up the NPL listing. A state may remove a possible site from its list if it finds that no problem exists.

When involved in a SMOA, both the lead and supporting agencies should review key documents and be involved in crucial decisionmaking processes as much as possible. Even without a SMOA, EPA must consult annually with the states to establish priorities, discuss potential ARARs, and generally develop a spirit of CERCLA cooperation.

Regardless of how involved a state becomes in the CERCLA program, however, §300.515(e) gives EPA the final word on selecting a remedy should there be a disagreement. EPA must notify the appropriate state at least 30 days prior to entering a consent decree if the selected remedy will not meet the ARARs. If the state agrees with the EPA, it may sign the consent decree. If the state does not agree to the consent decree, it has the right to go to court to force the remedy to meet the ARARs. If there is not substantial evidence that the waiver of the ARARs was appropriate, the remedy must be modified to meet that requirement.

Prior to having Superfund dollars spent on sites within their borders, states may be required to fund 10% of the cost of remediation under §500.510, and up to 50% if the site was publicly operated when it received hazardous substances. States do **not** have to share in the cost of state or EPA-lead fund-financed **removal** actions unless the site was operated by the state, or one of its subdivisions, at the time of disposal of hazardous substances, and a remediation action eventually takes place there. States also must agree to assume responsibility for all future maintenance of the response action throughout its expected life.

40 CFR §300.515 sets forth nonfinancial requirements for state involvement in EPA-led remedial and enforcement responses and also for EPA involvement in state-led remedial and enforcement responses. In effect, the requirements for these partnerships is that the agencies review major documents, coordinate decisionmaking procedures, conduct programmatic reviews, and coordinate other CERCLA activities as well as possible.

Given the inherent confusion that results when any two organizations work together on a project, it is not surprising that EPA–State CERCLA efforts have resulted in considerable duplication of efforts. To help resolve this problem, EPA Region I has set up a pilot program with the Commonwealth of Massachusetts to test new approaches to reducing risk at environmentally and economically sensitive areas. If successful, this approach may be a model for other State-EPA partnership programs.

NATIONAL PRIORITIES LIST

The National Priorities List (NPL) is, in theory, the official list of the most contaminated sites in the country. 40 CFR §300.425 states that only NPL sites may be eligible for Superfund monies for remediation, defined as removal actions, including remedial planning activities. Remedial investigations and feasibility studies are not limited to NPL sites in order to qualify for Superfund dollars. The higher a site stands on the NPL, the more priority it may have for Superfund expenditures, although there is no guarantee that an NPL listing of any kind will result in federal money for response actions. Sites appear on the NPL depending on how they fare under the Hazardous Ranking System (HRS), which is a model that EPA uses to determine a site's hazard potential. Each state may place one site on the NPL without having to complete the HRS review if the site meets certain conditions. The other sites are taken from the various state lists in their order in the HRS. Nicknamed the "Superfund list," the NPL is located in 40 CFR §300 Appendix B.

The workings of the HRS are explained in detail in Appendix A to 40 CFR §300. EPA considers such diverse factors as type and amount of contamination, proximity of human habitation and aquifers, and groundwater flow and precipitation in determining the HRS value given to a particular site. At this writing, any site with a HRS value of 28.5 or greater may be put on the list, but interested parties may go to court to appeal EPA's decision to do so. For comparison, nationally known NPL sites such as Love Canal, Valley of the Drums, and the Stringfellow Acid Pits have HRS values of anywhere from 50.5 to 70.5.

SETTLEMENTS

Once a party has been identified as being a potentially responsible party (PRP), it may wish to settle with the government or other PRPs. Settlements with other PRPs are essentially like indemnification contracts, only being enforceable to the settling parties. In the case of the federal government,

§9622(a) **directs** EPA to enter into agreements to perform response actions "whenever practicable" as long as they are in the public interest and consistent with the NCP. If the agency declines to enter into a settlement with any PRPs, it must inform them of that decision in writing and include an explanation of why settlement is not an option. Two examples of situations where EPA may opt not to enter into a settlement with a PRP are if it is unlikely to agree to a settlement or if it does not have adequate resources to properly carry out the response actions.

EPA will review all evidence relevant to a site, from old tax returns to shipping manifests to labels on drums found at the site, to determine who may be a PRP. These PRPs then receive a "notice letter" informing them of their potential liability and, generally, identifying other PRPs. The EPA may also include a request for information under §9604(e). Information provided pursuant to a §104(e) request is generally available to the public except where the PRP shows a need for confidentiality under 18 USC §1905.

§9622(b) allows the EPA to provide reimbursement to PRPs who carry out response actions pursuant to a settlement on behalf of the agency.

Once an organization enters into an agreement under §9622, subsection (c) dictates that the EPA enter into a covenant not to sue as in subsection (f). The basic theme of the covenant not to sue is that settling PRPs limit their potential liability for response costs at the site. In effect, by settling, these PRPs have paid their dues for the relevant site contamination. This limitation is not absolute, however, for all covenants must include a "reopener" clause that allows EPA to seek recovery for conditions that were not known at the time the covenant took effect. EPA also may include any type of "reopener" clause it thinks necessary to protect public health, welfare, and the environment. PRPs must meet their obligations under the settlement to be eligible for a covenant not to sue, and the covenant itself must be in the public interest. The covenant does not take effect until the Agency certifies that the remedial action has been completed to its satisfaction.

Settlements are desirable for some PRPs because, under §9613(f), their liability to other PRPs for response actions is limited by the terms of the settlement. If an organization has entered into an agreement to pay a certain amount for a certain type(s) of response action, a different PRP may not seek a contribution from the settling organization for its costs in carrying out that response action(s). PRPs who do not settle may find themselves liable for the "leftover" costs of the response action. The "leftover" amount is the cost of the action minus the amounts received by the government through settlements, and it may be considerable should the contamination be more severe or treatment more problematic than the Agency had believed when it settled with other PRPs. In private actions for cost recovery, non-settling PRPs may be able to reduce their liabilities to the plaintiff by the amount a PRP who settled with the plaintiff would have been liable for had it not settled.

While this settlement protection may seem desirable, it does not come without its costs. First, there is the possibility that a PRP may settle for more than it would have otherwise paid as its share of response costs. Further, a PRP may have to pay a premium over and above its projected share of the response costs in order to obtain a settlement. This premium varies in size depending on cost overruns and additional remediation needed when the initial remedy is not properly protective. The attraction of a settlement further diminishes when one looks at the EPA's model RD/RA consent decree published at 56 FR 30996 (8 July, 1991). This model contains several provisions that are exceptionally favorable to EPA, such as EPA's position being binding in any disputes over the implementation of the decree and its reserving the right to require additional response actions not in the decree if it believes that those actions are needed to meet stated performance standards.

De minimus PRPs may be eligible for special settlements under §9622(g) if the amount and the toxicity of hazardous substances for which they are responsible at the site are both minimal. Additionally, the owner of a site who did not permit the treatment, storage, or disposal at the site and who did not contribute to the contamination through any action or omission also may be eligible for a *de minimus* settlement. As long as settlements are practicable and in the public interest, the Agency may grant these settlements under essentially the same conditions, and with the same benefits accruing to the settling PRP, as for non-*de minimus* settlers. *De minimus* PRPs generally will settle for a premium of between 60 and 100 percent of their estimated liability. If the total response costs exceed $500,000, the Attorney General may have to approve the settlement agreement before it can take effect.

CERCLA LIABILITY

Overview

Given that the average EPA Superfund cleanup costs approximately thirty million dollars, it is appropriate that the most arresting aspect of CERCLA frequently seems to be its ability to attach massive liabilities to organizations that only minimally contaminated a site. It is important to emphasize that CERCLA liability only covers "response" costs. These costs, as discussed below, are the costs incurred by a party that cleans up a contaminated site in accordance with the National Contingency Plan (NCP). CERCLA liability, as set out in §9607, also includes damages for injury to natural resources and the costs of any health assessment carried out in accordance with the Act. CERCLA liability does not extend to personal injury suits, lost profits, or even some relocation costs, although civil courts addressing these issues may consider CERCLA requirements in establishing relevant liability.

Who May be Liable?

CERCLA liability only attaches to parties as described in §9607 of the Act. These parties include the present owner and operator of the site, as well as any other owner or operator of the site during the time it was contaminated, any transporters who selected the site and anyone who "arranged" for treatment or disposal of the hazardous substance. This aspect of CERCLA applies retroactively, which allows liability to attach to parties that long ago ceased to be involved with a particular site. CERCLA's retroactivity, along with the broad interpretations as to who qualifies as a §9607 responsible party, greatly increase the number of CERCLA potentially responsible parties (PRPs). In civil suits, these PRPs are frequently referred to as "defendants."

In particular, the term "Owner and Operator" is broader than it may appear. In addition to its clear meaning of anyone who actually has title to or is involved in day to day operations of a facility, the term may include off-site entities whose actions magnified CERCLA contamination (such as a party who spreads PCB-contaminated oil over a construction site to keep the dust down), lessors and lessees who had control over the contaminated property, and even lenders who conceivably may have influenced its treatment of hazardous substances. Similarly, generators and any other party that "arranged" disposal at a site may include an organization which sells a product that is intended to be released into the environment as well as the more basic generator who sends hazardous wastes to a site which eventually becomes contaminated and requires remediation under CERCLA. Courts also have found CERCLA liability for successor corporations and parents whose corporations have been involved in the offending organization's business operations to any extent.

Theories of Liability

The two legal theories that combine to create CERCLA's impressive potential liability are the theory of joint and several liability and the theory of strict liability. These two theories are court imposed and not statutorily created. Thus, the actual limits of liability may vary significantly among court districts. The theory of joint and several liability simply means that each defendant is responsible for the damages as a whole. Thus, if one defendant cannot pay its share of the damages, the other defendants must make up the difference. Because the plaintiff has no requirement to name all potential defendants, this theory frequently becomes the "deep pockets" phenomenon: plaintiffs sue the defendant(s) with the deepest pockets and leave it up to the defendants to sort out who pays for what. The second theory, that of strict liability, means that a plaintiff does not have to actually prove that a defendant's particular activities caused the plaintiff's specific injuries. It is enough that the defendant took part in activities that, in the aggregate, caused the plaintiff the harm.

Defenses to CERCLA Liability

There are several defenses to CERCLA liability, three of which are set forth in §9607(b) of the Act. The most effective defense, which is not described in §9607(b), is for a defendant to prove that it did not contribute **any** hazardous substances to the site. Failing that circumstance, a defendant may escape liability by proving that an Act of God or an Act of War caused the defendant's contamination. An "Act of God" receives attention in §9602(1), where it is specifically defined as including unanticipated grave natural disasters. A defendant also may avoid CERCLA liability by showing the release was caused by an unforeseeable act or omission of a third party. In this case, the third party must not have a contractual relationship with the defendant and the defendant must have exercised due care to prevent the actions of the offending third party. For example, a vandal opening a tank car valve might not suffice for this third party defense unless the vandal had to climb over a barbed-wire fence and evade roving security guards to get at the car. The final defense, contained in §9707(j), is that the contamination occurred as a result of a federally-permitted release, such as that provided in a permit pursuant to the Clean Air or Clean Water Acts. It is not clear if this defense holds true for violations of those permits. In general, if a facility has both permitted and non-permitted releases, it must establish that the harm from the permitted releases is separate from the harm caused by its non-permitted releases in order to avoid response cost liabilities for all of its releases. This final defense only avoids CERCLA liability, and response costs may still attach under other theories of liability.

An extension of the third person defense is known as the "innocent landowner" exception. This exception allows landowners to avoid CERCLA liability if they did not know and did not have any reason to know of the presence of hazardous substances on their property and who took proper actions upon learning of their presence. The landowner need only be ignorant as to the existence of the types of hazardous substances that incurred the response costs. For example, if a service station owner finds out that a recently purchased station is contaminated with something unexpected, such as cadmium from a past illegal disposal act of some rogue transporter, the owner may avoid liability for any response costs caused by the cadmium. The innocent landowner must have conducted "all appropriate inquiry into the previous ownership and uses of the property" according to §9601(35)(B). Factors that indicate whether the owner conducted an "appropriate" inquiry include the purchase price of the land, the obviousness of the presence or likely presence of contamination at the property, commonly known or reasonably ascertainable information about the property as developed in an environmental survey, and any specialized knowledge or experience on the part of the defendant.

Once CERCLA liability has attached, there are limits to its extension. First, a defendant who can prove that the harm, which in this discussion means the response costs, is divisible will be liable only for the portion of the harm he or she caused. If it is possible to sort out which hazardous substance(s) caused what damage, joint and several liability may not be appropriate. By and large, though, it is difficult to establish exactly which specific drum or load of hazardous substances belongs to whom and how much particular damage it did, so joint and several liability is always a significant threat to a potentially responsible party (PRP). Further, it is generally up to the PRPs to prove that the harm is truly divisible and that they are only responsible for a given percentage of it. This proof is a difficult and resource intensive judicial hurdle to clear.

Liability Between Defendants

As discussed above, a plaintiff, whether it is the government or another PRP seeking to recover response costs, must name only one defendant in order to recover funds. It is up to the defendants to include other PRPs in the suit in order to widen the pool from which the plaintiff may draw a recovery. Courts are willing to apportion liability between defendant PRPs, but generally they will not do so at the expense of lessening the award granted the plaintiff.

Indemnity Contracts

One way PRPs may lessen their liability to private parties is to enter into indemnification contracts. These contracts allow an individual or an organization to agree that, vis-a-vis the other contracting parties, CERCLA liability will be as stated in the contract. For example, a company may wish to buy some industrial land but fear of the potential cleanup costs prevents it from completing the purchase. To protect itself against future liability, the company may purchase the land subject to an indemnity contract stating that the seller will be liable for any response costs incurred by the purchaser or any other party as a result of contamination on the purchased property. These contracts are good only against contracting parties. Parties outside the contract, such as the state and federal government or neighbors may seek contribution from the purchaser despite the indemnification contract. It will be up to the purchaser to obtain relief from the seller who agreed to cover response costs. If the seller cannot cover its obligation, the purchaser may have to bear the costs itself.

Insurance

Insurance companies are concerned about spending millions of dollars on remediating land for which they provide policies. There have been numerous lawsuits in which PRPs sue their insurance companies to pay for Superfund site cleanups. The insurance companies, in turn, claim that these costs are not covered by their policies. Consequently, most insurance policies now contain some sort of "pollution exclusion" provision that specifically limits their exposure to remediation, removal or response costs. In many cases these policies will have a cap of $25,000.

Firms that may be subject to high cleanup costs are actively seeking other insurance. One approach is called "stacking." This technique may allow an organization to collect insurance coverage for every policy they had throughout a contamination event. Thus, if a leak took place over the course of six or seven years, and an organization renewed its policy each year during that period, it may be able to use stacking to get all six or seven policies to cover contamination that occurred during those years.

CERCLA Subchapter IV sets out a statutory program by which organizations may develop or join a "risk retention group." These groups are designed to assume and spread out the pollution risk of their members. This subchapter also sets out guidance for the operation of "purchasing groups," which are organizations which have banded together to purchase pollution insurance.

Federal and State Liability

§9620 states that both state and federal governments are liable to the same extent that private parties incur CERCLA liability. If a governmental agency is controlling operations at a certain site and that site becomes contaminated, it is probable that the government will be subject to CERCLA liability unless it fits under one of the general CERCLA defenses discussed above. Similarly, if the government owns a site and either contaminates the property itself or allows a contractor to contaminate it, the government probably will be subject to CERCLA liability. Governments generally will not be liable for carrying out regulatory-type actions, such as permitting or conducting OSHA inspections, at a site unless there was some gross negligence on the part of the government that helped lead to the contamination. Similarly, responding to an emergency created by another party, §107(d)(2) precludes the government from incurring CERCLA liability unless it acted in a grossly negligent fashion.

§9620(j) allows the President of the United States, in the interests of national security, to exempt such Department of Defense or Department of Energy sites from CERCLA requirements as he/she deems necessary. These exemptions may last for only one year, although follow-on exemptions may be granted. Presidential exemptions must be accompanied by a statement of the reasons for the exemption, and they are not an excuse for not proceeding with relevant response actions as expeditiously as possible.

Under §9601(20)(D)'s definition of "owner or operator," tax delinquency or abandonment which results in government ownership or control of a contaminated site will not expose the government to CERCLA liability. This exclusion does not include instances where the government caused or contributed to the release or threatened release at the site. Furthermore, the reality of such situations is that there may be no one else besides the government to carry out or finance remediation and removal actions on abandoned lands.

Federally Owned Property

§9620 specifically addresses how CERCLA affects federal facilities. [This section is not to be confused with the Federal Facilities Compliance Act, which waives the Federal Government's sovereign immunity under the Resource

Conservation and Recovery Act (42 USC §6961)]. §9629(a) explicitly waives the Federal Government's sovereign immunity under CERCLA. All guidelines, rules, regulations, and criteria that would apply to private parties in similar circumstances also apply to the Federal Government. §9620(e) sets out a list of required actions and a strict timeline that the agency owning the property must follow within six months of being listed on the NPL. Federal facilities also must comply with state laws concerning removal and remedial action at sites that are not on the NPL. If the Federal Government wishes to transfer land on which any hazardous substance was stored for at least 1 year, was released or was disposed of, the transferring agency must provide all relevant information concerning those hazardous substances to the potential buyer under §9620(h).

ENVIRONMENTAL COMPLIANCE

Notification Requirements

Checklist :

Review facility's stock of chemicals. Compare quantities on hand to reportable quantities under 40 CFR §302.4 and the consolidated list of chemicals.

No reportable
quantities of chemicals: No need for compliance program.

Reportable quantity: Review procedures to prevent a release and familiarize staff with procedures to follow in case of a release. Post number for National Response Center (NRC) and notification information in conspicuous places and by phones.

If there is a release, is the release pursuant to a federal permit?

    Yes: No notification required.
    No: Is release "continuous"?

Continuous release: Follow reduced notification guidelines of 40 CFR §302.8.

Notification Requirements (continued)

> **Checklist (continued):**
>
> Release is not pursuant
> to a federal permit and
> is not continuous: Notify the National Response Center of reportable quantity releases within 24 hours.

The compliance officer should review the definition of "hazardous substance" in §9601(14), noting that the term generally excludes petroleum and natural gas. The term does include far more than just hazardous wastes, and such materials as the Clean Air Act's Hazardous Air Pollutants, the Clean Water Act's toxic pollutants, and any substance specifically found by EPA to be hazardous are considered to be CERCLA hazardous substances. The compliance officer also should review the Consolidated List of Chemicals Covered in Title III of Superfund Amendments and Reauthorization Act (SARA). This list, available from EPA (800-535-0262), sets forth reportable quantities (RQs) of both hazardous and extremely hazardous substances. 40 CFR §302.4 consists of a similar list of hazardous substances and also should be reviewed. Unless the Agency sets a different RQ in these lists, the RQ will probably be one pound in accordance with §9602(b). Some of the more likely release notification concerns are asbestos (one pound) and lead (one pound). If the quantity of one or more of the hazardous constituents of the release is unknown, 40 CFR §302.6(b) requires notification when the total amount of the release equals or exceeds the RQ for the known hazardous constituent with the lowest RQ.

The consolidated chemical list and §302.4 are not completely inclusive, as many hazardous chemicals are identified by broad criteria rather than enumeration and therefore cannot be listed. If a compliance officer is not sure if one of his chemicals has a reportable quantity, EPA should be contacted for guidance, remembering to document the agency's response. Should the compliance officer determine that the facility has any hazardous substances that could be released in reportable quantities, he/she should review the measures taken to prevent a release. The compliance officer should also ensure that there is a procedure in place to determine if a release has occurred and to provide proper notification.

Release notification to the NRC consists of the following information: Continuous releases receive special treatment under §302.8 even if they are in excess of the relevant RQ. These releases, which must be either uninterrupted or routine, anticipated, intermittent and incidental to normal operations, are subject to the reduced notification requirements of §302.8(c). An example of a potential continuous release eligible for reduced reporting would be lead dust emissions from an indoor rifle range. Reduced requirements include initial telephone notification, written notification within 30 days, and notification of defined significant increases in releases. The reduced report must provide EPA with the geographical area of the release, the local population density, the name and phone number of the person in charge of the facility, the identity of the hazardous substance, the upper and lower bounds of the normal range of the release over the past year, the source of the release, and a variety of other relevant information. Failure to properly comply with the reduced notification requirements of a continuous release will subject a facility to the reporting requirements of §302.6 and the penal provisions discussed above. Within 30 days of the first anniversary of the initial written notification, the person in charge of the facility must verify and update release information in a follow-up notification.

Remediation Actions

While public attention and corporate concerns may focus on the dollar amount of the potential liability resulting from a remediation action, a compliance officer must understand how this liability develops. The compliance officer must be able to explain to corporate staff why a company may be forced to spend millions of dollars removing or treating contaminated soil and equipment, chasing and treating huge plumes of contaminated groundwater and even, in some cases, resettling residents of contaminated neighborhoods.

The compliance officer should ensure that the facility does not commit itself to a §9604 cleanup program without planning on following through with the program.

Response Actions

The compliance officer must be familiar with §9604, know when it may apply to the facility and be prepared to act accordingly.

Abatement Actions

These are expensive actions that often can be foreseen. Therefore, a compliance officer should strive to avoid conditions that lead to a release or perceived threat of a release.

In the event that his facility receives a §106 Order, the compliance officer should ensure that there is a strong case that the facility is not responsible for CERCLA response actions before suggesting a §106 Order be ignored. It generally is good policy to go along with the Order.

Voluntary Abatement Actions

The compliance officer should be alert for the need for Voluntary Abatement actions so that the firm will be praised for its action instead of being subjected to an EPA §106 Order. If the compliance officer believes that a voluntary abatement action is desirable, he/she should present it to management in a well-documented report that includes the reasons for the action, its compliance with the NCP, a listing of other PRPs, and as definitive a statement as possible on abatement costs and the possibility of recovering part or all of them from other PRPs.

Cleanup Standards

The compliance officer must learn what these standards may be for any possible CERCLA problem for the area of responsibility. In case of an actual cleanup, the compliance officer should determine the organization's ability to clean up to the required levels.

National Contingency Plan

The compliance officer should contact the local EPA on-scene coordinator to determine if the facility needs to concern itself with release response planning.

CERCLA Remediation

A compliance officer whose facility is undergoing, or will undergo, a CERCLA response action should review a copy of the ROD to ensure that he/she understands the program's requirements as they pertain to the facility. He/she then should evaluate the situation to decide the needed extent of the organization's participation, or lack of participation, in the remediation activity.

State Involvement

Checklist :

Is your facility on the state list of possible Superfund sites?

    No: No further action required
    Yes: Try to get the state agency to evaluate the site rapidly.
           If the state evaluation shows

State Involvement (continued)

Checklist (continued):

a.	No problems with the site:	Make sure the state agency removes your site from its list.
b.	Problems at the site:	Make a recommendation to your management as to whether you should clean up the site or wait for state or federal action.

National Priority List

The compliance officer should maintain up-to-date files on the contents of the NPL and the criteria for being on that list. He/she should be ready to notify management of any sites placed on that list that may be close enough geographically to affect the facility.

Settlements

While EPA is desirous of entering into settlements with PRPs whenever possible, the Agency usually is not willing to wait very long for remedial action to start. Accordingly, EPA is quite likely to carry out initial studies, or even the cleanup itself if the PRPs do not appear capable or willing to carry out the necessary actions. It therefore behooves the compliance officer who is a notified PRP to quickly align the organization with other organizations if he/she believes a settlement would be in the employer's best interest.

The decision as to whether to settle is a complex one. On the one hand, it resolves a problem and often is the most cost-effective approach. On the other hand, the settlement may be skewed in EPA's favor and against the company.

Unpleasant examples of PRP notification include the hypothetical one of the EPA's sending out invitations to organizations to attend meetings at hotel conference rooms or convention centers. Once there, the Agency informs everyone that they are all PRPs for a particular site and should a settlement agreement not be reached by the close of business that day, EPA is going to proceed on its own and seek reimbursement later. Organizations attending meetings such as these without proper preparation may well find themselves making decisions to settle or not to settle without an adequate opportunity to assess the relative risks.

CERCLA Liability

Compliance officers should be particularly concerned with CERCLA's ability to attach liability to an organization's officers, directors, and even its employees. Specifically, courts have been willing to find personal liability as an owner/operator where the individual in question either participated in the decisions that led to the contamination or was involved personally in the contaminating activities. Further, officers or directors may be liable if they were in positions to have prevented the contamination and failed to do so. Even lack of knowledge of the contaminating activity is not a sure defense, for a court may find that an individual's duty to know or his/her affirmatively refusing to learn about activities may lead to liability. Individual employees who were in a position to control the contamination, such as employees who actually place hazardous waste in a dumpster, may be liable under CERCLA for not preventing the resultant harm. In actuality, however, EPA uses its limited enforcement resources in a very discretionary manner. Individuals whose attachment to a CERCLA cost-recovery suit will have no impact on the overall recovery, are less likely to be named as PRPs by EPA.

§9607(d) specifically provides that no person shall be liable for costs or damages as a result of actions taken, or omitted, in the course of rendering assistance or advice in accordance with the NCP. This liability exemption extends to parties acting under the direction of an on-scene coordinator during an incident creating a danger to public health, welfare, or the environment. As is usually the case with any action, the party may start to incur liability should he or she behave in a negligent fashion. Accordingly, compliance officers should ensure that their organizations have sufficient proof to show that they did not act negligently when responding to any CERCLA issue.

Defenses to CERCLA Liability

The compliance officer should ensure that proper "due diligence" is conducted when purchasing or leasing property in order to avoid contaminated property whenever possible and to utilize the "innocent landowner" defense when precautions against buying contaminated property fail.

The theory of joint and several liability, and its divisibility defense, also applies to civil suits involving personal liability. Since CERCLA PRPs may be defendants in suits to recover personal damages due to sickness caused by a particular contamination episode, a compliance officer should be aware that the defenses to actions for response costs may also apply to other actions.

Liability Between Dependents

When the organization is likely to become a party to cost recovery for response actions, the compliance officer should carefully examine the notes of other possible PRPs so that the "pool" of defendants may be addressed and the cost to the compliance officer's company reduced.

Indemnity Contracts

The compliance officer should be aware of the pros and cons of entering into indemnification contracts.

GLOSSARY

Unpermitted Release . . . . A discharge of a liquid into the environment for which a permit has not been issued.

National Contingency Plan . . . . A regulation developed by EPA that details procedures to be used in responding to spills of hazardous materials.

Responsible Party . . . . The person(s) or organization(s) that is (are) at fault for the creation of a spill or an abandoned hazardous waste site.

Carcinogenicity . . . . The relative ability of a chemical to cause cancer in humans.

Systemic Toxicants . . . . Toxic chemicals that affect the body generally rather than at specific parts.

On-Scene Coordinator . . . . The federal person who assumes responsibility for all of the activity at a spill location.

Record of Decision (ROD) . . . . A document signed by the head of the federal agency that is responsible for a decision on a remedy for cleanup at a specific site. The ROD sets forth the rationale for the selection of the particular selected remediation approach.

De minimus . . . . A legal term that means the very least possible.

REFERENCES AND SELECTED READINGS

ECON Magazine, July, 1995, "Teamwork Speeds Methane Remediation," PTN Publishing, Inc., Melville, NY.

General Accounting Officer, September, 1994, "Superfund – Status, Cost, and Timeliness of Hazardous Waste Site Cleanups," GAO/RCED-94-256, Washington, D.C.

Mackenthun, K.M. and Bregman, J.I., 1992, *Environmental Regulations Handbook*, Lewis Publishers, Boca Raton, FL.

National Association of Manufacturers, 1989, "Waste Minimization: Manufacturers' Strategies for Success," Washington, D.C.

U.S. Army Corps of Engineers, Construction Engineering Research Laboratories, Revised, September, 1995, "The Environmental Assessment and Management (TEAM) Guide," USACERL Special Report EC-95/05, Champaign, IL.

U.S. Department of Energy, August, 1995, "Guidance Document Publications List," Office of Environmental Policy and Assistance, RCRA/CERCLA Division (EH-413), Washington, D.C.

U.S. EPA, May 8, 1991, "Protecting the Nation's Groundwater: EPA's Strategy for the 1990s," EPA Groundwater Task Force, Washington, D.C.

U.S. EPA, July 31, 1995, "National Oil and Hazardous Substances Pollution Contingency Plan – Revised Rule Issues," Environmental Guidance Regulatory Bulletin, Office of Environmental Policy and Assistance, RCRA/CERCLA Division (EH-413), Washington, D.C.

9   Toxic Substances Control

GENERAL OVERVIEW

While CERCLA governs response actions to releases and threatened releases of hazardous substances and RCRA governs the treatment, storage, and disposal of hazardous wastes, the actual use of hazardous substances is governed by a potpourri of applicable laws and regulations. Chief among the laws that relate to hazardous substance use and possession are the Toxic Substances Control Act (TSCA), 15 U.S.C. §§2601–2692, the Federal Insecticide, Fungicide, and Rodenticide Act (FIFRA), 7 U.S.C §§136–136y, and the Emergency Planning and Community Right to Know Act (EPCRA) 42 U.S.C. §§11001–11050. They are discussed in this chapter.

TOXIC SUBSTANCES CONTROL ACT (TSCA)

TSCA is the Federal legislation governing the use, production, and distribution of toxic substances and is implemented by 40 CFR §§700–766. The Act has four major sections covering toxic substances, asbestos hazard emergency responses, indoor radon abatement, and lead exposure reduction. The latter three items are discussed in the last chapter of this book. In the present chapter, we will confine ourselves to the toxic substances section.

TSCA is the result of Congressional findings that people and the environment are exposed to numerous chemical substances and mixtures every year and that many of these chemicals present an unreasonable risk of injury to health or the environment through their manufacture, processing, distribution, use, or disposal. The policy behind TSCA is that the manufacturers or processors of chemical substances must develop adequate data to understand the effects of their products on human health and environment. Where circumstances dictate, the government should regulate chemical substances that present an unreasonable risk of injury to health and the environment and take action where chemicals present imminent hazards. In implementing TSCA, with its multitude of testing, reporting, and warning requirements, EPA is directed to minimize regulatory interference with economic development.

Manufacturing, Processing, and Distributing Chemical Substances

According to the statute, when EPA finds that the manufacturing, distributing, processing, use, or disposal of a chemical substance or mixture may present an unreasonable risk of injury to health or to the environment, the Agency may require, by rule, that testing be conducted on the substance(s) in question. EPA also has power to require testing for substances for which there is insufficient data and experience to determine the substance(s)' effect(s) on health or the environment. The rule requiring chemical testing must include identification of the substance, standards for development of test data, the time period for carrying out the test, and submittal of the results to the Agency. Various testing procedures are listed in 40 CFR §§796–799.

Should EPA feel that the test results indicate that a chemical substance or mixture presents, or will present, a significant risk of serious or widespread harm to humans from cancer, gene mutations, or birth defects, it must take action within 180 days of receipt of the information to prevent or reduce such risk to an acceptable level. An EPA finding that the risks posed by a chemical substance or mixture are not unreasonable must be published in the *Federal Register*.

Most manufacturing of new chemical substances or manufacturing or processing existing chemical substances for **new uses**, as listed in §721, cannot be done unless the maker submits a notice of its intent to do so at least 90 days before starting his manufacturing or processing. These notices are called "Section Five notices" and, under §700.45, must be accompanied by fees of $100 for small business concerns and up to $2,500 for non-small business concerns. They also may need to be accompanied or preceded by the test results discussed above. Per §2613, test result data may be made available to a variety of parties for a variety of purposes, although disclosure of designated confidential material is guided by strict notification standards.

Premanufacture notification is discussed in §720 and is submitted via a specified notice form. §720.45 discusses the information that must be included on a notice form, including the chemical name, anticipated impurities, and a description of the byproducts resulting from the manufacture, processing, use, and disposal of the new chemical substance. §2604(h) allows for exemptions where a manufacturer or processor satisfactorily demonstrates that its product will not result in unreasonable risks to health or the environment and accepts such restrictions as EPA deems appropriate. §§720.30, 720.36 and 720.38 carve out specific exemptions for a variety of substances, including new chemicals made in small quantities solely for research and development, chemicals made for test marketing, and any byproduct which is not used for commercial purposes. Additional specific exemptions are noted in §723 Subpart B for manufacturers of less than 1,000 kg per year of a chemical substance, peel-apart film canisters, and polymers as long as certain requirements are met.

Parties must also notify EPA of significant new uses of chemical substances as described in §721. As a rough rule of thumb, if a new use requires additional protective personal equipment and procedures, it is likely to be a significant new use. Each specific significant new use is listed separately and may have unique notification requirements, in addition to the general notification requirements of §721.25. §721.45 describes the exemptions to this new use notification rule, including those parties who have applied for and been granted a test marketing exemption, parties who manufacture, import, or process the substance only as an impurity, and parties who import or process the substance as part of an article. A written hazard communication program, proper labeling of substances, availability of Material Safety Data Sheets, and worker training are some of the requirements facilities must meet under §720.

Reports

There are fairly complicated reporting and record-keeping requirements for TSCA. Small manufacturers, as defined in §704.3 and §710.2(x), are frequently exempted from these requirements, but they may have to submit some reports if EPA so decides. These reports may be referred to as 8(a) reporting, based on the section of TSCA that sets forth the requirements. Reporting information varies among chemicals, but typically involves use of specific EPA forms and includes such items as the number of workers who may be exposed to a chemical, engineering controls to prevent release of the chemical, and a description of the chemical's identity. Confidentiality of data submitted to EPA is generally possible for all reporting requirements as long as specific procedures are followed.

The first reporting system is outlined in §704. Nine specific chemicals, such as 11-aminoundecanoic acid and chlorinated terphenyl, are given specific reporting procedures in Subpart B. Subpart D lists an additional number of chemicals which are to be reported, according to the format described in Subpart C on the Comprehensive Assessment Information Rule (CAIR). §704.9 provides the address to which reports must be sent.

The second reporting process is somewhat more extensive than that described above. In order to prepare and keep current an accurate inventory of TSCA chemical substances imported or manufactured for commercial purposes, the Agency requires additional reporting under §710 Subpart A and updating under Subpart B. While impurities, byproducts, and other chemical substances noted in §710.4 do not fall within the scope of this inventory, and thus do not have to be reported, any other chemicals designated "for commercial purposes" must be reported, including chemicals substances related to test marketing. Note however, that only "chemical substances" are subject to this inventory requirement. §710.2(h) specifically excludes tobacco, firearm shells, mixtures, and a variety of other products from the legal definition of this term. §710.5 gives detailed instructions on how to properly report chemical substances. §§710.32 and 710.33 give detailed instructions on the information and timing concerning inventory updates.

Manufacturers and importers must submit a single EPA Form No. 7710-35 for each plant-site manufacture or import of a chemical substance listed in §712.30. Limited exemptions exist under §712.25 for parties involved in research, making or importing less than 1100 pounds, or being small manufacturers or importers of certain chemical substances.

Record Keeping, Certifications, Prohibitions, and Enforcement

Facilities must record incidents and alleged incidents of **significant** damage to human health or the environment per §717. Manufacturers and processors must collect any such allegations identifying a chemical substance they make or process or allegations concerning the harmful effects of emissions, distribution, etc. Allegations must name the specific substance in question, present an article containing the substance or identify the substance in some other adequate manner per §717.10. A facility should inform an alleger of the final outcome of the allegation. Significant adverse reactions, as described in §717.12 to include such varied issues as birth defects, cancer, and fishkills, must be recorded unless directly attributable to an accidental or excessive discharge which has already been reported to the proper federal authorities. EPA may, via a letter or notice in the *Federal Register*, require submission of these reports.

Reports and records, along with supporting documentation, copies of notices to customers informing them of their relevant reporting obligations (remember, customers do not have to file TSCA reports unless they manufacture, process, or import chemical substances), and signed return receipts of such notification must be kept for anywhere between three and 30 years, although it would be wise to keep such records indefinitely. Each type of report will have unique characteristics as noted above and detailed in the specific sections of the CFR.

Per §702.20, importers of chemicals must either certify that the imported chemicals meet TSCA regulations or are not subject to TSCA (e.g., pesticides). It is up to the importer to make a good faith effort to determine the applicability of TSCA to its imports. Customs will refuse entry to any shipment without proper certification, and also will detain a shipment if there are reasonable grounds to believe that it violates TSCA. Detained shipments must be brought into compliance, exported, destroyed, or voluntarily abandoned within the time periods prescribed in 19 CFR 12.124. Similarly, exports of TSCA regulated items are governed under §707 Subpart D. In general, these regulations require exporters to notify EPA of proposed shipments of various TSCA chemicals.

Parts 747 and 749 set forth a variety of prohibitions on the use of certain metal working and cooling fluids. Facilities may only use the listed substances as prescribed in the CFR, and must be sure not to mix certain listed substances with those substances subject to the CFR. Additionally, warning labels and letters instructing potential users of these substances of their danger are required for several of these substances.

Should EPA feel it necessary, the Agency may commence a civil action in U.S. District Court to seize imminently hazardous chemical substances, to seek relief against any person who manufactures, processes, distributes, uses, or disposes of such substances, or both seizure and relief. Citizens also have specific legislative authority per §2619 to use a Federal Court to force companies or EPA to comply with TSCA's requirements.

EPA has a wide variety of enforcement and inspection powers through TSCA. Penalties for noncompliance can be high. Aiding the Agency in its enforcement efforts are provisions in TSCA protecting employees from retaliation for participating in TSCA enforcement actions. Failure to comply with the testing and notification procedures outlined by TSCA, knowingly using substances processed, manufactured, or distributed in violation of TSCA, or failure to keep proper records may result in civil penalties of up to $20,000 per day per violation as well as criminal penalties of up to $25,000 per day per violation, up to one year imprisonment, or both.

EMERGENCY PLANNING AND COMMUNITY RIGHT TO KNOW ACT

In 1984, over 3,500 people were killed and another 200,000 injured in Bhopal, India when a leak at a local Union Carbide plant released a cloud of highly toxic methyl isocyanate gas. While this was perhaps the most famous air pollution incident in history, significant disasters have occurred several times in the U.S. Fortunately for U.S. citizens, good management and lucky wind directions have minimized the damage caused by these releases.

In response to the dangers posed by leaking toxic chemicals, Congress passed the Emergency Planning and Community Right-to-Know Act (EPCRA) as part of its Superfund Amendments and Reauthorization Act of 1984. EPCRA, codified at 42 U.S.C. §§11001–11050, requires facilities which use or store certain amounts of various listed chemicals to provide lists of those chemicals to local authorities, notify those authorities of certain-sized chemical releases and provide inventories of various chemicals manufactured, imported, processed, or otherwise used at the facility. The point behind these requirements is that Congress believed that communities, and their respective emergency services, should be aware of the chemical hazards posed by their industrial residents. For example, fire fighters responding to an alarm at a warehouse should not be surprised when the burning building turns out to contain thousands of gallons of mercuric chloride.

EPCRA is divided into several main parts which have the following different reporting requirements.

EMERGENCY PLANNING AND EMERGENCY PLANNING NOTIFICATION is covered in 40 CFR 355.30. This section applies only to extremely hazardous substances (EHS). A facility which contains an amount of an EHS equal to or greater than its threshold planning quantity (TPQ) or designated state quantity, at any one time, must comply with the emergency planning requirements. In addition, for the purposes of this section, any EHS must be present in concentrations of greater than 1% by weight, regardless of location, number of containers, or method of storage. A list of EHSs and their TPQs is located in the appendices to §355. In cases where the TPQ is two numbers, the lower quantity applies only in certain circumstances, such as when a solid exists in a powdered form and has a particle size of less than 100 microns. These circumstances are detailed in §355.40 (e)(2)(i).

A facility which meets these criteria must notify the State Emergency Response Commission (SERC) that it is a facility subject to the emergency planning requirements. In addition, the facility must designate a facility emergency coordinator who will participate in the local emergency planning process and must furnish any information relevant to emergency planning as requested.

EMERGENCY RELEASE NOTIFICATION is covered under §355.40. This section applies to two groups of chemicals: CERCLA hazardous substances and EHS's. Only a "reportable quantity" of either type of substance is covered in this subsection. The reportable quantities for each type of substance are not the same. The reportable quantities for EHS's are located in Appendix B to Part 355; those for CERCLA hazardous substances are located in the table at 40 CFR §302.4.

There are exceptions to the reporting requirements of this section. Emergency release notification is not required for any release which results in exposure to persons solely within the boundaries of a facility or for any release which is a federally permitted release as defined in §101 (10) of CERCLA. Additionally, reporting is not required for any release that is continuous and stable in quantity and rate per 40 CFR 302.8(b), of CERCLA. Natural radionuclide releases, releases which do not meet CERCLA's definition of "release" under Section 101(22) of CERCLA, and releases of pesticide products which are exempt from CERCLA §103(a) reporting are, in general, exempt from release reporting requirements as well.

Should a facility experience a release of a reportable quantity of either EHS or CERCLA hazardous substance, and that release is not covered under any of §355.40's exceptions, the facility is responsible for properly reporting the incident. According to 40 CFR §355.40(b), these requirements include immediate notification of the community emergency coordinator of any area likely to be affected by the release and the state emergency response commission of any state likely to be affected by the release. If there is no local coordinator, the facility must notify relevant local emergency response personnel, such as the local fire department.

Initial notification must include: (1) the chemical name or identity of any substance involved in the release; (2) an indication of whether the substance is an extremely hazardous substance; (3) an estimate of the quantity of any such substance that was released into the environment; (4) the time and duration of the release; (5) the medium or media into which the release occurred; (6) any known or anticipated acute or chronic health risk associated with the emergency along with relevant advice for treating exposed individuals;

(7) proper precautions to take as the result of the release, including evacuation, unless that information is readily accessible in the community emergency plan; and (8) the names and telephone numbers of the person(s) to be contacted for further information. Follow-up written notification containing all of the above information, plus information on how the facility responded to the release, should be submitted as soon after the release as practicable. The National Response Center (1-800-424-8802) must also be notified when a spill of a reportable quantity of a CERCLA hazardous substance occurs.

For releases during transportation, or during storage incident to transportation, the information described above may be initially provided to the 911 emergency operator per 40 CFR §355.50. If there is no 911 emergency telephone number in operation, this information may be submitted to the regular operator. Naturally, follow-up written notification and information updates would be via the normal procedures, not the local operator.

The penalties for not complying with emergency release notification procedures are stringent. Any person who fails to comply with the requirements of §355.40 is subject to civil penalties of up to $25,000 for each violation in accordance with section 325(b)(1) of the EPCRA. Civil penalties may be incurred of up to $25,000 for each day during which the violation continues. In the case of a second or subsequent violation, a person may be subject to civil penalties of up to $75,000 for each day the violation continues. Criminal penalties apply as well. Any person who knowingly and willingly fails to provide notice in accordance with §355.40 can, upon conviction, be fined up to $25,000 or imprisoned for up to two years, or both. In the case of second or subsequent conviction, a person can be fined up to $50,000 or imprisoned for up to 5 years, or both.

Hazardous Chemical Inventory Reporting is explained in 40 CFR Part 370. This subsection applies to any chemical or material which requires a Material Safety Data Sheet (MSDS) under the Occupational Safety and Health Act (OSHA). If any chemical is present at a facility in amounts equal to or greater than the threshold of 10,000 pounds at any point in time during the calendar year, reporting is required. If the chemical is also an EHS, the threshold is less — either 500 pounds or its TPQ, whichever is lower. Hazardous chemicals are mainly those chemicals defined under 29 CFR 1910.1200(c) (OSHA). Extremely hazardous chemicals are those chemicals listed in the appendices to 40 CFR 355.

The basic requirements of this program are that any facility which meets a threshold value must submit an MSDS to the local emergency planning committee, the state, or tribal emergency response commission and the fire department with jurisdiction over the facility, for each hazardous chemical present at the facility in threshold amounts. Per §370.21(b), facilities may elect to submit a list of chemicals for which an MSDS is required, with the common or chemical name and relevant hazardous components, instead of submitting individual MSDSs. Should the facility learn of new information concerning the hazards of a submitted chemical, or meet the thresholds with a new chemical, it must submit that information within three months. In addition to the submission of MSDSs for chemicals present in TPQ amounts, a facility must provide an MSDS for non-TPQ chemicals if requested to do so by the local emergency planning committee.

In addition, inventory reports are submitted on specific EPA forms per 40 CFR §370 Subpart D. Many states have their own required forms. There are two types, Tier I and Tier II. Tier I forms are used when the submission is due to chemicals being present at the facility above TPQ or threshold amounts. This form is submitted to the State Emergency Response Commission (SERC), the Local Emergency Planning Committee (LEPC), and the local fire department. Tier II forms are used when the information is being requested by the proper authorities, although Tier II forms are often submitted in lieu of Tier I forms. Subpart D in 40 CFR Part 370 provides detailed instructions on which chemicals are covered by the forms and how to fill them out. Tier II reports are due within 30 days of receipt of a written request for the information.

If hazardous chemicals are contained in a mixture, the MSDS and inventory form reporting requirements may be met by submitting the required information for each hazardous chemical in the mixture or by providing the required information on the mixture itself.

The general public may request MSDS and Tier II information from the local emergency planning committee. If the committee does not have the requested information, it will request that information from the relevant facility.

TOXIC CHEMICAL REPORTING is the final reporting requirements under EPCRA and is explained in 40 CFR Part 372. The main purpose of this requirement is to collect information to inform the general public and the communities surrounding relevant facilities about toxic chemical releases.

Not all facilities need to worry about toxic chemical release reporting. Only facilities meeting all of the criteria set forth in §372.22 must comply with these report requirements. These criteria include having 10 or more full-time employees, being in Standard Industrial Classification Codes 20 through 39, and making, processing, or using a toxic chemical in excess of the threshold quantities set forth in §372.25. These threshold quantities are "manufacturing" or "processing" greater that 25,000 pounds and/or "otherwise using" greater than 10,000 pounds of the chemical per calendar year with some exceptions. The term "otherwise using" is subject to varying interpretations and should become the subject of litigation. If toxic chemicals are recycled/reused at the facility, the amount used must include the chemicals added during the year. The actual toxic chemicals are listed in Subpart D.

Executive Order 12856, dated August 3, 1993, orders federal compliance with right-to-know laws and pollution prevention requirements. Thus, federal facilities must comply both with EPCRA and the Pollution Prevention Act of 1990.

The reporting requirements and schedules are set forth in §372.30. Essentially, any owner or operator of a facility covered by this section must file an EPA Form R (EPA Form 9350-1) in accordance with the instructions contained in Subpart E. The CFR also covers a variety of scenarios, such as where an owner or operator knows it is using some sort of toxic chemical, but is uncertain of the amount because the concentration of the chemical is unknown or the specific chemical identity is unknown. In these cases, the CFR explains how the facility can determine its relevant reporting requirements. The reports for each calendar year must be submitted on or before July 1 of the following year. Form R may be obtained from EPA Section 313 Document Distribution Center, POB 12505, Cincinnati, OH 45212. The Agency encourages use of magnetic media for submittals. These forms must be verified and signed by a senior management official. Form Rs include a wide variety of information such as an indication of the maximum amount of the chemical on site at any time during the reporting year, the name of the chemical reported, and an estimate of total releases from the facility based on point source emissions, fugitive emissions, underground injection, and releases to land. The Form R also includes a description of various waste stream and treatment procedures.

There are five categories where toxic substances at a facility may not lead to specific reporting requirements. These exemptions are detailed in §372.38 and include:

1. *De minimus* concentrations – toxic chemicals in a concentration below 1% or below 0.1% if a specifically listed carcinogen, in a mixture
2. Toxic chemicals in "articles" that are used on site without resulting in a release. Articles are defined as clothing, containers, etc.
3. Toxic chemicals "used" for specific purposes such as structural components of a facility, routine janitorial or facility grounds maintenance, personal use by employees of such items as cosmetics and food, maintaining the facility s motor vehicles, and certain air or water processes
4. Certain laboratory activities when under the supervision of a technically qualified individual as defined in 40 CFR §720.3(ee)
5. When property is leased, the owner may not have to meet any reporting requirements if he/she has no other business interests in the covered activity.

Under §372.45, a variety of facilities which sell or otherwise distribute substances containing toxic chemicals to a covered facility, or to someone who might in turn sell the chemical substance to a covered facility, must comply with certain notification requirements. These requirements include that there be a statement that the item contains a toxic chemical(s), the name of each toxic chemical and the percent by weight of each toxic chemical present in the mixture or product. Notification should be provided, in writing, with the first shipment of the chemical to the receiver in each calendar year. If the material is subsequently altered by adding, removing, or altering the percentage of any toxic chemical, the next shipment should be accompanied by a notification to that effect. If an MSDS is required per 29 CFR 1910.1200, this notification should either be attached to or incorporated into the MSDS. Notification is not required for defined *de minimus* concentrations of toxic chemicals, defined articles, food, drugs, and so forth packaged for distribution to the general public or defined consumer products per the Consumer Product Safety Act.

Confidential Information

The information provided by the TRI reports is provided to the general public. EPA puts out an annual nation-wide report approximately 16 months after the end of the calendar year, in addition to providing quicker public access to this information via an on-line database. Additionally, information submitted to the local emergency planning committee or any other emergency response organization by a Hazardous Chemical Inventory Report may become available to the public, as may the information on a Form R toxic chemical release report. Because some of the information contained in these reports may be trade secrets, EPA allows the reporting facility to claim trade secret confidentiality in the reports. The methods for requesting such confidentiality are detailed in 40 CFR §350.

There are four methods of asserting a claim of trade secrecy under §350.5, depending on which section of EPCRA demands submittal of the relevant information. For example, if §311 demands submission of information for chemicals requiring a Material Safety Data Sheet under the Occupational Safety and Health Act, the method of asserting a claim of trade secrecy would be detailed in §350.5(c). Subsections (b), (d), and (e) contain similar instructions.

The basic process of applying for trade secret status is as follows. The facility submits to EPA both a sanitized and an unsanitized version of the trade secret substantiation required in §350.7. The facility must also give EPA a copy of the information that it is submitting to the relevant emergency planning committees, with a generic class of chemicals put in place of the specific chemicals claimed as trade secrets. If EPA determines that the chemicals are, in fact, subject to trade secret protection, then that information is treated as confidential. Under certain circumstances, states and medical health professionals may gain access to specific trade secrets. If EPA decides that the information is not eligible for trade secret status, and that decision stands, then the Agency may disclose the relevant information to the general public.

FEDERAL INSECTICIDE, FUNGICIDE, AND RODENTICIDE ACT (FIFRA)

The Federal Insecticide, Fungicide, and Rodenticide Act (FIFRA) is located at 7 USC §§136–136y. The Act is primarily implemented by 40 CFR

§§152–186. This Act, and its implementing regulatory programs, is basically designed to manage the development, storage, application, and disposal of pesticides. Pesticides, by their very nature, as well as by their legal definition in the Act, are chemicals that are designed to prevent, destroy, repel, or mitigate pests. Pests include insects, rodents, fungus, or just about any other living organism designated as a pest by EPA. These definitions mean that pesticides are designed to kill or harm unwanted creatures. Common sense dictates that chemicals designed to kill rats, for example, could also, if misused or improperly stored, kill or injure unintended animals such as cattle, dogs or even humans. Hence FIFRA has become, in effect, the Toxic Substances Control Act (TSCA), the Resource Conservation and Recovery Act (RCRA), and, in some ways, the Occupational Safety and Health Act (OSHA) of the agricultural world. This analogy becomes more apparent when one reviews the numerous exceptions in other regulatory programs for farmers, fertilizers, and other agricultural entities.

Like all regulatory programs, it is essential to understand the basic definitions in FIFRA before one can properly implement or monitor a compliance program. Basic definitions are found in 40 CFR §152.3. Subsequent sections that refer to "new use," "residential use," and "institutional use" may only be understood through proper interpretation of these terms as described in the Code of Federal Regulations (CFR). The two most important definitions, as noted above, are "pesticide" and "pest." If an item is not intended for use against pests, it is not a pesticide per §152.8. Accordingly, chemicals for controlling fungi or bacteria on humans or animals are not pesticides. Many fertilizers or other chemicals or organisms used to increase either the fertility of the soil or the ability of plants to absorb nutrients through the soil are similarly defined as not being pesticides. 40 CFR §152.10 expands this list of nonpesticides to include products that are not deemed to be used for a pesticidal effect. Bleaches, cleaning agents, deodorizers, and physical barriers (such as certain pruning paints for trees) are examples of these types of non-pesticides. Naturally, if the CFR states that an item is not a pesticide, then a compliance officer need not worry about ensuring that use of the item follows FIFRA requirements, although OSHA, RCRA, and TSCA may be relevant.

In addition to providing several categories of "nonpesticides," the CFR also provides several groups of pesticides that are excepted from FIFRA under 40 CFR §152 Subpart B. §152.20 explains that if EPA feels that another agency is sufficiently regulating a substance, there is no need for EPA to regulate it under FIFRA. Many biological control agents and human drugs are exempted from FIFRA under this section. §152.25 exempts other chemicals when used in specific fashions. Wood treated against insects, pheromone traps, natural cedar, and vitamin hormone products are examples of chemicals which may, if their use meets certain conditions, be exempted from FIFRA. §152.30 allows limited distribution of certain pesticides without proper registration. Transferring an unregistered pesticide for export, for disposal, under an emergency exemption, or for experimental use are several examples of these distribution exemptions. Even when a pesticide falls under this exemption for distribution, however, there are still labeling, packaging, or other specified requirements the compliance officer must ensure are met.

Registration

§136a of FIFRA requires that, except for the exemptions discussed above, no person may distribute or sell unregistered pesticides. While anyone may apply to register a new pesticide product, it is most likely that the producer would ensure that the item is registered. In some cases, though, such as where a facility wishes to import a pesticide or desires another party to manufacture a new pesticide for a particular use, the end user or the importer may wish to register the product. Whatever the rationale for deciding who applies to register the pesticide, the compliance officer must make sure it is registered prior to distributing or selling it. When information pertinent to the registered pesticide changes, such as a change in its labeling or composition, the compliance officer may have to submit an application for an amended registration per 40 CFR §152.44. Minor changes may only require Agency notification and certain administrative-type changes to the label do not even require that. Subparts C through H of 40 CFR §152 describe the registration process in great detail, including the information required in the application, the rights of parties submitting data and the Agency review process.

It is important to note that a new use of a pesticide requires registration, even if the pesticide is already registered for an existing use. New use, has a specific meaning within the regulatory program under §152.3. As a rough rule of thumb, if a pesticide is being used in a way that increases exposure to humans, invokes the Federal Food, Drug, and Cosmetic Act, or puts a new active ingredient into the environment, it is probably a new use and may require registration.

Perhaps the most important part of the registration process is Subpart E data submission requirements. The goal of this data submission is to allow the Agency to determine that use of the pesticide in accordance with widespread and commonly recognized practices will not generally cause unreasonable adverse effects on the environment. Applicants may conduct their own studies, refer to federal studies, or refer to already registered constituent pesticides when submitting their data. 40 CFR §158 describes in detail the exact requirements of this data submission. As with many data submission programs, applicants may ask that their data be treated confidentially.

Registrants must also certify that their pesticide packaging meets the standards of §157.32 if they are subject to the child-resistant packaging regulations described below.

In lieu of registering a pesticide, a party may wish to apply for an Experimental Use Permit under §172. This permit may be used for unregistered pesticides or for pesticides which are being considered for a new use. Sale or distribution of pesticides under an Experimental Use Permit is limited to participants in the program, and use of the pesticides is only proper when a person grants express permission to use the pesticide on his or her property under the conditions of the permit. Permits are generally valid for one year, depending on the crop or test program, and they may be extended if necessary. Under §172, EPA may grant states the authority to run their own experimental use programs and issue the relevant permits.

Labeling

According to 40 CFR §156.10, every pesticide must bear a label which clearly and prominently shows certain information. All labels must be in English, although the Agency may require additional languages as necessary to protect the public. Information on the label must include the name under which the product is sold, the net contents of the product, prescribed warning statements and directions for use. The label must be on the actual pesticide container and, if the container is placed inside something else, such as a cardboard box, a label must be attached to the exterior container also. While in transit, labeling of pesticides must also meet the labeling, marking, and placarding requirements of 49 CFR §§179–189 Department of Transportation regulations.

Packaging

Pesticides must also meet the packaging requirements of 40 CFR §157. In general, a pesticide must be distributed and sold in approved child-resistant packaging if it meets certain toxicity criteria as discussed in §157.22 *and* the product's labeling either directly recommends residential use or reasonably can be interpreted to permit residential use. For example, a small jar of rat poison would probably require child-resistant packaging, assuming it meets one of the five toxicity criteria, but 55 gallon drums of the same material would probably not require such packaging. §157.24 spells out specific exemptions from the requirement for child-resistant packaging requirements. Large sized packages, as defined in the regulations, products classified for restricted use and specific pesticides for which EPA has approved an exemption application fall under these exemptions. The Agency may decline to approve an exemption when it believes the threat to public safety warrants such action. Exempted pesticides may still be packaged in a child-resistant manner, but only with the same Agency certification as is required for non-exempt pesticides.

Child-resistant packaging must meet the standards set out by 16 CFR 1700. Additionally, when in use as a pesticide container, these standards must continue to be met. For example, an acidic pesticide should not eat away at the safety features of its container. The safety features also should continue to function throughout the probable lifetime of the container, i.e., plastic safeguards should not get loose and metal rings should not suffer from metal fatigue as a container is opened and shut over the years.

Record Keeping

40 CFR §169 requires that producers of pesticides or of the active ingredients used in pesticides subject to FIFRA keep a variety of records. Basic records must include the product name, EPA registration number, amounts per batch of all pesticides produced, and the Experimental Permit Number, if appropriate. Other records must include the name and address of the shipper and carrier of active ingredients received by the producer, records of any tests done on humans, and research data. Even copies of all domestic advertising of the restricted uses of a pesticide registered for restricted use may have to be retained. These records must be kept for a varying amount of time, depending on the record. Records of tests on humans must be kept for 20 years, while records containing research data relating to registered pesticides must be kept as long as the registration is valid. It would probably be wise for the compliance officer to keep these records for as long as possible.

Worker Protection

40 CFR Part 170 details the standards designed to reduce the risks of illness or injury resulting from workers' and handlers' occupational exposure to pesticides on agricultural establishments. In addition to traditional exposure, this Part attempts to mitigate accidental exposure. To accomplish these goals, §170 requires workplace practices designed to reduce or eliminate exposure to pesticides and establishes procedures for responding to exposure-related emergencies. Liability for violations of this section by a facility's workers also is expressly assumed by the facility under §170.9(c).

Subpart B sets the specific standards for worker protection. This subpart also provides several exceptions to these standards, including exceptions for a variety of pesticide applications such as mosquito control and other wide-area pest control programs sponsored by government entities, use of pesticides on the harvested portions of agricultural plants, and exposure to family members on a family-owned agricultural establishment.

§§170.110 and 170.112 detail how these worker protection standards apply. Tables 1 and 2 in these sections provide a quick reference to find how long workers must stay out of an area after a certain type of pesticide application given a certain amount of ventilation. The type of protective gear, ranging from eye protection to respirators, also is detailed in respect to how recently pesticides have been applied to an area and what type of work is going to be done. Where the proper authorities declare an "agricultural emergency," workers may enter a treated area under a restricted-entry interval as long as certain listed safeguards are met.

Anytime workers enter a treated area, it is the employer's responsibility to ensure that they have been properly informed of the dangers, symptoms, and first aid responses involved with any relevant pesticides. Under §170.120, an agricultural employer must also inform workers of pesticide applications unless it is certain that the workers will not enter a treated area. Warnings should include posted notices in English and Spanish saying "Danger," "Pesticides," and "Keep out." Additional pesticide safety posters conveying basic pesticide safety concepts such as "no eating or drinking in a treated area" also may be required if pesticides have been applied within the previous 30 days.

Agricultural employers also are responsible for ensuring that their employees are properly trained. Proper training depends on the potential each employee has for exposure, and is detailed in §170.130. Safety training is generally required if an area has been treated in the past 30 days. Safety training includes discussions of the hazards posed by pesticides, the routes by which pesticides may enter the body and signs and symptoms of common types of pesticide poisoning. The person conducting the training must meet one of four criteria, including being a certified restricted-use pesticide applicator.

If there is potential for worker contamination, an agricultural employer should provide an area for decontamination. This decontamination area is described in §170.150 and includes having enough water for routine washing and emergency eye flushing, soap, and single use towels. This area must be no more than one-quarter mile from where the workers are located. Should a worker be poisoned by pesticides, the employer has an affirmative duty to provide emergency transportation to an appropriate emergency medical facility.

§170 Subpart C and all of §171 provide much more detailed guidance on how Pesticide Handlers and Pesticide Applicators must be trained and certified. Although the regulations are quite detailed, the basic thrust is pesticides must be handled and applied in such a manner that no pesticide will contact, either directly or through drift, any worker or other person besides a properly trained and equipped handler or applicator. Warning posters concerning the application must be properly displayed, the handlers and applicators must be properly trained, and they must understand and be able to implement the particular labeling requirements of the applied pesticide. Depending on the dangers posed by the pesticides, and whether the application is via ground or aerial spraying or some other means, these groups of workers must utilize protective equipment as specified on the pesticide labels. Different types of pesticide applicators must be properly certified according to their status as detailed in §171.

Pesticides in Foods and Animal Feeds

Although many pesticides are used on golf courses, on tree plantations, and in other situations where pesticide residues may pose only indirect health threats to humans, a large percentage of pesticide use is on crops intended for human or animal consumption. Not surprisingly, this use of pesticides on crops has led to regulations concerning pesticide residue on food additives, food, and animal feed. These regulations are primarily found in 40 CFR Parts 177, 178, 180, 189, 185, and 186.

The regulatory programs limiting the pesticide residues in the products mentioned above basically function as follows. Someone petitions the Agency to set standards for these products. The petition may have to be accompanied by a fee of over $58,000 in some cases. Following traditional administrative procedures, EPA may or may not set standards, depending on how serious a threat the Agency feels is posed by the product. During the process of determining a relevant standard, the Agency will accept comments from interested parties. After a standard is set, a party may continue to petition the Agency to erase, strengthen, or otherwise modify the standard.

§180 sets out specific amounts of pesticide residues that are acceptable on raw agricultural commodities (RAC). RACs do not necessarily include the whole product, so a compliance officer should check §180.1(j) to determine which parts of a product to measure for residue. §180.2 lists a variety of pesticide chemicals generally considered safe, although the compliance officer should check with EPA to make sure this list is accurate prior to relying on it for his compliance program. The tolerance limits vary from chemical to chemical and from agricultural product to agricultural product. For example, the herbicide atrazine is tolerable in 0.02 parts per million (ppm) in cattle meat but is acceptable at up to 15 ppm in fodder corn while the herbicide terbacil is approved for residues of 0.1 ppm in cattle meat. Some pesticides will have a zero tolerance for residues under certain circumstances. The Food and Drug Administration "Pesticide Analytical Manual" describes the methods to be used for determining whether pesticide residues are in compliance with established tolerances.

§185 and §186 are similar to §180 in that they set out specific tolerances for pesticides in food for human and animal consumption. Like the pesticides in §180, these pesticides are listed by name and are given various tolerance limits depending on the type of pesticide and its final use in food or food products. Some pesticide tolerances are accompanied by directions for permitted use, such as the application directions for Chlorpyrifos which prohibit use near uncovered food. A compliance officer concerned with pesticide levels in these agricultural products or with how to apply pesticides in areas where these products are present should refer to these sections for guidance on the pesticide in question. A follow-up call to EPA should ensure that the regulations concerning the pesticide have not changed.

ENVIRONMENTAL COMPLIANCE

A compliance officer should review organization records to determine if the facility needs to initiate or monitor a compliance program for any aspect of TSCA. It is quite possible to have a major compliance program in one area without having a compliance program with another area.

Manufacturing, Processing, and Distributing
Chemical Substances

Checklist :

- Does facility manufacture, process or distribute chemical substances?

     Yes or No. Continue as below

- Is the facility going to manufacture or process a chemical substance for a *new use* as listed in §721?

     No. Stop here
     Yes. Continue

- Is the substance covered by any of several exemptions?

     Yes. Make certain of exceptions and stop here
     No. Continue

- File premanufacture notices, new use notification, test results, and section 8(a) reports and inventories as necessary.

Compliance officers must ensure that their facilities file premanufacture notices for new chemicals that they are planning on making, processing, or distributing. Significant new uses of chemicals as described in §721 will also require notification.

A compliance officer must compare the list of chemical substances which EPA has determined to pose unreasonable dangers against substances manufactured, processed, or distributed at the facility. Substances on this list should not require further testing. If the substances are not on this list, testing may be required should EPA believe the substances may pose unreasonable dangers.

If the manufacturing or processing of a substance is for a new use, as listed in §721, the facility must first file a Section Five notice, which would be accompanied by a fee and the results of the testing required above.

Premanufacture notices are discussed in §720 and must be submitted via a specific notice form.

Manufacturing, Processing, and Distributing
Chemical Substances (continued)

Checklist (continued):

Section 8(a) forms are required for production of several listed chemicals in Subparts B and D.

Inventory reports of many chemicals designated "for commercial purposes" are required under §710 Subpart A and updating is required under Subpart B. §§710.5, 710.32, and 710.33 contain inventory and updating requirements.

Facilities making or importing chemical substances listed in §712.30 must file a single EPA Form No. 7710-35.

The compliance officer should ensure that his/her activity(s) or product(s) are not covered under any of the several exemptions in the regulations.

EMERGENCY PLANNING AND
COMMUNITY RIGHT TO KNOW ACT

Emergency Plans and Notification

Checklist :

- Determine if the facility contains TPQ amounts of extremely hazardous substances and triggers the regulatory requirements.

   No: No Compliance Program Necessary

   Yes: Notify SERC and designate a facility emergency coordinator to participate in local emergency planning.

- Does the facility store CERCLA hazardous substances or extremely hazardous substances?

   No: No reporting necessary.

Emergency Plans and Notification (continued)

Checklist (continued):

> Yes: Facility must have in place spill reporting procedures per 40 CFR 355.40(b)

Hazardous Chemical Inventory Reports

Checklist :

- Determine if the facility contains hazardous chemicals in excess of threshold amounts. These amounts are 10,000 pounds for hazardous chemicals and the lower of 500 pounds or the threshold planning quantity of extremely hazardous chemicals.

- Are chemicals present above these thresholds?

    > No: No compliance program necessary

    > Yes: Submit MSDS for these chemicals to local Emergency Planning Committee, State Emergency Reponse Commission, and local fire department
    >
    > Submit Tier I or Tier II inventory reports per 40 CFR §370 Subpart D in a timely fashion.

Toxic Chemical Release Reporting

Checklist :

- Does the facility meet the size, SIC, and threshold quantity criteria set forth in 40 CFR §372.22, or is it a federal facility?

    > No: No compliance program is needed.

    > Yes: Is facility covered by any of §372.28's exemptions?

Toxic Chemical Release Reporting (continued)

> **Checklist (continued):**
>
>   Yes: No compliance program is needed.
>
>   No: File EPA Form R per §372.30.
>
>   Facilities which distribute substance containing toxic chemicals may have to comply with notification requirements per §372.45.

Confidential Information

> **Checklist :**
>
> • Are industrial secrets potentially at risk under EPCRA reporting process?
>
>   No: No need to claim secrecy.
>
>   Yes: Claim trade secrecy under §350.5.

FEDERAL INSECTICIDE, FUNGICIDE, AND RODENTICIDE ACT

Distribution of Pesticides

> **Checklist :**
>
> • Does the facility make, distribute, or use chemicals that meet the statutory definition of pesticides under §152.3, are not non-pesticides per §152.10, or are not excepted under Subpart B?
>
>   No: Document. No compliance program needed.
>
>   Yes: Compliance program is needed and must be tailored to the use of pesticides in the facility.

Distribution of Pesticides (continued)

> **Checklist (continued):**
>
> - Does the facility distribute a new pesticide or a pesticide with a new use?
>
>   No: No registration necessary.
>
>   Yes: Facility must ensure pesticides are registered with EPA per 40 CFR §152. Note: Facility may apply for Experimental Use Permit per §172.
>   - Pesticides must be properly labeled per 40 CFR §156. Labels must be on exterior boxes of pesticide containers as well as on the containers themselves.
>   - Pesticides in transit must meet Department of Transportation regulations for hazardous material transportation.
>   - Pesticides must meet packaging requirements of 40 CFR §157. Child-resistant packaging may be required if the pesticides meet certain toxicity criteria and the product is labeled or can be expected to be used in residences. Some large containers of pesticides or certain noted pesticides are excepted.

Pesticide Production

> **Checklist :**
>
> - Does the facility produce pesticides or active ingredients for pesticides?
>
>   No: No compliance issues raised.
>
>   Yes: Facility must keep a variety of records under 40 CFR §169. Some of these records must be kept for up to 20 years or as long as a registration is valid.

Worker Protection

Checklist :

- Is the facility an agricultural establishment which employs agricultural workers?

    No: No compliance program needed. Note: Contract-ed lawn and garden workers may raise specific worker protection compliance issues depending on state laws of agency. A compliance officer should seek legal counsel on facility responsibil-ity for outside pesticide workers.

    Yes: The facility must ensure worker protection regu-lations are met. Note: Regulatory requirements are excepted for various pesticide applications noted in Subpart B.
    - Workers may only enter areas treated with pesticides after a prescribed period of time or wearing certain protective equipment.
    - Workers must be properly trained and warned of the dangers posed by pesticides and in-formed of symptoms of contamination and first aid issues.
    - Treated areas must be posted with "Keep Out" signs.
    - Decontamination areas must be provided if there is potential for worker contamination.

- Do facility workers apply or handle pesticides?

    No: No compliance program needed. Concerns for contract pesticide workers are discussed above.

    Yes: Facility must ensure that Pesticide Handlers and Applicators are trained and certified per §§170 and 171.
    - Warning posters concerning pesticide applica-tions must be displayed.
    - Workers must utilize proper protective equip-ment based on pesticide and method of appli-cation.

Pesticides in Foods and Animal Feeds

Checklist :

- Does the facility produce any crops that are used for food additives, food, or animal feed?

 No: No compliance program needed.

 Yes: The facility must ensure that specific listed tolerances for pesticide residues in various agricultural products are not exceeded. 40 CFR §§180, 185, and 186 list the amounts of various pesticide residues that are permissible on agricultural products intended for consumption.

GLOSSARY

By-Products . . . . Materials that are produced in a chemical reaction that are not those for which the reaction is carried out.

Designated State Quantity . . . . A value set by an individual state for concentrations of extremely hazardous substances below which the emergency planning requirements do not apply.

Material Safety Data . . . . A sheet provided by the supplier of a chemical that describes the chemical's properties, dangers, and actions to be taken in case of a spill.
 Sheet(MSDS)

Pheromone Traps . . . . Traps to attract insects that are baited with sexual stimulants.

Plant Nutrients . . . . Chemicals that feed plants and are absorbed by them through the soil.

Reportable Quantity . . . . Amount of a hazardous substance that, upon release, triggers the Emergency Release Notification procedure.

Respirators . . . . Face masks worn by the worker without external supplies of air.

Sanitized Version . . . . A description of a material or a process in which confidential information is not included.

Threshold Planning Quantity . . (TPQ) — Federal designation of extremely hazardous substances below which the emergency planning requirements do not apply.

ACRONYMS

CAIR . . . .   Comprehensive Assessment Information Rule

EPCRA . . . .   Emergency Planning and Community Right to Know Act

FIFRA . . . .   Federal Insecticide, Fungicide, and Rodenticide Act

MSDS . . . .   Material Safety Data Sheet

OSHA . . . .   Occupational Safety and Health Act

RAC. . . . .   Raw Agricultural Commodities

TPQ . . . .   Threshold Planning Quantity

TRI . . . .   Toxic Chemical Release Inventory

REFERENCES AND SELECTED READING

Mackenthun, K. and Bregman, J., 1991, *Environmental Regulations Handbook*, Lewis Publishers, Boca Raton, FL.

MORGAN, LEWIS, and BOCKIUS, 1993, *Environmental Deskbook*, New York, NY.

U.S. Army Corps of Engineers, Construction Engineering Research Laboratories, Revised, September, 1995, "The Environmental Assessment and Management (TEAM) Guide," USACERL Special Report EC-95/05, Champaign, IL.

10   Storage Tanks

UNDERGROUND STORAGE TANKS

Introduction

Many hazardous or other regulated materials (ORM) are manufactured, stored, transported, or used in liquid form. While in many instances these materials may be placed in relatively small containers, such as 5-gallon buckets or 55-gallon drums, in many other instances they are stored in much larger tanks. These larger tanks may be either above or below ground, and may raise many environmental compliance and liability issues. Regardless of the type of tank, there are numerous regulatory programs governing the construction, maintenance, and use of storage tank systems. Some tank systems have specific regulatory programs governing them, such as the tanks used in Hazardous Waste Treatment, Storage, and Disposal Facilities discussed in RCRA 40 CFR §264, Subpart J. Similarly, 49 CFR §173 discusses the standards tanks must meet when being used to transport hazardous materials.

The primary regulatory program for Underground Storage Tanks is RCRA Subtitle I, which is codified in the Solid Waste Disposal Act at 42 USC §6991(a)–(i). The federal regulations implementing this law are located at 40 CFR §280. The UST regulatory program is detailed and comprehensive, and violations of the regulations may lead to enforcement actions, including Agency compliance orders and subsequent fines for non-compliance.

The federal UST program is broken down into eight separate subparts. Each subpart has specific requirements of its own, but all of them are interrelated. Further, the subparts are listed in a logical progression, with the program scope and definitions up front, followed by standards for new USTs, operating requirements, release detection, release response, and so forth.

The federal UST regulations contain a large number of exceptions. However, many states have implemented stricter regulatory programs, such as the Massachusetts Chapter 21E program. Additionally, other compliance issues associated with USTs may make it prudent for a facility to follow the regulatory programs even if it does not have to. That leaking USTs are almost synonymous with CERCLA or other remediation programs such as the military s Installation

Restoration Program (IRP) supports this cautious policy. The U.S. Army, as an example, considers USTs such a major compliance issue that it has formally excused itself from some of the UST exemptions which otherwise would remove many of its tanks from specific compliance programs (AR200-1, 1990).

The largest concerns with USTs revolve around whether they leak, how to keep them from leaking and what to do if they are leaking. As far back as 1984, Congress estimated that there were between 75,000 and 100,000 leaking USTs in the U.S. (House of Representatives, 1984). This number has since grown (1995) to over 295,000 confirmed releases (EPA, 1995).

Despite their well-known problems, underground storage tanks were popular for a time because they posed less of a fire threat than above ground storage tanks (ASTs). In fact, fire code regulations prohibited the storage of various hazardous materials in ASTs throughout much of the country for many years. Hence, gas stations, home owners, and other parties put many of their storage tanks underground. Unfortunately, underground tanks are virtually impossible to inspect visually, and sophisticated leak detection systems only recently have become widely available. Tanks placed in the ground decades ago frequently were made of metal, which rusted over time. Eventually, many of these USTs began to leak, and have resulted in mammoth restoration efforts including soil removal programs and even moving houses.

It is easier to understand the regulatory program governing USTs after a brief discussion of the mechanical aspects of a UST system. Individual tanks will vary somewhat depending on their use and their surroundings, but they all will have some of the following characteristics in common. A UST will have at least one wall, which is what holds the liquid in place. When there is only one wall, the tank is referred to as a "single-walled tank." When the tank has two walls it is referred to as a "double-walled tank." Double-walled tanks have a space between the two walls called an interstitial space. In theory, this space allows material leaking through the first wall to pool up at the second wall without being released to the environment. Interstitial space monitoring equipment and alarms should sense that material has entered the space, allowing compliance personnel to address the leak before the material escapes through the second wall.

Most underground storage tanks have a fill pipe which allows the liquid to be transferred into the tank. On a typical oil tank, this pipe either sticks out of the ground fairly close to the tank, or is located in an enclosed "manway" below the ground but directly above the tank. The fill pipe may be surrounded by a collar or catch basin, which should contain any spills that may occur during filling. The fill pipe, or access to it, may have a locking mechanism to protect the integrity of the tank's contents. The tank also should have a vent pipe, which may be near the fill pipe or some distance away, depending on the size of the tank. An underground storage tank also will have a piping system to remove the materials from the tank. In the case of a heating oil tank, this system may be a simple copper tube that runs from the tank to the boiler. In the case of a more complex chemical tank farm, the piping may be several inches in diameter and run through a variety of distribution systems.

RCRA Regulatory Program Scope

40 CFR §280.12 defines an underground storage tank. It states that a UST is a single tank or combination of tanks, with their associated piping, that is used to contain an accumulation of **regulated substances**, the volume of which is 10% or more below the surface of the ground. Many types of tanks are specifically excluded from this definition, including septic tanks, farm, or residential tanks of 1,100 gallons or less which are used to store motor fuel for noncommercial purposes, and tanks used for storing heating oil for use on the premises. USTs also do not include storage tanks situated in an underground area, such as a basement or mine shaft, if the tank is situated on or above the surface of the floor. Flow-through process tanks forming an integral part of a production process also are excluded from the regulations.

Even these exclusions are not all-encompassing. §280.10(b) specifically excludes tanks that hold RCRA hazardous wastes, which have their own regulatory requirements, equipment or machinery that contains regulated substances for operational purposes such as hydraulic lift tanks, and any emergency spill or overflow containment UST system that is expeditiously emptied after each use. Additionally, Part §280 is inapplicable to UST systems whose capacity is 110 gallons or less or which contain *de minimus* concentrations of regulated substances.

§280.10(c) sets out an additional group of USTs that do not have to comply with Subparts B, C, D, and E of Part 280. This group of USTs includes wastewater treatment systems, UST systems containing radioactive material regulated under the Atomic Energy Act, UST systems that are a part of a nuclear power plant's emergency generator system, and airport hydrant fuel distribution systems. Although exempt from most of §284 standards, these UST systems still must comply with Subparts F and G s release response and closure requirements.

Finally, any UST storing fuel solely for use by emergency power generators does not have to comply with Subpart D release detection requirements, per §280.10(d).

UST Systems: Design, Construction, Installation, and Notification

Newly installed USTs must meet the requirements of 40 CFR §280 Subpart B. These requirements are designed to prevent releases due to structural failure, corrosion, or spills and overfills for however long the system is used to store regulated substances. Owners and operators are responsible for meeting these regulations.

In addition to the general requirement that all tanks be properly designed and constructed, any portion of a UST that is underground and routinely contains product must be protected from corrosion as specified in §280.20. Each type of tank, whether it be fiberglass, metal, steel-fiberglass-reinforced-plastic composite or any other material, must meet specific standards. Steel and cathodically protected tanks have the most complex construction requirements, with the manner of cathodic protection being specified. Where a UST is installed at a site that a corrosion expert determines should not have a release due to corrosion during its operating life, the tank may be constructed of metal without additional corrosion protection measures. In such a case, the compliance officer should maintain records demonstrating the site's lack of corrosive properties. Fiberglass, cathodically protected steel, and steel-fiberglass reinforced plastic composite USTs may comply with construction standards by meeting listed industry codes, such as Underwriters Laboratories Standards. The implementing agency, whether it be state or federal, may approve other UST construction methods if it determines that the construction and corrosion protection of a UST adequately prevent a release. The piping associated with USTs must meet virtually identical requirements if it routinely contains regulated substances and is in contact with the ground.

Spill and overfill prevention equipment is required on new USTs for product transfer to them. The spill prevention equipment must prevent the release of product to the environment when the transfer hose is detached from the fill pipe. A spill catch basin is a simple example of such equipment — product is caught by the basin as the transfer hose is detached and does not enter the environment.

Overfill prevention equipment is somewhat more complicated. Filling a UST system may take a long time, and the person manning the transfer hose may not remain at the transfer point for all that time. An example is when a fuel oil delivery man hooks up his hose to the UST and then returns to the cab of his truck until the fuel is delivered. If the oil is spilling out of the hose and not entering the tank, he may not realize it until the release has occurred. The overfill protection should automatically shut off flow into the tank when the tank is no more than 95% full; alert the transfer operator when the tank is no more than 90% full, or restrict flow 30 minutes prior to overfilling; alert the operator with an alarm one minute before overfilling, or automatically shut off flow into the tank so that none of the fittings located on top of the tank are exposed to product due to overfilling. If the UST system is filled by transfers of no more than 25 gallons at one time, or if alternative equipment is used that the agency finds to be protective of human health and the environment, the owners and operators do not have to use the spill and overfill protection specified above.

Tanks and piping must be properly installed in accordance with an accepted code of practice. Certification of proper installation is mandatory and can take a variety of forms per §280.20(e), including that the installer has been certified by the tank and piping manufacturers or that the installation has been inspected and approved by the agency. This certification, along with notification of financial responsibility, release detection, and other requirements, must be submitted to the agency within 30 days of bringing a tank into use. One notification may be used for several tanks located on one site, but owners of tanks located at more than one place of operation must file a separate notification form for each place of operation. Specific notification requirements are listed in §280.22. The notification forms themselves are published in Appendix I of 40 CFR §264 and the agencies to which notification should be sent are listed in Appendix II.

By December 22, 1998, all existing tank systems must meet one of three sets of standards discussed in §280.21. These are the new UST system performance standards, the upgrading requirements of paragraphs (b) through (d) of this section, or the closure and corrective action requirements of Subparts G and F. The CFR lists specific upgrades for tanks and provides relevant timelines. Steel tanks must be upgraded to meet listed requirements by either installing a proper internal lining, by installing cathodic protection or a combination of the two. Interior lining requires internal inspections 10 years after installation and at five year intervals thereafter. Cathodic protection may only be used where the integrity of the tank has been verified prior to installing the protection. Piping that routinely contains regulated substances and is in contact with the ground must be cathodically protected in accordance with the standards set forth in §280.20. Spill and overfill prevention must be upgraded to meet the new UST system spill and overfill prevention equipment requirements specified in §280.20(c).

General Operating Requirements

It is up to the owner and operator of the UST to ensure that releases due to spilling or overfilling do not occur. 40 CFR §280.30(a) sets out the common sense requirement that it is the owner's and operator's responsibility to ensure that the volume available in the tank is greater than the volume of product to be transferred into it. The owner/operator should make sure of this **before** the transfer begins. The owner/operator should also constantly monitor the transfer process to prevent overfilling and spilling. This clear delineation of responsibility is important because a facility will not be able to escape liability for spills during filling by claiming it was the delivery person's fault. The facility has an affirmative responsibility to make sure things go smoothly and without mishaps. If a facility complies with the transfer procedures described in National Fire Protection Association (NFPA) 30 "Flammable and Combustible Liquids Code," Section 5-4.4 (1993), and NFPA 385 (1990), it will be meeting these requirements. Owner and operators also have the affirmative responsibility to report, investigate, and clean up any spills in overfills in accordance with 40 CFR §280.53. The CFR has removed any confusion over who ultimately may be responsible for a spill or overfill at a facility. The facility is the responsible party, although it may seek contributions from other parties in the case of a release.

Owners and operators have the responsibility, under §280.32, of using a UST system that is either made of or lined with materials that are compatible with the substance stored in the UST system. Compliance officers should ensure that their facilities clearly delineate which types of materials go into which tanks and that the two are compatible. Additionally, although this is not in the CFR, compliance officers should ensure that tanks do not hold mixtures that are mutually incompatible.

The owners of steel USTs have additional operating requirements under §280.31. For as long as a steel UST is used to store regulated substances, the owner/operator must ensure that all corrosion protection systems are operated and maintained to provide continuous corrosion protection to any portion of the tank and piping that routinely contains regulated substances and is in contact with the ground. Naturally, areas of the tank system that are above ground or do not generally contain regulated substances, such as an overfill area, will not have to be protected. All cathodic protection systems must be tested within six months of installation and at least every three years thereafter, or according to a schedule set forth by the implementing agency. The National Association of Corrosion Engineers Standard RP-02-85, "Control of External Corrosion on Metallic Buried, Partially Buried or Submerged Liquid Storage Systems" is an acceptable code of practice by which to inspect such protection. If the steel UST is using impressed current cathodic protection, the protection system also must be inspected every 60 days to ensure that the equipment is running properly. Records of the operation of the cathodic operation protection system, including the results of the last two or three inspections, must be kept to demonstrate compliance with these corrosion protection requirements.

Like any other mechanical system, at some point in its serviceable life an underground storage tank system may break or threaten to break. These mechanical problems may occur because of frost heaves, rusty valves, poor maintenance, or any of a variety of other reasons. When repairing USTs, a facility must ensure that it follows §280.33's requirement that repairs will prevent releases due to structural failure or corrosion for as long as the system is used to store regulated substances. As with virtually every action involving a UST system, repairs to USTs must be properly conducted in accordance with a code of practice developed by a nationally recognized association or an independent testing laboratory. The CFR lists several codes and standards which facilities may use to comply with this requirement, including the National Fire Protection Association Standard 30, "Flammable and Combustible Liquids Code" (1993). Repairs to fiberglass-reinforced plastic tanks may only be made by the manufacturers authorized representatives or in accordance with a proper code of practice. This section requires specific actions in certain circumstances, such as the replacement of metal pipe sections and fittings that have released product as a result of corrosion or other damage, tightness testing within 30 days after completion of a repair, with some exceptions, and retaining repair records for the remaining operating life of the UST system. Facility compliance officers need to be aware of these standards in order to avoid the "jury rigging" solutions that many floor managers may be tempted to apply to their UST systems in order to save time, money, or production costs. If a repair is not in accordance with a relevant standard, it will not be acceptable.

§280.34 spells out the reporting and record-keeping requirements for UST systems, in addition to requiring facility compliance with agency inspections and requests for relevant documents. Owners and operators are required to notify the agency of all UST systems, to include certification of installation for new UST systems. The facility must also report all releases, including suspected releases, spills and overfills, notify the agency before permanent closure or change-in-service and inform that agency of corrective actions planned or taken. Records, including documentation of operation of corrosion protection equipment, documentation of UST system repairs and recent compliance with release detection requirements, must be maintained at the UST site or at a readily available alternative site.

Release Detection

While underground storage tank systems may present fewer fire hazards than aboveground systems, and while they may allow facilities to more efficiently utilize working space, USTs do have one major drawback. They may leak. In fact, the problems caused by leaks, or potential leaks, in UST systems are at the heart of the whole UST regulatory program. 40 CFR §280 Subpart D requires owners and operators of new and existing UST systems to provide a method, or combination of methods, of release detection that can detect a release from any portion of the tank and the connected underground piping that routinely contains product. This leak detection system must be installed, operated, and maintained in accordance with the manufacturer's instructions and must meet listed performance standards. Release detection for all UST systems should have been provided by December 22, 1993. Any UST that could not apply a proper method of release detection should have completed the closure procedures of subpart G by the date on which it was supposed to have provided release detection.

The release detection requirements differ for petroleum UST systems than for hazardous substance UST systems. §280.41 requires that petroleum USTs be monitored every 30 days for releases using an approved release detection method. There are a few exceptions. For example, USTs meeting certain criteria may use tank tightness testing every five years until December 22, 1998 or until 10 years after the tank is installed or properly upgraded, whichever is later. Other USTs may be able to use monthly inventory controls and annual tank tightness testing until December 22, 1998, at which point the tank must be properly upgraded or closed. Tanks with a capacity of 550 gallons or less may use prescribed weekly tank gauging as a method of release detection. In accordance with §280.41(b), underground piping which routinely contains regulated substances must be monitored for releases in various fashions, depending on whether it is pressurized piping or suction piping.

Existing hazardous substance UST systems must meet the requirements for petroleum UST systems discussed above. In addition, by December 22, 1998, all existing hazardous substance UST systems must meet the release detection requirements for new systems set out in §280.42(b). These requirements include a) providing secondary containment systems for regulated substances released from the tank until they are detected and removed and b) inspecting those containment systems for evidence of a release at least every 30 days. 40 CFR 265.193 may be used to comply with these requirements.

Double-walled USTs must be designed, constructed, and installed so that the outer tank contains any releases from the inner tank and failures of the inner wall are detected. External liners, including vaults, must be able to contain 100% of the capacity of the largest tank within the liner, prevent precipitation or groundwater intrusion from interfering with the system's ability to contain and detect releases, and must completely surround the tank. Underground piping associated with these USTs must also contain specific release detection devices. A facility may design its own release detection compliance program, independent of the requirements of the CFR, as long as it obtains proper agency approval prior to installing and operating a new UST system under an alternative compliance program.

The methods for release detection for USTs and piping are varied. Listed in §§280.43 and 280.44, each method must follow certain guidelines. The following methods of release detection for USTs are described in the CFR: *inventory control, manual tank gauging, tank tightness testing, vapor monitoring, groundwater monitoring*, and *interstitial monitoring*. According to paragraph (h), any other type of release detection may be used if it can detect a 0.2 gallon per hour leak rate or a release of 150 gallons within a month, with a probability of detection of 0.95 and a probability of false alarm of 0.05. As noted above, a facility also may gain approval for a unique release detection system as long as it is as effective as any of the above-listed methods of detection. Piping release detection devices may use any of the methods noted for USTs, as long as they are designed to detect a release from any portion of the underground piping that routinely contains regulated substances. Automatic line leak detectors and line tightness testing also may be used if they meet the standards noted in §280.44. Compliance officers should determine which type(s) of leak detection their facilities are using and the exact requirements of these particular methods of detection. The compliance officers then should compare the system requirements with actual implementation of the release detection methods at the facility and correct any discrepancies.

Release Report, Investigation, and Confirmation

40 CFR §280, Subpart E sets the regulatory standards for reporting, investigating, and confirming releases from underground storage tanks. §280.50 requires that owners and operators of UST systems must report suspected or known releases of regulated substances from a UST to the agency within 24 hours or within some other reasonable time period specified by the agency. Suspected or known releases are described in paragraphs (a), (b), and (c) of this section. The discovery of released regulated substances at the UST site or in the surrounding area, unusual operating conditions involving the UST such as sudden loss of product from the system or the unexplained presence of water in the tank, or monitoring results that indicate a release generally are enough evidence of a known or suspected release to inform the agency. Unless the circumstances clearly indicate a UST release has occurred, prior to informing the agency, compliance officers should do some preliminary investigation to ensure that the monitoring equipment was working properly or that discovered product cannot be otherwise explained. The results of this preliminary investigation should be kept with the UST records, and any malfunctioning equipment must be immediately repaired or replaced.

The presence of a regulated substance offsite or far from the UST system may still implicate a facility. Product released into the ground tends to migrate just as any liquid would, downhill (or "down gradient," to use the technical term) and by the path of least resistance. The exact migration pattern of the product depends on many factors, such as the characteristics of the product itself, the amount of precipitation in the area, the existence of groundwater, and the physical characteristics of the ground in the area. The resulting underground contamination is called a "plume." Plumes may be as large as miles in length, thousands of yards in width and hundreds of feet in thickness. Some plumes will not be discovered until the product seeps into a stream or a well, years after the initial release from a location that is miles away. Some of these releases, and their resulting cleanups, may be governed by CERCLA, but initial investigation and confirmation is governed by §280.50. Compliance officers also should be aware of any CERCLA reporting requirements concerning potential releases from their activities.

Unless corrective action is implemented in accordance with 40 CFR §280, Subpart F, owners and operators of a UST suspected of releasing product must investigate and confirm the suspicions within seven days or some other reasonable time frame established by the agency. A facility must conduct a tightness test in accordance with Subpart D for any parts of the UST system that routinely contain product. If the tightness test indicates a leaky system, a facility must repair, replace, or upgrade the UST system and begin corrective actions in compliance with Subpart F. If environmental contamination is not the basis for suspecting a release, a facility may stop its investigation after the tightness testing. If environmental contamination is the basis for suspecting a release, however, the facility must conduct a site check as described in

§280.52(b). Site checks consist of measuring for the presence of release at locations where contamination is most likely to be present at the UST site. These locations will differ depending on the site conditions. If test results indicate a release has occurred, a facility must take corrective action under the CFR. If the test results do not indicate a release has occurred, further investigation is not needed. All records of these investigations should be kept with the relevant UST records.

Corrective Action and Release Response for UST Systems

Once a facility realizes that one of its UST systems has had a release, whether it be through a faulty system, a spill or an overfill, the facility must take corrective actions as detailed in Subpart F of 40 CFR §280. USTs that are excluded from §280 requirements in accordance with paragraph .10(b) and UST releases that are governed by corrective action plans of RCRA are not required to comply with these standards. Compliance officers who are concerned with RCRA releases should review those standards. Officers concerned with releases from USTs exempted by .10(b) should consult their local laws concerning release and spill response.

The basic thrust of Subpart F is that owners or operators of a UST system which has had a release have 24 hours, or some other reasonable time set by an agency, to report the release to agency by telephone or E-mail, to take action to stop any further releases and to identify and mitigate fire, explosion, and vapor hazards. §280.62 lists the specific initial abatement measures facilities must perform, although the agency may direct otherwise if the circumstances so dictate. Among the specific measures the facility must carry out are (a) removing as much of the regulated substance as needed to prevent further releases to the environment, (b) visually inspecting any exposed releases and preventing further migration of the released substance, and (c) monitoring and mitigating fire and safety hazards as vapors or free product migrate from the UST excavation zone. Within 20 days after release confirmation, the facility must give the agency a report explaining its initial abatement steps along with any resulting information or data.

After the initial 24-hour response, the facility may still have more work to do, depending on how much contamination remains from the release. §280.63 lists the methods a facility should use to determine how extensive the remaining contamination is. The information a facility is required to submit to the agency within 45 days includes the nature and estimated quantity of the release, surrounding populations, water quality, use and approximate locations of wells potentially affected by the release, and the results of a site check. More extensive investigations may be required if free product removal is needed or if there is possible groundwater contamination. If there is free product in the area, it must be removed to the maximum extent practicable as determined by the agency. Free product removal must follow the standards set by §280.64, which are basically common sense procedures such as preventing the spread of free product into uncontaminated areas and properly handling flammable products. Forty-five days after confirming a release, a facility must submit a free product removal report.

Facilities may be required by an agency to submit a corrective action plan after a release, or they may wish to submit such a plan voluntarily. In either case, the requirements of §280.66 apply. Like any other corrective action plan, this plan must adequately protect human health, safety, and the environment in order to be approved by the agency. The agency will consider several factors when deciding whether to approve a plan, including the toxicity of the released substances and the proximity and potential uses of nearby surface and ground water. Once the agency has approved the plan and following the proper public notification, the facility must proceed with the plan and must obtain agency approval of any needed changes.

Out of Service UST Systems and Closure

If a facility is not using a UST, it must comply with the closure require-ments of 40 CFR §Subpart G. UST systems may be shut down temporarily, as might happen between production periods, or they may be shut down permanently, as might happen when a facility changes its production processes or ceases operations at a particular location. When a tank is temporarily closed, the facility must continue with the operation and maintenance of corrosion protection and release detection, unless the tank meets the requirements of being "empty," in which case release detection is no longer required.

If the system is only temporarily closed, compliance officers should con-tact local authorities to determine how long a UST may be closed before it must be removed. Compliance officers should also ensure that closed systems have their fill pipes locked or tagged, or even removed, to prevent inadvertent filling of product. If they are planning on removing a UST, compliance officers should inform the local Fire Marshall of those intentions. The Fire Marshall, and possibly a representative of the state, may wish to observe the UST removal, and pass judgment on whether the area around the tank is contami-nated prior to backfilling the UST hole. Typically, soil samples from both sides and ends of a UST are taken to determine if there has been a release. In cases where the hole is filled with water as the tank is removed, a clean sample of water should be taken to analyze for contaminants.

In some cases, impediments such as buildings or other tanks may exist that essentially preclude removal of a UST. In such cases, compliance officers should consult with the local environmental and fire protection agencies to determine the best course of action. These consultations should be well doc-umented, with copies sent to all interested parties prior to taking action. In general, the action probably will be to empty the tank system of all product to the maximum extent possible and then to fill the tank with concrete slurry or other approved material.

When a tank has been removed, compliance officers should ensure that *all* possible fill pipes, or anything that could be confused with a fill pipe, have been removed or rendered inoperable. There are many horror stories of thousands of gallons of product being pumped through a piping system to a tank that had been removed. Needless to say, the immediate result is a considerable release with corresponding remediation expenses.

State UST Programs

Most states operate their own UST programs as opposed to having the EPA run the program. 40 CFR §281 allows this transfer of authority as long as the state program is as stringent as the Federal program. In many cases, the state program may be more stringent or more detailed than the federal program, but the basic requirements are similar. If a state is not enforcing its UST program to EPA's satisfaction, then EPA may remove the authority of the state to run the program. Some examples of state regulations follow.

Arkansas

> *Regulated Storage Tanks* is a guide to the statutes and regulations that govern certain underground storage tanks in Arkansas. Edited by Arkansas attorneys Allan Gates and Walter G. Wright, Jr., this 244 page handbook is available free of charge by writing Mitchell, Williams, Selig & Tucker, 1000 Savers Federal Building, 320 West Capitol Avenue, Little Rock, AR 72201, Attn: Walter G. Wright, Jr.

Michigan

> New rules for underground storage tank systems took effect on January 3, 1991. The rules adopt by reference, with Michigan amendments, U.S. EPA technical and financial responsibility requirements for underground storage tanks. The regulations mandate technical standards for USTs including corrosion protection, release detection, spill and overfill protection, and compliance and reporting schedules. The rules also provide financial responsibility requirements for tank owners and operators. Administration and enforcement of the rules is the responsibility of the Michigan Department of State Police's Fire Marshal Division. Questions concerning the UST rules should be directed to the Fire Marshal's Hazardous Materials Section at (517) 334-7079. Copies of the rules may be obtained from the State Fire Safety Board, Michigan Dept of State Police, General Office Building, 7150 Harris Dr., Lansing, MI 48913.

Massachusetts

> The Massachusetts Board of Fire Prevention Regulations requires all tanks used for the keeping, storage, or dispensing of gasoline be installed under-

ground. These tanks also are subject to the approval of the head of the fire department and must meet all applicable fire prevention regulations. The requirement does not apply to bulk storage facilities unless the head of the fire department and/or local licensing authority requires such provisions.

Minnesota

Tank owners must hire state-certified contractors for installing, repairing, or closing USTs. Tank owners who use an uncertified contractor for tank closure may lose some or all of their financial reimbursement fund (Petrofund). To receive state certification, companies must employ at least one supervisor who has a minimum of two years of work in tank service, has taken a 5-day training course approved by the state, and has passed a written examination based on that training. The company must also submit proof that it has sufficient financial resources to pay for cleanup of any releases that it might cause while working on a tank. At present, there are approximately 174 certified contractors and 362 certified supervisors in the state. A list of state-certified contractors can be obtained from the Minnesota Pollution Control Agency.

Nevada

The State Environmental Commission has promulgated rules that require individuals providing services related to the handling and testing of underground storage tanks to be certified by the Division of Environmental Protection (DEP). The regulations set forth requirements for education, experience, and performance.

Texas

The installation, repair, or removal of underground storage tanks must be performed by Texas Natural Resources Conservation Commission (TNRCC) registered contractor who uses either a licensed installer or on-site supervisor. To qualify for the installer or on-site supervisor license, applicants must have two years of experience in the installation, repair, or removal of USTs, public underground utilities, or other engineering construction. In addition, the applicant must pass an exam administered by the TNRCC.

Compliance officers should determine if their state(s) are implementing their own UST programs or if the EPA is running them. If a state is running the program, the compliance officer should ascertain the differences between the state and the federal programs, ensuring compliance with the stricter standard. If the federal standard appears to be the stricter one, the compliance officer should request guidance in writing from both the federal and state environmental agencies as to which standard to follow.

ABOVEGROUND STORAGE TANKS

Introduction

Aboveground storage tanks (ASTs) are not regulated under 40 CFR in the same manner that underground storage tanks are regulated. The major Federal regulatory activity concerning ASTs is the Oil Pollution Act of 1990 that expands the scope of public and private planning and response activities associated with discharges of oil. That application to ASTs, as well as USTs, will be discussed later in this chapter in the section on Facility Response Plans.

For most facilities, the regulatory standards which govern ASTs are set forth in the state Fire Code or its equivalent due to the flammable nature of much of the material that is stored in ASTs. While state fire codes governing ASTs differ, the basic patterns are fairly consistent. Additionally, many AST management techniques make good business sense from a safety and increased productivity standpoint even if they are not required under the law.

As with any set of regulations, compliance officers should first review the regulations' definitions. Not all ASTs will be covered by regulatory programs. Generally, the tank must be above a certain size to be considered an AST, although that size may be as small as 10 gallons. Further, even large tanks may not be considered to be ASTs if they do not contain flammable or combustible materials. A large water tank, for example, would not be subject to most AST regulations, although it would be wise to comply with the regulations setting out basic engineering considerations, such as ensuring that the site can support the weight of the tank. Because different liquids respond to heat differently, AST regulations may set different standards depending on the flashpoint of a liquid. By and large, though, the regulations will be very similar regardless of the liquid in the tank.

Mechanical and Physical Requirements

AST programs are designed to minimize the risks of fire and, as such, frequently require the use of fire-resistant tanks when certain classes of flammable liquids are stored. An effective way to minimize fire risks posed by an AST is to minimize leaks. Accordingly, AST regulations focus on construction and management techniques that will keep leaks from occurring and locate them when they do occur. Basic site engineering is one way of keeping ASTs from leaking, and compliance officers should ensure that their ASTs are constructed on ground that can support the weight of the full AST. Clay, earth, or reinforced concrete dikes may be required to enclose an AST system. If so, the dikes may be limited to one-half the height of the highest tank enclosed. There may be additional requirements for tanks containing fluids susceptible to boilovers or AST systems of more than a certain number of gallons. Tanks may have to be a certain distance from the nearest property line and a certain distance, such as the diameter of the tank, from each other.

Further, they may need physical protection such as a surrounding fence and no vegetation.

The individual ASTs may be governed by specific regulations. Larger tanks may require "manholes" for access. The roofs of tanks may have to withstand superimposed loads (to prevent workers or debris from falling through). Tanks of a certain volume may have to meet certain measurements and be made of a certain thickness of metal depending on the size of the tank. Any part of an AST in contact with soil should have cathodic protection. Like USTs, ASTs must have proper venting, must be made out of materials appropriate to the liquid to be stored, and may be repaired only following approved methods. Once installed, new or replacement tanks may have to be properly tested prior to filling with liquid. ASTs covered by 40 CFR §112's Oil Pollution Prevention program must be inspected and tested on a regular basis as in §112.7(e)(2). Because of the specific requirements for ASTs, it may be illegal, and it is certainly unwise, to use a tank designed for underground use for aboveground storage.

The piping systems for ASTs generally must meet the same physical requirements as the tanks. Where the effects of jarring or vibration will damage rigid connections, flexible grounded hose may be appropriate. Otherwise, standard cast iron, steel, or brass with standard fittings or seamless copper, brass, or some other nonferrous tubing with standard fittings should be used.

ASTs and their associated piping systems should have an alarm that sounds when the tank is filled to a certain capacity, such as 90%. An automatic cutoff may be required when the system is filled to 95% capacity. While it may seem illogical for a tank to be "full" at 95% capacity, liquids expand when heated and a tank must always have space to accommodate this expansion, so as to avoid literally bursting at the seams.

Operating and Closure Requirements

The requirements for operating an AST system are as much concerned with common sense as they are with regulatory standards. Delivery vehicles should stay a minimum distance, perhaps 25 feet, from any AST unless they are filling the tanks by gravity. The delivery person should determine how much ullage (available capacity) is available in a tank prior to filling it, and the AST/delivery vehicle connections must be such as to minimize the risk of a spill due to improperly fitted connections, tampering, or physical damage.

Tanks which have been abandoned should be emptied of product and cleaned. It is good operating procedure to either lock or tag the fill pipes for these tanks to avoid accidental filling in the future. In some cases, where the AST held gasoline or another petroleum product, the fire marshall may dictate that the tank be removed if tank integrity has been compromised. If an AST has been abandoned and a facility wishes to bring it back into operation, compliance officers should notify the fire marshall and conduct an independent test on the integrity of the tank.

Waste Oil Tanks

A particularly important type of AST is the waste oil storage tank. In many areas these tanks are regulated differently from other ASTs, including smaller size limitations, although they still must meet certain specifications. Use of jury-rigged waste oil tanks, such as old heating fuel tanks, may seem practical but may not meet regulatory standards or basic health and safety concerns. These waste oil tanks, frequently found in auto maintenance areas, often may be stored inside a building as well as outside, although, in either case, their locations should be carefully designated. These tanks should be vented, have a funnel or hopper system to minimize spills while filling, and should be protected from vehicular traffic. A security system should keep unauthorized parties from filling the tank. Outside tanks may require diking, while inside tanks probably will not. Because waste oil tanks are site specific, the fire marshall may waive many of the requirements if the situation seems appropriate.

Vaults

Another special type of AST is the AST in a vault. Vaults are structures which completely enclose a tank, but which, unlike USTs, allow for ready access to the tank. Vaults generally have limited openings, allowing access only for inspection, filling, venting, and emptying the tank. Vaults must meet certain construction standards, including material thickness and fire prevention, and should be tight enough to prevent released material from escaping. In addition, vaults should have (a) a method of detecting liquids, including water, (b) a liquid recovery system, and (c) a suitable means to introduce a fire suppression agent. Only one AST should be in an individual vault.

State Laws and Regulations

Until the late 1980s, regulation of ASTs by states was accomplished in a piecemeal way through the National Fire Protection Association Code, the Uniform Fire Code, and state statutes dealing with water pollution, bulk storage, and hazardous substances. Then, two events occurred that changed this situation. The first was the collapse of an aboveground Ashland Oil storage tank in Pennsylvania in 1988 and resulting spill into the Monongahela River. The second was the passage of the Oil Pollution Act of 1990. Subsequently, several states have passed legislation regulating aboveground tanks as stringently as underground tanks. Much of this legislation authorizes comprehensive regulatory programs including design, construction, registration, tank testing and inspections, leak detection, spill prevention plans, closure, financial responsibility, and trust fund coverage for cleanup costs and third-party liability.

Eighteen months after the Ashland Oil spill, Pennsylvania enacted a storage tank law requiring registration of aboveground storage tanks containing

250 gallons or more of regulated substances. The statute excluded farm and municipal tanks of 1,100 gallons or less and home and business heating oil tanks from the requirements.

California's Aboveground Petroleum Storage Tank Act which became effective January 1990, includes provisions requiring owners and operators of regulated ASTs to file a storage statement every two years with the State Water Resources Control Board; take specific actions to prevent spills; immediately warn local agencies of any release of one barrel or more into the state's waters; prepare a spill prevention control and countermeasure plan; and, in certain instances, implement a groundwater monitoring program.

In Florida, ASTs over 550 gallons that contain pollutants have been regulated for several years and new rules require tough new standards for construction, installation, registration, maintenance, removal, disposal, and financial responsibility.

FACILITY RESPONSE PLANS

EPA's Oil Pollution Prevention regulation, also known as the Spill Prevention Control and Countermeasure (SPCC) regulation, was first published on December 11, 1973. This regulation is designed to prevent discharges of oil from onshore facilities and to contain such discharges when they occur. The principal authority for the SPCC program is Section 311(j)(l)(C) of the Clean Water Act (CWA), which authorizes the President of the U.S. to issue regulations establishing procedures, methods, and equipment to mitigate discharges of oil.

Congress enacted the Oil Pollution Act of 1990 (OPA) to help prevent major spills and ensure efficient response to spills when they occur. The OPA contains significant modifications to many provisions of section 311 of the CWA. New Section 311(j)(5), added by OPA Section 4202(a)(6), requires owners and operators of onshore facilities where a discharge could reasonably be expected to cause "substantial harm" to the environment to prepare plans for responding to a worst case discharge and the substantial threat of such a discharge. OPA Section 4202(b)(4) required that the President issue these regulations not later than 24 months after the OPA was enacted. A facility for which a response plan is required may not handle, store, or transport oil unless the owner or operator has submitted such a plan to the President (or his agent). According to the OPA, the President may authorize a facility to operate without an approved response plan not later than two years after the plan for the facility has been submitted if "the owner or operator certifies that the owner or operator has ensured by contract or other means approved by the President the availability of private personnel and equipment necessary to respond, to the maximum extent practicable, to a worst case discharge or a substantial threat of such a discharge."

The SPCC program regulates nontransportation-related facilities with above ground storage of oil of any kind greater than 1,320 gallons (or 660

gallons in a single tank). The Phase Two revisions to the Oil Pollution Prevention regulation now require owners and operators of SPCC-regulated facilities that could cause "substantial harm" to the environment by discharging
oil into navigable water bodies or adjoining shorelines to prepare and submit
a facility-specific response plan to EPA. The agency reviews it for approval.

Owners and operators must provide information such as facility-specific
emergency response instructions and a discussion of spill scenarios (including
a worst case discharge and lesser spill amounts, as appropriate) as required
elements of the response plan. EPA has integrated into the response plan a
number of response plan requirements from other federal and state agencies
to avoid the necessity of preparing duplicate plans. EPA also coordinates with
the other federal agencies to implement OPA response plan requirements for
transportation-related facilities to ensure a consistent approach.

As a result of the OPA, the President of the U.S. delegated the authority
to regulate nontransportation-related onshore facilities to the Administrator of
EPA by Executive Order (E.O.) 12777. By this same E.O., the President
delegated the authority to regulate tank vessels and transportation-related
facilities to the Department of Transportation and non-transportation-related
offshore facilities to the Department of the Interior. As part of the Phase Two
revisions, owners and operators are required to evaluate their facility against
a set of established criteria that include: storage capacity, proximity to sensitive
environments and drinking water intakes, marine transfer operations, adequacy
of secondary containment, and spill history. In addition, the EPA Regional
Administrator (RA) has the authority to determine that any SPCC-regulated
facility has the potential to cause "substantial harm" based on risk-based
criteria and taking into account site-specific characteristics and environmental
factors.

The RA may further assess the risks of a facility posing a threat of
"substantial harm" to determine if that facility could cause both "significant
and substantial" harm to the environment. To make this determination, the RA
uses the "substantial harm" criteria as well as other information that includes:
information from submitted plans, facility compliance history, tank age, proximity of discharge sources to navigable water, additional areas of environmental concern, and regional site characteristics.

Owners and operators may use a self-selection process to determine
whether their facility could cause "substantial harm" to the environment in
the event of a discharge. Owners and operators are required to evaluate their
facility against a set of criteria including: storage capacity, proximity to sensitive environments and drinking water intakes, marine transfer operations,
adequacy of secondary containment, and spill history. EPA reviews for
approval all facilities identified as having the potential to cause "significant
and substantial harm" to the environment. In addition, EPA RAs have the
authority to determine that any SPCC-regulated facility, regardless of the
results of the self-selection screening process, has the potential to cause "sub-

stantial harm" based on the same risk-based criteria and taking into account site-specific characteristics and environmental factors. The RA uses the "substantial harm" criteria in combination with other information that includes: tank age, proximity of discharge sources to navigable waters, additional areas of environmental concern, and regional site characteristics.

After completion of the "substantial harm" screening process, facility owners and operators that are required to prepare and submit response plans, must calculate the worst case discharge volume for their respective facility. Facility owners and operators use worksheets developed by EPA to calculate the worst case discharge volume for their facilities. Although it is anticipated that most production facilities may not meet the "substantial harm" criteria (due to the one million gallon cutoff), all production facilities remain subject to RA discretion for response plan submittal. In addition, owners and operators of facilities not submitting response plans must complete and maintain at the facility, with the SPCC Plan, a certification form that indicates that the facility does not have the potential to cause "substantial harm" to the environment.

Owners and operators of production facilities and multiple storage tank facilities without secondary containment for each storage tank or group of tanks at the facility must base the worst case discharge volume on the total production volume (for production facilities). Storage and production facilities where the nearest opportunity for discharge (i.e., storage tank, piping, or flowline) is located adjacent to navigable waters, must define a worst case discharge volume as equal to 110% of the capacity of the largest aboveground storage tank or group of aboveground storage tanks permanently manifolded together plus the entire production volume (if applicable). The remaining facilities must define a worst case discharge as the contents of the largest tank or group of tanks permanently manifolded together (if the manifold tanks function as one storage unit) plus the entire production volume at the facility (if applicable).

In addition to the implementation of the OPA requirements for response planning and worst case discharge determination, the Agency requires that SPCC-regulated facilities adopt a tiered approach to response planning in order to consider appropriate emergency response actions for small, more common spills. EPA has adopted a three tier approach to response planning, with a small spill, medium spill, and a worst case discharge.

The regulation also includes elements for response planning, which are designed to guide a facility owner and/or operator in gathering information needed to write a response plan for the facility's worse case discharge and for discharge and small and medium discharges. The elements of the response plan include the following: an emergency response action plan; facility information; emergency response information; hazard evaluation; discharge scenarios; discharge detection methods; plan implementation strategies; facility self-inspection logs; training and meeting logs; site diagrams; and a description of security measures.

The regulation also implements other non-technical requirements. These include: (1) providing RAs the authority to require amendment, modification, and resubmission of a Plan when it does not meet the requirements of 40 CFR part 112; (2) giving RAs authority to require preparation of Plans by owners or operators of previously exempted facilities when necessary to achieve the goals of the CWA; and (3) requiring submission of the Plan when an owner or operator invokes a waiver to certain technical requirements of the regulation.

ENVIRONMENTAL COMPLIANCE

As was the situation with the previous section of this chapter, the environmental compliance activities are broken down into three segments as follows:

- Underground Storage Tanks (UST)
- Aboveground Storage Tanks
- Facility Response Plans

Underground Storage Tanks

Basic Applicability

Checklist :

- Is the tank a UST? (at least 10% of the tank system underground and stores a regulated substance?)

  Yes: Determine if any exceptions apply under §280.10 or §280.12.

  No: The tank is not a UST, no compliance program is needed.

- Does the tank fall under any of the size, use, or placement exceptions of §280.10 or §280.12?

  Yes: No- or partial-compliance program needed depending on the exception. Review exceptions to determine which Subparts, if any, apply to the facility s tanks. Document.

  No: The tank must comply with §280's regulatory program.

Installation, Equipment, and Design

Checklist :

- Are the tanks and piping newly installed?

    Yes: Ensure and document compliance with:
    * Corrosion protection where in contact with corrosive ground.
    * Spill protection.
    * Overfill protection meeting specific standards.
    * Proper installation certificate filed with implementing agency within 30 days of bringing tank into use.
    * Regular, recorded inspections of cathodic protection systems.

    No: Ensure and document compliance with §280.21's upgrade requirements of corrosion, spill, and overfill protection.

- Are repairs necessary for the tank system?

    Yes: Ensure that repairs are conducted in accordance with an accepted code of practice. Ensure parts are replaced as required by §280.33. Document repairs.

    No: No compliance issues raised.

Release Detection

Release detection is required. Specific release detection requirements are set forth in compliance §§280.43 and .44. If a release detection method is not present, the tank must be closed.

Checklist :

- Does the tank store petroleum or hazardous substances?

    Petroleum: Most tanks must be properly monitored for releases every 30 days. Some tanks may use tightness testing every five years or weekly tank gauging.

Checklist (continued):

> Hazardous Substances: Tanks must meet standards for petroleum UST systems and, by December 1998, requirements of §280.42(b), including secondary containment and 30 day inspections of such containment.

Release Report, Investigation, and Confirmation

Checklist :

- Has there been a release or suspected release of product from a UST?

    No: No compliance program necessary for this item.
    Yes: Determine the source of the suspected release.

- Is the suspected release attributable to some cause other than a leaking UST?

    Yes: Correct that cause. Document.
    No: Inform the implementing agency of the suspected release per §280.50. Conduct a site investigation if environmental contamination is the basis for suspecting a release, and tightness testing if there is no environmental contamination.

- Does further investigation confirm the suspected release?

    No: Document. No corrective action needed.
    Yes: Conduct corrective action per Subpart F.

Corrective Action and Release Response

Checklist :

- Has there been a release from a UST?

Corrective Action and Release Response (continued)

Checklist (continued):

      No: No compliance issues raised for this item.

      Yes: Within 24 hours report release, take action to stop further releases and identify and mitigate hazards per §280.62.

- Does 40 CFR §280.63 indicate more contamination remains after initial response?

      No: Document. Submit a post-release report to implementing agency.

      Yes: Conduct a more extensive investigation on the release's impacts. Remove free product as appropriate. Contact the implementing agency to determine if a formal corrective action plan is necessary.

Out-of-Service UST Systems and Closure

Checklist :

- Is the facility not using any of its UST systems?

      No: No compliance program needed for this item.

      Yes: Determine whether the tanks are closed temporarily or permanently.

- Are tanks permanently closed?

      No: Continue with operation and maintenance of corrosion protection for all tanks and release detection systems for tanks that are not empty. Ensure tank is not closed for a period beyond which local regulations consider it permanently closed.

      Yes: Empty the tank, contact the fire marshal and remove the UST, checking for soil contamination as appropriate. If the tank cannot be removed, consult with environmental and fire protection agencies as to the best course of action. Ensure all fill pipes are removed or rendered clearly inoperable.

Aboveground Storage Tanks

Mechanical and Physical Requirements, Operation, and Closure

Checklist :

- Does the AST contain regulated or flammable substances?

    No: Compliance program is probably unnecessary.

    Yes: Check local fire or environmental codes to determine exact program requirements. Ensure ASTs are built in suitable area, have appropriate containment and are properly constructed.

- Does the AST system have appropriate physical protection and leak and overflow detection systems?

    Yes: Inspect and maintain as needed. Document.

    No: Install fences and remove vegetation as needed. Install fill system alarm and automatic shutoff as appropriate.

- Has the AST been removed from use?

    No: Comply with operational requirements as appropriate.

    Yes. Empty and clean tank. Remove or lock fill pipes. Contact fire marshal prior to bringing tank back into service.

Facility Spill Response Plans

Requirement for Facility Response Plans

Checklist :

- Does the facility handle enough petroleum products to fall under 40 CFR §112?

Requirement for Facility Response Plans (continued)

Checklist (continued):

No: No compliance program needed, although a spill response plan would be wise at any site where there is the potential to release any hazardous material that would significantly affect the environment.

Yes: Develop a SPCCP or a Facility Response Plan as needed. Ensure these plans accurately reflect the site's potential for a release to the environment, that personnel are properly trained in accordance with the plan in spill response, and that the necessary equipment and containment devices are available and installed. Obtain approval for Facility Response Plans from the implementing agency.

Emergency Response Action Plan

Checklist :

- EPA and the Coast Guard require that an Emergency Response Action Plan be developed as part of the Federal plan and maintained in accessible locations within the facility. The action plan is designed to provide the facility owner or operator with information on critical steps to stabilize the source of the spill, notify the appropriate people, and prevent the spread of spilled oil. The plan is kept in the front of the facility plan or in a separate binder that accompanies the overall plan.

- The following information must be contained in the action plan:

  * Identity and telephone number of emergency response coordinator.
  * List of emergency notification telephone numbers.
  * Information needed for spill response notification form.
  * List and location of facility response equipment.

Emergency Response Action Plan (continued)

Checklist (continued):

* Composition and capabilities of facility response team.
* Plans to evaluate facility and surrounding community.
* Description of immediate actions to control and contain spilled oil.
* Diagram of facility.

Examples of Spill Contingency Plans

Spill contingency plans must meet EPA requirements. When the plan is prepared for a federal agency, it also must meet that agency's requirements.

Thus, EPA regulations on oil pollution prevention require the preparation of Spill Prevention Control and Countermeasure Plans (SPCCP) containing the elements shown in the checklist below.

SPCC Plan Contents

Checklist :

The complete SPCC Plan must describe the facility's physical plant and include a facility diagram which must have the location and contents of all tanks marked. In accordance with 40 CFR 112.7 (a)(3)(i–ix), the SPCC Plan must also address the following:

* Unit-by-unit storage capacity;
* Type and quantity of oil stored;
* Estimates of quantity of oils potentially discharged;
* Possible spill pathways;
* Spill prevention measures, including procedures for routine handling of products (loading, unloading, and facility transfers, etc.);
* Spill controls such as secondary containment around tanks and other structures, equipment, and procedures for the control of a discharge;
* Spill countermeasures for spill discovery, response, and cleanup (facility's capability and those that might be required of a contractor);

SPCC Plan Contents (continued)

Checklist (continued):

- Disposal of recovered materials in accordance with applicable legal requirements;
- Contact list and phone numbers for the facility response coordinator, the National Response Center, cleanup contractors, fire departments, the Local Emergency Planning Committee, the State Emergency Response Commission, and downstream water suppliers who must be contacted in case of a discharge to navigable waters.

Inspections and tests required by the revision of 40 CFR 112 are to be in accordance with written procedures developed for the facility by the owner or operator or the certifying engineer. The written procedures and a record of the inspections and tests, signed by the appropriate supervisor or inspector, are required to be maintained with the SPCC Plan for a period of five years.

Under the proposed revisions, training is emphasized. Owner/operators are required to schedule and conduct spill prevention briefings for their operating personnel at least once a year to insure adequate understanding of the SPCC Plan for that facility. All personnel who are involved in oil-handling activities are to receive at least 8 hours of training within one year of the effective date of the Final Rule revising 40 CFR 112. In each subsequent year, 4 hours of training will be required annually. The training will consist of instruction on correct equipment operation and maintenance, general facility operations, discharge prevention laws and regulations, and the contents of the facility's SPCC Plan. Additionally, oil transfer personnel are to participate in annual unannounced drills.

SPCC Plans require review and certification by a Registered Professional Engineer (PE). The PE must attest that (1) he/she is familiar with 40 CFR Part 112 requirements, (2) that he/she has visited and examined the facility, (3) that the SPCC Plan has been prepared in accordance with good engineering practice, meeting the requirements outlined in 40 CFR Part 112, and (4), *that required testing has been completed*.

From AMSEC and BREGMAN & COMPANY, 1995.

As an example of an agency-specific plan, presented in the checklist below are the requirements for an Army Installation Spill Contingency Plan in conformance with U.S. Army Regulation (AR) 200-1 Update.

Army Installation Spill Contingency Plan

Checklist :

- Specify responsibilities, duties, procedures, and resources to be used to contain and cleanup spills. [AR-200-1, para. 8.5 b (1)];
- Describe immediate response actions that should be taken when a spill is first discovered. [AR-200-1, para. 8.5 b (2)];
- Identify resources for possible use by a Regional Response Team when implementing the National Contingency Plan. [AR-200-1, para. 8.5 b (3)];
- Identify the name, responsibilities, and duties of the Installation On-Scene Coordinator (IOSC). [AR-200-1, para. 8.5 b (4)];
- Provide specifications, composition, and training plans of the Installation Response Team (IRT). [AR-200-1, para. 8.5 b (5)];
- Identify a pre-planned location for an installation response operations center. [AR-200-1, para. 8.5 b (5)];
- Identify procedures for IRT alert and mobilization. [AR-200-1, para. 8.5 b (6)];
- Identify access to a reliable communications system for timely notification. [AR-200-1, para. 8.5 b (6)(a)];
- Identify Public Affairs Office involvement. [AR-200-1, para. 8.5 b (6)(b)];
- Provide a current list of persons and alternates, organizations and agencies who are on call to receive notice of an oil or hazardous substance spill. [AR-200-1, para. 8.5 b (7)];
- Identify surveillance procedures for early detection of spills. [AR-200-1, para. 8.5 b (8)];
- Develop quantities and locations of personnel, equipment, vehicles, supplies, and material resources for use in spill response. [AR-200-1, para. 8.5 b (9)];
- Identify specific actions for various magnitudes of potential spills. [AR-200-1, para. 8.5 b (9)];

Army Installation Spill Contingency Plan (continued)

Checklist (continued):

- Provide a prioritized list of critical water resources that must be protected in the event of a spill. [AR-200-1, para. 8.5 b (9)];
- Identify other resources to be used if the spill exceeds the response capability of the installation. [AR-200-1, para. 8.5 b (10)];
- Prescribe a prearranged procedure to request assistance and agreements to acquire resources during a major disaster or response situation. [AR-200-1, para. 8.5 b (10)];

- Indicate procedures and techniques used to identify, contain, disperse, reclaim, and remove oil and hazardous substances used in bulk quantities on the installation. [AR-200-1, para. 8.5 b (11)];
- Identify chemicals that may be used to concentrate, neutralize, collect, disperse, and remove oil or hazardous substance spills. [AR-200-1, para. 8.5 b (11)];
- Identify procedures for reporting, both by telephone and in writing, an oil or hazardous substance spill resulting from Army activities. [AR-200-1, para. 8.5 b (12)];
- Identify Army resources on your installation/activity useful to the Regional Response Team to aid in the cleanup of spills not used by Army activities [AR-200-1, para. 8.5 b (13)];
- Provide a description of safety precautions for known hazardous substances on the installation. [AR-200-1, para.8.5 b (14)];
- Include a Public Affairs appendix that describes procedures, responsibilities, and methods of releasing information in the event of a spill.[AR-200-1, para. 8.5 b (15)];

From AMSEC and BREGMAN & COMPANY, 1995.

Finally, the compliance officer must be aware of State requirements for discharge, contingency, or spill prevention plans.

Appendix D contains a listing of the state lead agencies in each of the following 21 states, as well as the applicable state laws and regulations, plus an overview of the general requirements.

Determination of State Requirements

> **Checklist :**
>
> - Is the installation/activity located in any of the following listed 21 states with known state requirements as of 1994?
>
> | | | |
> |---|---|---|
> | - Alabama | - Alaska | - California |
> | - Colorado | - Connecticut | - District of Columbia |
> | - Florida | - Kentucky | - Louisiana |
> | - Maine | - Maryland | - Michigan |
> | - Minnesota | - New Jersey | - Ohio |
> | - Oregon | - Pennsylvania | - Rhode Island |
> | - Texas | - Virginia | - Washington |
>
>   No: No known requirement to submit plans to state.
>   Yes: Does contact with state lead agency, indicate requirement for submission of state and/or federal plans to the state?
>
>   No: Stop here.
>   Yes: Develop and submit proper plans to State.

GLOSSARY

CFR . . . . Code of federal regulations.

Cathodic protection . . . . Prevention of metal corrosion of a tank by the use of a sacrificial metal that corrodes instead of the tank.

Fill pipes . . . . Pipes through which liquid is pumped unto an underground storage tank.

Installation Restoration . . . . The Department of Defense program to
  Program (IRP)   clean up abandoned hazardous waste sites. It is analogous to EPA's Superfund program.

Regulated Materials . . . . Those materials that are subject to federal laws or regulations. They usually are toxic or hazardous.

Release . . . . Movement of a liquid from a tank to the tank's surroundings.

Vent pipes . . . . Pipes that allow accumulated vapors from underground storage tanks to escape to the atmosphere.

REFERENCES AND SELECTED READING

40 CFR Part 112, October 22, 1991, "Oil Pollution Prevention: Non-Transportation-Related Onshore Facilities."

40 CFR Part 112, February 17, 1993, "Oil Pollution Prevention: Non-Transportation-Related Onshore Facilities."

40 CFR Part 194, December 28, 1992, "Response Plans for Onshore Oil Pipelines."

40 CFR Part 300, October 22, 1993, "National Oil and Hazardous Substances Pollution Contingency Plan."

40 CFR Part 194, January 5, 1993, "Response Plans for Onshore Oil Pipelines."

American Systems Engineering Corporation (AMSEC) and BREGMAN & COMPANY, Inc., 1995, *Model Plan Format for 1) Installation Spill Contingency Plan, 2) Spill Prevention Control and Countermeasure Plan, 3) State Discharge, Contingency or Spill Prevention Plans and 4) Federal Facility Response Plan*, Volume I, Environmental Planning Manual, Bethesda, MD.

National Association of Corrosion Engineers, 1990, Standard RP-02-85, Houston, TX.

National Fire Protection Association, 1990, Publication 385, Quincy, MA.

National Fire Protection Association, 1993, Standard 30, "Flammable and Combustible Liquids Code" Section 5-4.4, Quincy, MA.

U.S. Army Regulations 200-1, April 23, 1990, "Environmental Protection and Enhancement," Paragraph 5-7.

U.S. EPA, August, 1995, "Leaking Underground Storage Tanks Quarterly Report."

U.S. House of Representatives, 1984, Report #1133, 98th Congress, 2nd Session.

11   Archaeological and Cultural Resources

INTRODUCTION

Efforts to protect and preserve important archaeological sites and historic sites, structures, and objects often are referred to as "cultural resources management." While some private individuals and groups acquired and preserved important historical structures in the nineteenth century, most contemporary resource management is carried out under the influence of a variety of state and federal laws and programs. Accordingly, this discussion will use those governmental programs as a framework. The basic principles found in these programs can be applied effectively, whether or not the resource management activity is compelled by the need to comply with particular laws and regulations. Private developers can and do use these concepts in circumstances where they are not required by law, and there are sometimes rewards available in the form of tax credits or grant support for these efforts.

LEGAL AUTHORITIES

The National Historic Preservation Act, first passed in 1966, is the principal legislation that establishes the protection of significant historical properties as a national policy. Recent amendments to that act have pulled together aspects of earlier and later legislation, such as the Antiquities Act of 1906, the Historic Sites Act of 1935, the Reservoir Salvage Act of 1960, and Executive Order 11593 and incorporated them into the National Historic Preservation Act. Other legislation has been passed that addresses aspects of cultural resources that are not covered by that Act.

- The Archaeological Resources Protection Act (93 Stat. 721, 16 U.S.C. aa–mm) makes it a crime to disturb archaeological sites on Federal land without a permit and provides criminal sanctions for transporting artifacts acquired illegally across state lines.

- The Abandoned Shipwreck Act (102 Stat. 432, 43 U.S.C. 2101) transfers the title of abandoned shipwrecks to the states and acknowledges their historical value. It allows for their entry into the National Register.
- The Native American Graves Protection and Repatriation Act (104 Stat. 3048, 25 U.S.C. 3001–13) defines an ownership interest by Native Americans, Alaskans, and Hawaiians in the remains of their ancestors' graves. The Act makes it illegal to buy or sell either the human remains themselves, or the associated grave goods interred with them. Federal agencies must inventory their collections of such remains and return them to legitimate groups requesting them.

In addition to these laws, there is a wide variety of regulations and guidelines put forward by several agencies to implement them and the National Historic Preservation Act. They cover topics such as the curation of artifacts standards for preservation projects, and many others. Historic Preservation specialists at State Historic Preservation Offices and federal agencies can assist in identifying the applicability of these regulations to particular situations.

What are Cultural Resources?

Like any specialized activity, cultural resources management has its own jargon. Some terms are defined in legislation, or, more often, in implementing regulations, while others are common in usage but flexible in definition and application. The term "cultural resources" is a general concept and does not appear in the major historic preservation laws. It is understood by professionals working in the field to refer to particular places (sites), buildings, and objects that symbolize either important historical events and people, or long-term trends and continuities that have helped form our common experience as a nation and society. Unique and unusual places, people, structures and objects may also be included. While these resources may be considered significant in particular situations or contexts, or to particular individuals or groups, they will not all necessarily meet the legal and regulatory definition of "Historic Properties".

What are Historic Properties?

Rather more specific definitions of historically significant resources are given by the U.S. Department of the Interior, National Park Service. The National Historic Preservation Act of 1966 authorizes the Secretary of the Interior to maintain the *National Register of Historic Places* to document "districts, site, buildings, structures, and objects significant in American history, architecture, archaeology, engineering and culture." These are normally referred to as "historic properties" in the legal and regulatory context. The criteria for entry to the *National Register* are provided in the Code of Federal Regulations, Title 36, Section 60.4:

> *The quality of significance in American history, architecture, archaeology, engineering and culture is present in districts, sites, buildings, structures, and objects that possess integrity of location, design, setting, materials, workmanship, feeling, and association and*
>
> (a) *that are associated with events that have made a significant contribution to the broad patterns of our history; or*
> (b) *that are associated with the lives of persons significant in our past; or*
> (c) *that embody the distinctive characteristics of a type, period, or method of construction, or that represent the work of a master, or that possess high artistic values, or that represent a significant and distinguishable entity whose components may lack individual distinction; or*
> (d) *that have yielded, or may be likely to yield, information important in prehistory or history (U.S. Department of the Interior, 1991: 251).*

Clearly, these criteria are still quite broad and allow the inclusion of a wide variety of different kinds of sites and properties, including archaeological sites, buildings and battlefield sites, to name a few. The U.S. Park Service has provided additional guidance on how to evaluate the significance of historic properties. They don't exist in isolation, but rather must be regarded in relationship to their physical or historical surroundings. These surroundings are referred to as context:

> *In order to decide whether a property is significant within its historic context, the following five things must be determined:*
>
> • *The facet of prehistory or history of the local area, state, or the nation that the property represents;*
> • *Whether that facet of prehistory or history is significant;*
> • *Whether it is a type of property that has relevance and importance in illustrating the historic context;*
> • *How the property illustrates that history; and finally*
> • *Whether the property possesses the physical features necessary to convey the aspect of prehistory or history with which it is associated (U.S. Department of the Interior, n.d.).*

The use of contexts to determine whether or not a cultural resource qualifies as an historic property is specified in the Secretary of Interior's Standards and Guidelines for Archaeology and Historic Preservation (Secretary of the Interior, 1983: 44714). The context ties the resource into the broader tapestry of the history and geography that defines its significance. The resource and its context can be complex, and the determination of significance (in regulatory terms) is not always obvious. Fortunately, several states have provided comprehensive schedules of historic contexts that apply within their borders. These listings have been prepared as part of the Statewide Preservation Plans that are required for states to qualify for financial support from the Department of the Interior. These plans, where they are available, should always be consulted when a project that may affect cultural resources is planned. They are usually available from the Office of the State Historic Preservation Officer at the state agency which is responsible for historic preservation activities. This may be a separate division or department of state government, or it may be contained within an agency whose responsibilities include general land management concerns, such as a Department of Natural Resources. The context lists represent those aspects of state history that are regarded as important to the people of the state and local experts, and they provide important clues to the significance of a particular property.

For properties that are already listed on the *National Register of Historic Places*, consultation with the State Historic Preservation Officer will always be required when there is any involvement in a project by a federal agency. This would be true in cases when federal funding, licensing, or permitting is a factor. In cases where a project is entirely private in nature, consultation with the State Historic Preservation Officer, even though not required, may reveal certain tax advantages or possible grant opportunities in exchange for efforts to preserve or enhance the listed properties.

A special class of historic properties is authorized by the National Historic Preservation Act. These are National Historic Landmarks which are historic properties whose significance transcends consideration of local or state context, and which are significant at the national level. The criteria for Landmark designation are the same as those for listing on the *National Register of Historic Places* with the additional requirement that they possess significance at the national level. A more detailed discussion may be found in Title 36, Part 65, of the Code of Federal Regulations (U.S. Department of the Interior, 1993). Landmarks are listed in the National Register, and require special attention from any federal agency whose funding, licensing, or permitting programs might affect them.

Integrity

The determination of significance for historic properties is not always a simple undertaking. As may be seen by the preceding discussion, a variety of factors enter into this determination; if legal or regulatory constraints apply, professional consultation by an archaeologist, an architectural historian and/or an historian, will always be required (a particular property may contain both archaeological resources and historic buildings). An important factor in determining whether or not a cultural resource qualifies as a historic property is whether or not it possesses integrity. This means that the property still retains important characteristics that it had either when it originated or during the period of time when it achieved historical significance.

At a practical level, if there are old buildings present within, or near, a project area, inspection by even an untrained observer may show that they have been changed, added to, or otherwise altered in a manner which compromises their integrity. Consultation by an expert may be needed to determine whether or not these changes are reversible and whether or not significant historical "fabric" (construction material) is present, concealed beneath more recent additions. It must be remembered that the visual context, or the developmental susceptibility of historic properties may be affected by adjacent projects, and these effects should be considered by developers, even if the historic property is not within the boundaries of their project.

Archaeological sites present an even more difficult problem when evaluating integrity. First, it may be difficult to determine whether or not they are even present. This issue is considered below. Even when the presence of an archaeological site, or sites, is known or suspected, the evaluation of the integrity of these cultural resources is a matter for professional consultation (see Secretary of the Interior, 1983: 44738–44739). There may be artifacts, or architectural remains visible on the surface of the ground, but whether or not the depositional context retains sufficient scientific integrity that significant data may be extracted from it, will depend on evaluation by a professional archaeologist. If there is information about previous ground disturbance from construction or landscaping, this should be gathered and provided to the archaeologist when evaluating a project. Most archaeological sites that qualify as historic properties, do so under Criterion D, as specified in the Department of the Interior's regulations. That is, they "have yielded, or may be likely to yield, information important in prehistory or history." The issue of site integrity is especially important for archaeological sites, since their ability to yield such information depends on how well the soil context, in which this information is preserved, has survived intact from the time that the archaeological remains were deposited. The evaluation of this integrity may only be determined by professional investigation, since the investigation itself may compromise the information if not properly conducted.

ENVIRONMENTAL COMPLIANCE

Process

Dealing with cultural resources — and historical properties — can and should be handled in a systematic fashion. This is true in any situation, and particularly when there is a legal or regulatory requirement to consider them. The National Historic Preservation Act (U.S. Congress, 1982) places specific requirements on federal agencies that manage property and provide funding, licensing, and permits. Federal property managers are obliged to establish programs to identify and preserve significant historic properties, following the requirements of Section 110 of the National Historic Preservation Act. Federal agencies that provide funding, licensing, or permits to nonfederal projects are obliged to take into account the effects of their actions ("undertakings") on historic properties, either known, or not yet identified, under Section 106 of the National Historic Preservation Act [NHPA] (additional information on these requirements is given below). In this way, nonfederal organizations that will require federal funding, licensing, or permits, also become subject to those requirements.

Requirement to Follow Section 106 of NHPA

Checklist :

- Are you part of a federal agency that manages property or provides funding, licensing, or permits?

  - Yes: Follow instructions in this section of the chapter

  - No: See next item in this checklist

- Are you part of a nonfederal organization that will require federal funding, licensing, or permits?

  - Yes: Proceed as below

  - No: Check on whether your project is subject to state or local historic requirements; if so, follow them. Also consider whether or not to follow the Section 106 process, even though you are not required.

Even when a legal or regulatory constraint is absent, the specified process is an effective method for dealing with cultural resources. There are four basic steps specified in the legislation and accompanying regulations (Advisory Council on Historic Preservation 1991):

- Planning
- Identification
- Evaluation
- Treatment

Planning

There are several reasons for including a concern for cultural resources in the planning process for any project or property. First, some kinds of projects may benefit from the historic values contained in these resources. An historic theme or reference may increase the sales appeal or public appreciation of a project, even if such a theme is not the primary function of a project. Housing subdivisions have been named for historic events that took place at or near their location. The significance of these events was revealed by studies carried out in the planning process. Second, the discovery of significant resources during construction may result in significant delays and economic losses, particularly where federal funding or permitting is a factor. An effort to identify these resources during the planning process may avoid this inconvenience and potential loss. Third, when resources are identified during the planning process, it is often possible to modify the design of a project in such a way that the resources can be protected, and the project can still be completed successfully. When resources are discovered after final design commitments have been made, changes can be difficult and expensive. Finally, historic properties are "nonrenewable." Once they have been damaged or destroyed, one cannot go back in time to repair or replace them. Anticipating the resources during the planning process is the right thing to do in order to protect the nation's cultural heritage. Even if a specific project is not planned, the basic process can be conducted for any property held by a private entity or governmental agency. It is required for federal agencies by Section 110 of the National Historic Preservation Act.

Checklist :

- Is your proposed project at a point where there is still an opportunity for effective planning?

    - No: Proceed to next checklist

    - Yes: Bring historic possibilities into the planning process. Advise your engineers about the reasons for identifying significant cultural resources or possible archaeological sites during the planning process. Assist them in that regard and advise them on the optimum planning method in the case of such resources

---

Identification

You can't protect what you haven't identified. An inventory of potential historic properties should be carried out early in the planning process.

• *Background Study.* This will normally consist of an examination of historic documents and records from various sources to see what the historical record has to say about past events on a property of the project area. Up-to-date listings of historic resources and properties are not usually available for casual inspection because of the danger that vandals will use these records to locate and disturb archaeological sites and steal artifacts. However, a professional consultant conducting a study for planning purposes for a particular project or property will usually be given access to these records. Prehistoric archaeological sites rarely are discussed in old documents and records, and statewide inventories are always far from complete. Archaeologists do synthesize the results of previous research and create "predictive models" for the location of these resources. Prehistoric Native Americans lived in close harmony with the natural environment and generally returned to the same kinds of locations to exploit resources and make camp. These kinds of locations can often be pinpointed on the modern landscape, so even if a particular location has not been previously surveyed, it may be possible to predict that sites are, or are not, likely to be present. Professional review of these kinds of research models can aid in the next step of the resource management process.

• *Field Inventory.* After the background study is complete, some types of field inventories will usually be carried out. An exception to this procedure would be a situation where the background study has revealed that a particular project area has been so thoroughly disturbed or demolished that there is no possibility of any historic properties remaining. In general, the field inventory involves a physical inspection of the project area, or other designated property. It will be guided by the results of the background study, checking particular locations that historical documents or predictive models suggest may contain significant resources, as well as other locations that may be subject to project effect. The field procedure for historical buildings and structures is somewhat different from that for archaeological sites, and the inventories are usually performed by different professionals. For structures, a windshield survey is usually conducted. The consultant looks at each building and makes a judgement about how likely it is that the structure is a significant historic property. In some cases this is fairly unambiguous. Some buildings are obviously significant from even a brief inspection, while others are obviously quite recent and undistinguished. Those that are questionable can be listed for further investigation during the next step.

The problem with archaeological sites is that they are usually not visible from just a drive-by inspection. Obvious exceptions to this include such sites as cliff dwellings and kiva remains in the Southwestern U.S. which could be identified by a "windshield survey" almost as easily as a structure from the historic period. Virtually all of these types of historic properties (remember, this term includes prehistoric archaeological sites) have already been identified — because they are so easy to identify — and they represent only a tiny percentage of all archaeological sites. The usual procedure for an archaeological field inventory is for a team of archaeologists to carry out one of two field procedures, or a combination of the two:

1. *Surface Inspection*
2. *Subsurface Inspection*

These procedures collectively are sometimes referred to by archaeologists and managers as "Phase I Investigations."

• *Surface Inspection* — In areas such as plowed fields, where the surface of the soil is exposed, the archaeological team will walk across the surface of the ground looking for artifacts or other archaeological remains such as bones. If they observe any, they may document their location and concentration and move on, or they may then move to sub-surface testing. This procedure is designed only to identify possible archaeological sites, not to determine if they are significant historic properties. Many states have particular guidelines for how far apart the archaeologists in a surface inspection must walk, and other specific requirements. The surface inspection is a valid method only in a situation where there is no reason to believe that resources are deeply buried by natural or artificial soil deposits. In locations that have been previously plowed for agriculture, but are now grown over, the surface is sometimes exposed by replowing the field.

• *Subsurface Testing* — Subsurface testing is used in situations where the surface of the soil is hidden by vegetation or other material that obscures the natural soil surface. The team of archaeologists digs relatively small holes with shovels to view possible archaeological remains such as artifacts or soil features. These are referred to as "shovel tests." Again, states often specify how large, how deep, and how far apart the shovel tests must be in order to satisfy the State Historic Preservation Officer that an adequate field investigation has been conducted. When artifacts or soil features that indicate human occupation are encountered in the shovel test, larger units are sometimes excavated to learn more about these deposits.

It may be seen that the amount of effort needed for field investigations for identifying structures and buildings normally is considerably smaller than that required for identifying archaeological sites simply because they are so easy to see. An exception to this would be found in a heavily urbanized area, where background study indicates that the modern placement of utilities, basements, underground parking garages, etc. has effectively destroyed all archaeological evidence from earlier times. Some architecturally significant buildings may still exist in such an area — sometimes concealed beneath modern facades — and the architectural field investigation would still be needed. It should be observed in this connection, however, that a surprising amount of archaeological evidence has been found in heavily urbanized areas such as downtown Manhattan, The presence of a paved-over parking lot does not necessarily mean that archaeological remains cannot be found beneath. When there is doubt, field investigations should be carried out.

> **Checklist :**
>
> This assumes that the EC Officer has decided that the identification and treatment processes are necessary
>
> - Conduct a background study as per the previous text. If the need is substantial or critical enough, utilize a professional consultant
>
> - Based on the background study, develop and carry out a plan for conducting a field inventory(ies)
>
>   - If the inventory is for structures, perform a windshield survey
>
>   - If the inventory is for archaeological sites, hire a team of archaeologists to perform a surface inspection, subsurface testing, or both

Evaluation

After background study and field investigations have been done and the Identification step of the cultural resource management process has been completed, the particular resources that have been identified must be evaluated to determine whether or not they are significant and thus qualify as historic properties. This step involves comparing the attributes of each resource to the criteria of significance specified by the Department of the Interior, discussed above, and making a judgement about whether the property meets the criteria. Activities carried out during the Identification step may have generated enough information about the properties to allow this comparison. The Evaluation step may then be completed based on this identification information, and the significant historic properties tabulated for further consideration.

It is more often the case that the information gathered during the Identification step is not adequate to complete the evaluation. This is particularly true for archaeological resources. In such cases, additional background research and field investigation, focusing on the particular properties in question, may be needed before it can be determined whether or not they are historic properties in the legal and regulatory sense. The specific procedures for evaluating a particular resource will depend on the nature of the resource, its location, and physical condition. For historic structures it may be necessary to make a detailed inspection of the property, including its interior, to analyze construction details and architectural style. Archaeological sites may require additional excavation to determine the period of occupation, the function, and the integrity of the resource. These "Phase II" investigations should be designed and carried out by a professional archaeologist and should be carefully limited, so that they do not damage or exhaust the information potential of the site. The basic objective of an evaluation study is to determine whether or not the resource is eligible for listing on the *National Register of Historic Places*.

Checklist:

- Compare each possible historic reource with the criteria of significance specified by the Department of Interior

  - If inadequate information is available, go back to the field studies and have Phase II studies performed to the extent necessary (see earlier text)

  - If information is adequate for evaluation, determine which resources may be deemed to be significant and proceed as in following section

---

Treatment

If a resource is significant, and qualifies as an historic property eligible for listing on the *National Register of Historic Places*, decisions must be made about how it should be treated. If it is going to be affected by a specific project, the nature of the project effects should be assessed and alternative plans considered that might enhance the protection of the property, or at least avoid damaging it. Even if the project will not damage the property, a specialized maintenance plan may be needed to prevent it from deteriorating. Historic buildings may be successfully used for some contemporary function that is different from the one that originally caused them to be built. A residence may be converted to office space in a way that minimizes the damage to the fabric of the building. This procedure is referred to as "adaptive reuse," and architects that specialize in dealing with historic properties can often achieve a surprising harmony between the character of the building and a contemporary use for it.

In the case of archaeological sites, the best option is always to leave them alone, if possible. Steps taken to protect them from erosion and vandalism may be all that is required, Archaeologists refer to this approach as "stockpiling." The pace of construction in general in this country has created a situation where the archaeological profession has all it can do to take care of archaeological identification and evaluation studies that are required by law. Resources that can be preserved in place provide a "stockpile" of knowledge for future archaeologists who can carry out research with more advanced knowledge, technical methods, and equipment than are presently available.

If there is no way to preserve an archaeological site that is a significant historic property, then one method of treatment can be used as a last resort. Since most archaeological sites are significant because of the information that they contain (Criterion d above), their value can be rescued by excavating them completely in a process usually referred to as "data recovery." This process destroys the site, but recovers its significant prehistoric or historical value by scientific methods. This procedure is not preferred for two major reasons. (1) It is invariably extremely expensive - so much so that the costs of this approach should be evaluated carefully against the costs of redesigning, or even abandoning the project that threatens the site. (2) A scientific data recovery effort carried out now, under the pressure of project deadlines, is not likely to do as good a job extracting the significant information from the site as by more cautious incremental studies carried out at some future time with the superior methods and equipment that will inevitably develop over time.

For any historic property that best treatment is one that will preserve and enhance the characteristics that defined it as significant during the inventory steps.

Checklist :

- Have the identification and evaluation steps resulted in a requirement for treatment of specific resources?

  - No: Stop here

  - Yes: Proceed as below

- Which treatment procedure should be selected? Use the advice of cultural resources experts to determine which of the following treatments to use:

  - Protection of property through avoidance of damage to it

  - Development of a maintenance plan to prevent deterioration

  - Adaptation to other contemporary uses

  - Avoiding archaelogical site, i.e., "stockpiling"

  - Excavation, removal of historic materials and protecting them in a museum or other facility (a last resort)

- Develop appropriate treatment plan and pursue it

FEDERAL AGENCIES – SECTION 106 REQUIREMENTS

To this point, the discussion has dealt with general concepts for properly dealing with cultural resources. Planning, Identification, Evaluation, and Treatment provide a sequence of steps to manage cultural resources that are useful in any situation, though they are based on government procedures. Agencies of the U.S. Government must comply with these in some rather specific ways following the requirements, in particular, of Section 106 of the National Historic Preservation Act and associated regulations published by the Department of the Interior and the Advisory Council on Historic Preservation. There has already been some reference to these in the preceding discussions but if you are an agency EC Officer (or if your property or project are dependent on federal actions) you should be aware of some more specific procedures that must be followed.

Section 106 of the National Historic Preservation Act requires agencies to consider the effects of their actions on historic properties and consult with others in the process. The Advisory Council on Historic Preservation, created by the Act, has published an excellent summary of the compliance process which any agency official who deals, or might deal with historic properties should have: **Section 106, Step by Step** (Advisory Council on Historic Preservation, 1986). This is based on the key regulations contained in Title 36, Part 800, of the Code of Federal Regulations. Some of the more important points from this guidance will be mentioned in the following sections.

Step 1, Identify and Evaluate Historic Properties

The planning, identification, and evaluation steps are required of all federal agencies, and these, taken together, are specified as "Step 1" by the Advisory Council.

Step 2, Assess Effects

When a federal action ("undertaking") may affect historical properties, the agency must apply the "criteria of effect and adverse effect" found in Sections 800.9(a–b) of the regulations referenced above (Advisory Council on Historic Preservation, 1991). These criteria (Section 800.9(b) are stated as follows:

"An undertaking is considered to have an adverse effect when the effect on an historic property may diminish the integrity of the property's location, design, setting, materials, workmanship, feeling, or association. Adverse effects on historic properties include, but are not limited to:

  (1) *Physical destruction, damage, or alteration of all or part of the property;*
  (2) *Isolation of the property from or alteration of the character of the property's setting when that character contributes to the property's qualification for the National Register;*

> (3) *Introduction of visual, audible, or atmospheric elements that are out of character with the property or alter its setting;*
> (4) *Neglect of a property resulting in its deterioration or destruction;*
> (5) *Transfer, lease, or sale of the property."*

If the agency official responsible for an action that may affect an historic property discovers there might be an effect on the property, he must initiate Step 3, Consultation.

Step 3, Consultation

Under normal circumstances, consultation will begin with the State Historic Preservation Officer (SHPO). This individual is appointed by the governor of each state to be responsible for coordinating federal actions that might affect historic properties within the state, and to prepare plans and documents to assist in this. It is prudent practice for an agency to consult with the SHPO early in the planning process. If inventory and evaluation are incomplete for the area of the project, the SHPO can recommend additional inventory and evaluation studies to be completed early enough in the planning cycle that adjustments to the federal action can be made with a minimum of disruption to the project. This is particularly true for actions that may affect a large area of land, such as a reservoir or timber lease. It is also good practice even for projects with smaller areas of effect, such as permits for residential development and the like, In some circumstances, an agency's regulations will make a private applicant for funding or permits responsible for completing inventory and evaluation studies, and the applicants should be made aware of these requirements as early as possible to properly plan and budget for their action. The general rule about consulting with the SHPO is "consult early, consult often" to avoid misunderstandings and delays.

In cases where significant historic properties subject to adverse effect have been identified, the Advisory Council on Historic Preservation (ACHP) must join the consultation between the SHPO and the agency. The agency must offer the public an opportunity to participate in the consultation, and heads of local governments and other interested parties may be invited to consult with the principal parties (agency, SHPO, ACHP) to find solutions for adverse effects.

The purpose of the consultation is to consider ways to avoid, reduce, or mitigate the adverse effects of an undertaking on historic properties. When mutually agreeable solutions for problems of adverse effects are found, the parties to the consultation will usually prepare a Memorandum of Agreement (MOA), which documents their agreement. The consulting parties sign this document to commit themselves to carrying out these solutions.

Step 4, Council Comment

This is the final step in the Section 106 compliance process. If the Advisory Council on Historic Preservation has been a participant in the preparation of an MOA, its signature on the document constitutes its comment, and agency compliance with Section 106 has been completed. If it has not, then the MOA must be submitted to the Advisory Council for comment, and the Council may request adjustments to the document in order to return a favorable comment. If a federal agency has not successfully completed an MOA with the SHPO, it must still give the Advisory Council an opportunity to comment on its undertaking. It must supply the Council with sufficient information so that it can understand and evaluate the undertaking and its effects on historic properties. Since this information is needed at all stages of consultation, a federal agency should assemble this information before or during the consultation process. The Council has provided a minimum list (other information may be needed depending upon circumstances) as follows:

- *A description of the undertaking, including photographs, maps, and drawings as necessary;*
- *A description of the efforts to identify historic properties;*
- *A description of the affected historic properties, using materials already compiled during evaluation of significance, as appropriate; and*
- *A description of the undertaking's effects on historic properties (Advisory Council on Historic Preservation, 1986:37).*

After the agency has received the comments of the Advisory Council, it may proceed with its undertaking. If it will not, or cannot carry out the recommendations the Advisory Council supplies in their comments, it must respond to the Council, acknowledging their comments and stating why it will not follow the Council's recommendations. At this point, compliance with Section 106 is complete.

If the agency proceeds with the undertaking before it has received the Advisory Council's comments, it is said to have "foreclosed the Council's opportunity to comment" and is in violation of Section 106 of the National Historic Preservation Act. Although there are no specific penalties for this violation, the agency and/or the individual agency officials may be sued by the National Trust for Historic Preservation and other interested parties in order to force compliance. This can completely disrupt the undertaking and create major, usually costly, delays in the project. The 106 compliance process may seem a little cumbersome at times, but if the agency includes it in its own planning processes, it can be carried out as a fairly routine procedure and will rarely be as disruptive as dealing with a "foreclosure" suit.

This discussion has provided a brief overview of what Federal agencies must do to be in compliance with Section 106 of the National Historic Preservation Act. More detailed guidance is provided in the ACHP publication mentioned above (Advisory Council on Historic Preservation, 1986), which is available from the Council and sometimes from State Historic Preservation Officers. A proposed revision of the regulations (35 CFR 800) is currently being reviewed which attempts to "streamline" the process, and these should also be consulted if, or when, they are adopted. The discussion has centered on Section 106 compliance not only because it provides a model for general resource management, but also because it is the process most likely to be encountered both by federal agencies, and by nonfederal entities seeking their assistance.

Protecting significant cultural resources is closely related to other types of environmental compliance activities. In any situation where an Environmental Impact Statement (EIS) is required, the Section 106 process should be initiated immediately. The results of the Identification, Evaluation, and Consultation activities should be incorporated into the EIS. Other types of environmental activities may affect historic properties as well. Land alteration activities designed for wildlife habitat enhancement may adversely affect archaeological sites. If the cultural resources are recognized and included in the planning process, on the other hand, both wildlife resources and cultural resources can benefit. Transportation projects such as highways and airports should always include a cultural resources component in the environmental assessment process. In general, there are few situations where environmental evaluation is necessary that does not also require an evaluation of effects on historic properties. Many consultants that specialize in environmental compliance activities, include historic preservation professionals on their staffs, or offer services through sub-consultants. There are also consultants that specialize in historic properties evaluations. Many SHPOs maintain a list of such specialists that are available for work in their states.

SECTION 106 PROCESS

Checklist :

- Is the project subject to the Section 106 process?

  - No: Stop here
  - Yes: Proceed as below

- Is an EIS required?

  - No: Start Sec. 106 process at a convenient time
  - Yes: Start Sec. 106 process at the same time that the EIS starts or even earlier

- Obtain the *Section 106, Step by Step* regulations and follow them closely

Checklist (continued):

- Step 1, Identification and Evaluation of Historic Properties

    - Proceed as described in earlier checklists in this chapter

- Step 2, Assess Effects

    - In assessing effects, apply the "criteria of effect and adverse effect" discussed earlier in this chapter, note that the adverse effects "include, but are not limited to" the 5 listed criteria. Therefore, examine any other possible adverse effects

- Step 3, Consultation

    If there are any adverse effects, then

    - Consult with SHPO, as early as possible
    - Include ACHP in the consultation
    - Have public participation and also heads of local governments and other interested parties involved participate
    - Complete consultation with mutually agreeable solutions for problems of adverse effects
    - Draft a Memorandum of Agreement (MOA) for all parties to sign

- Step 4, Council Comment

    - Make sure ACHP is involved in the procedure, that they are in accord with the MOA, and that they sign it
    - If the ACHP does not agree with the MOA, respond to their comments and explain why you will not follow their recommendations

- General

    - The above Step 4 concludes the 106 process
    - Do not, under any circumstances, proceed with the project before receiving the ACHP comments and responding to them

CONCLUSION

Managing cultural resources and complying with the various laws and regulations can be a complicated process, and this introduction cannot provide detailed guidance that will cover every situation. The general outline of concepts and processes given here should be of assistance in understanding the expectations and actions of agency officials and consultants that will be involved in dealing with the management process. The key concept for these activities is planning. Anticipation of the various steps in the management and compliance process will allow timely consultation with the appropriate experts when the answers to questions are not readily apparent.

GLOSSARY

Artifact . . . . An object showing human workmanship or modification, usually found in an archaeological survey.

Federal Register . . . . A daily publication by the U.S. Government that presents actions, notices, regulations, etc., of government agencies. The publishing of these items serves to comply with legal notification to the general public.

Kiva . . . . A Pueblo Indian structure used as a ceremonial council, work, and lounging room for men that is usually round and partly underground.

MOA . . . . Memorandum of Agreement.

SHPO . . . . State Historic Preservation Officer.

Windshield Survey . . . . A survey of facilities conducted during a drive through a large area. Information developed is literally as seen through the windshield of the vehicle.

REFERENCES AND SELECTED READING

Advisory Council on Historic Preservation, 1986, "Section 106, Step-by-Step."
Advisory Council on Historic Preservation, 1991, "Part 800–Protection of Historic and Cultural Properties," (7-1-91 Edition): 466–478.
Secretary of The Interior, 1983, "Archaeology and Historic Preservation; Secretary of the Interior's Standards and Guidelines," *Federal Register*, 48 (190), 44716–44740.
U.S. Congress, 1982, "The National Historic Preservation Act of 1966 (as amended)," 16 U.S.C. §§470–470w-6.

U.S. Department of the Interior, 1991, "Part 60-National Register of Historic Places," Title 36, *Code of Federal Regulations* (7-1-91 Edition): 247–263.

U.S. Department of the Interior, 1993 "Part 65-National Historic Landmarks Program," Title 36, *Code of Federal Regulations* (Edition by National Park Service), Washington, D.C.

U.S. Department of the Interior, n.d. "How to Apply the National Register Criteria for Evaluation," *National Register Bulletin*, 15, National Register of Historic Places, National Park Service, U.S. Department of the Interior, Washington, D.C.

12   Biological Resources

Environmental compliance studies should examine all of the possible biological entities in all of the possible locations: air, land, and water. These locations, in turn, may be subdivided into factors such as deserts, tundras, wetlands, coastal areas, fresh and salt water, etc., (Bregman and Mackenthun, 1992).

Plants and animals have to be taken into account. The various families and taxa that may be present in the area under study should be examined.

It is the purpose of this chapter first to examine the legislation that requires biological compliance studies, then to review the items that should be examined, and finally to suggest environmental techniques to accomplish compliance.

LEGISLATION

There are a number of laws and regulations requiring environmental compliance which must be considered in examining the biological setting for an area. Some that are the most pertinent are discussed briefly below.

Endangered Species Act

The Endangered Species Act provides authority for the Secretary of the Interior to preserve species of animals and plants that are in danger of extinction and to conserve the ecosystems upon which they depend. The Secretary may acquire habitats and conduct investigations. The Act provides for cooperative agreements between the federal and state governments that have made up lists of endangered or threatened species. It provides for the development of a state conservation plan which typically includes objectives, the problems that a species is facing, and the strategy for a corrective program. The Endangered Species Act was signed into law on December 28, 1973, as Public Law 93-205 (Mackenthun and Bregman, 1991).

At this writing, the Act is under consideration in the U.S. Congress for reauthorization and possible changes.

Fish and Wildlife Coordination Act

The Fish and Wildlife Coordination Act was first passed in 1934 and has been amended a number of times since then. The Act, in its declaration of purpose states that:

> "...wildlife conservation shall receive equal consideration and be coordinated with other features of water-resource development programs through the effectual and harmonious planning, development, maintenance, and coordination of wildlife conservation and rehabilitation...to provide assistance to, and cooperate with, federal, state, and public or private agencies and organizations in the development, protection, rearing, and stocking of all species of wildlife, resources thereof, and their habitat, in controlling losses of the same from disease of other causes, in minimizing damages from overabundant species, in providing public shooting and fishing areas, including easements across public lands for access thereto, and in carrying out other measures necessary to effectuate the purposes of said sections."

The Act then goes into detail regarding how federal agencies are to work together to achieve the above objectives. It discusses protection of fish and wildlife, specifically in relation to aquatic habitat impacts and cooperative project modifications having diminished effect. Provision also is made for the acquisition of lands to be exempt from development. Lands that have value to the National Migratory Bird Management Program are among those protected.

Coastal Zone Management Act

The preamble to this Act states the Congress find that...

> "(d) The coastal zone, and the fish, shellfish, other living marine resources, and wildlife therein are ecologically fragile and consequently extremely vulnerable to destruction by man's alterations.
> (e) Important ecological, cultural, historic, and aesthetic values in the coastal zone which are essential to the well-being of all citizens are being irretrievably damaged or lost."

As a result of this Act, programs to protect the coastal zone have been developed by each of the coastal states. The programs vary from state to state, but basically they restrict new construction in coastal areas to varying degrees. In addition, they place considerable emphasis on the protection of fish and wildlife (Bregman and Mackenthun, 1992).

Marine Protection, Research and Sanctuaries Act of 1972 (Ocean Dumping)

The Marine Protection, Research and Sanctuaries Act of 1972, better known as the Ocean Dumping Act, regulates the ocean dumping of all types of materials that may adversely affect human health, the marine environment, or the economic potential of the oceans. EPA is authorized to designate sites where ocean dumping may be permitted or prohibited and to issue permits for material other than dredged materials. The U.S. Army Corps of Engineers is responsible for issuing permits to dump dredged material at sites designated by EPA or by the Corps of Engineers under its authority under Section 102.

The Act prohibits the dumping of radiological, chemical, and biological warfare agents and high-level radioactive wastes. For other wastes, EPA must determine through applicable criteria that their permitting for dumping will not unreasonably degrade or endanger human health, welfare or amenities, or the marine environment, ecological systems, or economic potentialities.

In establishing criteria to regulate ocean dumping, the Act requires that consideration be given, but not necessarily limited to:

- The effect of such dumping on fisheries resources, plankton, fish, shellfish, wildlife, shorelines and beaches
- The effect of such dumping on marine ecosystems, particularly with respect to the transfer, concentration, and dispersion of such material and its byproducts through biological, physical, and chemical processes; potential changes in marine ecosystem diversity, productivity, and stability; and species and community population dynamics

Wetlands

In contrast to other ecological features, no one law controls wetlands. They are the subject of a number of laws and regulations designed primarily for other purposes, but covering wetlands as well. A table summarizing the major federal programs that affect the use of wetlands is presented below (Office of Technology Assessment, 1993).

BIOLOGICAL ITEMS TO BE IDENTIFIED

The survey should identify the presence of any of the following biological items that may be present on the property:

Terrestrial Organisms

Flora

- Ground Cover
- Other Vegetation
- Brush
- Trees, etc.
- Other Terrestrial Flora

**Exhibit 12.1   Major Federal Programs
Affecting the Use of Wetlands**

Program or Act	Primary implementing agency	Effect of program
I. Discouraging or Preventing Wetlands Conversions		
A. Regulation		
Section 404 of the Clean Water Act (1972)	U.S. Army Corps of Engineers	Regulates many activities that involve disposal of dredged or fill material in waters of the United States, including wetlands
B. Acquisition		
Migratory Bird Hunting and Conservation Stamps (1934)	Fish and Wildlife Service (FWS), Dept. of the Interior (DOI)	Acquires or purchases easements on wetlands from revenue from fees paid by hunters for duck stamps
Federal Aid to Wildlife Restoration Act (1937)	FWS	Provides grants to states for acquisition, restoration, and maintenance of wildlife areas
Wetlands Loan Act (1961)	FWS	Provides interest-free federal loans for wetlands acquisitions and easements
Land and Water Conservation Fund (1955)	FWS, National Park Service (DOI)	Acquires wildlife areas
Water Bank Program (1970)	Agriculture Stabilization and Conservation Service (USDA)	Leases wetlands and adjacent upland habitat from farmers for waterfowl habitat over 10-year period
U.S. Tax Code	Internal Revenue Service (IRS)	Provides deductions for donors of wetlands to not-for-profit organizations
C. Other general policies or programs		
Executive Order 11990, Protection of Wetlands (1977)	All federal agencies	Minimizes impacts on wetlands from federal activities
Coastal Zone Management Act (1972)	National Oceanic and Atmospheric Administration, Dept. of Commerce	Provides federal funding for wetland programs in most coast states

**Exhibit 12.1   Major Federal Programs
Affecting the Use of Wetlands (continued)**

Program or Act	Primary implementing agency	Effect of program
II. Encouraging Wetlands Conversion		
U.S. Tax Code	IRS	Encourages farmers to drain and clear wetlands by providing tax deductions and credits for all types of general development activities
Payment-in-Kind (PIK) Program	USDA	Indirectly encourages farmers to place previously unfarmed areas, including wetlands, into production

Fauna

- Amphibians
- Reptiles
- Birds
- Mammals (e.g., mice, rabbits, deer, etc.)
- Insects
- Other Terrestrial Fauna

Aquatic Organisms

Flora

- Algae
- Phytoplankton
- Other Aquatic Flora

Fauna

- Zooplankton
- Benthic Organisms
- Pelagic and Inland Water Organisms (e.g., fish)
- Other Aquatic Fauna (e.g., mammals, etc.)

ENVIRONMENTAL COMPLIANCE

The first part of this environmental compliance section will discuss methods of compliance with the legislation described earlier in this chapter. That will be followed by a section that describes the mechanisms for conducting surveys for the various biological resources that may be present on the organization's property.

LEGISLATION

Endangered Species Act

The purpose of the environmental compliance survey is to determine the presence or absence of threatened or endangered species on the property in question. Since many of these species are quite mobile, the survey may also include adjoining properties.

Endangered Species

> **Checklist :**
>
> - Has a survey of endangered species on the property and in the vicinity been done?
>
>   - If yes, when was it done and was it done in accordance with state or federal guidelines?
>
>   If the survey is older than 5 years, undertake a new one. If less than 5 years old and adequate, no further survey work is required
>
>   - If no, or if survey was inadequate, conduct new survey as directed by text that follows

A literature review and field survey are required of the rare, threatened, and endangered species which occur, or which potentially occur, on the site or nearby. The literature review is conducted for the potential occurrence of both state and federally listed species of plants and animals. This is augmented by contacts with the appropriate state and federal agencies. An on-site survey then is made, if required, in order to confirm the potential occurrence of these species on the site. If any protected species are found on the site, their location and habitat is noted. An estimate of the potential occurrence of both plants and animals on the site also is made based on the results of the field survey and literature review. This analysis is required because of the highly mobile nature of many animals and because plant species are typically highly seasonal in their occurrence. Additional literature review is conducted if a species is found to actually occur on the site or if the site has a very high potential as a habitat (Bregman and Mackenthun, 1992).

Endangered Species or Critical Habitats Found

> **Checklist :**
>
> - Coordinate with federal and/or state officials on plans to minimize or eliminate negative effects on rare, threatened, or endangered plants or animals
>
> - If federally protected species are present, begin informal Section 7 process (see Endangered Species Act) with U.S. Fish and Wildlife Service or, for marine species, the National Marine Fisheries Service

Fish and Wildlife Coordination Act

> **Checklist :**
>
> - Survey property for any items regulated by this Act, especially in areas used for public shooting and fishing, or those that could be involved in development, protection and stocking of wildlife, as well as lands used by migratory birds
>
> - Coordinate with state and federal fish and wildlife agencies for actions required to comply with this Act

Coastal Zone Management Act

If the property to be surveyed is not in a coastal zone as defined by the state, no further action is needed. If it is in a coastal zone, then the specific regulatory requirements of that state should be checked against the proposed activity on the property.

> **Checklist :**
>
> - Is property in a Coastal Zone?
>
>   - No: No further action
>   - Yes: Check state requirements for validity of proposed action on that property

Marine Protection, Research and Sanctuaries Act of 1972

Ocean Dumping

> **Checklist :**
>
> - If no ocean dumping is involved, Act does not apply.
>
> - If ocean dumping proposed, then the following actions should be taken:
>
>   - Check to be certain that the dumping is done at an EPA designated site and under an EPA permit unless the dumped material consists of dredgings. If it is dredged material, the permit must be from the Corps of Engineers. Make certain that all permit requirements are being met.
>
>   - Verify that the dumped material does not contain radiological, chemical, and biological warfare agents or high-level radioactive wastes and meets Corps of Engineers/EPA ocean dumping criteria as specified in 40.CFR 220–228.

Wetlands

As indicated earlier, a large number of federal programs regulate activities in wetlands. The environmental compliance surveyor is not expected to check all of them. Rather, his responsibility is to determine whether any wetlands exist on his organization's property, or a property close enough to it, to be affected by activity on that property.

> **Checklist :**
>
> - Determine whether any previous wetlands surveys have been performed. If so, obtain copies of the survey to compliment your own survey.
>
> - In some states, e.g., Florida, the county has a detailed wetlands survey as well as a determination of the degree of protection to be afforded to these wetlands. In other states, the state has similar information on wetlands. In addition,

Checklist (continued):

the local district of the U.S. Army Corps of Engineers and the U.S. Fish and Wildlife Service may have information on wetlands on the site and nearby. All this information should be obtained and reviewed.

• A literature survey, along with contacts with nearby universities may yield wetlands information.

• The Fish and Wildlife Service maintains the National Wetlands Inventory (NWI) at its branch office in St. Petersburg, Florida. In this inventory, areas conforming to a detailed wetlands classification are delineated on maps developed from aerial photographs. Five major classes of wetlands are identified: Estuarine, Marine, Palustrine (marshy), Lacustrine (lake-formed), and Riverine. These maps, in which potential wetlands are presented overlaid onto USGS Quadrangles, should be obtained and examined for the identification of possible wetlands at the property. The authors of this book have found that the maps may be in error. Wetlands may be designated on the map that do not exist and conversely, wetlands may be on the property that do not show up on the aerial map. The presence or absence of wetlands should be verified in the field.

Delineation of Wetlands

Checklist :

• A field survey for wetlands should be undertaken by the ECAS surveyor. The document used as a guide to wetlands delineation is the *Corps of Engineers Wetlands Manual*, issued by the U.S. Army Corps of Engineers Environmental Laboratory, Vicksburg, MS in January, 1987. Subsequent manuals (1989, 1991) have been rescinded in favor of the 1987 manual. In essence, this 1987 manual identifies three parameters to be used for wetlands delineation: (1) soil; (2) hydrology; and (3) vegetation. For a parcel of land

Delineation of Wetlands (continued)

Checklist (continued):

to qualify as a wetland, it must show specified characteristics for all three parameters. **Exhibit 12-2** reproduced from the manual, shows six steps for determining that a given parcel is a wetland, leading to Step 7, by which the wetland boundaries are established.

A procedure that can be adopted for a more detailed study is to concentrate on areas that are marked on the NWI maps as potential wetlands, and to declare such areas as genuine wetlands only if in close scrutiny on foot the presence of hydrophytic plants (rushes, reeds, punks, cattails, etc.) is in evidence along with the presence of hydric soils. This procedure combines visual data and documentation. Considering that the delineated areas on the NWI maps are likely areas for the presence of wetlands but are not per se positive proof thereof, the ground truth observations should emphasize the presence or absence of hydrophytic vegetation. Even if not found in the field investigation, the presence of hydrophytic plants can be assumed if it is well documented in reliable literature for another season of the year.

The results of this survey should be accepted by the responsible federal, state, and local agencies as an authoritative delineation of wetlands.

BIOLOGICAL RESOURCES DETERMINATION

Checklist :

Detailed biological sampling techniques are presented below. It is recommended that they be carried out by biologists who have had considerable experience in these types of studies.

BIOLOGICAL RESOURCES DETERMINATION (CONTINUED)

Checklist (continued):

In determining the state of the natural biological environment, one may utilize existing data, acquire information from the field, or do both. When the time frame is short, then reliance on data in the literature or previously gathered by other groups or agencies becomes almost imperative. For environmental field surveys, time and funds to gather data must be allocated properly. In many cases this may mean acquiring data for a species at the same location in each season of the year and then taking a fifth sampling during the first season of the second year to check for any substantial change that may have occurred during the year of observation (Bregman and Mackenthun, 1992).

In general, the approach to biology in a survey includes the following:

- Assess existing literature and information concerning the organisms and environment in the study area and surrounding region
- Determine the need for field studies
- Design a qualitative and/or quantitative field sampling program, if needed

For many locations, data are readily available. Such information is normally acquired from the following sources:

- U.S. Fish and Wildlife Service
- USDA Soil Conservation Service
- U.S. Army Corps of Engineers
- U.S. Environmental Protection Agency
- State departments of natural resources
- Colleges and universities
- Interest groups (Audubon Society, Nature Conservancy, etc.)
- Contacts with the federal, state, and local officials

Where additional information is necessary, aquatic and terrestrial field surveys are conducted as described below.

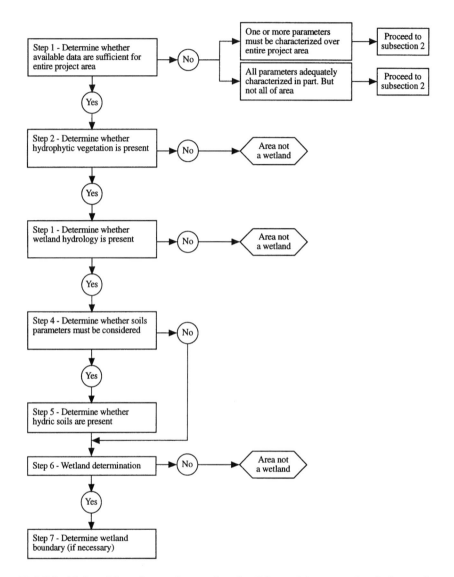

Exhibit 12-2. Flowchart of steps involved in making a wetland determination when an onsite inspection is necessary. (From 1987 Corps of Engineers Wetlands Delineation Manual.)

TERRESTRIAL FIELD SURVEY

Checklist :

The field survey reviews major terrestrial communities, including important species and their roles and functions in the system. Detailed species lists of flora and fauna are referenced or appended.

If no recent vegetation map is available, vegetation of the property can be mapped by the interpretation of aerial photographs and/or by field inspections.

A narrative description is prepared for each type of major plant community. The appearance and structures of the community are described and a list of dominant plant species in each layer of the vegetation is presented.

At the conclusion of the identification phase, the following sensitive types are depicted graphically and discussed:

- areas where endangered and threatened plants may occur
- wetlands
- coastal zone area (where applicable)
- remnant and relict botanical areas

WILDLIFE

Checklist :

Amphibians, reptiles, birds, and mammals normally are included in an existing conditions inventory. In some instances, insects, soil organisms, or other terrestrial life forms are also considered.

An inventory can be performed at different levels of detail, depending on the availability of previously collected and/or published information; the recognition of a significant environmental component, such as the presence of an endangered species and critical habitat for such a species; funding or time restrictions and other factors. In general, the inventory begins with a review of available literature to obtain a description of the project area and of the important species that may inhabit or use the area. Parks or wildlife refuges located in or near the project area also are noted.

WILDLIFE (CONTINUED)

Checklist (continued):

The major sources consulted for such information include in-house reference materials; computerized information bases; public, private, college, university, and museum libraries; federal, state, regional, county, and local agency files and publications; state academies of science; park managers and area game biologists; local arboreta, nature centers, zoological societies, state or national Audubon chapters and environmental groups; biology departments at nearby colleges or universities; and local citizens knowledgeable of wildlife populations, such as hunters, trappers, and birders. Many government publications are available for use in depository libraries. Masters' theses usually can be obtained by standard interlibrary loan procedures, and doctoral dissertations can be purchased in hardcover or on microfilm from several sources (Bregman and Mackenthun, 1992).

The first step is identification of endangered and threatened species that may be present in the project area. If one or more federal or state endangered or threatened species potentially is present, a description of the habits, habitat requirements (food plants or prey, vegetable cover requirements for shelter or breeding, and size of territory), and tolerance to pollution and human activity is prepared. If no list of species is available, a working list is compiled by examination of field guides for each group of animals and identification of those whose ranges are included in the property area. Many of these publications also provide information on the distribution and abundance of each species as obtained from publications for specific regions, states, and localities.

Animal habitats in the property area are identified as part of the vegetation survey, which normally includes the preparation of a land cover map. The species that may be present in these habitats are estimated with the aid of general references.

The species lists and text materials prepared for each group of animals include those species known or expected to breed in the project area. The land cover map prepared in the vegetation survey serves as the source of habitat-type information for correlation of species with their habitats. Information on species habitat affinity often is presented in tabular form as habitats used per species, or species present per habitat type, or in graphic form as maps or overlays.

WILDLIFE (CONTINUED)

Checklist (continued):

The final step in the preparation of a survey dealing with wildlife is the estimation of the value of existing habitats. The location and areal extent of these habitats are determined as part of the identification of sensitive areas. General descriptions of cover density usually are available from the vegetation survey. Areas with food sources required by particular species, and areas that support economically valuable game species or unique communities of plants and animals that may have high scientific, educational, or recreational values are described.

AQUATIC ORGANISMS

These organisms include:

- algae
- phytoplankton
- zooplankton
- benthic organisms
- fish in various stages from larvae to adult

The areas to be studied include all water bodies on the property or adjacent to it. In all of these cases, examination over a four-season period is essential because of the wide variation of aquatic communities and life stages that can be expected to occur.

Methods used for aquatic biological sampling comply with recommended and accepted methods as outlined in EPA's "Biological Field and Laboratory Methods for Measuring the Quality of Surface Water and Effluents" (1973) and the American Public Health Association's "Standard Methods for the Examination of Water and Wastewater" (1981). A detailed discussion of sampling methods follows. It is taken from Bregman and Mackenthun (1992).

Algae and Phytoplankton

Checklist :

Algae are sampled at the surface or just beneath it as indicated above. Phytoplankton collections usually are made at several

---

Algae and Phytoplankton (continued)

Checklist (continued):

designated biological sampling stations. Whole water samples of approximately 2 liters are collected at each station. In a river that is well mixed, only one sample at a 3- to 5-foot depth would be necessary; in a lake or reservoir, the mid-depth and near bottom both may be below the thermocline and thus 3 evenly spaced samples from surface to the thermocline should be taken (Weber, 1973). The samples are immediately preserved. Each bottle is labeled with the sample type, date of collection, location, time of day, and collector and returned to the laboratory for analysis.

The numbers and types of the following major algal groups, as indicated in American Public Health Association (APHA et al., 1980) and Weber,(1973), are determined:

- greens
- blue-greens
- diatoms
- golden
- flagellates
- dinoflagellates
- others

Phytoplankton identification and enumeration can be conducted with an inverted microscope and a phase microscope. The Utermohl method of sample analysis described by Weber (1973) frequently is utilized. This method is chosen because the sample material receives a minimum of handling and the sampling and analytical protocol includes the nannoplankton. Counting procedures follow those outlined in Weber (1973). At least two strips (perpendicular to each other) across the bottom of the chamber are counted. The volume of water sedimented is adjusted to yield counts that will include at least 100 individuals of each of the most abundant species.

Phytoplankton density can be calculated and reported as numbers per milliliter for each species or major group. Relative abundance of each species and group can be calculated as the percent of the total algal density. Species diversity can be calculated using the Shannon-Weiner index (MacArthur and MacArthur, 1961) for each sampling station.

Zooplankton

> **Checklist :**
>
> Zooplankton samples are collected at each of the sampling stations where phytoplankton were collected. Triplicate vertical (horizontal, if necessary) tows are made at each station, utilizing a number 20 mesh plankton net. The line used to lower and raise the net through the water column is marked at 0.5 meter increments. The length of each tow is determined by the water depth at each specific sampling station. Samples are transferred to individual, labeled bottles and preserved.
>
> The numbers, densities, and types of the following zooplankton groups then are determined microscopically.
>
> - copepods
> - cladocerans
> - rotifers
> - others
>
> Relative abundances of each species and each major taxonomic group, and species diversity are determined as previously described for phytoplankton.

Benthic Organisms

> **Checklist :**
>
> Benthic samples are collected from designated sampling stations which should include areas representative of the physical and bathymetric variations within the site. Samples may be collected with any one of a number of benthic sampling devices including an Ekman dredge in soft areas or a Ponar sampler. Samples are washed through a standard No.30 mm mesh sieve and the organisms and debris transferred to containers and preserved. Organisms in each sample are hand-picked or floated with a high density solution and are transferred to vials and preserved.
>
> The numbers and types of the following major benthos groups usually are determined:

Benthic Organisms (continued)

Checklist (continued):

- aquatic oligochaetes
- aquatic chironomids
- other dipterans
- ephemeropterans
- tricopterans
- others

Oligochaetes and chironomid larvae are mounted on microscope slides for identification and examined with a compound microscope. The microscopic mouth parts and teeth of chironomid larvae are important features of identification. Other taxonomic groups are examined with a dissecting scope. Organisms are identified to the lowest practical taxon, using standard taxonomic references. Sampling, sorting, and subsampling procedures used often follow those described by Weber (1973).

Densities of each taxon and each major group are calculated as numbers per square meter for each sample. Relative abundance (percent of total density), species diversity, and species richness are calculated for each station.

Fish

Checklist :

An accurate analysis of the fish population in a water body requires a sampling program that will account for all segments of the fish community. This may be accomplished by using the following methods:

Electrofishing

Electrofishing, using a boat-mounted 230 V alternate current generator, is conducted to sample fishes along the bank, shallow areas, vegetated areas, and other productive or protected areas. Shocked fish are dipnetted from the lake and placed in a live well. The number, size, and weight of individuals of each species are recorded. Scale samples for age determination may be secured. All fish are released unharmed as a result of the experience.

Fish (continued)

Checklist (continued):

Gill Netting

Experimental mesh monofilament gill nets are set at each of the sampling stations for approximately 24 hours. Each net consists of five panels of different size mesh. Additional individual nets may be set at the surface, thermocline, or near the bottom, depending on the specific situation. Should anoxic conditions exist at the bottom, the net should be set as close to the bottom as possible in oxygenated water. Fish are removed from each net and processed (weighed measured). Following gill netting, there are few, if any, recoverable fish except for a few bullheads. Scale samples are taken as appropriate.

Seining

Fish are collected with a haul seine in the shallow littoral areas. Seining will effectively sample young-of-the-year and other small fishes. Seining should be conducted for a predetermined period at each station. Fish are processed after each seine haul, then released. Individuals not readily identified in the field are preserved and transported to the laboratory for positive identification.

The following parameters are determined for individual fish collected by each method:

- species
- total length
- overall condition
- reproductive condition
- presence of disease and/or parasites
- age of at least representative size groups

The combined efforts of electrofishing, gill netting, and seining will ensure the collection of a large number of individuals of each of the dominant species in the water body.

Fish (continued)

> **Checklist (continued):**
>
> *Fish Tissue Analysis*
>
> Fish tissue analysis is often performed to determine presence of trace metals and chlorinated hydrocarbon pesticides. About five individuals of each species collected at each of the sampling stations are tested for trace metals. Two individuals of each species collected at each station are tested for pesticides.
>
> A tissue sample (filet) is collected from each individual fish and wrapped in plastic bags (for metal analysis) or aluminum (for pesticides analysis), placed on ice, and transported to the laboratory. The objectives of some studies may require that whole fish be examined for bioaccumulative substances.

GLOSSARY

Algae	A major group of lower plants usually found on still water surfaces.
Amphibians	Animals or plants adapted to life both on land and in the water.
Benthic	Occurring on the bottom, underlying a body of water.
Community Population Dynamics	Rate of change, growth or movement of specific types of organisms living in water bodies.
Dredged or Fill Materials	Material dredged from the bottom of a water body, either to deepen that water body or else for use to fill in land areas.
Estuarine	In a water area where the tide meets the current of a stream.
Habitat	The place where an animal or vegetable species naturally lives or grows.
Hydric Soils	Soils having a strong affinity for water.
Phytoplankton	Planktonic plants.
Plankton	Passively floating or weakly swimming minute animal or plant life in a body of water.

Relict Botanical Areas	Areas that show evidence of certain botanical species having previously existed there.
Remnant Botanical Areas	Areas showing remains of specific botanical species.
Species	A class of individuals having common attributes.
Terrestrial Biota	Life found on land.
Zooplankton	Planktonic animals.

REFERENCES AND SELECTED READING

American Public Health Association, "Standard Methods for the Examination of Water and Wastewater," 15th ed., 1980, American Water Works Association, and Water Pollution Control Federation, Washington, D.C.

Bregman, J.I. and Mackenthun, K.M., 1992, *Environmental Impact Statements*, CRC Press, Boca Raton, FL.

MacArthur, R. and MacArthur, J.W., 1981, "On Birds Species Diversity," *Ecology* 42:594–598.

Mackenthun, K.M. and Bregman, J.I., 1991, *Environmental Regulations Handbook*, Lewis Publishers, Boca Raton, FL.

Office of Technology Assessment, 1993, "Major Federal Programs Affecting the Use of Wetlands," Washington, D.C.

U.S. Fish and Wildlife Service, 1990, "National Wetlands Inventory," St. Petersburg, FL.

U.S. Army Corps of Engineers Environmental Laboratory, 1987, "Wetlands Manual," Vicksburg, MS.

Weber, C.I., 1993, "Biological Field and Laboratory Methods for Measuring the Quality of Surface Waters and Effluents," EPA-670/4/73-001, National Environmental Research Center, U.S. EPA Office of Research and Development.

13 National Environmental Policy Act (NEPA)

Until 1969, the national philosophy concerning negative environmental effects of major projects was to ignore them during the planning stages of the project. After the work was completed and the negative environmental effects were apparent, the attitude was generally one of "Too bad, but it couldn't be avoided." On a rare occasion, small mitigative measures would be installed after the project was finished.

Recognizing this attitude of "build now and worry about it later," the U.S. Congress in 1969 enacted the National Environmental Policy Act (NEPA). This Act, in effect, said that environmental impacts should be considered **before** the plans for a project were finalized. "Look before you leap" became the approach to be taken (Bregman and Mackenthun, 1992).

The NEPA approach is a common sense one. It requires that one think through the environmental consequences of an action before doing it. If those consequences include undesirable effects, then NEPA asks either that consideration be given to mitigating measures that can be built into the action, or that alternatives to the action be considered that would produce a similar end result but be less damaging to the environment. The mitigation process involves avoiding, minimizing, rectifying, reducing, or compensating for adverse impacts. The national policy now is one of answering the question "What is the impact on the environment of the planned action and how can it be minimized or avoided altogether?" before starting a major action. This is a common sense approach that required a law to make it happen.

NEPA has caused all federal, state, local, and private interests to incorporate environmental values in their decision-making. For most organizations, the NEPA review is now an integral part of program planning. The primary benefit has been enhanced environmental awareness leading to development and implementation of alternatives which reduce the potential for adverse effects on the environment. This has come about because of the NEPA review process and resultant changes in projects, such as alterations in project design, location, or operation; consideration of a greater range of alternatives; imple-

311

mentation of mitigation measures; and enhanced opportunity for public involvement in the decision-making process. An additional benefit often has been a reduction in project costs because environmentally sound projects consistently are more economical in the long run. The NEPA review process also has enabled organizations to address compliance with other environmental laws as part of a single review process rather than separate reviews under each law, thereby reducing the amount of paperwork, staff time, and effort (EPA, 1989). Many actions taken before NEPA was instituted would have been modified or changed if Environmental Impact Statements (EISs) had been required. Three are readily apparent are listed below:

- Mounds of radioactive dirt that almost destroyed Grand Junction, Colorado as a residential and resort center would not have been put there if an EIS had been done on the uranium extraction project at that location
- Chemical plants that are found in the flood plains of the Ohio River would not have been placed there
- Thousands of acres of wetlands that were destroyed for highways and housing projects would have been saved (Bregman and Mackenthun, 1992).

The NEPA Laws and Regulations

NEPA (42V.S.C. 4321 et seq) was enacted by the Congress in 1969. The essence of the Act is stated in the Purpose of the Act (Sec. 2) as follows:

To declare a national policy which will encourage productive and enjoyable harmony between man and his environment; to promote efforts which will prevent or eliminate damage to the environment and biosphere and stimulate the health and welfare of man; to enrich the understanding of the ecological systems and natural resources important to the Nation; and to establish a Council on Environmental Quality.

Under Title I of the Act, the purpose of the national environmental policy is expanded as follows:

...It is the continuing responsibility of the federal government to use all practicable means, consistent with other essential considerations of national policy, to improve and coordinate federal plans, functions, programs, and resources to the end that the nation may -

(1)   Fulfill the responsibilities of each generation as trustee of the environment for succeeding generations;

(2)   Assure for all Americans safe, healthful, productive, and aesthetically and culturally pleasing surroundings;

(3)   *Attain the widest range of beneficial uses of the environment without degradation, risk to health or safety, or other undesirable and unintended consequences;*

(4)   *Preserve important historic, cultural, and natural aspects of our national heritage, and maintain, whenever possible, an environment which supports diversity, and variety of individual choice;*

(5)   *Achieve a balance between population and resource use which will permit high standards of living and a wide sharing of life's amenities; and*

(6)   *Enhance the quality of renewable resources and approach the maximum attainable recycling of depletable resources.*

Section 102 of the Act creates the environmental impact report process as follows:

Include in every recommendation or report on proposals for legislation and other major Federal actions significantly affecting the quality of the human environment, a detailed statement by the responsible official on:

(i)   *The environmental impact of the proposed action,*

(ii)   *Any adverse environmental effects which cannot be avoided should the proposal be implemented,*

(iii)   *Alternatives to the proposed action,*

(iv)   *The relationship between local short-term uses of man's environment and the maintenance and enhancement of long-term productivity, and*

(v)   *Any irreversible and irretrievable commitments of resources which would be involved in the proposed action should it be implemented.*

The federal official responsible for an EIS is required to request comments from all federal, state, and local agencies that may be affected. States are allowed to prepare their own EISs, provided that the responsible federal official is involved in the process and evaluates the statement. That federal official is responsible for ensuring that federal, state, and local agencies, as well as the public and special interest groups, have an opportunity to participate in the scoping meetings where the items to be addressed in the EIS and the concerns of the attendees are addressed, as well as in Public Hearings to review the draft EIS and present their comments.

Title II of NEPA establishes the Council on Environmental Quality (CEQ) in the Executive Office of the President. Most important of all, CEQ is given the authority to issue regulations for implementing NEPA. The Council has the responsibility of preparing an annual Environmental Quality Report for transmittal by the U.S. President to Congress. It also gathers information on trends in environmental quality, reviews federal programs for compliance with NEPA, conducts studies, and recommends national environmental policies and legislation. In exercising its powers, CEQ consults with the Citizens Advisory

Committee that was established by Executive Order No. 11472, May 29, 1969 (Bregman and Mackenthun, 1992).

CEQ Regulations for Implementing NEPA

CEQ has issued regulations for implementing NEPA under the authority of NEPA and Executive Order 11514 as amended by Executive Order 11991, "Regulations for Implementing the Procedural Provisions of the NEPA of 1969," (40 CFR 1500–1508, 29 Nov. 1978). The CEQ regulations apply to all federal agencies and require that those federal agencies issue their own sets of regulations that clarify how they will comply with the CEQ requirements.

A key provision of the regulations is that paperwork shall be kept to a minimum and the EISs are to be written in a manner that is understandable to the general public. Consequently, EISs generally are limited to 150 pages, have executive summaries, and are easy to understand. The detailed technical information that supports the EIS conclusions usually is usually provided in accompanying appendices (which have no page limit).

The CEQ regulations require that environmental factors be considered while the opportunity exists to make adjustments in the project to accommodate environmental concerns.

The regulations allow agencies to perform an Environmental Assessment (EA) as a part of the process of determining whether an EIS should be prepared. The result of the EA is either the preparation of a Finding of No Significant Impact (FONSI), or publishing a Notice of Intent (NOI) to prepare an EIS in the *Federal Register*. When it is obvious that an EIS will have to be prepared, the agency may go directly to the EIS step and skip the EA. The criteria for that action include such factors as obvious major negative impacts, national scope and concerns, etc.

Each EIS has a "lead agency." Where more than one agency is involved in a project, a determination of the lead agency is made by the agencies involved. The remaining agencies then become "cooperating agencies." In case of a disagreement as to who should be the lead agency, the determination is made by CEQ.

Cooperating agencies participate in the NEPA process and may develop some of the information required for the EIS.

As soon as a decision is made by an agency to prepare an EIS, the agency must publish a Notice of Intent in the *Federal Register*. The scoping meeting is the next step in the EIS process. Scoping meetings are held at a very early time in the EIS process for the purpose of determining the scope of the issues to be addressed and for identifying the significant environmental factors related to a proposed action. The lead agency invites "the participation of affected federal, state, and local agencies, any affected Indian tribe, the proponent of the action, and other interested persons (including those who might not be in accord with the action on environmental grounds)."

The CEQ regulations define the requirements of an EIS and discuss its implementation. EISs are required for major federal actions which are defined as projects requiring federal permits, or adoption of new agency programs or regulations. CEQ regulations state that "An agency shall commence preparation of an environmental impact statement as close as possible to the time the agency is developing or is presented with a proposal so that preparation can be completed in time for the final statement to be included in any recommendation or report on the proposal. The statement shall be prepared early enough so that it can serve as an important contribution to the decision-making process and will not be used to rationalize or justify decisions already made."

EISs are to proceed in two stages as follows:

1. Draft EISs according to the decisions made in the scoping process.
2. Final EISs which respond to comments made on the Draft EISs.

In addition, supplementary EISs may be prepared if the situation warrants. The proposed EIS format is as detailed in 40 CFR 1502:

a. Cover Sheet
b. Summary
c. Table of Contents
d. Purpose of and Need for Action
e. Alternatives Including Proposed Action
f. Affected Environment
g. Environmental Consequences
h. List of Preparers
i. List of Agencies, Organizations, and Persons to Whom Copies of the Statement Are Sent
j. Index
k. Appendices (if any)

The cover sheet is to contain a list of the responsible agencies; the title of the proposed action and its location; identification of the person who can supply more information; a designation of the EIS as draft, final, or supplementary; an abstract; and the date by which comments on the EIS must be received.

The summary contains the major conclusions, areas of controversy, and issues to be resolved. It is not to exceed 15 pages.

The CEQ regulations state that the discussion of alternatives must present "the environmental impacts of the proposal and the alternatives in comparative form, thus sharply defining the issues and providing a clear basis for choice among options by the decision maker and the public." If preferred alternatives exist, they are to be identified. Also, appropriate mitigative actions for negative impacts are to be shown.

The affected environment means the environment of the area that may be affected as it exists prior to the proposed action.

The environmental consequences of each of the alternatives form the basis for their comparison. Especially critical factors include any adverse environmental effects which cannot be avoided, the relationship between short-term uses of man's environment and the maintenance and enhancement of long-term productivity, and any irreversible or irretrievable commitments of resources which would be involved in the proposal should be implemented. Both direct and indirect effects are to be considered. Conflicts with plans, policies, and controls for the area concerned are to be noted.

Consequences are defined so as to include environmental effects, energy and resource requirements, as well as urban quality, historic, and cultural resources.

The list of preparers should include a description of their qualifications. The appendix comprises all of the backup material prepared or obtained during the EIS and is to be circulated with the EIS.

The CEQ regulations require that circulation of the Draft EIS and Final EIS should be made to:

(a) *Any federal agency which has jurisdiction by law or special expertise with respect to any environmental impact involved and any appropriate federal, state, or local agency authorized to develop and enforce environmental standards.*

(b) *The applicant, if any.*

(c) *Any person, organization, or agency requesting the entire environmental impact statement.*

(d) *In the case of a final environmental impact statement, any person, organization, or agency which submitted substantive comments on the draft.*

Whenever a broad EIS has been prepared (such as a program or policy statement) and a subsequent supplemental EIS (SEIS) or EA is then prepared on an action included within the entire program or policy (such as site specific action), the subsequent SEIS or EA need only summarize the issues discussed in the broader statement by reference. It should only concentrate on the issues specific to the subsequent action. Similarly, in order to reduce EIS size, material which is readily available to the public may be incorporated by reference.

Cost-benefit analyses details may be placed in the appendix with only the results discussed in the EIS. Methodologies used in the EIS are to be named in the EIS and discussed in the appendix.

The regulations emphasize the need to prepare Draft EISs concurrently with, and integrated with, related documents required by the following:

- Fish and Wildlife Coordination Act
- National Historic Preservation Act
- Endangered Species Act
- Other environmental review laws and executive orders

The Draft EIS must list all federal, state, and local permits, licenses, etc., that must be obtained in order to implement the proposal.

After preparation of the Draft EIS, the agency sponsoring it must obtain comments from the following:

- Federal agencies
- State and local agencies
- Indian tribes, when affected
- Any other interested agency
- The applicant, if any
- The interested public, by soliciting comments from persons and organizations

Comments to the Draft EIS are to be responded to in any of the following methods:

- Modification of alternatives, including the proposed action
- Development of new alternatives
- Modification of analyses in the EIS
- Factual corrections
- Explaining why the comments do not apply

The comments and the responses should be incorporated into the Final EIS. This is usually done in the appendix for those comments that are not accepted.

There may be cases where proposed major federal actions may cause unsatisfactory environmental effects as determined by the U.S. EPA in its authority under the Clean Air Act. In that event, or if another federal agency makes a similar determination in its NEPA review, and differences cannot be resolved with the lead agency, the matter is referred to CEQ for judgment. Every possible attempt is to be made to minimize this from happening, with emphasis on mitigating the unfavorable environmental consequences or switching to a more favorable alternative.

A public Record of Decision (ROD), as specified in 40 CFR 1505.2, must be prepared in cases where EISs were required. This ROD must discuss the alternatives and describe any practicable means of avoiding or minimizing environmental harm, including possible monitoring and enforcement programs. Permits and funding of the actions are to have mitigation and monitoring as conditions of approval where necessary.

40 CFR, part 1506 covers other requirements of NEPA. The first requirement places limitations on any actions that may be taken on a proposal subject to NEPA until the EIS process is completed, thus preventing a *fait accompli* and ensuring that the NEPA process will work. No administrative action is taken until 90 days after the Draft EIS is filed or 30 days after the Final EIS

is filed with EPA. Another requirement encourages federal agencies to cooperate with State and local agencies to reduce duplication between NEPA and comparable state and local requirements.

Agencies are allowed to adopt EISs prepared by other agencies if the proposed actions are essentially the same, or to combine them with other agency documents. EISs prepared by contractors are to be chosen by the lead agency or, where appropriate, by a cooperating agency. In any event, there is to be no conflict of interest concerning the contractor.

Public involvement in the NEPA process is stressed in 40 CFR 1501.7. Adequate public notices of the availability of NEPA documents is emphasized. Actions with effects of national concern are to have a notice published in the *Federal Register*. In addition, national organizations that may be interested are to be notified. For actions of local interest, notices are to be given to Indian tribes of effects that may occur on reservations. In addition, notices are to be published in local newspapers (rather than legal papers) and also are to be given to community organizations, small business associations, newsletters, and the like. Further, information about the EIS may be distributed by direct mailing to owners and occupants of nearby affected properties. A notice may be posted at the location where the action will take place.

The federal agency may decide to hold public hearings if substantial environmental controversy exists, if there is substantial interest in a hearing, or if another agency with jurisdiction over the action feels that a hearing will be helpful. When a public hearing is held on an EIS, a notice to the public must be given at least 15 days in advance.

EISs, comments received, and all the underlying information are to be made available to the public either without charge, or for the actual costs of reproduction.

From time to time, the CEQ may provide federal agencies with further guidance concerning NEPA by using any of several procedures available to it. Conventional draft and final EISs for congressional legislation are to be prepared under any of the following conditions, according to the CEQ regulations:

(i)   *A Congressional Committee with jurisdiction over the proposal has a rule requiring both draft and final environmental impact statements.*

(ii) *The proposal results from a study process required by statute (such as those required by the Wild and Scenic Rivers Act and the Wilderness Act).*

(iii) *Legislative approval is sought for federal or federally assisted construction or other projects which the agency recommends be located at specific geographic locations. For proposals requiring an environmental impact statement for the acquisition of space by the General Services Administration, a draft statement shall accompany the Prospectus or the 11(b) Report of Building Project Surveys to the Congress, and a final statement shall be completed before site acquisition.*

(iv) An agency decides to prepare draft and final statements. Comments on the legislative statement are given to the lead agency which forwards them along with its own responses to the Congressional committees with jurisdiction.

EISs, along with comments and responses, are filed with the U.S. EPA, which delivers a copy to the CEQ.

EPA publishes a weekly notice in the *Federal Register* that lists the EISs filed during the preceding week. Decisions by agencies on the proposed actions cannot be made until 90 days after a Draft EIS or 30 days after a Final EIS. Exceptions are made in the case of appeals by other agencies or the public. Exceptions also may be made when rulemaking for the purpose of protections of the public health or safety is involved. In any event, not less than 45 days is to be allowed for comments on draft statements. The lead agency may extend the prescribed periods. EPA may reduce the periods for compelling reasons of national policy. Provision is made for emergency situations where it is necessary to take an action with significant environmental impact without observing the regulations.

Several of the definitions in Part 1508 of the CEQ regulations are worthy of repetition, and are presented below. They are particularly important in the EIS process.

Categorical Exclusion means a category of actions which do not individually or cumulatively have a significant effect on the human environment and which have been found to have no such effect in procedures adopted by a federal agency in implementation of these regulations (§1507.3) and for which, therefore, neither an environmental assessment nor an environmental impact statement is required. Most agencies develop such listings.

Finding of No Significant Impact (Part 1508.13) is a document prepared by a federal agency which briefly presents the reasons why an action, not otherwise excluded, will not have a significant effect on the human environment and for which an EIS will not be prepared. The FONSI concludes the EA process.

Major Federal Actions are defined as including the following categories:

(a) Adoption of official policy, such as rules, regulations, and interpretations; treaties and international conventions or agreements; and formal documents establishing an agency's policies which will result in or substantially alter agency programs.

(b) Adoption of formal plans, such as official documents which guide or prescribe alternative uses of Federal resources, upon which future agency actions will be based.

(c) Adoptions of programs, such as a group of concerted actions to implement a specific policy or plan.

(d) Approval of specific projects, such as construction or management activities located in a defined geographic area. Projects include actions approved by permit or other regulatory decision as well as Federal and federally assisted activities.

Mitigation includes:

(a) Avoiding the impact altogether by not taking a certain action or parts of an action.
(b) Minimizing impacts by limiting the degree or magnitude of the action and its implementation.
(c) Rectifying the impact by repairing, rehabilitating, or restoring the affected environment.
(d) Reducing or eliminating the impact over time by preservation and maintenance operations during the life of the action.
(e) Compensating for the impact by replacing or providing substitute resources or environments.

Notice of Intent means a notice that an environmental impact statement will be prepared and considered. The notice shall briefly:

(a) Describe the proposed action and possible alternatives.
(b) Describe the agency's proposed scoping process including whether, when, and where any scoping meeting will be held.
(c) State the name and address of a person within the agency who can answer questions about the proposed action and the environmental impact statement (Bregman and Mackenthun, 1992).

Executive Order 11514, Protection and Enhancement of Environmental Quality

Executive Order 11514 was promulgated on March 5, 1970 and amended by Executive Order 11991 (Sections 2(g) and 3(h)) on May 24, 1977. It requires federal agencies to conform with NEPA under the guidance of the CEQ.

Section 3 of the Executive Order sets forth the responsibilities of the CEQ. It gives CEQ overview responsibility for federal policies and activities directed to pollution control and environmental quality. With regard to environmental impacts, CEQ is to

(e) Promote the development and use of indices and monitoring systems (1) to assess environmental conditions and trends, (2) to predict the environmental impact of proposed public and private actions, and (3) to determine the effectiveness of programs for protecting and enhancing environmental quality.
(f) Coordinate federal programs related to environmental quality.
(h) Issue regulations to federal agencies for the implementation of the procedural provisions of the Act.

NEPA Regulations by Other Agencies

As indicated above, the CEQ regulations call for the development of regulations by each Federal agency on how it will implement NEPA. This has been done by most agencies, but there is a substantial degree of variation from agency to agency regarding the type of projects and policy matters that will have to conform to the EIS process. The individual agency regulations therefore make provision for these variations while, at the same time, adhering to NEPA and the CEQ regulations. Probably the two organizations that are the most involved with NEPA are the U.S. Environmental Protection Agency and the U.S. Army Corps of Engineers. A discussion follows that summarizes the approaches that each of these agencies has taken in the development of regulations for the implementation of the NEPA process.

EPA's NEPA Regulations (40 CFR Part 6)

EPA's compliance procedures with NEPA establish a straightforward, step-by-step approach for ensuring that agency decision-making includes careful consideration of all environmental effects of proposed actions, analysis of potential environmental effects of proposed actions and their alternatives, provision for public understanding and scrutiny, and avoidance or minimization of adverse effects to the extent possible. The process is designed to incorporate consideration of environmental factors into the decision-making process at the earliest possible point.

The first document prepared in the EPA NEPA process is an "environmental information document" which is prepared by applicants, grantees, or permittees and submitted to EPA. The environmental information document must include adequate information to enable the responsible official to prepare an environmental assessment. The environmental information documents, at a minimum, should include the following information:

- Overview of the proposed action, including purpose and need
- Description of the existing environment
- Description of the future environment
- Development and evaluation of alternatives
- Description of the environmental impacts of the action

One of the key requirements for the environmental information document is ensuring a thorough evaluation, particular consideration of indirect impacts, and evaluation of the no-action alternative (Bregman, 1995).

Based on the information prepared by the applicant, or permittee, EPA then carries out an environmental review, and prepares an Environmental Assessment (EA) of the proposed action. Based on the EA, a decision is made as to whether an Environmental Impact Statement (EIS) or Finding of No

Significant Impact (FONSI) is required. If it can be determined ahead of time that an EIS will be required, it is not necessary to prepare a formal EA.

Where it is determined that an EIS is necessary, EPA must issue a Notice of Intent in the *Federal Register*. Following this announcement, the formal scoping process begins and the EIS is prepared. When the requirement for an EIS is determined early enough in the planning of the proposed project, it is possible to carry out a "piggyback" EIS, where the EIS is prepared jointly with the environmental information document.

Regardless of the approach taken, the key steps in the EIS process include the following:

- *Conduct Scoping Meeting* — an early, open process for determining the scope of issues to be addressed and for identifying the significant issues related to the proposed action
- *Prepare purpose and need* — for the project
- *Develop alternatives* — including the proposed action
    - alternative considered by the applicant
    - the no-action alternative
    - alternatives available to EPA
    - alternatives available to other permitting agencies
- Identify the *preferred alternative*
- Describe the *affected environment* and *environmental consequences* of each alternative
- *Coordinate* with other Federal, State, and local agencies
- *Provide for participation of the public* through hearings, meetings and other activities

After completion of the EIS, the responsible official then prepares a concise public Record of Decision (ROD). The ROD includes mitigation measures implemented to make the selected alternative environmentally acceptable.

The final step in the general series of actions taken to comply with NEPA is monitoring. This includes all actions taken by the responsible official to ensure that decisions based on the EIS are properly implemented (Bregman and Mackenthun, 1992).

Department of the Army, Office of the Chief of Engineers – Policy and Procedures for Implementing NEPA

Engineering Regulation (ER) No. 200-2-2, dated March 4, 1988 (33 CFR 230), describes the implementation of NEPA by the Corps of Engineers. This regulation is applicable to all offices of the Chief of Engineers (OCE) elements and all field operating activities having responsibility for preparing and processing environmental documents in support of Civil Works functions. The

Corps also has military and regulatory functions. The discussion in this section relates to the Civil Works program only. The Corps of Engineers states as policy that it will implement NEPA vigorously in carrying out its Civil Works mission.

The regulation lists types of Corps of Engineers actions which will require EISs or EAs:

- Legislation
- Feasibility studies
- Survey studies
- Post-authorization advanced engineering and design (AE&D) planning reports
- Continuing authorities studies (e.g., under Flood Control or River and Harbor Acts)
- Projects in a construction status
- Real estate management and disposal actions
- Regulatory permits

District Engineers are allowed to bypass NEPA requirements in emergency actions that are necessary to prevent or reduce risks to life, health, or property, or to prevent severe economic losses. When the emergency action may have a significant environmental impact, the Corps consults with CEQ about appropriate alternative NEPA arrangements.

District Engineers are encouraged to prepare EAs where applicable. After receiving comments on the EA, if the District Engineer believes that no significant environmental impact will occur, he issues a FONSI. If he determines that there is a possibility of significant negative impacts, then he directs that an EIS be prepared. In the case of a FONSI, both the FONSI and the EA are sent to EPA for comments within 15 working days as required under the Clean Air Act.

When an EIS is prepared, it is to follow a specific format outlined in the appendix to the Corps regulations. The Corps issues a Main Report (Feasibility Report) on projects, which will include a concise EIS. The average length of an EIS included with the Feasibility Reports normally is not to exceed 50 pages, single-spaced.

The contents of the EIS are to be as follows:

- Cover Sheet
- Summary
- Table of Contents
- Need for, or Objectives of the Action
- Alternatives
- Affected Environment
- Environmental Effects of Alternatives

- List of Preparers
- Public Involvement
  - Means of involving the public
  - Their views
  - Incorporation of their views in the decision-making process. Other comments are included in the Appendix
- Index, References, and Appendices.

A Notice of Intent is to be issued as soon as the array of alternatives to be studied is determined, even if the preferred alternative has not yet been selected.

Formal Scoping Meetings, on the other hand, are not required, but are held at the discretion of the District Engineer. Coordination (informal scoping) with Federal, state and local agencies and the interested public, takes place throughout the NEPA process. Other requirements for the Corps Civil Works program which are somewhat different than for other agencies, are as follows:

- The Environmental Assessment normally should not exceed 15 pages.
- Cost-benefit analyses are not required in the EIS. However, economic impacts on the public definitely should be included.
- Supplements to Draft EISs may be prepared in the EIS format and require a 45-day comment period.

The Corps allows Final EISs to be abbreviated documents if the response to the comments and the Corps review results in only minor changes. In these cases, the Draft EIS and its appendix are incorporated by reference.

The Corps ROD tends to be more comprehensive than that of other agencies. It includes the following items: (a) a statement of what the decision was, (b) an identification of the environmentally preferable alternative or alternatives, (c) a discussion of economic and technical considerations and agency statutory missions and other essential considerations of national policy, and (d) a statement of whether all practicable means to avoid or minimize environmental harm from the alternative selected are to be employed, and if not, why not.

The ROD (c) identifies mitigation measures and includes a summary of any monitoring or enforcement program applicable for any mitigation committed as part of the decision. In addition, it discusses compliance with Section 404 of the Clean Water Act and other environmental statutes or Executive Orders having a bearing on the decision.

At a minimum, Corps EAs or EISs must include discussion of compliance with the following Acts:

- Clean Water
- Coastal Zone Management

- Endangered Species
- Estuary Protection
- Federal Water Project Recreation
- Fish and Wildlife Coordination
- Land and Water Conservation
- Marine Protection, Research and Sanctuaries
- National Historic Preservation
- River and Harbor Act
- Watershed Protection and Flood Prevention
- Wild and Scenic Rivers (Bregman and Mackenthun, 1992)

33 CFR Part 325, Appendix B provides procedural guidance for preparing and processing NEPA documentation for Corps regulatory actions. Army Regulation 200-2 (23 December, 1988), *Environmental Effects of Army Actions* has been referred to in this section. This regulation covers the following areas, as described in its summary:

This regulation establishes policy, procedures, and responsibilities for assessing the environmental effects of Army actions. It implements the Council on Environmental Quality's National Environmental Policy Act regulations, Executive Order 12114, DOD Directive 6050.1, and DOD Directive 6050.7.

The regulation is stated to have the following applicability:

This regulation applies to the Active Army, Army National Guard (ARNG), and the U.S. Army Reserve (USAR). It applies to proposals and activities of the ARNG involving Federal funding. It does not apply to the Civil Works functions of the Corps of Engineers nor to combat or combat-related activities in a combat zone.

This revision to the previous Army Regulation 200-2 (Sept., 1981) is complete and makes the following changes in the old regulations:

- Clarifies organizational responsibilities for assessing environmental impacts of Army actions (chap 1).
- Clarifies the term "proponent" and how the proponency is defined for the purposes of the Army National Guard (para 1–6 and glossary).
- Deletes the former requirement of affixing the legend "RCS DD-M(AR)1327" (chap 2-2)
- Requires mitigation measures identified in the environmental assessment and Environmental Impact Statement to become a line item in the proposed budget (para 2-7).
- Defines the role of the life cycle environmental document (para 3-1).
- Defines Army policy relative to compliance with the National Environmental Policy Act when projects are undertaken pursuant to

Comprehensive Environmental Response Compensation Liability and Superfund Amendments Reauthorization Act (para 3-1).
- Emphasizes the role of the Deputy for Environment, Safety, and Occupational Health in approval of EISs (para 6-5)
- Incorporates categorical exclusion screening criteria as a requirement for application (app A).
- Deletes the former categorical exclusion for forestry operations (para A-3).
- Deletes the former categorical exclusion for proposed actions determined to be insignificant (para A-28).
- Adds methodology for implementing a monitoring and mitigation program (app F)."

State and Municipal Equivalents of NEPA

Many states and municipalities have developed their own modifications of EIS requirements and utilize them as part of the permit-granting process for major new construction. This includes facilities such as industrial plants, schools, highways, shopping centers, etc. The requirements tend to vary from state to state and from municipality to municipality as a function of the environmental concerns that are of greatest importance to the local authorities.

As would be expected because of its pollution problems, local control is the most intensive in the State of California. Requirements have existed for many years for documents that are the equivalent of environmental assessments for most new construction, even of relatively small size. In a number of other states, EPA has delegated the NEPA process. EPA maintains oversight authority on these environmental documents and may overrule the state if it believes the documents are inadequate.

ENVIRONMENTAL COMPLIANCE

NEPA covers all major federal actions, which have been defined as to include new, or substantially renovated facilities that require federal permits, such as those for water discharges or air effluents. Thus, all practically new or substantially expanded major facilities also are subject to NEPA (Bregman, 1995).

When does the compliance officer become involved with NEPA? The answer to this in the case of industry is at the point where planning begins for a major action that will require a federal permit. Industry also may be subject to state NEPA-like laws for those projects that must be approved by the state. In the case of federal agencies, NEPA and the implementing regulations come into play in the case of every major federal action that may have an impact on the environment. Federal actions are defined as both project and programmatic types and have been described earlier in this book.

This section on environmental compliance will be structured so as to take the Environmental Compliance Officer through the NEPA process. Details of the types of studies can be found in Bregman and Mackenthun, 1992. Much of it describes policy, procedures, and responsibilities for assessing environmental effects of Army actions (AR 200-2), but the discussion is general enough to apply to all other types of facilities.

The major difference between the actions required by NEPA and those in the other chapters of this book are that NEPA becomes a concern of the compliance officer when new actions are planned, whereas the other requirements apply to already existing situations where compliance may have been overlooked. That will be the thrust of the initial checklist that follows.

Is a NEPA Action Required?

Checklist :

- For federal agencies - Is the proposed action one that can be defined as a major federal action?

  - If no, stop here.
  - If yes, proceed with the NEPA process.

- For federal agencies - Is the proposed action covered by the agency list of Categorical Exclusions?

  - If yes, stop here.
  - If no, proceed as below.

- For industrial firms - Will the proposed action require federal, state, or local permits?

  - If no, stop here.
  - If yes, proceed with NEPA process for federal permits, or with appropriate state or local NEPA equivalents for their permits. If both apply, the federal NEPA process takes precedence.

In the case of industrial firms that are subject only to state or local NEPA type requirements, the compliance officer will have to find out what the requirements are and conform to them. They will vary from location to location and generally are fairly brief in both time and funding requirements.

Industrial State or Local NEPA-Type Requirements

Checklist :

- Find out what the requirements that must be completed are

- Discuss them with the appropriate state and local officials

- Draw up a compliance plan. Be as specific as possible with regard to time and cost

- Obtain management approval and proceed

Industry generally becomes involved in the NEPA process because of the need to obtain federal permits for air or water discharges.

In preparation for the NEPA process, and as a part of its study of the activity requiring a new permit, an industrial firm usually will examine various alternative actions and decide on a preferred one. In addition, it will perform environmental studies that will enable it to predict the effects of the proposed action (e.g., construction of a new plant, expansion, or overhaul of an existing one, etc.). These studies on alternatives and their effects on the environment have to be turned over to EPA as the first step in the NEPA process. Together they make up the first document prepared in the NEPA process called an "environmental information document." This environmental information document must include adequate information to enable the EPA to prepare an Environmental Assessment, which is described further below. The environmental information document was described earlier in this chapter.

Industrial Federal Environment Information Document

Checklist :

- Assemble all information related to project planning with emphasis on alternatives

- Prepare environmental information document

- Submit above materials to the appropriate U.S. EPA regional office

If at some point EPA decides that an EIS will be required for the industrial discharger's construction, the Environmental Compliance Officer has the option of letting EPA proceed with the EIS procedure or of recommending to his/her management that a "third party" approach be taken. In the third party approach, the permit applicant selects the contractor who will do the NEPA study with the approval of the agency. The applicant pays for the EIS, but the contractor reports directly to the agency. The applicant sits in on all of the meetings between the contractor and the agency. This approach, while costly to the applicant (since otherwise the agency would pay for the EIS) has the following advantages:

- The work on the EIS usually starts earlier, since the applicant generally can make funds available more rapidly than the government agency.
- The applicant is in a better position to contribute information to the EIS as it goes along.
- By sitting in on meetings, the applicant receives a preview of some of the facts that will be developed in the EIS. This allows the applicant to plan ahead and to consider possible project changes long before the normal time. This factor alone could result in considerable savings in time and money.

Third Party EIS

Checklist :

- For industrial compliance officers, decide whether a third party EIS would be worthwhile

  If no, take no further action
  If yes, recommend this course to management

- If management approves the third party approach, negotiate details with EPA Regional Office and proceed

Various government agencies have established "categorical exclusion" lists. These are lists made up by the agency of actions that always have no significant impact on the environment, such as minor program changes, small modifications of an industrial plant, etc. Having such a list means that the lengthy NEPA process can be avoided on what boils down to everyday-type minor actions. This "categorical exclusion" list usually applies to agency actions of a housekeeping nature and rarely affects industrial activities.

Categorical Exclusions

Checklist :

- Check agency "categorical exclusion" list

  If action is on list, this ends the NEPA activity, but the project must comply with all other environmental laws and statutes. However, if a Record of Environmental Consideration (REC) is required by the agency involved, then this will have to be done

  If action is not on the list, proceed to Environmental Assessment (EA) or, if it is obvious that an EIS will be required, go directly to EIS

If the proposed action is not on the "categorical exclusion" list, then, based on the information prepared by the applicant, EPA or any other federal Lead Agency, carries out an environmental review, and prepares an Environmental Assessment (EA) on the proposed action. EAs have the same basic contents as EISs, but they are abbreviated in content and are performed in a much shorter time period, e.g., 6 weeks to 3 months. This is because the Environmental Assessment is the forerunner of the EIS and determines whether an EIS will be required. If it is apparent that there will be major negative impacts, then the Agency has the option of going directly to an EIS and bypassing the EA.

A typical EA will contain the following information:

- Purpose of, and need for the project
- Alternatives to be considered
- The existing environment
- Possible environmental effects of the alternatives

The EA concludes with a recommendation that one of the two following courses be pursued:

1. Because of possible significant negative impacts, an EIS should be performed, or
2. Since there will not be any significant impacts, a Finding of No Significant Impact (FONSI) should be prepared.

Major differences between the EA and EIS, in addition to the shortened time period, include the following:

- No formal scoping meeting is held
- Almost all of the data collected is that which is already available, rather than new material
- No publication of the availability of the Draft EA is placed in the *Federal Register*
- Comment period is shorter if comments are requested.

Environmental Assessment (EA)

Checklist :

- Have the EA prepared, either within the agency or by a contractor

- Determine whether, as a result of the conclusions of the EA, a Finding of No Significant Impact (FONSI) or an Environmental Impact Statement (EIS) is required

If the EA determines that there will not be any significant impacts, a FONSI is prepared, thus allowing the project to proceed without further environmental studies.

FONSI

Checklist :

- For the Department of Defense – All EAs and FONSIs must be reviewed by the installation or activity Staff Judge Advocate or chief legal advisor at the installation before submission to the commander

- Prepare the FONSI and have it published in the *Federal Register* if the FONSI is of national interest; if it only is of local or regional interest, then have it published in local media

- Allow an appropriate period of time for any public comments (30 to 60 days)

 If no comments of substance are received, proceed with the project

FONSI (continued)

> **Checklist (continued):**
>
> If comments are received that raise serious possibilities about negative impacts, reconsider the validity of the FONSI and then either go ahead with the project or else go to an EIS

If an EIS is to be prepared, a Notice of Intent is first published in the *Federal Register*. A contractor is selected, a scoping meeting is held and the EIS is prepared. After the EIS is concluded, a Record of Decision is prepared and published in the *Federal Register*. The project then proceeds.

EIS

> **Checklist :**
>
> - Prepare a Notice of Intent and insert it in the *Federal Register*
>
> - Select a contractor
>
> - Prepare the EIS. Follow the procedures described in Chapter 3, Bregman and Mackenthun, 1992, and shown as *Appendix A* in this book. That process includes the following items:
>
>   - Notice of Intent
>   - Scoping Meeting
>   - Preparation of Draft EIS
>   - Comment Period – Public Hearings Optional
>   - Incorporate Comments into Final EIS
>   - File Final EIS with EPA
>   - Mandatory Waiting Period
>
>   However, the contents and timing will vary somewhat between agencies
>
> - Prepare the Record of Decision (ROD). Insert it into the *Federal Register* and allow 30 days for comments

EIS (continued)

> **Checklist (continued):**
>
> If no comments of substance are received during that period, proceed with the project
>
> If comments of substance are received, respond to them. Then either proceed with the project or revise the EIS, depending on the contents of the comments

GLOSSARY

Notice of Intent.............. A written statement by a federal agency describing an EIS to be performed. This is published in the *Federal Register* and precedes any work on the EIS itself.

REFERENCES AND SELECTED READINGS

Bregman, J.I., "NEPA Requirements for Industrial Companies," August 1995, *J. Environ. Law Practice*.

Bregman, J.I. and Mackenthun, K.M., 1992, *Environmental Impact Statements*, CRC Press, Boca Raton, FL.

Canter, L.W., 1977, *Environmental Impact Assessment*, McGraw-Hill, Inc., New York, NY.

Jain, R.K., Urban, L.V., Stacey, G.S., and Balbach, H.E., 1993, *Environmental Assessment*, McGraw-Hill, Inc., New York, NY.

U.S. Environmental Protection Agency, 1989, "Facts About the National Environmental Policy Act," Washington, D.C.

14   Other Federal and State Laws and Regulations

INTRODUCTION

In addition to the federal and state laws and regulations that have been covered thus far in this book, there are several others of which the compliance officer must be knowledgeable. May of these apply only in specific situations and to include them all in this book would turn it into an encyclopedia in size. For that reason, this chapter will focus on a small number of additional areas that must be considered by the compliance officer, with emphasis being given to those areas that will be of concern to most of the officers.

In this chapter, therefore, the following topics are considered:

1. Asbestos
2. Lead Paint
3. Noise
4. Radon
5. PCBs

ASBESTOS

Asbestos is a naturally occurring mineral whose crystals form into long thin fibers. Deposits of asbestos are found throughout the world. Asbestos minerals are divided into two groups: serpentine and amphibole.

Serpentine minerals have a sheet or layered crystal structure, amphiboles have a chain-like crystal structure. Chrysotile, the only mineral in the serpentine group, is the most commonly used type of asbestos and accounts for approximately 95% of the asbestos found in buildings in the United States. Chrysotile is commonly known as "white asbestos," so named for its natural color.

Five types of asbestos are found in the amphibole group. Amosite, the second most likely type to be found in buildings, is often referred to as brown asbestos. Crocidolite, blue asbestos, is utilized in high temperature insulation applications. The remaining three types of asbestos in the amphibole group are anthophyllite, tremolite, and actinolite. These are extremely rare, and occasionally are found as contaminants in asbestos-containing materials.

EPA distinguishes between friable and nonfriable forms of asbestos-containing materials (ACMs). Friable ACMs can be crumbled or reduced to powder by hand pressure. Friable ACMs release fibers into the air readily.

EPA identifies three categories of ACM used in buildings:

• *Surfacing Materials* — ACM sprayed or troweled on surfaces (walls, ceilings, structural members) for acoustical, decorative, or fireproofing purposes. This includes plaster and fireproofing insulation.

• *Thermal System Insulation* — Insulation used to inhibit heat transfer or prevent condensation on pipes, boilers, tanks, ducts, and various other components of hot and cold water systems and heating, ventilation, and air conditioning (HVAC) systems. This includes pipe lagging, pipe wrap, insulation, cements, and "muds," and a variety of other products such as gaskets and ropes.

• *Miscellaneous Materials* — Other largely nonfriable products and materials such as floor tile, ceiling tile, roofing felt, concrete pipe, outdoor siding, and fabrics.

The concern about friable asbestos is its effects on human health. Inhalation of friable asbestos can cause the following diseases:

Asbestosis — a scarring of the lung
Lung cancer — A malignant tumor of the bronchial coating
Mesothelioma — Enlarging of the linings of the chest or the abdominal walls

Each of these three diseases may ultimately lead to death, as may several other rarer diseases caused by asbestos. For smokers, the exposure to asbestos causes a synergistic effect that is claimed to increase the risk of developing lung cancer ten-fold for people who smoke 20 cigarettes a day or more.

ASBESTOS LAWS AND REGULATIONS

Two federal agencies are primarily responsible for regulations for asbestos control conformation. These two agencies are the U.S. Environmental Protection Agency (EPA) and the Occupational Safety and Health Administration (OSHA). Those regulations will be discussed here.

Other federal agencies promulgating regulations regarding asbestos include the Department of Transportation (DOT) regulations regarding the transport of asbestos, the National Bureau of Standards which establishes standards and protocols for laboratory accreditation, and the Consumer Product Safety Commission which bans asbestos in some products.

Asbestos Hazard Emergency Response Act (AHERA)

Included in this Act, which was passed in 1986, are provisions directing EPA to establish rules and regulations addressing asbestos-containing materials in schools. Specifically, EPA was directed to address the issues of (1) identifying, (2) evaluating, and (3) controlling ACMs in schools. These regulations, or simplified versions thereof, also are followed for asbestos in buildings other than schools, depending on the various state requirements. The final AHERA regulations became effective on December 14, 1987. They are found in 40 CFR 763 Subpart E §763.80–§763.99 under the Toxic Substances Control Act (TSCA).

Schools' responsibilities under the rule (§763.82) are as follows:

- To designate a person to ensure that AHERA requirements are properly implemented
- To inspect and identify friable and non-friable ACMs
- To monitor and periodically reinspect ACMs
- To develop and update management plans
- To determine and implement response actions
- To develop and implement operations and maintenance programs
- To notify parents, building occupants, and outside contractors of ACMs identified in the building
- To ensure that accredited persons perform these required activities under AHERA.

School buildings were to be inspected by October 12, 1988 (§763.85) and inspections conducted thereafter by accredited inspectors at least every 3 years, and by anyone every 6 months (§763.851). Areas that are suspected to contain ACMs are sampled and analyzed. However, schools may elect to assume that any or all materials contain asbestos. If they choose to make this assumption, no sampling is necessary. Bulk samples are to be analyzed for asbestos by laboratories accredited by the National Bureau of Standards, or laboratories with interim accreditation from EPA (§763.87). Analysis is by polarized light microscopy (PLM), using the prescribed method.

All friable asbestos-containing building materials (ACBMs) and assumed ACBMs must be located and categorized as to present condition, potential for damage, and type of material (§763.88). Non-friable ACBMs and assumed ACBMs must be identified and documented. Consideration may be given to the following control actions:

- encapsulation
- enclosure
- operations and maintenance
- repair
- removal (§763.81).

Particular conditions require specified response actions (§763.90). When an operations and maintenance program (O&M) is required, the following conditions must be met:

- Any building where friable ACBMs are present or assumed to be present must develop and implement an O&M program
- OSHA Construction Standards (29 CFR 1926.58) and/or EPA Worker Protection Rule (40 CFR 763.121) that cover workers performing O&M and repair activities must be followed
- The O&M program must provide for surveillance of ACMs at least every 6 months
- Additional requirements and directions for responding to fiber release episodes are specified in the regulations.

Warnings must be posted adjacent to any ACBMs located in maintenance areas of a building. They must read: **CAUTION: ASBESTOS. HAZARDOUS. DO NOT DISTURB WITHOUT PROPER TRAINING AND EQUIP-MENT.** Failure to comply can result in fines ranging from $5,000 to $25,000 per day of violation. Criminal penalties can be invoked. Under AHERA, training is required for building inspectors, management planners, design professionals, abatement supervisors, and abatement workers.

National Emission Standards for Hazardous Air Pollutants (NESHAP) (40 CFR 61 Part M)

This Act was discussed earlier in this book in the chapter on air quality. NESHAP is the governing law concerning worker protection. EPA rules concerning the application, removal and disposal of asbestos-containing materials were issued under NESHAP. Also included in NESHAP are rules concerning manufacturing, spraying, and fabricating of asbestos-containing material.

Notification requirements specified under NESHAP are as follows:

- At least 20 days advance notice must be filed when a building is to be demolished or as early as possible before renovation begins, if more than 260 linear feet of asbestos pipe covering or 160 square feet of asbestos surfacing material are to be removed during building renovation.
- At least 10 days advance notice must be filed before demolition if the amount of friable asbestos materials in the facility being demolished is less than 260 linear feet or 160 square feet.
- If less than 260 linear feet or 160 square feet of friable ACMs is being removed at a facility being renovated, no notice is required.

If more than 160 linear feet or 260 square feet of ACMs are present, then under NESHAP:

- Removal is required prior to demolition and prior to renovation if the renovation would break up the ACMs.
- No visible emissions of dust to the outside air are permitted during removal or renovation.

Disposal requirements specified under NESHAP include the following:

- No visible emissions to the outside air are allowed during collection, packaging, transportation, or deposition of ACM waste.
- Wet ACM must be sealed in a leak-tight container.
- Containers must be labeled with OSHA labels.

State and Local Regulations

Several provisions in AHERA encourage states to develop their own regulatory programs. States are encouraged to establish and operate training and certification programs for the various categories of asbestos professionals, as long as the programs are at least as stringent as AHERA's Model Plan. Some states have established requirements that exceed EPA's in the area of notification of abatement actions, abatement work practices, and transportation and disposal of asbestos-contaminated waste.

OSHA Asbestos Standards

The Occupational Safety and Health Administration (OSHA) has established three sets of regulations which address asbestos exposure:

29 CFR 1910.1001 - General Industry
29 CFR 1926.58   - Construction Industry
29 CFR 1910.134 - Respirators

The construction industry standard, which is the one most applicable to this discussion, covers employees engaged in demolition and construction. It includes the following activities that could involve asbestos exposure: removal, encapsulation, alteration, repair, maintenance, insulation, spill/emergency clean-up, transportation, disposal, and storage of ACMs. The respirator standards cover their proper use.

OSHA coverage includes all private sector employers and employees under federal jurisdiction. Those not covered under the standard include: self-employed persons, certain state and local government employees, and federal employees covered under other federal statutes. Persons engaged in inspection, management planning, and other asbestos-related work in schools, fall under OSHA's construction industry standard.

OSHA is authorized to conduct workplace inspections. In addition, employees have the right to file an OSHA complaint without fear of punishment from the employer. OSHA may not conduct a warrantless inspection without the employer's consent. Citations are issued by OSHA during an inspection if the inspecting officer finds a standard being violated. The citation informs the employer and employees of the regulations or standards alleged to have been violated and of the proposed length of time allowed for correction. Monetary penalties may also be imposed.

The OSHA asbestos exposure limits under their standards are as follows:

- *The permissible exposure limit* (PEL), is 0.2 fibers per cubic centimeter (f/cc), time weighted average (TWA); TWA means exposure concentration averaged over an 8 hour period.
- An *action level* of 0.1 f/cc TWA triggers certain regulatory requirements

If an employee is required to wear a negative pressure respirator, the employer must:

- Establish a medical surveillance program
- Institute an employee training program

If employees are exposed to airborne asbestos at or above the PEL, then in addition to the steps taken when the action level is exceeded, the employer also must institute the following procedures:

- Establish a respiratory protection program
- Conduct daily personal air sampling to record employee exposure to asbestos. If air-supplied respirators are being worn, this sampling is not necessary
- Employees must be notified as soon as possible of the results of air sampling
- The employer must establish a regulated area wherever concentrations of airborne asbestos exceed the PEL
- Access to the regulated area is to be limited
- A negative pressure enclosure must be established around the regulated area
- Eating, smoking, drinking, and gum chewing are prohibited in the regulated area
- A designated competent employee must monitor the integrity of the area and enforce the above requirements
- Exceptions are allowed for "small scale, short duration projects"

A "competent person" is defined as a person who by training and experience is qualified to oversee the various asbestos activities. This person has the following attributes:

- Capable of identifying asbestos hazards
- Authority to take corrective action to eliminate the hazards

The responsibilities of the competent person are as follows:

- Determine the need for the negative pressure enclosure and ensure its integrity
- Control entry to and exit from the enclosure
- Supervise employee exposure monitoring as required by OSHA
- Ensure that all employees working within a restricted area wear appropriate personal protective equipment
- Ensure that engineering controls in use are functioning properly

The following engineering and/or housekeeping controls are encouraged to achieve compliance with exposure standards:

- High Efficiency Particulate Air (HEPA) Filter ventilation systems and vacuum cleaners
- Wet methods (wetting agents, cleaning processes)
- Proper disposal
- Proper work practices
- Appropriate respirator and protective clothing

Required hazard communication measures are as follows:

- Warning signs that contain specific words for a regulated area must be posted
- Warning labels that contain specific wording and colors must be attached to any product containing asbestos and to all waste containers

Employers must provide employees with training that covers the following topics:

- The risks of asbestos exposure
- Work practices and control measures to minimize exposure
- The OSHA standard
- Medical surveillance and employee rights
- Relationship between smoking and exposure to asbestos

The medical surveillance program covers:

- All employees exposed to fiber levels at or above the action level (0.1 f/cc TWA) for 30 days or more per year
- All employees who are required to wear Negative Pressure Respirators.

Recordkeeping requirements specified by OSHA include the following:

- Employee air sampling exposure data and medical records must be maintained for 30 years
- Sampling data showing that the exposure level was below the action level must be retained for 30 years
- Training materials must be retained one year after termination of employment for each employee
- All records must be made available to the employee, to OSHA, and, with permission, to the employee's union representative
- Special provisions are established for records when an employer goes out of business

Any employer who falls under the jurisdiction of OSHA must provide:

- Respirators at no cost to employees
- Protective clothing, when appropriate, at no cost to employees
- A medical surveillance program at no cost to employees
- Awareness training (communication of potential hazards)

The OSHA respirator rule specifies what type of respirators must be worn for different levels of contaminants in the air. A half- or full-face mask negative pressure air purifying respirator with HEPA filters should be sufficient for conducting inspections and collecting bulk samples. Exceptions requiring a higher level of protection would be extremely dusty or contaminated areas such as crawl spaces.

Lead Paint

Exposure to lead can cause health problems ranging from delays in neurological and physical development to nervous and reproductive system disorders. Acute exposure to lead can cause blindness, coma, and even death. Children under 6 years of age are especially at risk from exposure to lead (EPA, 1994). In 1991, the Secretary of the Department of Health and Human Services characterized lead poisoning as "the number one environmental health threat to the health of children in the United States."

Lead accumulates in the body. Lead poisoning usually results from many small exposures over a period of weeks or years. Lead is stored throughout the body and stays in the blood for several months, and it can be stored in the bone for many decades.

In 1994, Henry G. Cisneros, U.S. Secretary of the Department of Housing and Urban Development, speaking of the danger of lead paint poisoning and the need to do something about it said, *This is an important and difficult American health and safety issue. HUD and EPA have worked to strike an appropriate balance in writing this regulation; the idea is to not overly burden the housing industry, yet take appropriate action to protect our children from the dangerous threat inherent in lead-based paint.*

Approximately 57 million homes and apartment units have lead-based paint, according to HUD. About three-quarters of pre-1980 housing contain some lead-based paint. The occurrence, extent, and concentration of lead-based paint increase with the age of the housing. 90% of privately owned housing units built before 1940 contain some lead-based paint, as do 90% of 1940–1959 units, and 62% of 1960–1979 units (HUD, 1990). Lead was widely used as a major ingredient in most interior and exterior oil-based paints prior to 1950. Lead compounds continued to be used as corrosion inhibitors, pigments, and drying agents from the early 1950s. In 1972, the Consumer Products Safety Commission limited lead content in new residential paint to 0.5% (5000 ppm) and, in 1978, to 0.06% (600 ppm).

EPA estimates that one in 11 American children have elevated blood lead-levels and one out of every five children in minority, low-income families have elevated blood lead levels. Properly maintained, lead-based paint poses little risk. Improperly managed, however, lead from paint can threaten the health of occupants, especially children under six years of age (Brown, 1994).

Lead Paint Laws and Regulations

In 1978, the use of lead in household paint was banned. Since that time, EPA estimates the lead blood levels in the United States have fallen by 80%. Regulations at the state and federal level, including but not limited to, 29 CFR 1910.1025 and 29 CFR 1926.62, as well as a number of guidance documents (e.g., the HUD Interim Guidelines for Hazard Identification and abatement in Public and Indian Housing), have been designed to protect the occupants of buildings where lead abatement or lead management projects occur, the workers involved in the projects, and the environment. Failure to follow regulations and guidelines may cause hazardous conditions, the assessment of fines or other penalties, and costly delays or revisions to project plans.

Blood lead tests are the only way to detect lead poisoning early and are part of the routine health care recommended for young children. Regulations which address and require that blood lead testing be conducted include 29 CFR 1910.1025 and 29 CFR 1926.62, the OSHA General Industry Lead

Standard and the Final Rule for the Lead in Construction Standard, effective June, 1993 (Christian, 1994).

According to HUDs 1990 Interim Guidelines, a lead content of 0.5% (5,000 ppm) by weight or an X-Ray Fluorescence Analysis (XRF) reading of 1.0 mg/cm^2 or greater are considered to be the action levels at which a hazard exists and lead paint should be abated. Some states have set standards for this "level of hazard" that may differ from the HUD standard.

Personnel who remove lead paint must follow all applicable respiratory requirements which include, but are not limited to, 29 CFR 1910.1020, 29 CFR 1926.62, and 29 CFR 1210.134.

In 1992, in an effort to protect families from exposure to the hazards of lead-based paint, Congress amended the Toxic Substances Control Act (TSCA) to add Title IV, entitled "Lead Exposure Reduction." Title IV directs EPA to address the general public's risk of lead exposure to lead-based paint hazards through regulations, education, and other activities. One particular concern was the potential lead exposure risks that can occur during renovations of housing containing lead-based paint.

Recognizing that many families might be unaware that their homes may contain lead-based paint, section 406(a) of TSCA directed EPA to publish, after notice and comment, a lead hazard information pamphlet providing comprehensive information to the general public on lead-based paint in housing, the risks of exposure, and the precautions for avoiding exposure. Section 406(b) of the law directed EPA to issue regulations requiring that renovators distribute the pamphlet to owners and occupants of most pre-1978 residential housing before beginning renovations (1987 is the year that lead-based paint was banned from residential use).

In early 1994, EPA therefore proposed regulations that would require renovators to provide an EPA pamphlet, entitled *Lead-Based Paint: Protect Your Family*, to owners and occupants of most pre-1978 housing before beginning renovations. The housing covered would include all housing built before 1978 with some exceptions. EPA's proposal would provide flexibility for renovations conducted in common areas (like stairways, lobbies, and hallways) of buildings containing several housing units (EPA, March 1994).

On October 16, 1994 EPA and the Department of Housing and Urban Development (HUD) proposed a new rule that would require sellers and landlords to disclose information on lead-based paint hazards before the sale or lease of most housing built before 1978. The proposed rule would require the following actions before ratification of a contract for housing sale or lease:

- Sellers and landlords or their agents would have to disclose any known lead-testing information regarding lead-based paint hazards in housing, or disclose if such testing or information is unknown.
- Sellers and landlords or their agents would have to indicate such information in disclosure forms, and retain them for three years following the sale or lease.

- Sellers and landlords or their agents also would be required to provide purchasers and renters with a copy of an EPA pamphlet on lead hazards obtainable from real estate agents or the government.
- Purchasers would be entitled to a 10-day opportunity to conduct a lead-based paint inspection or risk assessment at their expense. Sellers would not be required to finance the inspection/risk assessment, and the length of time could be changed by mutual agreement.
- Contracts for sale or lease of the housing will include general information on the hazards lead can pose as part of the Federal disclosure form.
- Selling and leasing agents would share responsibility for ensuring compliance by sellers and landlords (Christian, 1994).

On September 2, 1994, EPA proposed a new rule governing lead-based paint activities. The proposed rule (59 FR 45872) provides a regulatory framework for addressing lead-based paint hazards and requires that individuals and firms conduct lead-based paint activities in a manner that safeguards the environment and protects human health, specifically that of building occupants and workers.

The proposal prescribes training for individuals working with lead-based paint, accreditation of training programs, and certification of contractors performing lead abatement. The proposed rule also includes a model state program which, when promulgated, may be adopted by any state that seeks to administer and enforce a state program under Title IV of the Toxic Substances Control Act (TSCA).

Buildings that are affected by this program include the following:

- Public housing and private residences built before 1978
- Public buildings such as day-care centers, schools, and other facilities frequented by children
- Commercial buildings and superstructures, including industrial warehouses, power plants, bridges, water towers, and other structures that have been painted with lead-based paint (Christian, 1994).

Noise

Health Effects

Noise at levels that may be objectionable in terms of health or nuisance effects generally will occur as a result of one of the following activities:

- Construction and plant operation
- Vehicular traffic
- Aircraft
- Population growth and urbanization
- Military activities (Bregman and Mackenthun, 1992).

The concern about noise is directly related to its negative impacts upon humans, animals and plant life. These ill effects have been summarized as follows:

- Annoyance
- Permanent or temporary hearing loss
- Speech interference
- Health impacts
  - cardiovascular effects
  - achievement scores
  - birth weight
  - mortality rates
  - psychiatric admissions
- Harm to animals and plant life
- Effects on productivity of domestic animals
- Vibration of walls and windows
- Radiation of secondary noise
- Human physiological response to intense low frequency sound
- Sonic booms (Newman and Beattie, 1985)

Hearing loss may be either permanent or temporary. Continuous exposure to high levels of noise will damage human hearing. The upper limit of hearing is about 120 decibels (dB) (Newman & Beattie, 1985), at which discomfort begins to occur. Pain usually starts at 140 dB with auditory fatigue or acoustical injury eventually being reached. However, even sounds below 90–100 dB may bring about short-term changes in hearing (Bregman and Mackenthun, 1992).

Harm to animals is difficult to quantify. One may divide the effects into two categories: wild and domestic animals. Wild animals are considered to be those that live in wildlife refuges, national parks and wilderness areas. In the case of short-time noises, e.g., construction, the animals may simply vacate the area. Whether or not they come back again depends on the nature of the project. However, for continuing noise such as from traffic or aviation, the response of animals appears to be species-dependent and varies from almost no reaction to no tolerance of the sound (Newman and Beattie, 1985).

Some birds will be driven away permanently from nesting areas as a result of a project that brings a human population into the area (e.g., eagles) whereas others do not seem to be affected at all. The same applies to vehicular traffic and aviation flights as well.

Noise Level Explanation

Noise is measured in decibels. This number is equivalent to the "sound pressure level." The human ear perceives sound, which is mechanical energy, as a pressure on the ear. The sound pressure level is the logarithmic ratio of that sound pressure to a reference pressure and is expressed as the decibel (dB).

Sound is measured by a meter which reads decibels. For highway traffic and other noises, an adjustment, or weighing, of the high- and low-pitched sounds is made to approximate the way an average person hears sounds. The adjusted sounds are called "A-weighted levels" (dBA).

The A-weighted decibel scale begins at zero. This represents the faintest sound that can be heard by humans with very good hearing. The loudness of sounds (that is, how loud they seem to humans) varies from person to person, so there is no precise definition of loudness. However, based on many tests of large numbers of people, a sound level of 70 is twice as loud to the listener as a level of 60. This principle is illustrated in Exhibit 14-1.

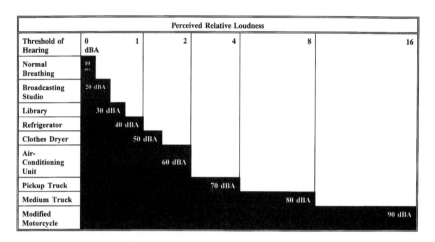

Exhibit 14-1.   Perception of sound levels.

Decibel levels are not additive, i.e., one cannot add a 70 dB noise to a 70 dB setting and obtain 140 dB. Instead, the final result would be between 73 and 74 dB, due to the fact that these levels are based on a logarithm scale. In addition, noise is three-dimensional in space because of its sound wave characteristics. Sound sources can also vary in intensity with the passage of time at a particular location (e.g., rush hour traffic on a usually quiet street corner). Consequently, in projecting noise effects on a specific setting, such as from a highway onto different levels of a nearby house, one must analyze a three-dimensional spatial model with a time of day factor as well. These models are frequently used for highway traffic and aviation effects on buildings (Bregman and Mackenthun, 1992).

The two most common statistical descriptors used for traffic noise are L_{10} and L_{eq}. L_{10} is the sound level that is exceeded 10% of the time. L_{eq} is the constant, average sound level, which over a period of time contains the same amount of sound energy as the varying levels of the traffic noise. L_{eq} for typical traffic conditions is usually about 3 dBA less than the L_{10} for the same conditions. The Federal Highway Administration (FHWA, 1990) has established noise impact criteria for different land uses close to highways. Some of the exterior criteria are summed up below.

Land use	L_{10}	L_{eq}
Residential	70 dBA	67 dBA
Commercial	75 dBA	72 dBA

The day-night noise level (L_{dn}) which is derived from hourly L_{eq} over a 24-hour period, takes into account increased nighttime sensitivity to noise.

Exhibit 14-2 presents comparative noise levels for activities encountered in daily life and shows which of these may be responsible for hearing damage from prolonged exposure.

Exhibit 14-2   Comparative Noise Levels

Typical decibel (dBA) values encountered in daily life and industry	dBA
Rustling leaves	20
Room in a quiet dwelling at midnight	32
Soft whispers at 5 feet	34
Men's clothing department of large store	53
Window air conditioner	55
Conversational speech	60
Household department of large store	62
Busy restaurant	65
Typing pool (9 typewriters in use)	65
Vacuum cleaner in private residence (at 10 feet)	69
Ringing alarm clock (at 2 feet)	80
Loud orchestral music in large room	82
Beginning of hearing damage for prolonged exposure over 85 dBA	
Printing press plant	86
Heavy city traffic	92
Heavy diesel-propelled vehicle (about 25 feet away)	92
Air grinder	95
Home lawn mower	98
Turbine condenser	98
150 cubic foot air compressor	100
Banging of steel compressor	104
Air hammer	107
Jet airliner	115

From Newman and Beattie, 1985

Noise Laws and Regulations

Noise Control Act of 1972 (Public Law (PL) 92-574, 42 USC 4901–4918) as amended. This Act:

- Establishes coordination of federal research and activities in noise control
- Authorizes the establishment of federal noise emission standards for products distributed in commerce
- Provides information to the public concerning the noise emission and noise reduction characteristics of such products.

The following categories of products which produce noise are covered by this Act:

- Construction equipment
- Transportation equipment (including recreational vehicles and related equipment)
- Any motor or engine (including any equipment of which an engine or motor is an integral part)
- Electric or electronic equipment.
  (Schell and Beckler, 1993)

Under this Act, the manufacturer of a product is required to give notice to the prospective user about the level of the noise the product emits, or its effectiveness in reducing noise (42 USC 4907 (b)). Such notice may not be removed from the product or its container (42 USC 4909 (4)). The manufacturer is prohibited from removing or rendering ineffective any device or element of design incorporated into the product to control noise (42 USC 4909 (2)).

As directed by this Act, EPA (EPA, 1974) prepared Exhibit 14-3, which summarizes the yearly equivalent sound levels identified as requisite to protect the public health and welfare with an adequate margin of safety. EPA also set noise source emission standards for various products, including transportation vehicles, construction equipment, and consumer products. EPA also proposed aircraft/airport regulations to the FAA following a special procedure specified in the Noise Control Act of 1972.

Quiet Communities Act of 1978 (95-609). This Act was designed to set up methods for EPA to assist communities in noise reduction. Thus, in a grants program under this Act, EPA initiated such technical assistance programs as the Quiet Communities Program (QCP) and Each Community Helps Others (ECHO).

Airport and Airway Development Act of 1970, as Amended. Under this Act, Airport Noise Control and Land Use Compatibility (ANCLUC) planning

**Exhibit 14.3   Yearly Average Equivalent Sound Levels
Identified as Requisite to Protect the Public Health
with an Adequate Margin of Safety Measured as L$_{eq}$(24)**

	Indoor activity interference	Indoor hearing loss[a]	Outdoor activity interference	Outdoor hearing loss
Residential with outside space and farm residences	45	70	55	70
Residential with no outside space	45	70		
Commercial		70		70
Inside transportation		70		
Industrial		70		70
Hospitals	45	70	55	70
Educational	45	70	55	70
Recreational areas		70		70
Farmland and general unpopulated land				70

[a] The exposure period that results in hearing loss at the identified levels is 40 years.

From U.S. EPA, 1974.

studies by the Federal Aviation Administration (FAA) integrate the master planning study activities, the environmental considerations, and the airport-land use compatibility planning activities at an airport. The objective is to achieve maximum noise and environmental compatibility within the constraints of safety, service, and economic viability.

The Aviation Safety and Noise Abatement Act of 1979 (PL 96-193, 49 USC Appendix 2103, 2104), as Amended. Any airport operator may submit to the Secretary of Transportation a noise exposure map. Such map shall set forth the noncompatible uses in each area of the map, a description of the projected aircraft operations at such airport, and the ways in which such operations will affect such map (49 USC 2103).

Any airport operator who has submitted a noise exposure map and the related information may submit to the Secretary of Transportation a noise compatibility program. This program shall include measures which the operator has taken or proposes for the reduction of existing noncompatible uses and the prevention of the introduction of noncompatible uses within the area covered by the noise exposure map submitted (49 USC Appendix 2104).

Under this Act, the Federal Aviation Administration (FAA) has a program to retrofit engines or equipment on noisy aircraft or to replace them with newer, quieter aircraft. It also includes the development of operational procedures which can reduce the aircraft's noise impacts.

Housing and Urban Development (HUD) Noise Regulations. The major purpose of HUD's noise regulations (24 CFR Part 51 Subpart B) is to assure that activities assisted or insured by the Department achieve the goal of a suitable living environment. The regulations apply to all HUD actions and provide minimum national standards to protect citizens against excessive noise in their communities and places of residence. HUD assistance for construction of new noise sensitive uses is prohibited for projects with normally unacceptable noise exposures, which are defined as noise levels above 75 dB (day-night average sound level (DNL) in decibels). These noise levels are to be based on noise from all sources (Bregman and Mackenthun, 1992).

Federal Aid Highway Act. As a result of this Act, the Federal Highway Administration (FHWA) is concerned with traffic and construction noise associated with Federally aided highways. It requires study of future noise exposures in conjunction with standards featuring highway design noise levels. FHWA also provides for noise mitigation on existing Federally aided highways. For each new highway, FHWA requires that state highway agencies furnish localities information on noise and land use.

Department of Veterans Affairs. The Department of Veterans Affairs policy for consideration of noise and land use planning is promoted in the VA Loan Guaranty Program, the Department of Medicine and Surgery (MD&S) and the Department of Memorial Affairs (DMA).

The VA Loan Guaranty noise policy governs VA decisions as to whether residential sites in airport environs are "acceptable" for loan guaranty programs to eligible veterans and active duty personnel. It sets three noise zones of increasing decibels. In the case of new construction, all new developments located in the two higher zones generally are not eligible for VA assistance. The policy for land acquisition, construction, and maintenance adhered to by DM&S and DMA considers noise in the environmental planning of all acquisition and construction programs.

Department of Defense Air Installations. The Department of Defense policy for noise compatible land use guidance is called the Air Installation Compatible Use Zone (AICUZ). Each military service studies noise exposure and land use at all DoD air installations. Each study contains noise contours, accident potential zones, existing and future land use compatibilities and incompatibilities, and land use planning/control recommendations. Department of Defense policy requires that all reasonable, economical, and practical measures be taken to reduce and/or control the generation of noise from aircraft.

U.S. Army Regulations. AR 200-1, Chapter 7, *Environmental Noise Abatement Program*, outlines the requirements for compliance with Federal laws and regulations on the control and abatement of environmental noise. These requirements include assessment of the impact of noise produced by proposed Army actions and maintenance of an active control program (Schell and Beckler, 1993).

State and Local Regulations. Most of the specific standards for allowable noise levels at specific locations are set by state and local agencies. These standards cover such activities as industrial development, military facilities, highways, civilian airports, etc. The compliance officer will have to check with the state or local governing body for allowable noise levels at the specific site or facility under consideration. As a general rule, states tend to treat environmental noise as a source-specific pollutant whose emissions will be controlled by the locally affected community.

Radon

Introduction

Radon is a colorless, odorless, tasteless, radioactive gas that occurs naturally in soil gas, underground water, and outdoor air. It exists at various levels throughout the United States. Prolonged exposure to elevated concentrations of radon decay products has been associated with increases in the risk of lung cancer. According to EPA, radon is the second leading cause of lung cancer. EPA has developed a radon risk evaluation chart (EPA, August, 1992) in terms of radon levels measured as pico Curies/liter (pCi/l). (See Exhibit 14.4).

Exhibit 14-4   Radon Risk Evaluation Chart

Annual radon level	If a community of 100 people were exposed to this level:	The risk of dying from lung cancer compares to:
100 pCi/l	About 35 people in the community may die from radon	Having 10,000 chest X-rays each year
40 pCi/l	About 17 people in the community may die from radon	Smoking 2 packs of cigarettes each day
20 pCi/l	About 9 people in the community may die from radon	Smoking 1 pack of cigarettes each day
10 pCi/l	About 5 people in the community may die from radon	Having 1000 chest X-rays each year
4 pCi/l	About 2 people in the community may die from radon	Smoking at least 5 cigarettes each day

Note: Levels as high as 3500 pCi/l have been found in some homes. The average radon level outdoors is around 0.2 pCi/l or less. The risks shown in this chart are for the general population, including men and women of all ages as well as smokers and nonsmokers. Children may be at higher risk.

From U.S. EPA, August, 1992.

The health risk due to radon is further complicated by the fact that radon concentrations in buildings may vary with time, and concentrations at different locations in the same building also may vary substantially (EPA, 1993). EPA has estimated that nearly 1 out of every 15 homes in the U.S. has elevated radon levels (EPA, May, 1992).

An elevated concentration is defined as being at or above the EPA suggested guidelines of 4pCi/l. Pico-Curies per liter is used as a radiation unit of measure for radon. The prefix pico means a multiplication factor of 1 trillionth. A Curie is a commonly used measurement of radioactivity (EPA, Aug, 1987).

Soil gas entering homes through crawl spaces, through cracks and openings in slab-on-grade floors, and through below-grade walls and floors is the primary source of elevated radon levels. Radon in outside air is diluted to such low concentrations that it does not present a health hazard.

Radon moves through the small spaces that exist in all soils. The speed of movement depends on the permeability of the soil and the presence of a driving force caused when the pressure inside a home is lower than the pressure outside or in the surrounding and underlying soil. A lower pressure inside a building may result from:

- Heated air rising
- Wind blowing past the building
- Air being used by fireplaces and wood stoves
- Air being vented to the outside by clothes dryers and exhaust fans in bathrooms, kitchens, or attics.

In the above instances, soil gas is driven into the building (EPA, August, 1987).

Radon Laws and Regulations

There is a relative paucity of federal laws and regulations relating to radon and its control. Major requirements are as follows:

The Toxic Substances Control Act as Amended in 1986 – U.S. Code (USC) 2601–2671. This is the federal legislation which deals with the control of toxic substances. The Act consists of three subchapters, one of which regulates indoor radon abatement. The national long-term goal of the United States with respect to radon levels in buildings is set that the air within buildings in the United States should be as free of radon as the air outside of buildings (15 USC 2661).

The head of each federal department or agency that owns a federal building had to conduct a study for the purpose of determining the extent of radon contamination in such buildings. The study had to be based on design criteria specified by the U.S. Environmental Protection Agency (U.S. EPA). The studies were completed and reported to the U.S. EPA.

Executive Order (EO) 12088, Federal Compliance with Pollution Standards, October 13, 1978. This EO requires federally owned and operated facilities to comply with applicable pollution control standards. It has been interpreted to include radon.

AR 200-1, Environmental Protection and Enhancement, Chapter 11, Army Radon Reduction Program (ARRP). This requirement describes policy and procedures for assessing indoor levels of radon and mitigating radon in structures where the levels are elevated. The program is decentralized; that is, each facility is responsible for funding, executing, documenting, and managing the radon monitoring and mitigation efforts based on the ARRP (Schell and Becker, 1993).

State Laws and Regulations

A large number of states have their own laws and regulations concerning radon. Many of them require that sellers of residential real estate must furnish the buyer with a disclosure form that includes radon levels and hazard information. Others require that all school buildings in the state be tested for radon and the results made available to the public.

PCBs

Polychlorinated biphenyls (PCBs) are a class of organic chemical compounds that are nonflammable and can conduct heat without conducting electricity. PCBs are used primarily in electrical equipment and heat transfer systems. They have been produced industrially since 1929 and have been mainly used as insulators or heat transfer liquids in electrical equipment such as transformers and capacitors. PCBs have also been used in paints, adhesives, caulking compounds, and certain plastics. From 1929 to 1975, an estimated 1.4 billion pounds of PCBs were produced in the United States.

If released into the environment, PCBs tend to persist and are considered a chronic toxic hazard since they are readily absorbed and retained in human and animal tissues. Short-term exposure to PCBs may cause skin problems, while long-term exposure may cause liver damage or impairment of the nervous system. PCB exposure also has caused reproductive problems and cancer in animals.

PCB fumes also can be dangerous. Although PCBs are used as fire retardants, when heated to decomposition in uncontrolled environments they emit highly toxic fumes. Thus, transformer fires potentially can be very hazardous (GAO, 1994).

PCB Laws and Regulations

Toxic Substances Control Act as Amended in 1986. The Act (15 USC § 2601–2692) directs the EPA to regulate chemicals that "pose an unreasonable risk of injury to health and the environment." The Act specifically bans the use, manufacture, processing, and distribution in commerce of PCBs and PCB items, except in certain limited circumstances.

The Act charges EPA to promulgate and enforce PCB regulations. These regulations (40 CFR 761) generally prohibit the manufacturing of PCBs and the use of PCBs unless they are totally enclosed. Some PCB items such as transformers or capacitors are permitted to remain in use for the remainder of their useful lives, subject to servicing, record keeping, and inspection conditions. The regulations also require proper disposal, labeling to indicate PCB content, and spill containment procedures.

Currently, the EPA regulations only address those PCBs found in electrical equipment, since the uses of PCBs in manners other than in electrical equipment generally present less of a risk to health and the environment.

Executive Order (EO) 12088, Federal Compliance with Pollution Standards. This EO requires federally owned and operated facilities to comply with applicable federal, state, and local environmental requirements. This includes all PCB requirements.

State Requirements. State PCB regulations may provide additional requirements to address a specific concern or activity sensitive in that state. State regulations may supersede the federal regulations in certain areas including the following:

- PCBs may be regulated as hazardous wastes.
- PCBs may be regulated to lower concentrations.
- Shipments of PCBs may require manifest documents.
- Analyses may be required to quantify the PCB concentration in all PCB items.
- Additional inspections of select PCB items and specific disposal requirements for PCBs and PCB items also may be required.
- Generators of PCBs and PCB items may be required to obtain disposal permits (Schell and Beckler, 1993).

U.S. Army Regulations. AR 200-1, Environmental Protection and Enhancement, Chapter 5, para 6, Polychlorinated Biphenyls (PCBs), mandates compliance with *TSCA* and outlines a record keeping system for PCBs and PCB-related items.

ENVIRONMENTAL COMPLIANCE

Asbestos

The compliance officer basically has the following duties with regards to asbestos:

- Survey the facilities to determine the presence or absence of asbestos

- If asbestos is present, develop either a) a management plan for its removal or b) an Operation and Maintenance (O&M) plan that will render it harmless
- Oversee removal or encapsulation to be certain that all OSHA requirements are met
- Make certain that the O&M plan is carried out properly.

The following discussion amplifies upon these points.

Is asbestos present anywhere in the facilities? A survey must be undertaken to answer this question. This survey includes both a review of building plans and a walk through visual inspection of the entire facilities. If the buildings have been built in the very recent past, asbestos may not be present, except possibly in floor tile or exterior shingles. If the building is more than 15 years old, the chances are very good that there is asbestos insulation present in several locations.

Survey

Checklist :

Is asbestos possibly present in your facilities?

No: No further action on asbestos

Yes: Perform a survey of the facilities for asbestos

The survey for asbestos will follow the AHERA formula (if the facilities are schools or public buildings), or a simplified version thereof for other facilities. In the latter case, it would be wise to check with the appropriate state agency to be sure that it approves of the procedure to be used.

The personnel doing the survey must be AHERA certified. In the course of obtaining that certification, they will learn the required AHERA survey techniques. This involves the types of materials to be examined, the nature and number of samples to be taken, the types of laboratory analysis required for them and the determination of the presence or absence of friable ACBMs.

What happens if friable asbestos is found in the survey?

What to Do if Friable Asbestos Is Present

Checklist :

Friable asbestos absent: No further studies on asbestos are required.

What to Do if Friable Asbestos Is Present (continued)

Checklist (continued):

Friable asbestos present:

1) On detailed drawing of the building, locate all ACBM and categorize as to present condition, potential for damage, and type of material

2) Determine appropriate response action

3) Develop management plan for the response action

The required response action, as shown earlier in this section, may be one of several, e.g., encapsulation, enclosure, operations and maintenance (O&M), repair, or removal.

Management Plan

Checklist:

Encapsulation/Enclosure/Repair/Removal: Develop a plan that shows in detail what has to be done and where

O&M: Prepare O&M manual specifying what has to be checked, when and by whom

The management plan for the four items in the above checklist should be prepared by an AHERA certified management planner. It should follow AHERA procedures and include such items as what is to be done, where it is to be done, monitoring and regulatory requirements, as well as a rough approximation of possible costs.

In the case of the O&M manual, it should be prepared in accordance with AHERA requirements. A foolproof method must be set up to ensure that the O&M requirements are followed.

Oversight of Encapsulation, Enclosure, Repair or Removal of Asbestos

---

- If requested, develop bid forms, list of firms to be solicited and assist in selection of contractor

- Oversee the work by the contractor. Make certain that it conforms with all required federal and state regulations

- Write report on work done after it has been completed

Lead Paint

Lead paint duties of the compliance officer include the following:

- Determine which buildings have lead paint in them
- For those where lead paint is present, determine amounts and locations
- Develop a management plan for the paint removal
- Oversee removal

These responsibilities are described below.

Which buildings that the organization owns have lead in them? This determination is made on the basis of two factors:

- Building age
- Paint chip samples for the older buildings

Lead Paint Determination

Checklist :

- Determine building age

- If built since 1978, paint is unlikely to contain excessive quantities of lead. If built since 1990, lead may be considered absent

- If built pre-1990, take a small number of paint chips for laboratory analysis for lead. Chips should be taken from the older peeling paint where possible

---

If lead paint appears to be present, a detailed survey should be conducted using either the portable X-Ray Fluorescence analysis method (XRF), or a detailed paint chip survey. The XRF method is performed on site, it is less destructive to paint surfaces than other methods and gives quick on-site results. The equipment is expensive, requires trained operators and suffers from the following difficulties:

- May not read accurately on some surfaces such as brick, metal, or radiators
- Can only take readings on smooth flat surfaces

The detailed paint chip method also has both advantages and disadvantages as follows:

- Advantages
  - Analyzed in laboratory, usually by atomic absorption spectrometry (AAS)
  - Very accurate
  - Results reflect lower as well as upper paint layers
- Disadvantages
  - Lengthy laboratory period and expense
  - Large number of samples required
  - Not too accurate if there are many paint layers
  - Destructive to painted surfaces

Detailed Survey

Checklist :

- Decide whether to use the XRF or paint chip method

- If the XRF method, carefully follow equipment manufacturer instructions. Use trained personnel for this analysis. Record readings

- If paint chip method, carefully take several paint scrapings (30–70 or more per building, depending on building size). Try to take multi-layer samples, as well as individual layers where possible

- Make arrangements ahead of time with a certified laboratory as to number of samples, QA/QC, size of samples, etc.

Detailed Survey (continued)

> **Checklist (continued):**
>
> - By either method, develop detailed analysis of locations of lead

The next step obviously is lead removal.

Lead Paint Removal

> **Checklist :**
>
> - Develop detailed plan that shows location and amounts of lead paint on blueprint of building
>
> - Develop scope of work for removal contractors. Scope must include training and work protection requirements listed earlier in this chapter. Send out bids to qualified contractors. Select winning bidder
>
> - Oversee paint removal. Make sure it conforms to all applicable EPA, OSHA, state and local requirements

Noise

Information first should be developed by the compliance officer on the existing situation with regard to noise as follows:

- The existing and anticipated land uses at and near the project or facility site
- The existence of sensitive receptors nearby at which noise measurements may be made
- Applicable noise standards and criteria for the area
- Existing noise levels at and in the facility and site and the "sensitive receptors"

This information is basic before any conclusions are reached concerning noise problems whether at an existing facility or site, or a proposed one.

Measurement of noise levels is a simple procedure that uses a hand-held instrument. The sound level meter is a battery operated device that contains the appropriate electronics to convert the sound pressure exciting the microphone diaphragm into a meter reading in decibels (dB). The concern with using a portable sound level meter is the possible effect the person holding the meter has on the sound field. Certain combinations of noise and distances of the sound level meter from one's body can alter the sound field by several dB. For precision measurements, these effects can be eliminated by simply placing a 2–3 meter cable between the sound level meter and the microphone, and mounting the microphone on a tripod.

For many measurements, it is sufficient to simply hand hold the sound level meter and record the levels directly from the meter reading. However, under certain circumstances it is necessary for the sound level meter to have additional capabilities. To record the noise using a portable tape recorder, the sound level meter must have an AV output terminal. In addition, in order to calibrate the entire sound recording system, a calibrator or pistonphone must be used.

For measuring vehicular pass-by levels or one-time, short duration (impulsive type) noise events, a "hold" circuit is a necessity for two reasons: (1) since the duration of the peak pass-by or impulse noise is often less than or equal to the response time of the meter, the hold circuit electronically holds the maximum value, permitting the meter itself sufficient time to respond, and (2) since the peak sound-pressure levels only last a brief moment, it would be difficult to accurately and consistently read the meter (if it could respond correctly) in such a short period of time (Bregman and Mackenthun, 1992).

Existing Noise Situation

> **Checklist :**
>
> - Determine existing and anticipated land uses at or near the project or facility site; record information
>
> - Determine which sensitive receptors are of concern
>
> - Determine noise standards and criteria for area
>
> - Measure noise levels at site or facility; record information

The question that has to be answered now is whether existing noise levels at the site or facility or at nearby sensitive receptors are in violation of state or local standards.

Existing Noise vs Standards

> **Checklist :**
>
> - Compare existing noise levels determined above for site, facilities and sensitive receptors with state, regional or local standards
>
> - Noise levels are not in excess of standards
>   No further action required
>
> - Noise levels are in excess of standards
>   Determine appropriate mitigation measures and carry them out

If existing noise levels are in violation of standards, it is necessary to determine the source of the noise and then develop appropriate quietening measures. Noise violations occur from individual sources such as the following:

- Power generating equipment
- Emergency generators
- Industrial facilities
- Airfields/heliports/helipads
- Vehicle motor parks or garages
- Highways
- Rock quarries.

Pinpointing Noise Violation Sources

> **Checklist :**
>
> - Determine source of violation by measurement of that source when and where noise from other sources is minimal
>
> - Develop a noise mitigation plan

The noise mitigation plan will vary with the source of the noise. Examples of possible noise mitigation approaches are shown later in this section.

Planning for new facilities must include provision for meeting noise standards during both the construction and operational stages. First, noise levels during both the construction and operational phases are projected. The calculated construction, operation, and induced population growth-associated noise levels then are compared with the measured existing sound levels. A comparison

of predicted noise levels is made with applicable state and local noise regulations, as well as EPA guidelines to protect the public health and safety.

In the case of highways, FHWA has developed three procedures whereby
traffic noise from freely flowing highway traffic can be reasonably well predicted. Two of these procedures are graphical and the third requires a digital
computer program. One of the graphical procedures uses a readily available
nomograph, which is valid for moderately high volume, freely flowing traffic
on infinitely long, unshielded, straight, level roadways. Adjustments are then
made to the values obtained from the nomograph to include some of the effects
of the roadway geometry and road surface characteristics.

There are many situations where the traffic flow is intermittent, where
cars and trucks operate in accelerating and decelerating modes, or where the
principal sound source is an intermittent line of low speed, low volume trucks
climbing a steep ramp grade. Simple and reliable noise prediction schemes
for such complicated situations are not yet readily available.

Projecting New Noise Levels

Checklist :

- Distinguish between construction of a facility and its operation

- Project the levels at the closest sensitive receptors

- Compare the projected levels with applicable standards

  If they are below the applicable standards, no further action
  is required

  If they exceed the applicable standards, then determine
  proper mitigation methods, being sure to distinguish between construction and operation

Mitigation methods include the following:

Construction Phase

Checklist :

- For trucks
  - Muffling devices
  - Keep speed low

Construction Phase (continued)

Checklist (continued):

- For machinery
  - Vibration reduction
  - Enclose noise source
  - Absorb sound waves in equipment

- For both
  - Schedule noise generating activities for hours when they will be least noticeable or have least effect
  - Insulate nearby sensitive receptors or soundproof them
  - Construct noise berm between noise generator and receptor

Operational Phase of Noise Generator

Checklist :

- Mitigation is to be tailored to the type of noise generator

- For an industrial plant

  - Use of quieter equipment, precesses, or materials
  - Enclosure of source of noise
  - Soundproofing plant and/or neighboring building receptors

- For highways

  - Traffic management measures
    one-way systems
    traffic lights
    speed limits
    mass transit
    parking controls

  - Buffer zones
  - Land use control
  - Planting vegetation
  - Insulating buildings alongside the highway
  - Highway relocation
  - Noise barriers

Operational Phase of Noise Generator (continued)

Checklist (continued):

- For aircraft

    - Modify aircraft design
    - Changes in aircraft operations and route locations
    - More frequent aircraft maintenance
    - Landscape architecture and acoustic insulation for near-by buildings
    - Land use zoning near airports

                                        (Bregman and Mackenthun, 1992)

Radon

Buildings

A radon compliance program for buildings is designed to assess radon levels in buildings after a priority list is established. Detailed assessments then are accomplished at the facilities where initial screening results identify a radon problem. Following mitigation, assessments are conducted on the effectiveness of the mitigation actions.

Priority List Establishment for Buildings

Checklist :

- Create priority list for radon survey

Each compliance officer will have to create his/her own building priority list, depending upon the nature of the facility being surveyed. Thus, for example (Schell and Becker, 1993), the major U.S. Army Reserve installations utilize the following prioritization:

Priority 1: Day-care centers, hospitals, schools, and living areas (that is, quarters, unaccompanied personnel housing, and billets).

Priority 2: Areas having 24 hour operations, such as operations centers and training and research, development, test, and evaluating facilities.

Priority 3: All other routinely occupied structures.

Conduct Screening Tests for Radon

> **Checklist :**
>
> - Conduct short-term radon tests on the facilities in the priority order shown above
>
>   For those facilities where the results are below 4pCi/l no more radon assessment activity is required
>
>   For the facilities with results above 4pCi/l, repeat the test

Equipment used for short-term tests remains in the building for 2 to 3 days, depending on the device. Charcoal canisters are most commonly used for short-term testing. The test kits are supplied by a manufacturer or laboratory and must be returned to them for their analysis after use.

In placing a short-term radon test, the compliance officer should follow the instructions that come with the test kit. If doing a short-term test, close windows and outside doors at least 12 hours **before** beginning the test, and keep them closed as much as possible during the test. Do not conduct short-term tests during unusually severe storms or periods of unusually high winds.

The test kit should be placed in the lowest used level of the building. Place it at least 20 inches above the floor in a location where it will not be disturbed — away from drafts, high heat, high humidity, and exterior walls. Leave the kit in place for as long as the package says. Once finished with the test, reseal the package and send it immediately to the lab specified on the package for analysis. Test results should be back within a week to 10 days.

The compliance officer should use a device and a testing company that is state certified, and/or listed in EPA's Radon Measurement Proficiency (RMP) Program. It should display the phrase *Meets EPA Requirements*. EPA's Program is designed to help assure that consumers are given reliable radon measurements. If it is decided to hire a professional to take the measurement, the environmental compliance officer should contact the state radon office for a current list of certified companies and individuals. They must follow quality assurance and EPA measurement procedures and have demonstrated the ability to take reliable measurements with specific devices. The state also may have additional requirements for professional radon testers.

Short-Term Repeat Testing

> **Checklist :**
>
> - If the repeat test is low enough so that the average of the two tests is well below 4.0 pCi/l, no further action is necessary

Short-Term Repeat Testing (continued)

Checklist (continued):

- If the average of the two short-term tests is near or slightly over 4.0 pCi/l, it may be desirable to do a long-term test

- If the average of the two short-term tests is well over 4.0 pCi/l, e.g., 8–10 pCi/l or more, it is desirable to proceed directly to corrective measures

Long-Term Testing

Checklist :

- Use one of several long-term tests, e.g., alpha track or electret ion chamber. The test should proceed for a minimum of 90 days and, preferably, for as long as possible. The closer the test is to 365 days, the more likely it is to give an accurate year-round average radon level

- If the long-term results are well below 4.0 pCi/l, no further action is required

- If the long-term results are at 4.0 pCi/l or higher, remedial actions should be started

There are simple ways to fix a radon problem that are not too costly. Even very high levels can be reduced to acceptable levels. A variety of methods are used to reduce radon in a building. In some cases, sealing cracks in floors and walls may reduce radon. In other cases, simple systems using pipes and fans may be used to reduce radon. Such systems are called "sub-slab depressurization," and do not require major changes to the building. These systems remove radon gas from below the concrete floor and the foundation before it can enter the building. Similar systems can also be installed in buildings with crawl spaces. Radon contractors use other methods as well. The right system depends on the design of the building and other factors. Methods of reducing radon levels are discussed in EPA's *Consumer's Guide to Radon Reduction* (U.S. EPA, August, 1992).

The cost of making repairs to reduce radon depends on how the building was built and the extent of the radon problem. Most buildings can be fixed for about the same cost as other common building repairs like painting or having a new hot water heater installed.

Lowering high radon levels requires technical knowledge and special skills. It is generally desirable to use a contractor who is trained to fix radon problems. The EPA Radon Contractor Proficiency (RCP) Program tests these contractors. EPA provides a list of RCP contractors to state radon offices. A contractor who has passed the EPA test will carry a special RCP identification card. A trained RCP contractor can study the radon problem in the building and assist the compliance officer in selecting the right treatment method.

Radon Reduction

Checklist :

- Develop a Request for Proposals (RFP) for the radon reduction program

- Go out on bids for the work, using a list of state and/or EPA certified contractors as bidders. Obtain that list from the state radon agency

- Select the winning contractor

- Oversee the remediation effort

- Check the radon level in the building about 7–10 days after the contractor has finished to be certain that the desired reduction has been obtained

EPA has developed an excellent checklist for evaluating and comparing contractors for radon reduction (EPA, 1992). That checklist follows:

Yes   No

☐ ☐ **Will the contractor provide references or photographs, as well as test results of *before* and *after* radon levels for past radon reduction work?**

☐ ☐ **Can the contractor explain what the work will involve, how long it will take to complete, and exactly how the radon reduction system will work?**

☐ ☐ **Does the contractor charge a fee for any diagnostic tests?**

☐ ☐ **Did the contractor inspect the building's structure *before* giving you an estimate?**

☐ ☐ **Did the contractor review the quality of the radon measurement results and determine if EPA testing procedures were followed?**

Do the contractors' proposals and estimates include:

Yes   No

☐   ☐   **Proof of liability insurance and being bonded and licensed?**

☐   ☐   **Proof of state certification and/or RCP listing?**

☐   ☐   **Diagnostic testing prior to design and installation of a radon reduction system?**

☐   ☐   **Installation of a warning device to caution you if the radon reduction system is not working correctly (an RCP requirement)?**

☐   ☐   **Testing after installation to make sure the radon reduction system works well (an RCP requirement)?**

☐   ☐   **A guarantee to reduce radon levels to 4 pCi/l or below, and if so, for how long?**

Finally, EPA has developed the following listing of important information that should appear in the contract (EPA,1992):

- The total cost of the job, including all taxes and permit fees; how much, if any, is required for a deposit; and when payment is due in full.
- The time needed to complete the work.
- An agreement by the contractor to obtain necessary licenses and follow required building codes.
- A statement that the contractor carries liability insurance and is bonded and insured to protect you in case of injury to persons, or damage to property, while the work is being done.
- A guarantee that the contractor will be responsible for damage and clean-up after the job.
- Details of warranties, guarantees, or other optional features, including the acceptable resulting radon level.
- A declaration stating whether any warranties or guarantees are transferable.
- A description of what the contractor expects the owner to do (e.g., make the work area accessible) before work begins.

Open Areas

Radon measurements in open areas generally are quite inaccurate because the radon dissipates into the air so rapidly under windy conditions. For that reason, the radon level is estimated by use of existing maps such as EPA's series of maps of radon zones in each state, which was developed by its Office of Radiation and Indoor Air. These maps show the percentage of radon readings above 4.0 pCi/l for various regions in each state. An example of such a map for the state of Maryland is presented in Exhibit 14-5.

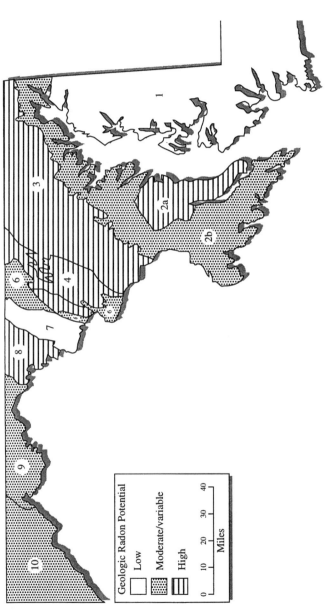

Exhibit 14-5. Geologic Radon Potential Areas of Maryland. (1) Eastern Shore - Quaternary; (2a) Western Shore - Tertiary; (2b) Western Shore - Cretaceous Quaternary, Minor Tertiary; (3) Eastern Piedmont - Schist and Gneiss; (4) Western Piedmont - Phyllite; (5) Frederick Valley - Carbonates and Clastics; (6) Mesozoic Basins - Culpeper/Gettysberg Basins; (7) Blue Ridge - Igneous and Sedimentary; (8) Great Valley - Carbonates and Clastics; (9) Valley and Ridge - Silurian and Devonian; (10) Allegheny Plateau.

In those cases where a significant (this term is to be determined by the environmental compliance officer) percentage of radon studies (in the region where the land is located) is above 4.0 pCi/l, then it is recommended that tests be taken of new buildings as they are being built. That is done when the bottom level of the building is in place and is completely covered from the air outside. Corrective measures, if necessary, can be instituted in the buildings under construction at that time.

Construction principles for new buildings that are designed to minimize radon levels include the following:

- Buildings should be designed and constructed to minimize pathways for soil gas to enter.
- Buildings should be designed and built to maintain a neutral pressure differential between indoors and outdoors.
- Features such as the following also can be incorporated during construction that will facilitate radon removal after completion of the home if prevention techniques prove to be inadequate.
  - Use of gravel in sub-floor area
  - Perforated drain pipes along interior or exterior of foundation
  - Insertion of standpipes in sub-slab aggregate and connection to venting at roof

If the building has been constructed and radon problems still remain, then corrective actions similar to those for existing buildings may be employed.

Open Areas Radon Levels

Checklist :

- If the area being surveyed is open to the air, obtain an EPA radon map of the area.

- Does the map show a high frequency of radon levels above 4.0 pCi/L?

  If no, no further action is required.

  If yes, a) take readings when enclosed buildings are constructed to the point where the lowest levels are enclosed, and b) construct the buildings in such a manner as to minimize radon levels.

- After construction, check radon levels.

  If below 4.0 pCi/l, no further action is required.

Open Areas Radon Levels (continued)

> **Checklist (continued):**
>
> If at or above 4.0 pCi/l, take steps similar to those de-
> scribed earlier in this chapter for existing buildings.

PCBs

The first thing required of the environmental compliance officer is to
determine the locations of items that may have PCBs in them.

Location of PCBs

> **Checklist :**
>
> - Plans and Maps to Review
>   - Spill plan
>
> - Records to Review
>   - Inspection, storage, maintenance and disposal records
>   for PCBs/PCB items
>   - PCB equipment inventory and sampling results
>   - Correspondence with regulatory agencies concerning
>   PCB noncompliance situations
>   - Annual reports
>
> - Physical Features to Examine
>   - PCB storage areas
>   - Equipment, fluids, and other items used or stored at the
>   facility containing PCBs
>
> - People to Interview
>   - Anyone who may be knowledgeable (Schell and Beck-
>   ler, 1993), such as building manager, engineers, main-
>   tenance personnel, etc.

As a result of the above review, a decision is made on which items to
survey for PCBs.

The EPA regulations do not specifically require activities to determine the
PCB concentration of fluid used in existing equipment, EPA assumes that
concentrations in those cases are at levels that are safe. However, if leaks occur
and PCB is identified, EPA then imposes requirements for monitoring, inspect-

ing, storing, and disposing of PCBs. EPA considers fluid or items containing fluid with PCB concentrations of

- 500 ppm or more to be PCB
- 50 ppm but less than 500 ppm to be **PCB-contaminated**, and
- Under 50 ppm to be non-PCB.

PCB items (500 ppm or greater) must be monitored when in use. For example, PCB items must be labeled and listed on an annual log. Their locations must be reported to local fire departments, and PCB transformers must be periodically inspected for leaks. PCB items that are no longer in use must be labeled and may be stored up to one year in a building that meets certain standards. The items must be disposed of in an incinerator or, in certain circumstances, chemical waste landfill.

The use of PCB-contaminated items (50 ppm but less than 500 pm) is not as stringently regulated. Once taken out of use, however, PCB-contaminated items are subject to storage and disposal requirements.

Laboratory tests may be used to determine PCB concentrations. For items not tested, users must assume they are PCB items if the nameplate indicates the equipment contains PCB fluid, there is any reason to believe the equipment contained PCB fluid at one time, or there is no nameplate on the equipment. Generally, untested items that do not meet the above conditions must be assumed to be PCB-contaminated.

PCB spills must be contained and cleaned up according to approved disposal methods. The cleanup must begin within 48 hours after a spill is discovered. In addition to the environmental hazard they create, PCB spills are expensive to clean up because of training and labor costs, testing requirements, and disposal expenses.

As an example of the continued prevalence of electrical equipment still in use that contains PCBs, it has been stated (GAO, 1994) that military installations have thousands of electrical transformers and other electrical equipment that either contain, or are suspected to contain, PCBs. The U.S. Air Force fiscal year 1990 inventory indicates 4,904 PCB and PCB-contaminated transformers were in service at air force installations. The calendar year 1993 Navy inventory shows a total of 6,461 PCB items in use or in storage, including 4,600 transformers. This total is a reduction from the 1992 data showing 6,984, including 4,891 transformers. The U.S. Army does not collect service-wide inventory data.

Survey For PCB Content

Checklist :

- From the previous determination of PCB locations, determine which electrical units may contain PCBs.

Survey For PCB Content (continued)

Checklist (continued):

- Examine the subject units
  - Look for signs of leakage
  - Look for notice on equipment for PCB content or lack thereof
  - Call container owners (e.g., utility company) if necessary to determine whether there is any PCB in container

- If no sign of leaking from units that contain PCBs, note location and condition for resurvey in one year

- If signs of leakage are evident, make arrangements for corrective action
  - Contact unit owners to have this done

- For PCB equipment taken out of service
  - Store for up to one year for disposal in a specially designated storage area
  - Dispose of PCB fluids by incineration in specially licensed incinerators
  - Dispose of PCB equipment (without the fluid) in a specially licensed chemical waste landfill

GLOSSARY

Abatement . . . . The removal of asbestos.

Capacitor . . . . A device for accumulating and holding a charge of electricity, consisting of conducting surfaces separated by a dielectric.

Diagnostic Tests . . . . Tests to determine presence or absence of items being sought.

Encapsulation . . . . Covering asbestos materials with a coating (usually polymeric) that does not allow the asbestos to come through.

Engine Retrofit . . . . Adding to existing engines or modifying them in a manner designed to achieve a specific objective, e.g., noise reduction.

High Concentration PCBs . . . .   PCBs that contain 500 ppm or greater PCBs, or those materials which the U.S. EPA requires to be assumed to contain 500 ppm or greater PCBs in the absence of testing (40 CFR 761.123).

LEAs . . . .   Local Education Agencies.

Mitigation . . . .   Reduction or elimination of an undesirable effect.

Negative Pressure Enclosure . .   A confined area wherein the air pressure is less than it is on the outside.

Nomograph . . . .   A graphical presentation of numerical relations.

Non-PCB Transformers . . . . . .   Any transformer that contains less than 50 ppm PCBs; however, any transformer that has been converted from a PCB Transformer or a PCB-contaminated transformer cannot be classified as a non-PCB Transformer until reclassification has occurred in accordance with the requirements of 40 CFR 761.30(a)(2)(v)(40 CFR 761.3).

Paint Chip . . . .   A small, thin, flat piece of paint.

PCB or PCBs . . . .   Any chemical substance that is limited to the biphenyl molecule that has been chlorinated to varying degrees or any combination of substances which contains such a substance (40 CFR 761.3).

PCB-Contaminated Electrical. .
Equipment   Any electrical equipment including, but not limited to, transformers, capacitors, circuit breakers, reclosers, voltage regulators, switches, electromagnets and cable, that contain 50 ppm or greater PCB, but less than 500 ppm PCB (40 CFR 761.3).

PCB Container . . . .   Any package, can, bottle, bag, barrel, drum, tank, or other device that contains PCBs or PCB articles and whose surface has been in direct contact with PCBs (40 CFR 761.3).

PCB Equipment . . . .   Any manufactured item, other than a PCB Container or a PCB Article Container, which contains a PCB Article or other PCB Equipment, and includes microwave ovens, electronic equipment, and fluorescent light ballasts and fixtures (40 CFR 761.3).

PCB Transformer . . . . Any transformer that contains 500 ppm PCB or greater (40 CFR 761.3).

Permeability of Soil . . . . Relative ability of a gas or liquid to move through a soil layer.

Personal Air Samplers . . . . Small units attached to the belts of asbestos abatement workers that measure the amounts of asbestos to which they are exposed.

Respirators . . . . Systems that are worn over the face that prevent the inhaling of asbestos.

Scope of Work . . . . A detailed description of the extent and nature of the work to be done under a contract.

Sensitive Receptor. . . . . A person, building, or facility that is especially sensitive to nearby noise.

Specially Designated. . . . . A facility that stores PCB waste. If a facility's storage of PCB waste at no time exceeds 500 gallons (gal) of PCBs, the owner or operator is not required to seek approval as a commercial storer of PCB waste (40 CFR 761.3).

Specially Licensed Chemical . . A landfill at which protection against risk
Waste Landfill for PCBs   of injury to health or the environment from migration of PCBs to land, water, or the atmosphere is provided from PCBs and PCB items deposited therein by locating, engineering and operating the landfill as required (40 CFR 761.3).

Synergism . . . . Cooperative action of discrete effects such that the total effect is greater than the sum of the two or more effects taken independently.

REFERENCES AND SELECTED READINGS

Bregman, J.I. and Mackenthun, K.M., 1992, *Environmental Impact Statements*, Chapter 11, CRC Press, Boca Raton, FL.

Brown, David, November, 1994, "EPA/HUD Propose Lead-Disclosure Rule," *Environmental Times*, Page 2, Washington, D.C.

Christian, Esther B., 1994, *Managing Lead Paint Hazards: Health and Safety Concerns*, Environmental Resource Center,

Federal Highway Administration, Sept., 1980, "Highway Traffic Noise," HEV-21/8-80(20-M), Washington, D.C.

Kling, David. J., U.S. EPA, May 10, 1988 *AHERA, 100 Questions Document and Implementation Update*, Memorandum to Interested Parties, Washington, D.C.

Newman, J.S. and Beattie, K.R., "Aviation Noise Effects," March, 1985, U.S. Department of Transportation, Report No. FAA-EE-85-2, Washington, D.C.

Schell, Donna J. and Beckler, Tina M., "Environmental Compliance Assessment Army Reserve (ECAAR)," September, 1993, U.S. Army Corps of Engineers, Construction Engineering Research Laboratories, USACE&L Special Report EC-93/07, Champaign, IL.

U.S. Department of Housing and Urban Development, December 7, 1990, "Comprehensible and Workable Plan for the Abatement of Lead-Based Paint in Privately-Owned Housing: A report to Congress," Washington, D.C.

U.S. Environmental Protection Agency, March, 1974, "Information on Levels of Environmental Noise Requisite to Protect Public Health and Welfare with Adequate Margin of Safety," Office of Noise Abatement and Control, Washington, D.C.

U.S. Environmental Protection Agency, August, 1987, "Radon Reduction in New Construction," Offices of Air and Radiation and Research and Development, OPA-87-009, Washington, D.C.

U.S. Environmental Protection Agency, October 30, 1987, "Asbestos-Containing Materials in Schools; Final Rule and Notice," 40CFR Part 763, U.S. Federal Register, Washington, D.C.

U.S. Environmental Protection Agency, May, 1992, "A Citizen's Guide to Radon," second edition, Air and Radiation, (ANR-464), Washington, D.C.

U.S. Environmental Protection Agency, August, 1992, "Consumer's Guide to Radon Reduction," Air and Radiation 66040, 402-K92-003, Washington, D.C.

U.S. Environmental Protection Agency, 1992, "Has Your Home Been Invaded by Radon," Ad Council, Washington, D.C.

U.S. Environmental Protection Agency, June, 1993, "Protocols for Radon and Radon Decay Product Measurements in Homes," Washington, D.C.

U.S. Environmental Protection Agency, March, 1994, "Environmental Fact Sheet – EPA Proposes to Require Distribution of Pamphlet on Lead Before Renovations," Office of Prevention, Pesticides and Toxic Substances, EPA 74S-F-94-003, Washington, D.C.

U.S. General Accounting Office (GAO), August, 1994, "Environmental Compliance – DOD Needs to Better Identify and Monitor Equipment Containing Polychlorinated Biphenyls," GAO/NSLAD-94-243, Washington, D.C.

Appendix A

EIS PROCESS

While each federal agency has its own approach to an EIS process, they tend to differ only in small details. The generally accepted process is discussed in this appendix. The approach that will be taken is that of the person or firm that would do an EIS. A series of tasks will be presented and each one discussed in terms of content and approximate elapsed time for the task. After this is completed, a discussion will follow concerning Environmental Assessments.

Environmental Impact Statements (EISs)

The major steps and analyses in the EIS process would be carried out in a series of discrete tasks as described below.

Task 1. Initial Meeting with Federal Agency Client

Within a day or two after EIS start, a meeting should be held between EIS project personnel and the federal agency sponsoring the EIS (Client). The purpose of the meeting will be to allow the client to transmit to the EIS preparer all available information on the project scope, existing site conditions, known feasible alternatives, and various studies and reports relevant to the project, including any other EISs near the site. Project issues will be defined and scoping meetings planned.

Task 2. Methodology Approval

Using the information developed in Task 1, the EIS methodology should be submitted to the client for approval within 15 days after project start. Any necessary revisions required by the client then are made.

Task 3. Scoping Meetings

Prior to the scoping meetings, it is often useful to prepare a 5 to 10 page Preliminary Environmental Analysis (PEA) that identifies the geographic area of the proposed project, reviews the alternatives, describes the important characteristics of the area, and discusses the significant project-related issues. It goes on to present a proposed outline of the EIS and gives a brief discussion of each item therein. This PEA then serves as the handout at the scoping meetings and the starting point for consideration of changes or additions to the EIS. Individuals are identified to whom invitations are sent to participate in the scoping meeting. Arrangements are made for the meeting areas and required newspaper advertisements. An agenda is prepared. The EIS scoping meeting(s) usually are held within 30 days of project start. The specific times and places of the scoping meetings usually are in the alternative areas to be served by the project. The scoping meetings are held in accordance with CEQ's EIS scoping requirements (40 CFR 1501.7) and minutes, or transcripts, of the discussion are taken.

The purpose of the scoping meeting(s) is to determine the scope of the Draft Environmental Impact Statement (DEIS) and to identify the major project-related issues to be addressed and emphasized in it. Comments to this effect by the attending agencies and public are solicited. Invited agency representatives consist of all of the federal agencies that may have an interest in project impacts and/or participate in the EIS as cooperating agencies. State and local agencies invited include all of the pollution prevention, natural resource, historical and archaeological agencies and any others who express an interest. Public participation includes groups or individuals.

The product of the scoping meeting is a brief paper (Scoping Report) that summarizes the significant alternatives and issues related to them. The paper reflects issues and extent of coverage to be contained in the Draft EIS. A brief discussion of the scoping process and the comments received from the public are included in the report.

Task 4. Data Collection and Description of the Existing Environment

The suitability of environmental data obtained from the client in Task 1 is evaluated for use in the descriptions of existing environmental conditions, the evaluation of project alternatives, and the assessment of alternatives impact upon the environment. Work in Task 4 focuses on the gathering of additional data, where necessary, in order to address the significant issues of the EIS. Every attempt should be made to avoid duplication of others' work in the gathering and analysis of data. A discussion of the data to be gathered and analyzed follows. It will be broken down into two major categories, identified as the natural environment and the man-made environment. The topics that go into each category are listed. They are discussed in detail in other chapters in this book.

a. **Natural Environment.** The natural environment as defined here consists of the local climatology, topography, geomorphology (including geology and soils), and biology.

b. **Man-Made Environment.** The discussion of the existing man-made environment includes, but is not limited to, the following topics: water quality, including surface waters and groundwater, noise, air quality, land use, historic preservation and archaeology, demography, housing, local economy and other socioeconomic aspects, hazards and nuisances, aesthetics and urban design, community services, and transportation.

Task 5. Assessment of Potential Environmental Impacts

The potential impacts of each proposed project alternative are assessed as well as for the "do nothing" alternative, on each of the environmental and social components delineated above under Task 4. The level of impact analysis is site specific, i.e., the specific impacts at the project site. Emphasis is placed on the key issues identified and discussed during the scoping phase of the project.

Identification is made of the potential short- and long-term impacts associated with the project. Short-term impacts resulting from the proposed project may be those associated with the construction phase, including such disturbances as noise, dust, erosion, and wildlife displacement. Long-term post-construction impacts may include such factors as pollution from stormwater runoff, added pollution, more noise, consumption of energy, depletion and contamination of groundwater sources, overloading of roadways and other infrastructure, and placing of heavy demands on community services such as sewage treatment and the disposal of solid wastes. These impacts are further characterized as "avoidable," "unavoidable," and "capable of being mitigated."

In doing the assessments, one should follow standards and utilize analytical procedures established and approved by EPA and other Federal agencies having applicable legal jurisdiction. The impacts on public services may be quantified by calculating usage based on actual per-household demand data for these areas. Air quality impacts are assessed in accordance with state requirements, as is noise. A summary of the impacts of each alternative should be presented in the EIS.

Irreversible and irretrievable resource commitments resulting from the implementation of the proposed action are described. The consumption of resources is categorized in terms of environmental and human effects.

Mitigative actions should be included in the discussion. Where possible, their costs and benefits should be quantified. These facts will be critical in the final decisions as to which alternative to select.

Task 6. Preparation of the Preliminary Draft Environmental Impact Statement (PDEIS)

A Preliminary Draft EIS (PDEIS) is prepared that addresses the major issues concerning the proposed project at the alternative sites and for the "no action" alternative. The Preliminary Draft EIS format should be in accordance with CEQ rules and regulations for the preparation of EISs by federal agencies. The Preliminary EIS also should be consistent with the procedures and requirements of the sponsoring agency. The format of the Preliminary Draft EIS usually will include the following items:

- Cover Sheet
- Summary
- Table of Contents
- Purposes and need for action
- Alternatives, including the proposed action
- Affected environment
- Environmental impacts, including a discussion of impacts that can and cannot be mitigated
- List of Preparers
- List of agencies, organizations and persons to whom copies of the EIS are sent
- Index
- Appendices

The cover sheet identifies the person in the agency to whom comments on the DEIS are to be sent. The appendices are bound separately from the rest of the EIS and contain materials such as the following:

Scoping Meeting details

Detailed data from which information in the EIS is drawn

Letters from agencies and the public

Task 7. Preparation of the Draft EIS (DEIS)

After the sponsoring agency has reviewed the PDEIS and suggested changes, a final version is prepared and is labeled as the Draft EIS (DEIS). After agency review and approval, copies are transmitted to previously identified interested parties. In addition, a notice is placed in the *Federal Register* that identifies the EIS, the agency, and the manner in which copies may be obtained. A date is given for the receipt of comments on the draft, usually 45 days.

Task 8. Response to Comments

The preparation of the Preliminary Final Environmental Impact Statement commences with transmittal of comments received by the agency during the

Draft EIS public comment period. Administrative or policy questions are answered by the agency and given to the EIS preparer, who develops answers to the technical comments, which then are submitted to the agency for approval.

Task 9. Preliminary Final EIS (PFEIS)

A Preliminary Final EIS (PFEIS) that includes the responses to comments, as well as presenting the full text of all comments in the appendix, then is prepared. It is reviewed and approved by the agency.

Task 10. Preparation of the Final EIS (FEIS)

The agency's approved revisions of the Preliminary FEIS are incorporated into the FEIS. Upon approval by the agency, the FEIS is distributed to appropriate parties.

Task 11. Record of Decision (ROD)

The agency prepares a Record of Decision after the EIS is completed.

Appendix B

EPA REGIONAL OFFICES

Region I
(Connecticut, Maine, Massachusetts, New Hampshire, Rhode Island, Vermont)

John F. Kennedy Federal Building
One Congress Street
Boston, MA 02203
617/565-3420

Region II
(New Jersey, New York, Puerto Rico, Virgin Islands)

Jacob K. Javits Federal Building
26 Federal Plaza
New York, NY 10278
212/264-2657

Region III
(Delaware, District of Columbia, Maryland, Pennsylvania, Virginia, West Virginia)

841 Chestnut Building
Philadelphia, PA 19107
215/597-9800

Region IV
(Alabama, Florida, Georgia, Kentucky, Mississippi, North Carolina, South Carolina, Tennessee)

345 Courtland Street, N.E.
Atlanta, GA 30365
404/347-4727

Region V
(Illinois, Indiana, Michigan, Minnesota, Ohio, Wisconsin)

77 West Jackson Boulevard
Chicago, IL 60604-3507
312/353-2000

Region VI
(Arkansas, Louisiana, New Mexico, Oklahoma, Texas)

First Interstate Bank Tower at Fountain Place
1445 Ross Avenue, 12th Floor, Suite 1200
Dallas, TX 75202-2733
214/655-6444

Region VII
(Iowa, Kansas, Missouri, Nebraska)

726 Minnesota Avenue
Kansas City, KS 66101
913/551-7000

Region VIII
(Colorado, Montana, North Dakota,
South Dakota, Utah, Wyoming)

999 18th Street, Suite 500
Denver, CO 80202-2405
303/293-1603

Region IX
(American Samoa, Arizona,
California, Guam, Hawaii, Nevada)

75 Hawthorne Street
San Francisco, CA 94102
415/744-1305

Region X
(Alaska, Idaho, Oregon, Washington)

1200 Sixth Avenue
Seattle, WA 98101
206/553-4973

Appendix C

STATE ENVIRONMENTAL AGENCIES

ALABAMA
Department of Environmental
Management
1751 Cong. W.L. Dickinson Drive
Montgomery, AL 36130
205/271-7700

ALASKA
Department of Environmental
Conservation
410 Willoughby, Suite 105
Juneau, AK 99801
907/465-5050

ARIZONA
Arizona Department of
Environmental Quality
3033 North Central Avenue
Phoenix, AZ 85012
602/257-2300

ARKANSAS
Department of Pollution Control and
Ecology
8001 National Drive
P.O. Box 8913
Little Rock, AR 72219-8913
501/562-7444

CALIFORNIA
California State Environmental
Protection Agency
555 Capitol Mall, Ste. 525
Sacramento, CA 95814
916/445-3846

COLORADO
CO Dept of Public Health and
Environment
4300 Cherry Creek Drive, South
Denver, CO 80222-1530
303/692-3099

CONNECTICUT
Department of Environmental
Protection
165 Capitol Avenue
Hartford, CT 06106
203/566-5599

DELAWARE
Department of Natural Resources and
Environmental Control
P.O. Box 1401
Dover, DE 19903
302/739-4403

DISTRICT OF COLUMBIA
Department of Consumer and
Regulatory Affairs
Office of Environmental Programs
2100 Martin Luther King, Jr. Avenue
Washington, D.C. 20020
202/404-1136

FLORIDA
Florida Dept of Environmental
Protection
3900 Commonwealth Building, MS-
10
Tallahassee, FL 32399-3000
904/921-4303

GEORGIA
Georgia Department of Natural
Resources
Floyd Towers East, Suite 1154
205 Butler Street, SW
Atlanta, GA 30334
404/656-4317

HAWAII
State Department of Health
Environmental Management Division
1250 Punchbowl Street
Honolulu, HI 96813
808/586-4424

IDAHO
Division of Environmental Quality
Department of Health & Welfare
410 North Hilton, 2nd Floor
Boise, ID 83706-1255
208/334-5840

ILLINOIS
Illinois Environmental Protection
Agency
2200 Churchill Road
Springfield, IL 62706
217/782-9540

INDIANA
IN Department of Environmental
Mgmt
P.O. Box 6015
Indianapolis, IN 46225
317/232-8612

IOWA
Department of Natural Resources
Henry A. Wallace State Office
Building
900 East Grand Avenue
Des Moines, IA 50319-0034
515/281-6284

KANSAS
Division of the Environment
Department of Health and
Environment
Forbes Field, Building 740
Topeka, KS 66620-0001
913/296-1535

KENTUCKY
Department for Environmental
Protection
Frankfort Office Park
14 Reilly Road
Frankfort, KY 40601
502/564-2150

LOUISIANA
Department of Environmental
Quality
7290 Bluebonnet Road
Baton Rouge, LA 70810
504/765-0222

MAINE
Department of Environmental
Protection
#17 State House Station
Augusta, ME 04333-0017
207/287-2812

MARYLAND
Maryland Department of the
Environment
2500 Broening Highway
Baltimore, MD 21224
410/631-3084

MASSACHUSETTS
Department of Environmental
Protection
Executive Office of Environmental
Affairs
100 Cambridge Street
Boston, MA 02202
617/727-3163

MICHIGAN
Department of Natural Resources
P.O. Box 30028
Lansing, MI 48909
517/373-2329

MINNESOTA
Minnesota Pollution Control Agency
520 Lafayette Road
St. Paul, MN 55155
612/296-6300

MISSISSIPPI
Department of Environmental
Quality
P.O. Box 20305
Jackson, MS 39289
601/961-5000

MISSOURI
Department of Natural Resources
Jefferson Building, 12th Floor
P.O. Box 176
Jefferson City, MO 65102
314/751-0763

MONTANA
Environmental Sciences Division
Cogswell Building, Room B-201
836 Front Street
Helena, MT 59620
406/444-2544

NEBRASKA
Department of Environmental
Quality
1200 N. Street, Suite #400
Lincoln, NE 68509
402/471-2186

NEVADA
Division of Environmental Protection
Department of Conservation and
Natural Resources
123 West Nye Lane
Capitol Complex
Carson City, NV 89710
702/885-4670

NEW HAMPSHIRE
Department of Environmental
Services
Health and Welfare Building
6 Hazen Drive
Concord, NH 03301
603/271-3503

NEW JERSEY
Department of Environmental
Protection
401 East State Street, CN 402
Trenton, NJ 08625
609/292-2885

NEW MEXICO
Department of Environment
P.O. Box 26110
Santa Fe, NM 87502
505/827-2850

NEW YORK
Department of Environmental
Conservation
50 Wolf Road
Albany, NY 12233
518/457-3446
Toll-Free: 1-800-631-0666 (in New
York)

NORTH CAROLINA
Department of Environmental Health
and Natural Resources
P.O. Box 27687
Raleigh, NC 27604
919/733-7015

NORTH DAKOTA
Environmental Health Section
Department of Health
P.O. Box 5520
Bismarck, ND 58502-5520
701/328-5150

OHIO
Ohio Environmental Protection
Agency
1800 Watermark Drive
P.O. Box 1049
Columbus, OH 43266
614/644-2782

OKLAHOMA
Department of Environmental
Quality
1000 Northeast 10th Street
Oklahoma City, OK 73117-1299
405/271-5338

OREGON
Department of Environmental
Quality
811 SW 6th Avenue
Portland, OR 97204
503/229-5300
Toll Free: 1-800-452-4011 (in
Oregon)

PENNSYLVANIA
Department of Natural Resources
P.O. Box 2063
Harrisburg, PA 17105-2063
717/787-5028

RHODE ISLAND
Department of Environmental
Management
9 Hayes Street
Providence, RI 02908-5003
401/277-2771

SOUTH CAROLINA
Department of Health and
Environmental Control
2600 Bull Street
Columbia, SC 29201
803/734-5360

SOUTH DAKOTA
Department of Water and Natural
Resources
523 E. Capitol Avenue
Pierre, SD 57501
605/773-3153

TENNESSEE
Department of Environment and
Conservation
L & C Tower, 15th Floor
401 Church Street
Nashville, TN 37247
615/532-0220

TEXAS
Environmental & Conservation
Health Protection
Department of Health
1100 W. 49th Street
Austin, TX 78756
512/458-7111

UTAH
Department of Environmental Health
P.O. Box 144810
Salt Lake City, UT 84114
801/536-4402

VERMONT
Department of Environmental
Conservation
Agency of Natural Resources
103 South Main Street - 1 S. Building
Waterbury, VT 05676
802/241-3808

VIRGINIA
Department of Environmental
Quality
629 E. Main Street
Richmond, VA 23219
804/762-4020

WASHINGTON
Department of Ecology
P.O. Box 47600
Olympia, WA 98504-7600
206/407-6000

WEST VIRGINIA
Division of Environmental Protection
Commerce, Labor and Environmental
Resources
10 McJunkin Road
Nitro, WV 25143-2506
304/759-0515

WISCONSIN
Environmental Standards Division
Department of Natural Resources
P.O. Box 7921
Madison, WI 53707
608/266-1099

WYOMING
Department of Environmental
Quality
122 West 25th Street
Cheyenne, WY 82002
307/777-7192

NONSTATE AGENCIES

AMERICAN SAMOA
Environmental Quality Commission
Office of the Governor
Pago Pago, AS 96799
684/633-2304

GUAM
Environmental Protection Agency
130 Rojas Street
Harmon, GU 96911
671/646-8863

**NORTHERN MARIANA
ISLANDS**
Environmental Quality Division
Public Health and Environmental
Services
P.O. Box 409
Saipan, MP 96950
670/235-1011

PUERTO RICO
Environmental Quality Board
P.O. Box 11488
San Juan, PR 00910-1488
809/767-8057

U.S. VIRGIN ISLANDS
Department of Planning and Natural
Resources
Nisky Center, Suite 231
St. Thomas, VI 00802
809/774-3320

Appendix D

STATE REQUIRED CONTINGENCY/RESPONSE PLANS

Alabama (AL)	STATE LEAD AGENCY
EPA Region: IV CG Districts: 2 & 8	Department of Environmental Management (ADEM) ATTN: Water Division (Industrial Branch) 1751 Congressman W.L. Dickinson Drive Montgomery, AL 36130 (205) 271-7852
APPLICABLE STATE LAWS & REGULATIONS - Alabama Code, Title 22 § 22 - Volumes 1 and 2, Water Quality Program, Division 6, ADEM Administrative Code	GENERAL STATE REQUIREMENTS & REMARKS - Alabama requires that facilities obtain a storm water discharge permit. A copy of the federal SPCC Plan for the facility must be included in the application.

Alaska (AK)	STATE LEAD AGENCY
EPA Region: X CG Districts: 17	Department of Environmental Conservation ATTN: Spill Prevention and Response Division 410 Willoughby Avenue, Suite 105 Juneau, AK 99801-1795 (907) 465-5250
APPLICABLE STATE LAWS & REGULATIONS	GENERAL STATE REQUIREMENTS & REMARKS
- Articles 1 and 2, Chapter 4, Title 46 of the Alaska Statutes. - Article 4, Chapter 75, Title 18 of the Alaska Statutes	- Prohibits operation of an oil terminal/pipeline/facility/vessel without an approved Oil Discharge and Contingency Plan. Exempts facilities with less than 5,000 barrels (210,000 gallons) crude oil capacity, or less than 10,000 barrels (420,000) refined oil capacity. - Provides details of procedures, format, contents, etc. for Oil Discharge and Contingency Plans in Alaska. NOTE: State law and regulations do not indicate if a federal plan is acceptable in lieu of a state plan.

California (CA)	STATE LEAD AGENCY
EPA Region: IX CG Districts: 11	Department of Fish and Game ATTN: Oil Spill Prevention & Response Office 1700 K Street Sacramento, CA 95818 (916) 445-9338
APPLICABLE STATE LAWS & REGULATIONS	GENERAL STATE REQUIREMENTS & REMARKS
- Article 5, Lempert-Keene-Seastand Oil Spill Prevention and Response Act, Sept. 90 - Subchapter 3, Chapter 2, subdivision 4, Division 1, Title 14 of the California Code of Regulations	- Establishes legislative requirement for Oil Spill Contingency Plans - Provides detailed guidance on preparation and submission of California Oil Spill Contingency Plans NOTE: California allows owner/operators to use their federal plan, with appropriate amendments, to satisfy the state requirement

Colorado (CO) EPA Region: VIII CG Districts: 2	STATE LEAD AGENCY Department of Health ATTN: Oil Inspections Office 1001 E. 62nd Avenue Denver, CO 80216 (303) 289-5644
APPLICABLE STATE LAWS & REGULATIONS - Colorado Revised Statutes, Title 8, Article 20, §§503-509 - Colorado Water Quality Control Act	GENERAL STATE REQUIREMENTS & REMARKS - 1992 legislation authorizes creation of regulations governing aboveground storage tanks (AST). The pending regulations include requirements for spill prevention and response plans. NOTE: It is not yet known if the state will accept compliant federal plans in lieu of a state plan

Connecticut (CT) EPA Region: I CG Districts: 1	STATE LEAD AGENCY Department of Environmental Protection ATTN: Oil & Chemical Spill Response Division 165 Capitol Street Hartford, CT (203) 566-4633
APPLICABLE STATE LAWS & REGULATIONS - Sections 448-453, Title 22a, General Statutes of Connecticut	GENERAL STATE REQUIREMENTS & REMARKS - Connecticut does not require a separate state plan, but does require that facilities submit a copy to the state of the facilities federal SPCC Plan that has been certified by a professional engineer registered in Connecticut, plus copies of any Federal Facility Response Plan(s) required by OPA-90

District of Columbia (DC)	STATE LEAD AGENCY
EPA Region: III CG Districts: 5	Department of Consumer and Regulatory Affairs ATTN: Environmental Regulatory Administration (Water Quality Control Branch) 2100 Martin Luther King Jr. Avenue, S.E. Washington, DC 20020 (202) 404-1120
APPLICABLE STATE LAWS & REGULATIONS - Section 6930, DC Water Pollution Act, DC Annotated Code §6-921 et. seq.	GENERAL STATE REQUIREMENTS & REMARKS - DC requires that any facility that stores a hazardous substance must have an approved SPCC Plan. However, DC does not provide any detailed guidance, and encourages facilities to use their federal SPCC Plan to satisfy the DC requirement

Florida (FL)	STATE LEAD AGENCY
EPA Region: IV CG Districts: 7 & 8	Department of Environmental Protection ATTN: Office of Coastal Protection Majory Stoneman Douglas Building 3900 Commonwealth Boulevard, mail stop 59 Tallahassee, FL 32399 (904) 448-2974
APPLICABLE STATE LAWS & REGULATIONS - Chapter 16N-16 of the Florida Administrative Code (The Pollutant Discharge Act)	GENERAL STATE REQUIREMENTS & REMARKS - Paragraph 16.033 provides details of procedures, format, contents, etc. for Terminal Facility Contingency Plans - Paragraph 16.036 provides details of procedures, format, contents, etc. for Vessel Spill Contingency Plans NOTE: Florida also accepts compliant federal plans as satisfying state requirements

Kentucky (KY)	STATE LEAD AGENCY
EPA Region: IV CG Districts: 2	Department of Environmental Protection ATTN: Division of Water Quality 14 Reilly Road Frankfort, KY 40601 (502) 564-3410
APPLICABLE STATE LAWS & REGULATIONS - Chapter 224, Kentucky Revised Statutes - Chapter 5, Title 401, Kentucky Administrative Regulations	GENERAL STATE REQUIREMENTS & REMARKS - Paragraph 5:090 incorporates by reference the federal requirements for an SPCC Plan. The state requires that a copy of the federal plan by submitted to the state only when the state determines that the facility owner/operator is unable or unwilling to properly manage the facility

Louisiana (LA)	STATE LEAD AGENCY
EPA Region: VI CG Districts: 8	Department of Environmental Quality ATTN: Governors Oil Spill Coordinator P.O. Box 94095 Baton Rouge, LA 70804 (504) 922-3230
APPLICABLE STATE LAWS & REGULATIONS - Chapter 19, Subtitle II, Title 30, Louisiana Revised Statutes of 1950	GENERAL STATE REQUIREMENTS & REMARKS - Paragraph 2470B requires that terminal facilities have an implemented Discharge Prevention and Response Plan NOTE: This paragraph further states that a Facility Response Plan that meets federal requirements will also satisfy Louisiana requirements

Maine (ME) EPA Region: I CG Districts: 1	STATE LEAD AGENCY Department of Environmental Protection (DEP) ATTN: Bureau of Oil/Hazardous Materials Control State House, Station 17 Augusta, ME 04333 (207) 287-2651
APPLICABLE STATE LAWS & REGULATIONS - Chapter 600, Code of Maine Regulations - Subchapter II-A, Chapter 3, Title 38, Maine Revised Statutes - Maine Public Law 454 (Act LD 77, June 1992)	GENERAL STATE REQUIREMENTS & REMARKS - Requires that marine terminals with over 500 gallon capacity register with DEP, and submit a spill response plan - Defines "oil terminal facility" as facilities with capability to store/handle more than 500 barrels (21,000 gallons), and requires licensing of such facilities - Requires that owners/operators file copies with the state of any required federal plans, or a statement that no such plan is required under federal law and/or regulations.

Maryland (MD) EPA Region: III CG Districts: 5	STATE LEAD AGENCY Department of the Environmental ATTN: Waste Management Administration 2500 Broening Highway Baltimore, MD 21224 (410) 631-3442
APPLICABLE STATE LAWS & REGULATIONS - §4-401, et. seq., Annotated Code of Maryland - Subtitle 10, Title 26, Maryland Department of Environmental Regulations	GENERAL STATE REQUIREMENTS & REMARKS - Defines and regulates oil storage facilities with capacity greater than 1,100 gallons. Directs development of regulations requiring spill contingency plans for facilities, vessels and barges. - Paragraph 26.10.26 requires that marine oil facilities have a spill contingency plan, and that it be in compliance with both USGC regulations (33 CFR 154) and EPA regulations (40 CFR 112). NOTE: Maryland accepts compliant federal plans in lieu of a state plan

Michigan (MI)	STATE LEAD AGENCY
EPA Region: V CG Districts: 9	Department of Natural Resources ATTN: Waste Management Division P.O. Box 30028 Lansing, MI 48809 (517) 373-2730
APPLICABLE STATE LAWS & REGULATIONS - Michigan Comprehensive Laws, §232.1 et seq. - Act 307 of 1982 (The Environmental Response Act)	GENERAL STATE REQUIREMENTS & REMARKS - Requires that facilities have State Pollution Prevention Plans NOTE: The state may accept federal plans in lieu of a State Pollution Prevention Plan

Minnesota (MN)	STATE LEAD AGENCY
EPA Region: V CG Districts: 2 & 9	Minnesota Pollution Control Agency ATTN: Tank and Spills Section 520 Lafayette Road St. Paul, MN 55155 (612) 297-8613
APPLICABLE STATE LAWS & REGULATIONS - S.F. No. 891, May 1991/Section 115E, Minnesota Statutes	GENERAL STATE REQUIREMENTS & REMARKS - Paragraph 115.04 requires Prevention and Response Plans for vessels, vehicles, facilities and pipelines. General criterion is storage or handling of more than 100,000 gallons per month NOTE: Minnesota accepts federal plans in lieu of state plans, provided that state required information under paragraph 115.04 is included in the federal plan

New Jersey (NJ)	STATE LEAD AGENCY
EPA Region: II CG Districts: 1 & 5	Department of Environmental Protection ATTN: Bureau of Discharge Prevention 301 E. State Street, CN-424 Trenton, NJ 08625-0424 (609) 633-0610
APPLICABLE STATE LAWS & REGULATIONS - New Jersey Annotated Statutes, 58:10-23.11, et seq. (New Jersey Spill Compensation and Control Act)	GENERAL STATE REQUIREMENTS & REMARKS - Requires that major facilities (more than 200,000 gallons storage capacity) have a Discharge Prevention, Containment, and Countermeasures (DPCC) Plan, and provides detailed guidance on content. NOTE: New Jersey may accept federal plans in lieu of a state plan, if State representatives determine it meets state requirements

Ohio (OH)	STATE LEAD AGENCY
EPA Region: V CG Districts: 2 & 9	Environmental Protection Agency ATTN: Division of Emergency & Remedial Response Spill Response Coordinator P.O. Box 1049 Columbus, OH (614) 644-3070/2078
APPLICABLE STATE LAWS & REGULATIONS - Chapters 3750 (Emergency Planning) and 6111 (Water Pollution Control), Ohio Revised Code	GENERAL STATE REQUIREMENTS & REMARKS - Requires that owners/operators maintain and submit lists of hazardous chemicals, to include Material Safety Data Sheets (MSDS), for inclusion in the appropriate local Emergency Response Plan - Authorizes development of regulations for spill plans. Spill plans must be consistent with and equivalent in scope, content coverage to federal SPCC Plans

Oregon (OR)	STATE LEAD AGENCY
	Department of Environmental Quality (DEQ) ATTN: Water Quality Division 811 S.W. Avenue Portland, OR 97204
EPA Region: V CG Districts: 13	(503) 229-5046

APPLICABLE STATE LAWS & REGULATIONS	GENERAL STATE REQUIREMENTS & REMARKS
- Senate Bill 242, 22 July 1991 - Chapter 340, Division 47, DEQ, Oregon Administrative Rules	- Legislation directing DEQ develop and adopt rules and procedures for the preparation of contingency plans for oil spill protection and emergency response - Requires contingency plans for vessels, and for facilities capable of storing more than 10,000 gallons of oil <u>if they receive the oil via tank vessels, barges or pipelines</u>. This regulation provides detailed instructions on plan preparations and submission NOTE: Oregon accepts submission of a federal plan in lieu of the state plan, <u>if</u> DEQ determines that the federal requirements equal or exceed the state requirements

Pennsylvania (PA)	STATE LEAD AGENCY
	Department of Environmental Resources ATTN: Bureau of Water Quality Management Division of Storage Tanks P.O. Box 8762 Harrisburg, PA 17105-8762
EPA Region: III CG Districts: 2, 5 & 9	(717) 772-5599

APPLICABLE STATE LAWS & REGULATIONS	GENERAL STATE REQUIREMENTS & REMARKS
- Act 32 (SB 280), 6 July 1989	- Chapter 9 of Act 32 requires a State Spill Prevention Response Plan for all facilities with aboveground storage tank (AST) capacity greater than 21,000 gallons. Section 902 specifies the content of the plan NOTE: Act 32 does not indicate if a federal plan is acceptable in lieu of a state plan

Rhode Island (RI) EPA Region: I CG Districts: 1	STATE LEAD AGENCY Department of Environmental Management ATTN: Division of Site Remediation 291 Promenade Street Providence, RI 02908 (401) 227-2234
APPLICABLE STATE LAWS & REGULATIONS - Rhode Island General Laws, §§42-17.1, 42-35, and 46-12	GENERAL STATE REQUIREMENTS & REMARKS - Requires a Spill Prevention and Emergency Plan for any aboveground storage facility with a capacity of more than 500 gallons NOTE: A compliant federal plan is acceptable in lieu of a state plan, if it contains the elements set forth in the State emergency plan regulations

Texas (TX) EPA Region: VI CG Districts: 8	STATE LEAD AGENCY Texas General Land Office ATTN: Oil Spill Prevention and Response Division 1700 N. Congress Avenue, Room 740 Austin, TX 78701-1495 (512) 463-5091
APPLICABLE STATE LAWS & REGULATIONS - Chapter 40, Subtitle C, Title II, Natural Resources Code (Oil Spill Prevention and Response Act of 1991) - Chapter 199, Part I, Title 31, Natural Resource Code	GENERAL STATE REQUIREMENTS & REMARKS - Requires that terminal facilities be registered and that they have an implemented Discharge Prevention and Response Plan which meets state and federal requirements - Requires that facilities provide the state with current copies of Federal discharge prevention and response plans for that facility, including the SPCC plan under 40 CFR 112 NOTE: Texas will accept a compliant federal terminal facility discharge prevention and response plan in lieu of a state plan

Virginia (VA)	STATE LEAD AGENCY
EPA Region: III CG Districts: 5	Department of Environmental Quality ATTN: Spill Response and Remediation Office P.O. Box 11143 Richmond, VA 23230-1143 (804) 527-5275
APPLICABLE STATE LAWS & REGULATIONS	GENERAL STATE REQUIREMENTS & REMARKS
- Virginia Regulation No. 680-14-07 (Oil Discharge Contingency Plans and Fee for Approval)	- Requires an Oil Discharge Contingency (ODC) Plan for all facilities with an aboveground oil storage capacity of 25,000 gallons or more (excluding oil in drums, barrels and portable tanks, of which no single container exceeds 110 gallons). Provides detailed guidance on content and preparation - Above facilities with more than 1,000,000 gallons capacity must also file a groundwater characterization study - This regulation also requires a state ODC Plan for tank vessels transporting or transferring more than 15,0000 gallons of oil, and for pipelines having an average daily pumped through volume (throughput) of 25,000 gallons or more of oil NOTE: Paragraph 5L provides that a federal plan may be accepted in lieu of a state plan, dependent on results of a review of the federal plan by DEQ

Washington (WA)	STATE LEAD AGENCY
EPA Region: X CG Districts: 13	Department of Ecology ATTN: Facility Spill Prevention and Response Rule Project Leader P.O. Box 47600 Olympia, WA 98504-7600 (206) 493-2819
APPLICABLE STATE LAWS & REGULATIONS - Washington Revised Code §88.44.005 (Washington 1991 Oil Spill Prevention and Response Act) - Washington Administrative Code §173-180D	GENERAL STATE REQUIREMENTS & REMARKS - Washington requires that all vessels and facilities have an Oil Spill Prevention and Response Contingency Plan. The state has prepared a publication, "Guidelines for Preparation and Review of Facility Oil Spill Prevention Plans", that provides a step-by-step guide to achieving a compliance plan NOTE: Federal plans may be accepted in lieu of state plans, if DOE determines that the federal plan possesses approval criteria that equal or exceed the state requirements

Appendix E

EPA AND STATE OFFICES

EPA Regional Emergency Response Offices

EPA Region I
Emergency Planning and Response
Section
Mail Code: EEP
60 Westview Street
Lexington, MA 02173
617-860-4300

EPA Region II
Response and Prevention Branch
Mail Code: MS-211
2890 Woodbridge Avenue
Raritan Depot, Building 209
Edison, NJ 08837
908/321-6656

EPA Region III
Superfund Removal Branch
Mail Code: 38HW-34
841 Chestnut Street, 9th Floor
Philadelphia, PA 19107
215/597-5998

EPA Region IV
Emergency and Response Removal
Branch
Mail Code: 8RRB
346 Courtland Street, NE, 1st Floor
Atlanta, GA 30365
404/347-4062

EPA Region V
Emergency and Enforcement Response Branch
Mail Code: HSA-5J
77 W. Jackson Boulevard
Chicago, IL 60604
312/353-2318

EPA Region VI
Emergency Response Branch
Mail Code: SE-E
1445 Rose Avenue, 9th Floor
Dallas, TX 75202-2733
214/665-2270

EPA Region VII
Emergency Planning and Response
Branch
Mail Code: (not required)
25 Funston Road, 2nd Floor
Kansas City, KS 66115
913/551-5000

EPA Region VIII
Emergency Response Branch
Mail Code: 8HWM-ER
999 18th Street, Suite 500
Denver, CO 80202-2466
303/293-1788

EPA Region IX
Field Operations Branch
Mail Code: H-8
75 Hawthorne Street
San Francisco, CA 94106
415/744-1500

EPA Region X
Superfund Branch
Mail Code: HW114
1200 6th Avenue, 11th Floor
Seattle, WA 98101
206/553-2139

EPA Locations

EPA Headquarters
401 M Street SW
Washington, DC 20460
(202) 260-4700

EPA Region I (Connecticut, Maine, Massachusetts, New Hampshire, Rhode Island, Vermont)
John F. Kennedy Federal Building
1 Congress Street
Boston, MA 02203
(617) 565-3400

Air Management Division.............................(617) 565-3402
Waste Management Division ....(617) 573-5700
Water Management Division ....(617) 565-3478
Environmental Services Division ....(617) 860 4315
Office of Regional Counsel...........................(617) 565-3451
Planning & Management Division ....(617) 565-3355
Office of External Programs..........................(617) 565-2713

EPA Region II (New Jersey, New York, Puerto Rico, Virgin Islands)
Jacob K Javitz Federal Building
26 Federal Plaza
New York, NY 10278
(212) 264-2525

Air & Waste Management Division ....(212) 264-2301
Water Management Division ....(212) 264-2513
Emergency & Remedial Response Division...............(212) 264-8672
Environmental Services Division ....(908) 321-6754
Regional Counsel ....(212) 264-1017
External Programs Division ....(212) 264-2515
Office of Policy & Management.......................(212) 264-2520

EPA Region III (Delaware, District of Columbia, Maryland, Pennsylvania, West Virginia, Virginia)
841 Chestnut Street
Philadelphia, PA 19107
(215) 597-9814

Hazardous Waste Management Division . . . . (215) 597-8181
Air Management Division. . . . . (215) 597-9390
Air Enforcement Branch . . . . (215) 597-3989
Air Programs Branch . . . . (215) 597-4713
Environmental Services Division . . . . (215) 597-4532
Office of External Affairs . . . . (215) 597-6938

EPA Region IV (Alabama, Florida, Georgia, Kentucky, Mississippi, North
Carolina, South Carolina, Tennessee)
3455 Courtland Street NW
Atlanta, GA 30365
(404) 347-4727

Air Pesticides & Toxics Management Division . . . . (404) 347-3043
Waste Management Division . . . . (404) 347-3454
Air Programs Branch . . . . (404) 347-2864
Air Enforcement Branch . . . . (404) 347-2904
Environmental Services Division . . . . (706) 546-3136
Office of Public Affairs. . . . . (404) 347-3004

EPA Region V (Illinois, Indiana, Michigan, Minnesota, Ohio, Wisconsin)
77 West Jackson Blvd.
Chicago, IL 60604-3507
(312) 353-3000

Air & Radiation Division . . . . (312) 353-2212
Environmental Sciences Division . . . . (312) 353-3808
Waste Management Division . . . . (312) 886-7579
Water Division . . . . (312) 353-2147
Office of Public Affairs. . . . . (312) 353-2072
Regional Counsel . . . . (312) 886-6675

Region VI (Arkansas, Louisiana, New Mexico, Oklahoma, Texas)
First Interstate Bank Tower at Fountain Place
1445 Ross Avenue, 12th Floor
Suite 1200
Dallas, TX 57202-2733
(214) 655-2100

Hazardous Waste Management Division . . . . (214) 655-6701
Air, Pesticides, & Toxics Division . . . . (214) 655-7200
Air Compliance Contract . . . . (214) 655-7220
Chief-Air Branch. . . . . (214) 655-7205
Environmental Services Division . . . . (214) 655-2210
External Affairs Division . . . . (214) 655-2200

Region VII (Iowa, Kansas, Missouri, Nebraska)
726 Minnesota Avenue
Kansas City, KS 66101
(913) 551-7006

Office of Public Affairs.............................(913) 551-7003
Air & Toxics Division...............................(913) 551-7020
Environmental Services Division ....(913) 551-5000
Waste Management Division ....(913) 551-7080
Water Management Division ....(913) 551-7030
Office of Inspector General...........................(913) 551-7878

Region VIII (Colorado, Montana, North Dakota, South Dakota, Utah,
Wyoming)
999 18th Street, Suite 500
Denver, CO 80202-1603
(303) 294-1616

Hazardous Waste Management Division ....(303) 293-1720
Air & Toxics Division...............................(303) 293-0946
Water Management Division ....(303) 293-1542
Environmental Services Division ....(303) 293-0994
Regional Counsel ....(303) 294-7550
Office of External Affairs ....(303) 294-1119

Region IX (Arizona, California, Hawaii, Nevada, Guam, American Samoa)
75 Hawthorne Street
San Francisco, CA 94105
(415) 744-1001

Office of Regional Counsel..........................(415) 744-1364
Office of External Affairs ....(415) 744-1015
Air & Toxics Division...............................(415) 744-1219
Hazardous Waste Management Division ....(415) 744-1730
Water Management Division ....(415) 744-2125

Region X (Washington, Oregon, Idaho, Alaska)
1200 6th Avenue
Seattle, WA 98101
(206) 553-0479

Air & Toxics Division...............................(206) 553-4152
Air Programs Branch ....(206) 553-1152
Hazardous Waste Division ....(206) 553-1261
Environmental Services Division ....(206) 553-1625
Air Compliance Contact ....(206) 553-8507
Office of External/Public Affairs ....(206) 553-1107

U.S. EPA OFFICES

Agency Locator Service .... (202) 260-2090
Air Docket.. (202) 260-7548
Center for Environmental Research Information .... (513) 569-7562
Drinking Water Docket................................ (202) 260-3027
FOIA Office .... (202) 260-4048
OUST Docket .... (202) 260-9720
Office of Air & Radiation............................. (202) 260-7400
Enforcement & Compliance .... (202) 260-4134
Office of General Counsel .... (202) 260-8040
Office of Intergovernmental Liaison..................... (202) 260-4454
Office of Pesticides & Toxics.......................... (703) 305-6244
Office of Public Affairs............................... (202) 260-4361
Office of Solid Waste .... (202) 260-4627
Office of Superfund .... (202) 260-2180
Office of UST .... (202) 308-8850
Office of Water .... (202) 260-5700
Pesticides Docket .... (703) 305-5805
Procurement Information .... (202) 260-5020
Public Info. Reference Unit .... (202) 260-2080
RCRA Docket....................................... (202) 260-9327
Superfund Docket .... (202) 260-3046
TSCA Assistance Info. Office .... (202) 554-1404
TSCA Docket .... (202) 260-3587

U.S. EPA Hotline

Asbestos Ombudsman................................. (800) 368-5888
Federal Facilities Docket .... (800) 548-1016
RCRA & Superfund Hotline........................... (800) 424-9346
SARA & R-T-K Hotline .... (800) 535-0202
Safe Drinking Water Hotline .... (800) 426-4791
Small Business Ombudsman............................ (800) 368-5888
Federal Facility Inventory............................. (800) 254-3793

U.S. EPA Library

Hazardous Waste Collection........................... (202) 260-5934
Headquarters....................................... (202) 260-5922
Enforcement Investigations............................ (303) 236-5122
RTP Library .... (919) 541-2777

STATE AGENCY CONTACTS

Alabama Department of Environmental Management .... (205) 271-7861
Alaska Department of Environmental Conservation............... (907) 465-5100
Arizona Department of Environmental Quality .... (602) 207-2381
Arkansas Department of Pollution Control and Ecology .... (501) 570-2872
California Department of Toxic Substances Control .... (916) 323-6042
Colorado Hazardous Materials & Waste Management Division ..... (303) 692-3300

Connecticut Department of Environmental Protection. . . . . (203) 566-8476
Washington, D.C. Environmental Regulation Administration. . . . . . . (202) 645-6080
Delaware Department of Natural Resources & Environmental Control (302) 739-3689
Florida Department of Environmental Regulation . . . . (904) 487-3299
Georgia Department of Natural Resources . . . . (404) 362-2537
Hawaii Department of Health . . . . (808) 686-4424
Idaho Department of Health & Welfare . . . . (208) 334-5879
Illinois Environmental Protection Agency . . . . (217) 782-6760
Indiana Department of Environmental Management . . . . (317) 232-3210
Iowa Land Quality Bureau. . . . . (515) 281-5145
Kansas Bureau of Waste Management . . . . (913) 296-1600
Kentucky Division of Waste Management. . . . . (502) 564-6716
Louisiana Department of Environmental Quality. . . . . (504) 765-0261
Maine Bureau of Hazardous Materials & Solid Waste . . . . (207) 287-2651
Maryland Waste Management Administration. . . . . (410) 631-3304
Massachusetts Department of Environmental Protection. . . . . (617) 292-5589
Michigan Department of Natural Resources. (517) 373-7023
Minnesota Minnesota Pollution Control Agency . . . . (612) 296-7300
Mississippi Department of Environmental Quality. . . . . (601) 961-5171
Missouri Department of Natural Resources . . . . (314) 751-5401
Montana Department of Health and Environment . . . . (406) 444-1430
Nebraska Department of Environmental Quality . . . . (402) 471-2186
Nevada Division of Environmental Protection . . . . (702) 687-5872
New Hampshire Department of Environmental Services. . . . . (603) 271-2905
New Jersey Department of Environmental Protection . . . . (609) 292-1250
New Mexico Environmental Department . . . . (505) 827-0047
New York Department of Environmental Conservation . . . . (518) 457-6934
North Carolina Department of Solid Waste Management. . . . . (919) 733-2178
North Dakota Department of Health & Consolidated Laboratories. . . (701) 221-5166
Ohio Environmental Protection Agency . . . . (614) 644-2917
Oklahoma Department of Environmental Quality . . . . (405) 271-5338
Oregon Department of Environmental Quality. . . . . (503) 229-5913
Pennsylvania Department of Environmental Resources. . . . . (717) 787-9870
Rhode Island Division of Air & Hazardous Materials . . . . (401) 277-2797
South Carolina Department of Health and Environment . . . . (803) 734-5200
South Dakota Department of Environmental & Natural Resources. . . (605) 773-3153
Tennessee Division of Solid Waste Management. . . . . (615) 543-0780
Texas Industrial & Hazardous Waste Division . . . . (512) 908-2334
Utah Division of Solid & Hazardous Waste . . . . (801) 538-6170
Vermont Department of Environmental Conservation . . . . (802) 241-3888
Virginia Department of Waste Management. (804) 225-2667
Washington Department of Ecology. . . . . (206) 407-6700
West Virginia Division of Natural Resources . . . . (304) 348-5929
Wisconsin Department of Natural Resources . . . . (608) 266-0833
Wyoming Department of Environmental Quality. . . . . (307) 777-7752

Index

A

Abatement actions, 190–191, 206
  voluntary, 191, 207
Aboveground storage tanks (ASTs), 25, 250–256, 260
  mechanical and physical requirements, 250–251
Acid rain, 104, 112, 118, 129–130, 133, 146
Adaptive reuse, 279
Advisory Council on Historic Preservation, 274, 282
Agricultural stormwater discharges, 36
Air, 101–148
  air quality, monitoring, 113–115
  Clean Air Act regulations, 117–118
  emissions trading, 115–117
  environmental compliance, 118–145
  federal laws and regulations, 101–108
  regulatory programs, 108–110
  state laws and regulations, 110–113
Air emissions, 19
Air emissions inventory, 134–135
Air quality standards, 101–108
Algae, 308
Antiquities Act, 269
Applicable or relevant and appropriate requirements, 195–196
Aquatic organisms, 293, 303–308
  algae and phytoplankton, 303–304
  benthic organisms, 305–306
  fish, 306–308
  zooplankton, 305
Aquifers, 24, 59–60, 63, 74, 76–77
  confined, 59
  karst, 60
  sole source, 59, 66, 74, 77, 84, 99
  unconfined, 59

Archaeological and cultural resources, 269–286
Archaeological Resources Protection Act, 269
Army installation spill contingency plan, 264–265
Arsenic, 80, 109
Artifact, 286
Asbestos, 16, 26, 86, 109, 205, 213, 335–342, 355–358
  Asbestos Hazard Emergency Response Act (AHERA), 337–339, 356–357
  friable, 337–338, 356–357
  laws and regulations, 336–342
  mesothelioma, 336
  National Emission Standards for Hazardous Air Pollutants (NESHAP), 338–339
  non-friable, 337
  OSHA asbestos standards, 339–342
  permissible exposure limit (PEL), 340
  surfacing materials, 336
  thermal system insulation, 336
Asbestos Hazard Emergency Response Act (AHERA), 337–339, 356–357
Attainment areas, 102, 108, 111, 114, 118, 122, 146

B

Beryllium, 80
Best available control technology (BACT), 32, 123, 146, 192
Best conventional pollutant control technology, 32
Best Management Practices (BMP) programs, 29, 33–34, 46
Biological resources, 289–308

411